KU-186-704

SPORTS AND RECREATION

PATRON

TUN DR MAHATHIR MOHAMAD

Editorial Advisory board

CHAIRMAN
Tan Sri Dato' Seri Ahmad Sarji bin Abdul Hamid

MEMBERS OF THE BOARD
Tan Sri Dato' Dr Ahmad Mustaffa Babjee
Prof. Dato' Dr Asmah Haji Omar
Puan Azah Aziz
Dr Peter M. Kedit
Dato' Dr T. Marimuthu
Dato' Mohd Yusof bin Hitam
Ms Patricia Regis
Mr P. C. Shivadas
Tan Sri Dato' Dr Wan Mohd Zahid Mohd Noordin

Sports and Recreation Committee

CHAIRMAN
Tan Sri Dato' Seri Ahmad Sarji bin Abdul Hamid

MEMBERS OF THE COMMITTEE
Prof. Dr Ghulam-Sarwar Yousof
Prof. Dato' Dr Khoo Kay Kim
Datuk Prof. Dr M. Jegathesan
Mr Lazarus Rokk
Dato' Noh Abdullah
Mr P. C. Shivadas
Tan Sri Dato' Dr Wan Mohd Zahid Mohd Noordin

EDITORIAL TEAM

Series Editorial Team

PUBLISHER
Didier Millet

GENERAL MANAGER
Charles Orwin

PROJECT COORDINATOR
Marina Mahathir

EDITORIAL DIRECTOR
Timothy Auger

PROJECT MANAGER
Martin Cross

PRODUCTION MANAGER
Sin Kam Cheong

DESIGN DIRECTORS
Annie Teo
Yusri bin Din

Volume Editorial Team

EDITORS
William Citrin
Kiri Cowie
Fong Min Yuan
Vinod Divakaran
Christy Yoong

ASSISTANT EDITORS
Chang Yan Yi
Lee Li Lian
Joane Sharmila

DESIGNERS
Muamar Ghadafi bin Ali
Theivani A/P Nadaraju
Yusri bin Din

ILLUSTRATORS
Chai Kah Yune
Lim Joo
Tan Hong Yew

EDITORIAL
CONSULTANTS
**Prof. Emeritus Datuk
Dr Alex Delilkan**
Gerald Martinez
Rizal Hashim

The Encyclopedia of Malaysia was first conceived by Editions Didier Millet and Datin Paduka Marina Mahathir. The Editorial Advisory Board, made up of distinguished figures drawn from academic and public life, was constituted in March 1994. The project was publicly announced in October that year, and eight months later the first sponsors were in place. In 1996, the structure of the content was agreed; later that year the appointment of Volume Editors and the commissioning of authors were substantially complete, and materials for the work were beginning to flow in. By early 2008, 15 volumes were completed for publication. Upon completion, the series will consist of 16 volumes.

The Publishers wish to thank the following people for their contribution to the first seven volumes:

Dato' Seri Anwar Ibrahim,
who acted as Chairman of the Editorial Advisory Board;
and
the late Tan Sri Dato' Dr Noordin Sopiee
Tan Sri Datuk Augustine S. H. Ong
the late Tan Sri Zain Azraai
Datuk Datin Paduka Zakiah Hanum bt Abdul Hamid
Datin Noor Azlina Yunus

SPONSORS

The Encyclopedia of Malaysia was made possible thanks to the generous and enlightened support of the following organizations:

- DRB-HICOM BERHAD
- MAHKOTA TECHNOLOGIES SDN BHD
- MALAYAN UNITED INDUSTRIES BERHAD
- MALAYSIA NATIONAL INSURANCE BERHAD
- MINISTRY OF EDUCATION MALAYSIA
- NEW STRAITS TIMES PRESS (MALAYSIA) BERHAD
- TRADEWINDS CORPORATION BERHAD
- PETRONAS BERHAD
- UEM WORLD BERHAD
- STAR PUBLICATIONS (MALAYSIA) BERHAD
- SUNWAY GROUP
- TENAGA NASIONAL BERHAD

- UNITED OVERSEAS BANK GROUP
- YAYASAN ALBUKHARY
- YTL CORPORATION BERHAD

PNB GROUP OF COMPANIES
- PERMODALAN NASIONAL BERHAD
- NCB HOLDINGS BERHAD
- SIME DARBY BERHAD
- MALAYAN BANKING BERHAD
- MNI HOLDINGS BERHAD
- PERNEC CORPORATION BERHAD

© **Editions Didier Millet, 2008**
Published by Archipelago Press *an imprint of* Editions Didier Millet Pte Ltd
121, Telok Ayer Street, #03-01, Singapore 068590
Tel: 65-6324 9260 Fax: 65-6324 9261 E-mail: edm@edmbooks.com.sg

First published 2008

Editions Didier Millet, Kuala Lumpur Office:
25, Jalan Pudu Lama, 50200 Kuala Lumpur, Malaysia
Tel: 03-2031 3805 Fax: 03-2031 6298 E-mail: edmbooks@edmbooks.com.my
Websites: www.edmbooks.com • www.encyclopedia.com.my

Colour separation by United Graphic Pte Ltd
Printed by Star Standard Industries (Pte) Ltd
ISBN 978-981-4155-61-8

All Rights Reserved. No part of this book may be reproduced, stored in a retrieval system, or transmitted in any form or by any means without permission from the publisher.

Note for Readers
Every effort has been taken to present the most accurate and up-to-date information about Malaysian athletes and administrators in this volume. We have also attempted to state accurately the titles awarded to persons mentioned as at the date to which their entry in this volume refers. We apologize for any errors or omissions that may have occurred.

CONTRIBUTORS

Abd. Hamid Majid
*Honorary Secretary, Malaysian
Chess Federation*

Abdul Malik Mohd Salleh
President, Selangor Tennis Association

Abdul Rahman Hussin
*Treasurer, Persatuan Seni Suara
Burung Ketitir (Merbok) Kelantan*

Peter Ibrahim Abisheganaden
Editor, Equestrian.Com.My

Ahmad Ismail
*President, Sepak Takraw Federation
of Malaysia*

Ahmad Sarji
President, Malaysia Lawn Bowls Federation

Haji Anuar Haji Abd. Wahab
*Founder and Main Instructor, Seni
Gayung Fatani Malaysia*

Arnaz M. Khairul
New Straits Times

Azlan Ismail
*President and Chief Instructor,
Kuala Lumpur Skydiving Association*

Aznir bin Abdul Malek
Chairman, Kelah Action Group of Malaysia

Maj. (retired) Baharuddin Jamil
First Vice President, Asian Archery Federation

Col. Basir Abdul Rahman
President, Malaysian Paramotor Association

K.M. Boopathy
New Straits Times

Chan Foong Keong
*Honorary Secretary, Table Tennis
Association of Malaysia*

Samantha Chan
Writer

Chee Yih Yang
The Star

Chin Chooi Ying
*Former Chairperson, Malaysian Dance
Sport Berhad*

Chuah Sim Swee
Committee Member, Penang Scrabble Club

Dan Guen Chin
New Straits Times (retired)

Dorairaj Nadason
The Star

Fu Chee Cheng
Chairman, Hash Heritage Foundation

Prof. Dr Ghulam-Sarwar Yousof
Universiti Malaya

M.K. Jacob
*Honorary Secretary, Kabaddi Association
of Malaysia*

Jaffry Zakaria
Universiti Pendidikan Sultan Idris

Maj. Jasni Shaari
*Executive Secretary, National Shooting
Association of Malaysia*

Assoc. Professor Dr Juli Edo
Universiti Malaya

Khalid Yunus
*President, National Adventure Association
of Malaysia*

Dr Selina Khoo
Universiti Malaya

Thomas Kok
*Former President, Malaysian Woodball
Association*

Paul Lam
President, Paintball Asia League Series

Tresa Lazaroo
Universiti Malaya

Christy Lee
The Star

Lee Yee Dian
Writer

Lee You Meng
*Technical Chairman for Volleyball,
Malaysian School Sports Council*

Pamela Lim
*Honorary Secretary, Malaysian Sport
Diving Association*

Dr Lim Teong Wah
*Chairman, Malaysian Contract
Bridge Association*

Low Beng Choo
President, Softball Association of Malaysia

C.K. Low
Writer

Loy Chee Luen
Universiti Pendidikan Sultan Idris

Dr M. Mahadevan
President, Iskandar Polo Club

Gerald Martinez
*New Straits Times (retired)
Executive Secretary, FT Amateur
Fencing Association*

Mazidah Musa
*Honorary Secretary, Malaysian
Netball Association*

Mohd Adam Ismail
Writer

Mohd Amin Mohd Taff
Universiti Pendidikan Sultan Idris

Mohd Nadzrin Wahab
Founder, SilatMelayu.Com

Heidi Munan
Writer

Terence Netto
Writer

Ng Num Thiam
*Honorary Secretary, Malaysian
Handball Federation*

Ng Peng Kong
*Former President, Selangor Rugby Union
Former Secretary, Malaysian Rugby Union*

Noh Abdullah
*President, Baseball Federation of Malaysia
Former Director General, National
Sports Council*

Andrew Oon Hock Beng
Coach, PISA Swimming Team Penang

Larry Parr
*Co-author with Dato' Tan Chin Nam
of 'Never Say I Assume!'*

Ian Pereira
The Malay Mail

**Assoc. Prof. Dr Jacqueline
Pugh-Kitingan**
Universiti Malaysia Sabah

Prof. Dr Rahmah Bujang
Universiti Malaya

Raja Morgan Veerapan
*Artistic Director, Abinaya Shetra
Dance Company*

Ram Derayan
New Straits Times

Ramzi Ramli
Universiti Malaya

Capt. Martins Rijkuris
Journalist, Asian Yachting Ventures Sdn Bhd

Rizal Hashim
The Malay Mail

B. Sarjit Singh
*Executive Director, Malaysian Association
of Hotels*

Percy Seneviratne
*Publisher, PNS Publishing Sdn Bhd
Former Deputy Sports Editor,
Singapore Straits Times*

Shazfinas Hashim
Coach, Pyramid Ice Rink

Joe Slowinski
*Director of Coaching and Certification for
Tenpin Bowling, National Sports Council*

Richard Nelson Sokial
Member, Sabah Society

Maj. (retired) B. Subramaniam
*Executive Councillor, Malaysian Amateur
Boxing Federation*

Sum Kwok Seng
*Former Secretary, Malaysian Weightlifting
Federation*

Gary Tan Khia Peng
*Coach, Kelab Hoki Ais Saga (KHAS)
Captain, Malaysian Ice Hockey Team*

Dr Tan Siew Eng
*National training institute in education
management and leadership, Ministry
of Education*

Moira Tan Siew See
*Honorary Assistant Secretary,
Olympic Council of Malaysia*

Ronnie Theseira
*Former President, Malayan Amateur
Fencing Association*

Royal Prof. Ungku A. Aziz
*President, Angkasa (National Co-operative
Organization of Malaysia)*

Luis J.A. Wee
*Founder and Event Director, International
Rainforest Challenge*

Yeoh Choo Hock
*Honorary Secretary, Malaysia Amateur
Basketball Association
Secretary General, FIBA Asia*

THE ENCYCLOPEDIA OF
MALAYSIA

Volume 15

SPORTS AND RECREATION

Volume Editor
Tan Sri Dato' Seri Ahmad Sarji bin Abdul Hamid
President, Malaysia Lawn Bowls Federation

ARCHIPELAGO PRESS

Contents

Above: Sepak takraw match being played at Stadium Negara, 1968.

Title page: Fans celebrating Malaysia's victory in the 1992 Thomas Cup in Kuala Lumpur.

Half title page: M. Jegathesan crossing the finish line to win the gold medal in the 100-metre event at the 1965 SEAP Games in Kuala Lumpur.

Drum festival held annually in Kelantan after the rice harvest in May or June. Groups of two men beat giant drums (*rebana besar*) and compete to determine which pair can play with the most skill, artistry and harmony.

Wong Peng Soon being held aloft
after winning the men's singles
event of the All England Badminton
Championships, 1952.

Sauber–PETRONAS car racing
during the F1 PETRONAS
Malaysian Grand Prix, 2005.

Stadium Merdeka on 31 August 1957. The inaugural Merdeka Football Tournament was held in conjunction with the Independence day celebrations.

RIGHT: Chrystal Lim Wen Chean performing during the rhythmic gymnastics competition at the Commonwealth Games in Melbourne, 2006. With her teammates Durratun Nashihin Rosli and Fong Seow Ting, Chrystal captured the silver medal in the team event.

Sports facilities in Malaysia

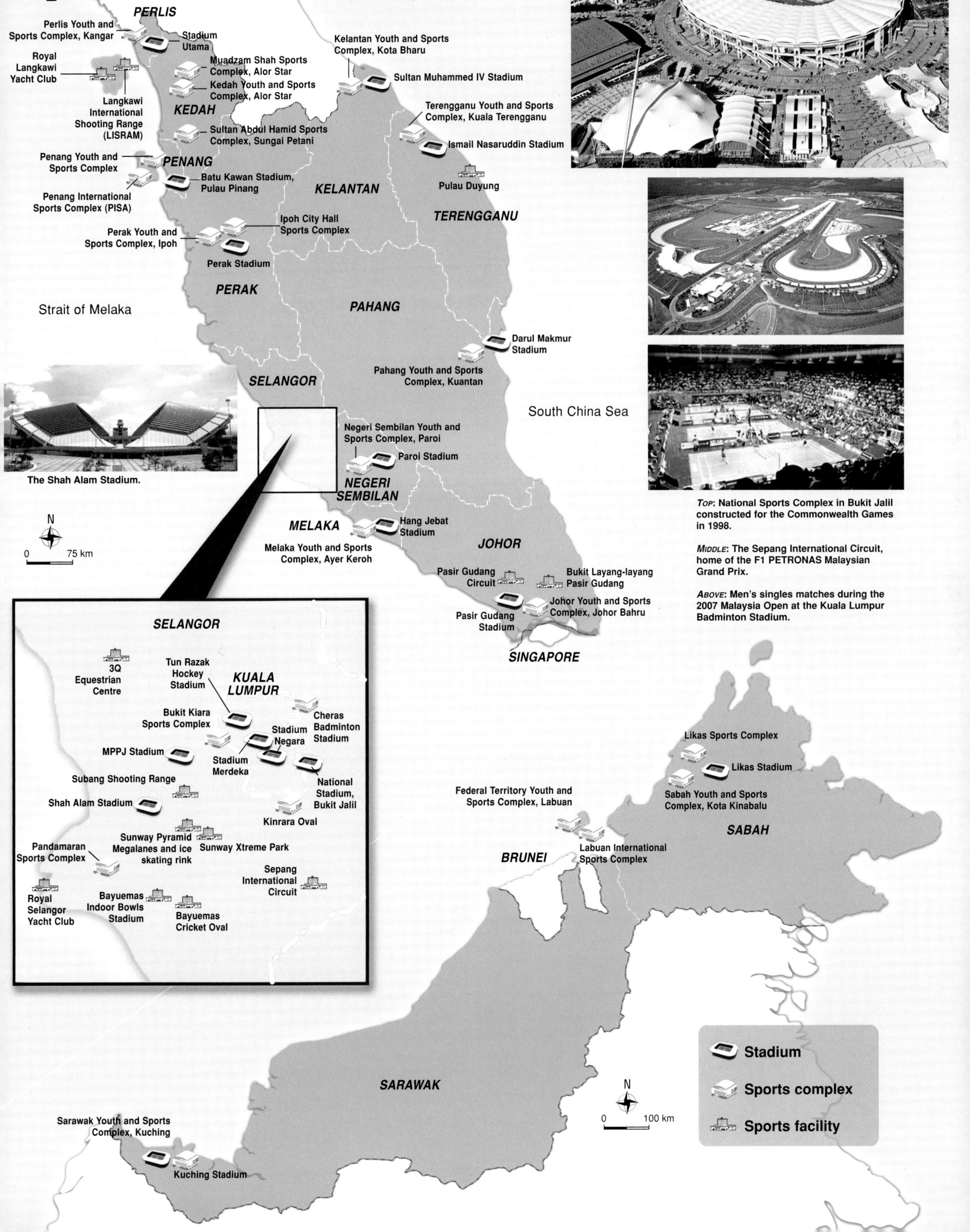

PERLIS
Perlis Youth and Sports Complex, Kangar
Stadium Utama
Royal Langkawi Yacht Club
Langkawi International Shooting Range (LISRAM)
Muadzam Shah Sports Complex, Alor Star
Kedah Youth and Sports Complex, Alor Star
KEDAH
Sultan Abdul Hamid Sports Complex, Sungai Petani
Penang Youth and Sports Complex
PENANG
Batu Kawan Stadium, Pulau Pinang
Penang International Sports Complex (PISA)
Ipoh City Hall Sports Complex
Perak Youth and Sports Complex, Ipoh
Perak Stadium
PERAK
Strait of Melaka
Kelantan Youth and Sports Complex, Kota Bharu
Sultan Muhammed IV Stadium
Terengganu Youth and Sports Complex, Kuala Terengganu
Ismail Nasaruddin Stadium
Pulau Duyung
KELANTAN
TERENGGANU
PAHANG
Darul Makmur Stadium
Pahang Youth and Sports Complex, Kuantan
SELANGOR
South China Sea
Negeri Sembilan Youth and Sports Complex, Paroi
Paroi Stadium
NEGERI SEMBILAN
MELAKA
Hang Jebat Stadium
Melaka Youth and Sports Complex, Ayer Keroh
JOHOR
Pasir Gudang Circuit
Bukit Layang-layang Pasir Gudang
Johor Youth and Sports Complex, Johor Bahru
Pasir Gudang Stadium
SINGAPORE
N
0 75 km
SELANGOR
3Q Equestrian Centre
Tun Razak Hockey Stadium
KUALA LUMPUR
Bukit Kiara Sports Complex
Cheras Badminton Stadium
Stadium Negara
MPPJ Stadium
Stadium Merdeka
National Stadium, Bukit Jalil
Subang Shooting Range
Shah Alam Stadium
Kinrara Oval
Sunway Pyramid Megalanes and ice skating rink
Sunway Xtreme Park
Pandamaran Sports Complex
Sepang International Circuit
Royal Selangor Yacht Club
Bayuemas Indoor Bowls Stadium
Bayuemas Cricket Oval
Likas Sports Complex
Likas Stadium
Sabah Youth and Sports Complex, Kota Kinabalu
SABAH
Federal Territory Youth and Sports Complex, Labuan
Labuan International Sports Complex
BRUNEI
SARAWAK
Sarawak Youth and Sports Complex, Kuching
Kuching Stadium
N
0 100 km
Stadium
Sports complex
Sports facility

The Shah Alam Stadium.

Top: National Sports Complex in Bukit Jalil constructed for the Commonwealth Games in 1998.

Middle: The Sepang International Circuit, home of the F1 PETRONAS Malaysian Grand Prix.

Above: Men's singles matches during the 2007 Malaysia Open at the Kuala Lumpur Badminton Stadium.

Introduction

Opening ceremony of the 3rd Southeast Asian Peninsular (SEAP) Games at Stadium Merdeka in Kuala Lumpur, 1965.

Top: Participants preparing to release their kites during an international kite flying festival in Kelantan, 2007.

Above: Spinner throwing his top during a competition held in conjunction with the birthday of the Sultan of Kelantan, 1961.

This volume showcases the diversity of sports and recreation which comprises the full spectrum of Malaysian games and pastimes, ranging from top spinning to badminton to Formula One. Each section of the volume is devoted to a separate category of sports or recreation, enabling readers to navigate easily the 86 topical articles. Each sport and pastime is examined systematically, with information on its origins and development, rules and methods, achievements and administration.

Celebrating culture and cultivating the intellect

The richness of Malaysian culture is reflected in the variety of traditional games and pastimes that have been played for centuries. A wide range of recreational activities is practised locally by the Malay, Chinese, Indian, Orang Asli, Sabah and Sarawak communities. Each ethnic group possesses its own forms of traditional recreation, rooted in its unique history, beliefs and practices. Inevitably, through inter-ethnic and cross-cultural contact, many games and pastimes have been shared between different peoples and changed in the process. Traditional pastimes such as top spinning, kite flying, bird singing, *congkak* and traditional water sports remain widely popular.

Conventional sports and recreation

Malaysians participate in a multitude of competitive sports and modern recreational activities. In addition to the 49 sports represented at the Olympic Council of Malaysia by their respective associations, a whole host of other established and popular sporting and recreational activities are played locally. Each sport and pastime played in Malaysia has a unique history, beginning with its origins, whether it was conceived here or introduced by foreigners, and proceeding with the key personalities and events that have shaped its evolution.

Of the team sports, football, hockey, cricket and rugby were introduced to Malaya by the British in the late 19th century. Football and hockey in particular are popular, with large participatory and fan bases, and have achieved a measure of international success. The Merdeka Tournament, inaugurated in 1957 in conjunction with the celebration of Independence, was Asia's premier football event, and the home team claimed the championship in 1958, 1959, 1960, 1968, 1974, 1986, 1993 and 2007. In 1972 and 1980, the men's football team emerged victorious from the gruelling qualifying matches to earn berths at the Olympic Games. The men's hockey team surprised the world by finishing fourth in the 1975 World Cup held in Kuala Lumpur at Merdeka Stadium. Football and hockey continue to dominate the sports headlines. Sepak takraw, a visually spectacular team sport which features lightning-fast exchanges and acrobatic manoeuvres, was derived from the ancient Malay game of *sepak raga*. Although the national teams from Malaysia and Thailand tend to dominate international competitions, other countries, in the region and beyond, have embraced the sport to become worthy competitors.

Racquet sports have been the source of some of Malaysia's greatest achievements in the international sports arena. Badminton, with a history in the Malay Peninsula dating all the

The Thomas Cup trophy. Malaysia has hosted the Thomas Cup competition five times (1970, 1984, 1988, 1992 and 2000) and won it five times (1949, 1952, 1955, 1967 and 1992).

The Malayan team (in stripes) playing in a match during the Merdeka Tournament at Stadium Merdeka, 1963.

way back to the early 1800s, thrust the country into the spotlight in 1948 with our success in the Thomas Cup tournament and the individual accomplishments of Wong Peng Soon and Eddy Choong in the All England Open Championships. This tradition of excellence has continued through the years, and Malaysian shuttlers remain at the pinnacle of the sport. Squash players, most notably reigning world champion Nicol David, have also brought honour to the country through their achievements.

Malaysian players (in light shirts) on the attack against India during a semi-final match at the 1975 Hockey World Cup in Kuala Lumpur.

Malaysian athletes have made an impact in precision sports as well. In 1979, national tenpin bowlers Koo Boon Jin, Edward Lim and Allan Hooi clinched the coveted FIQ World Championships in the three-man event. Through youth development programmes, Malaysia has produced a long line of high-calibre players including 2001 World Tenpin Masters champion Shalin Zulkifli and 2005 FIQ–WTBA World Champion Esther Cheah. Lawn bowlers have also risen to the top of the world rankings. Siti Zalina Ahmad created history by winning the women's singles lawn bowls gold medal at consecutive Commonwealth Games in 2002 and 2006. In 2005, Nor Iryani Azmi emerged as the women's singles World Champion of Champions. World-number-one Safuan Said clinched the men's singles title at the 2008 World Bowls Championships.

Although informal running, jumping and throwing contests have been present in the country since time immemorial, athletics was introduced to Malaya on an organized basis by the British in the early 1900s. The golden age of Malaysian track and field was in the 1960s, when runners M. Jegathesan and M. Rajamani and javelin thrower Nashatar Singh blazed a trail for future athletes.

Sazali Abdul Samad, a four-time winner of the Mr Universe title in 2000, 2004, 2006 and 2007. Sazali was voted the 'Best Bodybuilder of the 20th Century in Asia' by the Asian Bodybuilding Federation.

Malaysia plays host to two of the world's most prestigious racing events—Tour de Langkawi and the Formula One Malaysian Grand Prix—as well as numerous other racing events. The Malaysian passion for speed is demonstrated by the large crowds that attend these events, and the emergence of World Rally Champion Karamjit Singh, the most successful rally driver ever from the Asia Pacific region.

The nation's paralympic athletes, too, have brought glory to the country by competing with as much passion as their able-bodied counterparts and achieving international success, most recently during the 2006 FESPIC Games held in Kuala Lumpur.

Above: Malaysian women's tenpin bowling team showing off the gold medals they won in the team event at the 2007 FIQ–WTBA World Championships in Mexico.

Below: Malaysian contingent marching at the opening ceremony of the Commonwealth Games in Kuala Lumpur, 1998.

Sporting events and structure

Since the 1950s, Malaysia has competed with distinction at numerous multi-sport events including the Olympic, Commonwealth, Asian and Southeast Asian (SEA) Games. The country has played host to the Commonwealth and SEA Games as well as single-sport championships including the World Cup of Hockey in 1975, the Thomas Cup in 1970, 1984, 1988, 1992 and 2000, a World Heavyweight title fight between Muhammad Ali and Joe Bugner in 1975, the World Cup of Golf in 1999 and the equestrian FEI World Cup Jumping Final in 2006. The most significant sporting event that Malaysia has hosted to date, however, was the Commonwealth Games in 1998, which saw the participation of 5000 competitors from 70 countries.

The formation of the National Sports Council in 1971 and the passing of the Sports Development Act in 1997 were important landmarks in the development of sports in the country. Structure and organization play as big a role as athletes do in sports, and sporting institutions govern and promote sports in Malaysia. These organizations work through the education system and the public to create a healthy nation and future athletes to build on the successes of their predecessors.

Awards and achievements

Sportsmen and Sportswomen of the Year

1966 M. Jegathesan–**athletics**
M. Rajamani–**athletics**

1967 Tan Aik Huang–**badminton**
M. Rajamani–**athletics**

M. Jegathesan (left) and M. Rajamani (right) standing with Deputy Prime Minister Tun Abdul Razak after being honoured as the inaugural sportsman and sportswoman of the year.

1968 Ng Boon Bee–**badminton**
Goh Koon Gee–**basketball**

1969 Punch Gunalan–**badminton**
Ong Mei Lin–**swimming**

1970 Ng Joo Ngan–**cycling**
Radika Menon–**badminton**

1971 Daud Ibrahim–**cycling**
Junaidah Aman–**athletics**

1972 M. Mahendran–**hockey**
Junaidah Aman–**athletics**

1973 Chiang Jun Choon–**swimming**
Gladys Chai–**athletics**

Punch Gunalan (left) and Rani Kaur with their awards.

1974 Punch Gunalan–**badminton**
Rani Kaur–**hockey**

1975 Khoo Chong Beng–**athletics**
Sylvia Ng–**badminton**

1976 Mokhtar Dahari–**football**
Marina Chin–**athletics**

1977 Shukor Salleh–**football**
Marina Chin–**athletics**

V. Subramaniam (left) and Sylvia Ng with their awards.

1978 V. Subramaniam–**athletics**
Sylvia Ng–**badminton**

1979 Koo Boon Jin–**tenpin bowling**
Shirley Chow–**tenpin bowling**

1980 Rabuan Pit–**athletics**
Katerina Ong–**swimming**

1981 Misbun Sidek–**badminton**
Helen Chow–**swimming**

1982 Rabuan Pit–**athletics**
Zaiton Othman–**athletics**

1983 Misbun Sidek–**badminton**
Norsham Yoon–**athletics**

1984 Michael Chuah Seng Tatt–**tenpin bowling**

1985 Rosman Alwi–**cycling**
Nurul Huda Abdullah–**swimming**

1986 Abdul Malek Mohd Noor–**bodybuilding**
Nurul Huda Abdullah–**swimming**

1987 M. Kumaresan–**cycling**
Nurul Huda Abdullah–**swimming**

1988 Jeffrey Ong Kuan Seng–**swimming**
Nurul Huda Abdullah–**swimming**

1989 Foo Kok Keong–**badminton**
Nurul Huda Abdullah–**swimming**

1990 Rashid Sidek–**badminton**
Lydia Kwah–**tenpin bowling**

1991 Rashid Sidek–**badminton**
Lisa Kwan–**tenpin bowling**

1992 Rashid Sidek–**badminton**
Lim Ai Lian–**golf**

1993 Ramachandran Munusamy–**athletics**
Lisa Kwan–**tenpin bowling**

1994 Nur Herman Majid–**athletics**
Shalin Zulkifli–**tenpin bowling**

1995 Sam Chong–**snooker and billiards**
Sharon Low Su Lin–**tenpin bowling**

1996 Rashid Sidek–**badminton**
Shalin Zulkifli–**tenpin bowling**

1997 Cheah Soon Kit and Yap Kim Hock–**badminton**
Shalin Zulkifli–**tenpin bowling**

1998 Lim Keng Liat–**swimming**
G. Shanti–**athletics**

1999 Shahrulneeza Mohd Razali–**cycling**
Nicol Ann David–**squash**

2000 Sazali Samad–**bodybuilding**
Noraseela Mohd Khalid–**athletics**

2001 Mohd Roslin Hashim–**badminton**
Shalin Zulkifli–**tenpin bowling**

2002 Karamjit Singh and Allen Oh–**rally racing**
Shalin Zulkifli–**tenpin bowling**

2003 Nazmizan Muhamad–**athletics**
Nicol David–**squash**

2004 Josiah Ng Ong Lam–**cycling**
Elaine Teo–**taekwondo**

Nicol David (left) and Lee Chong Wei with their awards.

2005 Lee Chong Wei–**badminton**
Nicol David–**squash**

2006 Sazali Samad–**bodybuilding**
Nicol David–**squash**

National athletes and administrators along with government and OCM officials, including Prime Minister Dato' Seri Abdullah Ahmad Badawi (front row, seventh from left), at the OCM Hall of Fame induction ceremony, 2004.

Olympic Council of Malaysia (OCM) Hall of Fame

Athletics
- 1966 4x100-metre relay team
- M. Jegathesan
- Ishtiaq Mobarak
- Rahim Ahmad
- Nashatar Singh
- M. Rajamani
- Rabuan Pit
- G. Saravanan
- Saik Oik Cum

Badminton
- 1949 Thomas Cup team
- Eddy Choong
- Razif Sidek
- Jalani Sidek
- Rashid Sidek
- Cheah Soon Kit
- Yap Kim Hock

- Wong Peng Soon
- Ong Poh Lim
- Teh Kew San
- Ooi Teik Hock
- Tan Aik Huang
- Tan Yee Khan
- Ng Boon Bee
- Punch Gunalan
- Rosalind Singha Ang
- Sylvia Ng
- Choong Tan Fook
- Lee Wan Wah

Basketball
- Goh Koon Gee

Boxing
- Sapok Biki
- Tiger Aman

Cricket
- Lall Singh

Cycling
- Daud Ibrahim
- Ng Joo Ngan

Football
- 1972 national football team
- Abdul Ghani Minhat
- Edwin Dutton
- Mokhtar Dahari
- M. Chandran
- Soh Chin Aun
- Santokh Singh
- M. Arumugam

Hockey
- 1975 national hockey team
- Wilfred Vias
- Ho Koh Chye
- R. Yogeswaran
- M. Mahendran
- Sri Shanmuganathan
- Rani Kaur

Swimming
- Nurul Huda Abdullah

Tennis
- Khoo Hooi Hye

Tenpin bowling
- P.S. Nathan
- Koo Boon Jin
- Holloway Cheah
- Allan Hooi
- Edward Lim
- Lee Kok Hong

OCM President Tunku Tan Sri Imran Tuanku Ja'afar (left) with some of the 2002 OCM Hall of Fame inductees including (foreground from left) M. Jegathesan, Ishtiaq Mobarak, Lee Wan Wah, Razif Sidek, Jalani Sidek and Rashid Sidek.

Olympic Council of Malaysia (OCM) Olympians of the Year

M. Ramachandran (left) and P. Jayanthi with their awards.

1993 M.Ramachandran–**athletics**
P. Jayanthi–**athletics**

1994 Asian Games sepak takraw team
Shalin Zulkifli–**tenpin bowling**

1995 Sam Chong–**snooker and billiards**
Sharon Low–**tenpin bowling**

1996 Cheah Soon Kit and Yap Kim Hock–**badminton**
Anastasia Karen Raj–**athletics**

1997 Zaki Sadri–**athletics**
Au Li Yen–**gymnastics**

1998 G. Saravanan–**athletics**
Nurul Huda Baharin–**shooting**
Lim Keng Liat–**swimming**
Nicol Ann David–**squash**

1999 Elvin Chia–**swimming**
Shalin Zulkifli–**tenpin bowling**

2000 Choong Tan Fook and Lee Wan Wah–**badminton**
Yuan Yufang–**athletics**

2001 Qabil Ambak–**equestrian**
Leong Mun Yee–**diving**

2002 Ho Ro Bin–**wushu**
Siti Zalina Ahmad–**lawn bowls**

2003 Nazmizan Muhamad–**athletics**
Wong Mew Choo–**badminton**

2004 Josiah Ng–**cycling**

2005 Ng Shu Wai–**gymnastics**
Wong Pei Tty and Chin Eei Hui–**badminton**

2006 Koo Kien Kiat and Tan Boon Heong–**badminton**
Esther Cheah–**tenpin bowling**

2007 Daniel Bego–**swimming**
Khoo Cai Lin–**swimming**

Deputy Prime Minister Dato' Sri Najib Tun Razak (third from right) with other officials and the 2007 OCM Olympians of the Year.

Malaysia's medal tally in major multi-sport events*

1950s

Commonwealth Games	Gold	Silver	Bronze
1950 Auckland	2	1	1
- Weightlifting	2	1	1
1954 Vancouver	did not participate		
1958 Cardiff	0	2	0
- Weightlifting	0	2	0

Asian Games	Gold	Silver	Bronze
1951 New Delhi	did not participate		
1954 Manila	0	0	0
1958 Tokyo	0	0	3
- Athletics	0	0	1
- Tennis	0	0	1
- Weightlifting	0	0	1

1960s

Commonwealth Games	Gold	Silver	Bronze
1962 Perth	0	0	1
- Weightlifting	0	0	1
1966 Kingston	2	2	1
- Badminton	2	2	1

Asian Games	Gold	Silver	Bronze
1962 Jakarta	2	4	9
- Athletics	1	2	4
- Badminton	1	2	2
- Cycling	0	0	1
- Football	0	0	1
- Hockey	0	0	1
1966 Bangkok	7	5	6
- Athletics	5	3	4
- Badminton	2	2	0
- Boxing	0	0	2

1970s

Commonwealth Games	Gold	Silver	Bronze
1970 Edinburgh	1	1	1
- Badminton	1	1	1
1974 Christchurch	1	0	3
- Badminton	1	0	3
1978 Edmonton	1	2	1
- Badminton	1	2	1

Asian Games	Gold	Silver	Bronze
1970 Bangkok	5	1	7
- Athletics	0	0	2
- Badminton	3	0	3
- Cycling	2	1	2
1974 Tehran	0	1	4
- Athletics	0	1	1
- Football	0	0	1
- Hockey	0	0	1
- Shooting	0	0	1
1978 Bangkok	2	1	3
- Athletics	1	1	1
- Boxing	0	0	1
- Hockey	0	0	1
- Tenpin bowling	1	0	0

1980s

Commonwealth Games	Gold	Silver	Bronze
1982 Brisbane	1	0	1
- Badminton	1	0	1
1986 Edinburgh	did not participate		

Asian Games	Gold	Silver	Bronze
1982 New Delhi	1	0	3
- Athletics	1	0	1
- Hockey	0	0	2
1986 Seoul	0	5	5
- Aquatics	0	2	2
- Athletics	0	0	1
- Shooting	0	1	0
- Taekwondo	0	1	0
- Tenpin bowling	0	1	2

1990s

Commonwealth Games	Gold	Silver	Bronze
1990 Auckland	2	2	0
- Badminton	2	2	0
1994 Victoria	2	3	2
- Badminton	2	2	2
- Weightlifting	0	1	0
1998 Kuala Lumpur	10	14	12
- Athletics	1	0	0
- Badminton	3	4	0
- Boxing	1	0	1
- Cycling	0	1	0
- Gymnastics	1	1	2
- Hockey	0	1	0
- Lawn Bowls	0	1	2
- Shooting	1	4	3
- Tenpin bowling	2	1	1
- Weightlifting	1	1	3

Asian Games	Gold	Silver	Bronze
1990 Beijing	2	2	4
- Aquatics	0	1	0
- Athletics	0	0	1
- Badminton	0	1	2
- Hockey	0	0	1
- Sepak takraw	2	0	0
1994 Hiroshima	4	2	13
- Athletics	0	0	1
- Badminton	0	1	2
- Karate	0	0	3
- Sailing	1	0	0
- Sepak takraw	1	0	0
- Taekwondo	0	0	3
- Tennis	0	0	1
- Tenpin bowling	2	1	2
- Wushu	0	0	1
1998 Bangkok	5	10	14
- Aquatics	1	1	1
- Athletics	0	0	1
- Badminton	0	0	2
- Equestrian	0	1	1
- Karate	2	0	4
- Sailing	0	3	0
- Sepak takraw	0	2	1
- Snooker	1	1	0

1998 Bangkok	Gold	Silver	Bronze
- Squash	1	0	1
- Taekwondo	0	1	1
- Tenpin bowling	0	0	1
- Wushu	0	1	1

Olympic Games	Gold	Silver	Bronze
1992 Barcelona	0	0	1
- Badminton	0	0	1
1996 Atlanta	0	1	1
- Badminton	0	1	1

2000s

Commonwealth Games	Gold	Silver	Bronze
2002 Manchester	7	9	18
- Aquatics	0	1	1
- Athletics	0	1	1
- Badminton	3	3	3
- Boxing	0	0	1
- Gymnastics	0	1	1
- Lawn Bowls	1	0	3
- Shooting	0	2	2
- Squash	0	1	0
- Tenpin bowling	0	0	1
- Weightlifting	3	0	5
2006 Melbourne	7	12	10
- Aquatics	0	2	0
- Badminton	4	3	0
- Gymnastics	0	5	2
- Hockey	0	0	1
- Lawn Bowls	2	0	0
- Shooting	0	1	4
- Weightlifting	1	1	3

Asian Games	Gold	Silver	Bronze
2002 Busan	6	8	16
- Aquatics	0	1	3
- Badminton	0	0	2
- Bodybuilding	0	1	0
- Boxing	0	0	1
- Cycling	0	1	0
- Equestrian	0	0	1
- Hockey	0	0	1
- Karate	2	1	2
- Sailing	0	1	0
- Sepak takraw	0	1	1
- Squash	1	1	2
- Taekwondo	0	0	2
- Tenpin bowling	2	1	1
- Wushu	1	0	0
2006 Doha	8	17	17
- Aquatics	0	1	3
- Athletics	0	1	1
- Badminton	1	0	3
- Bodybuilding	0	1	0
- Cycling	0	1	0
- Equestrian	0	1	2
- Gymnastics	0	1	0
- Karate	0	4	3
- Sailing	1	0	1
- Sepak takraw	0	2	1
- Snooker	0	1	0
- Squash	2	1	1
- Tenpin bowling	3	3	0
- Wushu	1	0	2

* See 'Chronology' for information on other major sports achievements and events.

Chronology*

* Malaysia's medal tally in major multi-sport events (Olympic Games, Commonwealth Games and Asian Games) appears on 'Awards and achievements'.

1940s and 1950s

1949 ◆ **BADMINTON**: Men's team wins the inaugural Thomas Cup competition in England.
◆ Ooi Teik Hock and Teoh Seng Khoon win the men's doubles event at the All England Open Championships.

Malayan contingent to the British Empire Games comprising from left) Thong Saw Pak, Ng Liang Chiang, Tho Fook Hung, E. Strickland (manager), Tan Kim Bee and Lloyd Valberg, 1950.

1950 ◆ **BADMINTON**: Wong Peng Soon wins the men's singles event at the All England Open Championships.

1951 ◆ **BADMINTON**: Wong Peng Soon wins the men's singles event at the All England Open Championships.
◆ Eddy Choong and David Choong win the men's doubles event at the All England Open Championships.

1952 ◆ **BADMINTON**: Men's team wins the Thomas Cup competition in Singapore.
◆ Wong Peng Soon wins the men's singles event at the All England Open Championships.
◆ Eddy Choong and David Choong win the men's doubles event at the All England Open Championships.

1953 ◆ **BADMINTON**: Eddy Choong wins the men's singles event at the All England Open Championships.
◆ Eddy Choong and David Choong win the men's doubles event at the All England Open Championships.
◆ **ORGANIZATION**: Formation of the Federation of Malaya Olympic Council, renamed the Olympic Council of Malaysia in 1963.

1954 ◆ **BADMINTON**: Ooi Teik Hock and Ong Poh Lim win the men's doubles event at the All England Open Championships.
◆ Eddy Choong wins the men's singles event at the All England Open Championships.

1955 ◆ **BADMINTON**: Men's team wins the Thomas Cup competition in Singapore.
◆ Wong Peng Soon wins the men's singles event at the All England Open Championships.

1956 ◆ **BADMINTON**: Eddy Choong wins the men's singles event at the All England Open Championships.
◆ **HOCKEY**: Men's team finishes ninth at the Olympic Games in Melbourne.
◆ **OLYMPICS**: Malaya makes its Olympic debut in Melbourne.

Malayan contingent marching during the opening ceremony of the 1956 Olympic Games in Melbourne.

1957 ◆ **BADMINTON**: Eddy Choong wins the men's singles event at the All England Open Championships.
◆ **FOOTBALL**: The first Merdeka Tournament staged in conjunction with the celebration of Independence.

1958 ◆ **BADMINTON**: Men's team finishes as runner-up in the Thomas Cup competition in Singapore.
◆ **FOOTBALL**: Men's football team wins the Merdeka Tournament.
◆ **ORGANIZATION**: Formation of the Malaysian Schools' Sports Council (MSSC).

1959 ◆ **FOOTBALL**: Men's team wins the Merdeka Tournament.

1960s

1960 ◆ **ATHLETICS**: M. Jegathesan runs in the 200-metre event in the Olympic Games in Rome.
◆ **FOOTBALL**: Men's team shares the Merdeka Tournament title with South Korea.

1962 ◆ **BODYBUILDING**: Clancy Ang becomes Malaysia's first Mr Universe, winning the short class category of the NABBA Mr Universe competition held in London.

1964 ◆ **ATHLETICS**: M. Jegathesan makes it to the semi-finals in the 200-metre event at the Olympic Games in Tokyo.
◆ **FENCING**: Ronnie Theseira becomes the first, and only, Malaysian fencer to take part in the Olympics.
◆ **HOCKEY**: Men's team finishes ninth at the Olympics.

1965 ◆ **BADMINTON**: Ng Boon Bee and Tan Yee Khan win the men's doubles event at the All England Open Championships.
◆ **BASKETBALL**: The Asian Basketball Confederation (ABC) Championship held in Kuala Lumpur.
◆ **SEPAK TAKRAW**: Sepak takraw officially made a sport and included as an event in the Southeast Asian Peninsular (SEAP) games.

1966 ◆ **BADMINTON**: Tan Aik Huang wins the men's singles event at the All England Open Championships.
◆ Ng Boon Bee and Tan Yee Khan win the men's doubles event at the All England Open Championships.

1967 ◆ **BADMINTON**: Men's team wins the Thomas Cup competition in Indonesia.

Teh Kew San (left) and Tan Aik Huang (right) holding the Thomas Cup during a victory parade in Kuala Lumpur, 1967.

1968 ◆ **ATHLETICS**: M. Jegathesan runs in the 200-metre event at the Olympic Games in Mexico.
◆ **FOOTBALL**: Men's team wins the Merdeka Tournament.

1970s

1970 ◆ **BADMINTON**: Men's team finishes second in the Thomas Cup competition in Kuala Lumpur.
◆ **TENPIN BOWLING**: Men's team wins eight golds at the Asian FIQ Championships in Hong Kong.

1971 ◆ **BADMINTON**: Ng Boon Bee and Punch Gunalan win the men's doubles event at the All England Open Championships.
◆ **FOOTBALL**: Men's team qualifies for the 1972 Olympic Games in Munich.
◆ **ORGANIZATION**: Formation of the National Sports Council (NSC).

1972 ◆ **HOCKEY**: Men's hockey team finishes eighth at the Olympic Games in Munich.

1975 ◆ **HOCKEY**: Men's team finishes fourth in the World Cup tournament held in Kuala Lumpur.

1976 ◆ **ATHLETICS**: Ishtiaq Mobarak competes in the 110-metre hurdles event at the Montreal Olympic Games and makes it to the semi-finals.
◆ **BADMINTON**: Men's team finishes as runner-up in the Thomas Cup competition in Bangkok.

Malaysian 1975 World Cup hockey team.

◆ **HOCKEY**: Men's team finishes eighth at the Olympic Games.

1979 ◆ **TENPIN BOWLING**: Allan Hooi, Edward Lim and Koo Boon Jin win a gold medal in the three-man event at the FIQ World Championships in Manila.

1980s

Malaysian 1980 Olympic football team.

1980 ◆ **FOOTBALL**: Men's team qualifies for the Moscow Olympic Games.

1982 ◆ **BADMINTON**: Razif Sidek and Jalani Sidek win the men's doubles event at the All England Open Championships.

1985 ◆ **SEPAK TAKRAW**: Men's team wins the King's Cup World Championship in Thailand.
◆ **NETBALL**: Women's team wins Asian Open Championship in Kuala Lumpur.

1988 ◆ **BADMINTON**: Men's team finishes as runner-up in the Thomas Cup competition in Kuala Lumpur.
◆ **PARALYMPICS**: P. Mariappan wins a bronze for powerlifting in Seoul, the nation's first Paralympic Games medal.
◆ **SEPAK TAKRAW**: Men's team wins the King's Cup World Sepak Takraw Championship in Thailand.
◆ **TAEKWONDO**: M. Vasugi wins Malaysia's first Olympic medal in a demonstration event, taking a bronze in the women's flyweight category in Seoul.

1990s

1990 ◆ **BADMINTON**: Men's team finishes as runner-up in the Thomas Cup competition in Tokyo.
◆ **SNOOKER**: Sam Chong wins the Asian Snooker Championship in Jakarta.

1991 ◆ **BODYBUILDING**: Abdul Malek Noor becomes the heavyweight Mr Asia for the sixth time. He previously won each year from 1985 to 1988 and again in 1990.

1992 ◆ **BADMINTON**: Men's team wins the Thomas Cup competition in Kuala Lumpur.
◆ Razif Sidek and Jalani Sidek win the bronze medal in the men's doubles competition at the Olympic Games in Barcelona.

Players and fans celebrating after Malaysia's victory in the Thomas Cup competition at Stadium Negara, 1992.

- **HOCKEY**: Men's team finishes ninth at the Olympic Games in Barcelona.
- **TAEKWONDO**: Sarah Chung wins a gold medal in the heavyweight category at the Asian Taekwondo Championships in Kuala Lumpur.

1994 ◆ **BADMINTON**: Men's team finishes as runner-up in the Thomas Cup competition in Jakarta.
- **SNOOKER**: Ooi Chin Kay wins the Asian Snooker Championship in Bangladesh.

1996 ◆ **BADMINTON**: Rashid Sidek wins the bronze medal in the men's singles competition at the Olympic Games in Atlanta.
- Cheah Soon Kit and Yap Kim Hock win the silver medal in the men's doubles competition at the Olympic Games in Atlanta.
- **CYCLING**: Debut of the Tour de Langkawi.
- **ORGANIZATION**: The first sports school is set up in Bukit Jalil, Kuala Lumpur.

1997 ◆ **MOUNTAINEERING**: M. Magendran and N. Mohandas become the first Malaysians to reach the summit of Mount Everest.
- **ORGANIZATION**: Passing of the Sports Development Act and creation of the office of the Sports Commissioner.
- **OFF ROAD RACING**: The 4x4 International Rainforest Challenge held for the first time.

1998 ◆ **BADMINTON**: Men's team finishes second in the Thomas Cup competition in Hong Kong.
- **BOXING**: Sapok Biki becomes the first Malaysian boxer to win a Commonwealth Games gold medal.
- **LAWN BOWLS**: Malaysia scores its first medals in lawn bowls at the Commonwealth Games.
- **ORGANIZATION**: Malaysia hosts the Commonwealth Games.

Miniature sheets issued in 1998 showing Malaysian individual and team gold medal winners at the Commonwealth Games in Kuala Lumpur.

1999 ◆ **FORMULA ONE**: The inaugural F1 PETRONAS Malaysian Grand Prix held at the Sepang International Circuit.
- **GOLF**: World Cup of Golf held in Kuala Lumpur.
- **SAILING**: Azhar Mansor becomes the first Malaysian to sail solo around the world.

2000s

2000 ◆ **BODYBUILDING**: Bantamweight bodybuilder Sazali Samad wins the Mr Universe title.
- **TABLE TENNIS**: World Table Tennis Championships held in Kuala Lumpur.
- **TRIATHLON**: Inaugural Ironman Langkawi Malaysia Triathlon staged.

2001 ◆ **LAWN BOWLS**: Malaysian team wins five gold and three silver medals at the Asian Lawn Bowls Championship in Hong Kong.
- **TENPIN BOWLING**: Shalin Zulkifli wins the World Tenpin Masters Championship in England, marking the first time a woman defeated a man in a major world bowling tournament.

2002 ◆ **BADMINTON**: Men's team finishes as runner-up in the Thomas Cup competition in China.
- **KARATE**: S. Premila wins a bronze medal in the women's open kumite event at the World Karate Championships in Madrid.
- **LAWN BOWLS**: Malaysian team wins seven gold medals and one bronze medal at the Asian Lawn Bowls Championship in Manila.
- **RALLY RACING**: Karamjit Singh becomes the first Asian to win the FIA Production Car World Championship for Drivers.

2003 ◆ **BADMINTON**: Mohd Hafiz Hashim wins the men's singles event at the All England Open Championships.
- **BOXING**: Adnan Jusoh wins the Commonwealth Amateur Boxing Championship in Kuala Lumpur.
- **LAWN BOWLS**: Malaysian team wins five gold medals at the Asian Lawn Bowls Championship in Kuala Lumpur.
- **TENPIN BOWLING**: Women's team wins the FIQ–WTBA World Championship in Kuala Lumpur.
- Men's and women's teams win the World Tenpin Team Cup in Denmark.

2004 ◆ **AQUATICS**: Lim Keng Liat makes it to the semi-finals of the 100-metre backstroke event at the Olympic Games in Athens.
- **BODYBUILDING**: Bantamweight bodybuilder Sazali Samad wins the Mr Universe title.
- **ORGANIZATION**: Appointment of the Cabinet Committee on Sports Development.
- **TAEKWONDO**: Elaine Teo qualifies for the Olympic Games after winning a silver medal in the 49-kilogram women's event at the Asian Taekwondo Olympic Qualifying Games.

2005 ◆ **LAWN BOWLS**: Nor Iryani Azmi wins the women's singles event at the World Champion of Champions tournament in Christchurch.
- Malaysian team wins five gold medals at the Asian Lawn Bowls Championship in Kuala Lumpur.
- **ORGANIZATION**: The National Women's Games is held for the first time.
- The Ministry of Education sets up the Sports Advisory Panel.
- **SQUASH**: Nicol David wins the women's singles title at the World Squash Open in Hong Kong and becomes the number one ranked player in the world.
- **TENPIN BOWLING**: Esther Cheah wins a gold medal in the singles event at the FIQ World Championships in Denmark.

2006 ◆ **BODYBUILDING**: Bantamweight bodybuilder Sazali Samad wins the Mr Universe title.
- **CYCLING**: Josiah Ng becomes overall winner of the World Cup keirin event. Coupled with his first success in 2003, he becomes the first cyclist in the world to have won it twice.
- **EQUESTRIAN**: The FEI World Cup Jumping Finals held in Kuala Lumpur.
- **LAWN BOWLS**: Nur Fidrah Noh wins the women's singles title at the New Zealand National Open.
- **PARALYMPICS**: Malaysia has its best ever performance at a FESPIC Games, winning 44 gold, 60 silver and 71 bronze medals at the competition held in Kuala Lumpur.
- **SQUASH**: Nicol David wins her second consecutive women's singles title at the World Squash Open in Belfast and retains her number one world ranking.

Nicol David holding up the 2005 World Squash Open trophy.

Tan Sri Dato' Seri Ahmad Sarji Abdul Hamid (centre), president of the Malaysia Lawn Bowls Federation, admiring the gold medals won by (from left) Nur Iryani Azmi, Nor Hashimah Ismail and Azlina Arshad in the women's triples event and Siti Zalina Ahmad (right) in the women's singles event at the Commonwealth Games in Melbourne, 2006.

2007 ◆ **BODYBUILDING**: Lightweight bodybuilder Sazali Samad wins the Mr Universe title.
- **BADMINTON**: Koo Kien Keat and Tan Boon Heong win the men's doubles event at the All England Open Championships.
- BWF World Badminton Championships held in Kuala Lumpur.
- **FOOTBALL**: Men's team wins the Merdeka Tournament.
- **LAWN BOWLS**: Siti Zalina Ahmad wins the women's singles event at the Australian Open.
- Asian Lawn Bowls Championship held in Kuala Lumpur. The Malaysian team wins six gold medals.
- Nur Fidrah Noh wins the women's singles event and Malaysia wins the mixed pairs event at the World Indoor Bowls Championships in Kuala Lumpur.
- Safuan Said becomes the number one ranked male player in the world according to the World Bowls Board ranking system.
- **MOUNTAINEERING**: Marina Ahmad becomes the first Malaysian woman to reach the summit of Mount Everest.

Josiah Ng (foreground) racing in the Under-23 World Championships in Stuttgart, 2007.

- **SQUASH**: Nicol David wins eight of the eleven tournaments she participates in on the World Tour Circuit and retains her ranking as the number one player in the world.
- **TENPIN BOWLING**: Women's team wins the FIQ World Championships in Mexico.

2008 ◆ **LAWN BOWLS**: Safuan Said wins the men's singles title at the World Bowls Championships in Christchurch.

The *New Zealand Herald* featured Safuan Said in its sport section following his victory the men's singles event at the 2008 World Bowls Championships in Christchurch.

1. Top spinning contest taking place during a cultural festival in Kelantan, 1961.

2. Gold medallist Azrin Abdul Malek (left) jumping to avoid a kick from his competitor from Vietnam in the silat event during the SEA Games in Brunei, 1999.

3. Female students playing in an inter-school *galah panjang* competition in Kuala Lumpur, 2005.

4. Students from various ethnic groups enjoying a friendly game of *batu seremban*, a Malay traditional pastime, during their school recess, 2000.

5. Children flying kites in Sabah.

6. Dignitary dotting the eye of the dragon's head to symbolically awaken it before the 14th Penang International Dragon Boat Festival, 1992.

7. Participants taking part in a blowpipe competition during the Borneo Games in Kuching, 2007. The recently revived multi-sport event includes competitions based on traditional skills.

8. Over 6000 exponents from *taiji quan* and *qigong* associations throughout Malaysia gathering together at the *padang* in Ipoh, Perak for a mass demonstration, 2003.

TRADITIONAL GAMES AND PASTIMES

The population of Malaysia comprises a diversity of cultures and a corresponding array of sports and recreational activities. Traditional recreation helps preserve the past and can be classified broadly according to three categories: activities that belong to the various indigenous peoples of Peninsular Malaysia, Sabah and Sarawak, activities associated with the Malays and, finally, activities practised by the various communities, such as the Chinese and Indians, who came into the country during the colonial period. Like much of Malaysia's multicultural landscape, these traditional recreational activities, engaged in by diverse communities and introduced in different time strata, exist side-by-side, engendering a unique heritage.

Some of these traditional games and pastimes, however, can be encountered throughout Southeast Asia and are shared especially among geographically contiguous communities in different countries. Top spinning, kite flying, silat and bird singing are all activities that transcend international borders. But there are clearly distinguishable features that make the Malaysian manifestations of these activities distinctive. Kelantanese tops, for example, are unique by virtue of their sheer size, and the manner in which they function as competitive as well as decorative objects. Although kite flying dates back at least 3000 years to China, Korea and Japan, perhaps nowhere more than in Malaysia is the making and flying of kites seen as such a serious art form, demonstrating consummate craftsmanship and skill and elaborate cultural symbolism. Traditional pastimes have thus evolved into highly significant representations of local culture.

Traditional recreation not only serves the purposes normally associated with sports and games. Indeed, amusement and competition are merely two of the many aspects of Malaysian traditional pastimes, which are often multifunctional in character and involve numerous levels of meaning. The recreation of the Orang Asli and other indigenous communities, for instance, fulfils social functions, playing an important role in determining an individual's standing in the community. By requiring the demonstration of physical prowess and mental capabilities, recreational activities such as dancing, hunting, fishing and cooking can lend prestige to members of a community, serving as means of proving self-worthiness and even attracting potential spouses. Other traditional games and pastimes are also connected with deeply embedded spiritual beliefs, mythologies and world views. Traditional games and pastimes are vehicles of social cohesion, and help to pass on the shared values of a community from one generation to the next.

Series of commemorative stamps issued in 2000 which feature popular traditional Malaysian children's games (from left) kite flying, *main guli* (marbles), bicycle rim racing, *tarik upih* and *ting ting* (hopscotch).

Top spinning

Some of the largest, heaviest and aesthetically outstanding tops in the world can be found in the Southeast Asian islands of Java and Bali and in Malaysia. In Malaysia, particularly among the Malay communities of the east coast of the Malay Peninsula, top spinning (main gasing) is a competitive sport. Contests are held throughout the year, and the pastime has developed into a major social, cultural and athletic phenomenon.

Gasing uri competition held in conjunction with the Sultan of Kelantan's birthday, 1998.

A living tradition

Archaeologists have discovered tops dating from 3500 BCE in the ancient city of Ur in Iraq. Other evidence of the early existence of tops comes from 1400 to 2000 years ago in Egypt. Tops which were found in China and Greece date back to 1250 BCE. Over the centuries, tops have been referred to in the works of some of the greatest writers of the world including Homer, Plato, Aristophanes, Virgil and Shakespeare.

Performer suspending and spinning his *gasing* on a piece of string.

In Malaysia, normal tops such as those handled by children are ubiquitous. The more unique gigantic tops, however, can commonly be found in the states of Kelantan and Terengganu.

Originally practised in village communities as a pastime during the months when the rice was ripening, top spinning in Kelantan spread through statewide competitions held in Kota Bharu. Such events continue to draw participants from near and far, and observers from all over Malaysia. The serious art of top spinning is also practised in Melaka, as well as on a lesser scale in other parts of the country.

Top spinning is a fascinating manifestation of the Malaysian cultural heritage. While it is certainly an important pastime and sport for local residents, tourists visiting the country are often amazed by the size of the tops, the energy required to spin them, the grace and beauty of the sport and the enthusiasm that it generates. Malaysian top spinners have travelled abroad to exhibit their tops as well as to demonstrate their spinning skills.

BELOW: Children in Kuala Lumpur playing with tops made from young betel nuts, 1994.

BOTTOM: Players taking part in a top spinning competition organized by the Batu Rakit league in Terengganu in 2005.

Competitive top spinning

Top spinning is essentially a friendly game meant for adults; it involves large tops, and requires a great deal of physical effort as well as training and skill. There are two methods for playing: *gasing pangkah* (top striking), and *gasing uri* (top spinning). In *gasing pangkah*, a top is spun and strikes an opponent's top that is already spinning in place with the intention of stopping it. In *gasing uri*, the objective is to outlast an opponent's top in terms of spinning

duration. In *gasing pangkah*, the participants are divided up into teams, each with two members, while *gasing uri* is played by individuals. In both contests, there are several assistants who help facilitate the proceedings.

Types of tops

In Malaysia, there is a wide range of tops which can be divided broadly into two categories: those that are used for ornamentation, and those utilized for playing. This second category may be subdivided

Two professional *gasing* makers from Kelantan demonstrating the art of top making at the Karyaneka Handicraft Centre in Kuala Lumpur, 1983.

into tops designed for children and those created for adults participating in serious contests.

To fashion the tops, any wood that is readily available can be used, including that of the mangosteen, guava or tamarind trees. The most suitable wood for making tops for competition, due to its hardness, comes from the merbau tree.

In terms of shape, there are several varieties of tops found in Malaysia. The most common ones are plate-shaped tops (*gasing piring*), heart-shaped tops (*gasing jantung*), flat-top tops (*gasing leper*), egg-shaped tops (*gasing telur*), tops shaped like the berembang fruit (*gasing berembang*) and betel nut-shaped tops (*gasing pinang*). *Gasing pinang* are usually used by children. A young betel nut is shelled by removing its husk and skin, and the wood is then shaped at the top and bottom, with a bamboo strip or nail attached to it.

A *gasing piring* (middle), *cokok* (left) and *lopak* (right) are used for *gasing uri* competitions.

Tops vary in weight, with the bigger and heavier ones meant for competition made of wood, iron and lead, and can weigh up to 5 kilograms.

Top spinning competitions

Contests

There are two types of top spinning contests: spinning tops (*gasing uri*) and striking tops (*gasing pangkah*). A contest typically takes place in a shed known as a *gelanggang*, measuring approximately eight metres square for *gasing pangkah* and nine metres square for *gasing uri*. In the centre of the *gelanggang* is a square or circular clay platform, called a *bong*, measuring between 60 and 90 centimetres across. As the top is spun and flies through the air, it is supposed to land on the *bong*.

Rope being coiled around a *top* in preparation for spinning.

Physics of spinning

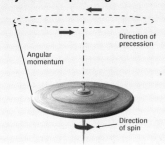

Angular momentum

Direction of precession

Direction of spin

A ritual specialist (*bomoh* or *pawang*) prepares the playing court by driving away the spirits and building an invisible security 'fence' around the area, thus preventing their return. When necessary a *bomoh* also conducts rites to prevent rain. Islamic invocations may also be read. Turmeric rice is scattered to prevent any mishaps, and gong-beats announce the beginning of the competition.

For the purpose of spinning the top, a rope which is 1.75 centimetres thick and 3–5 metres in length is used. One end of the rope is tightly wound around a tiny knob called the *jambul*, so that the entire surface of the top is covered. The other end of the rope is circled four or five times around the wrist of the spinner. The top is thrown, and the string withdrawn quickly to give the top the momentum for its spin.

Throwing a top

ABOVE: Participant in a *gasing uri* contest spinning his top as his assistant, the *juru cokok*, looks on and prepares to scoop up the *gasing* with a wooden paddle called a *cokok*.

ABOVE RIGHT: Juru lopak balancing his *gasing* on a wooden post or *lopak*, on which the top continues to spin.

RIGHT: After the *juru lopak* positions his *gasing* on the ground, it will spin, along with the competitors' tops, for as long as possible.

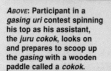

The gasing uri contest

Two assistants, commonly referred to as *juru* or *jong*, are required for each participant in the *gasing uri* competition. One of them, the *juru cokok*, is responsible for holding the *cokok*, a wooden scoop or paddle approximately 60 centimetres in length. The *cokok* is used to pick up the top immediately after it touches the ground. The other assistant, the *juru lopak*, is responsible for handling the *lopak*, a wooden post with a height of 40–45 centimetres and a metal surface with a shallow indentation at the top. The *gasing*, while spinning, is scooped into this indentation by the *juru cokok*, where it continues to spin for as long as possible. The player whose top spins the longest is declared the winner. A *gasing uri* typically spins for over an hour.

1. The top spinner raises the *gasing* above his shoulder before taking several quick steps forward.
2. The top spinner, using great force, hurls the *gasing* at a 30-degree angle toward the clay platform.
3. After releasing the *gasing* with one hand, the top spinner uses his other hand to pull the string back, thereby giving the *gasing* its momentum.

The gasing pangkah contest

G*asing pangkah* is usually played in teams called *regu*, often with five or more teams participating at a time. Each team comprises two to five, but typically four, persons. To determine which team will launch their tops first, (*pasukan menanti*), and which team will strike (*pasukan pemangkah*), a *gasing uri* contest is held with each team represented by a single top. The team whose top spins longer becomes the first team to strike.

The competition begins with the *pasukan menanti* launching their tops onto the *bong*. Several tops may be spun at the same time. The *pasukan pemangkah* then put their tops into play with the intention of hitting the tops of the *pasukan menanti*, so that the latter either cease spinning altogether, are broken or, at least, with their balance affected, are unlikely to spin for too long. Once the tops of the two teams have been launched and struck respectively, those that are still spinning are carefully scooped up and transferred to the *lopak*, as in the *gasing uri* competition. If at least one of the tops of the *penanti* team outlasts the tops of the *pemangkah* team, the roles are reversed, with the *penanti* team now becoming the *pemangkah*.

A participant in a *gasing pangkah* contest smashes his *gasing* into an opponent's, hoping to break it, or at least stop its spin, with the impact of the collision.

Kite flying

Malaysian kites range from simple to highly elaborate in style and construction. Kites from the states of Kelantan and Terengganu called wau, *demonstrate the greatest variety in terms of type and intricacy of design and ornamentation. Kite flying is a popular recreational and competitive activity in Malaysia. Participants and spectators come from all over the country and abroad to attend various kite flying festivals and competitions.*

Competitors preparing to release their kites into the air at the beginning of a kite flying contest in Terengganu, 2000. According to accounts in the *Sejarah Melayu*, these competitions date back to the 15th century.

Children flying *wau* in Kelantan, a state which is famous for its many traditional arts and crafts activities.

Wau-making

The process of making a *wau* is complicated and can take up to two weeks for a particularly ornate kite. It begins with the preparation of the kite frame, which is made of thin-jointed sections of bamboo. The various sections of the frame are assembled and tied with thread. The frame of the kite consists of several sections: the head, the wings, the tail or tail fin, and a spine which runs through the length of the kite and joins the wings and the tail. Bamboo struts, braced to the wing-tips, are often wound with vibrantly coloured paper streamers, and bunches of streamers with long paper tassels are attached to the head and the thick nose of the kite to act as stabilizers in strong wind. In the largest of the kites, which are about 3 metres high and have a 2.5-metre wing span, the backbone may be braced by two cross-sections, fixed with rattan slip-knots, to provide additional strength. After the frame is completed, the wings are covered with two or three layers of paper. The first layer consists of plain coloured paper, while the second and third layers are artfully designed and decorated.

Traditional Kelantanese *wau* maker using bamboo to make the frame of a kite.

Origins of kite flying

The history of kite flying reaches back over 3000 years, with actual written records dating back to the 5th century BCE. Most historians believe that China was the first country to develop the art of kite flying and Buddhist missionaries later spread it to Korea and Japan where people eventually created their own styles of kites. However, other theories argue that this art form could have arisen independently in several different countries including India, Malaysia, Myanmar and Indonesia or that Genghis Khan and his Mongol warriors could have introduced kite flying to Central and South Asia as well as to Europe.

There is no clear indication as to the origins of the Malaysian kite. It is possible that the idea may have been initially borrowed from China, India or Indonesia, with the eventual evolution of a style unique to Malaysia. Indigenous techniques and designs are typically encountered in the eastern states of the Peninsula.

Apart from the more well-known, intricate and elaborate kites of Kelantan and Terengganu called *wau*, there are many varieties of kites found in other states of Malaysia. Small diamond-shaped Chinese kites, for instance, are commonly seen in urban centres on the west coast of the Peninsula.

The *wau* derives its name from the resemblance of its wings to the Arabic letter which is pronounced the same way. This term has now gained national acceptance as a means of generally referring to kites. The terms *layang-layang* and *layangan* are also used, primarily in Johor, Negeri Sembilan, and Penang, to speak about kites in general.

The functions of kites

Kite making is considered a serious art form because it requires consummate skill and craftsmanship. Principally, *wau* are appreciated for their aesthetic beauty, and they are often explicitly made for this purpose, utilizing batik printed fabric instead of paper. They also serve as prized pieces for collectors and hobbyists.

In Kelantan, *wau* are sometimes used to drive away evil spirits. For this purpose, a *busul*, a device that makes a humming sound, is attached to the kite as it floats in the air. This device is shaped like a violinist's bow, with a piece of split-leaf fibre (*daun busar*) held taut between the ends of the bow. When the wind blows across the kite's path, the *daun busar* gives out a loud low-pitched sound or harmony of notes.

In many countries, including Malaysia, kite flying is a celebration of a good harvest, and hence contests are usually held after the harvest season. Kite flying is highly regarded as a recreational activity in Malaysia, and the sport of kite flying has become a bona fide competition among *wau* enthusiasts.

Kite flying competitions

When there is a kite flying contest, the competitors and spectators from neighbouring villages or districts gather at the chosen ground, usually an open field. People of all ages arrive in droves, prepared to spend a good portion of the day at the site. In the event that there are too many competitors, qualifying heats are conducted to select the finalists.

The winner of the contest is the competitor or team whose kite reaches and sustains the greatest vertical height above the ground. A string is tied to each kite, the same thin twine that is used for making fishing-nets, and is sometimes marked in even lengths with coloured thread for better visibility. When a dozen or more kites are all flying close together in the distance, it is almost impossible for the naked eye to distinguish which one is the highest. Consequently, the competitors, after stabilizing their kites in the air, must tie their strings to a horizontal wooden bar anchored five metres above the ground by two stakes. The judges can then easily measure the length of each string and its angle of inclination to the ground, and thereby estimate the height at which the respective kites are flying. A half of a coconut shell with a hole in its centre is submerged in a bucket of water and at the moment it sinks the judges determine which kite is the highest and declare the winner. The judges' decision is very rarely contested.

Winning a contest depends upon the skill of the flyer in handling the kite and whether he is able to take advantage of the prevailing wind conditions. However, the actual design of his kite, the positioning of stabilizers and the manner in which the string is fastened to the kite can also make a difference.

The type of kite most favoured for serious competitions is the *wau bulan* (moon kite) which remains steady in variable wind conditions after being launched. Other types of kites seen at competitions, but primarily used for display purposes, include *wau puyuh* (quail kite), *wau kucing* (cat kite), *wau ikan* (fish kite), and *wau kikir* (file kite).

In another type of competition, simply designed and easily manoeuvrable 'fighter kites' are employed. The section of the string nearest the kites is smeared with crushed glass and glue.

In flight, the kites are then manoeuvred in an effort to knock each other down by severing the string connected to the opponent's kite. Kite fighting competitions are not officially organized, and participants in such contests get involved on an informal basis.

Kites are also judged competitively based on the beauty of their design and ornamentation and the musicality of the humming sound which their *busul* makes during flight.

Named for its crescent-shaped tail, the *wau bulan* (moon kite) is the most common variation of the traditional Malay kite. With the right wind conditions, the *wau bulan* can reach heights in excess of 450 metres.

Kite flying festivals and competitions

In Malaysia, kite flying festivals and contests are not confined to any particular season. The harvesting season in certain states is a popular time for these events, but they are also held at various other times of the year. Kite festivals and competitions are organized in various states on a rotational basis as well as in conjunction with special cultural events and celebrations.

Kite-flying stamp issued in 1982.

Modern interpretation of a *wau burung* (bird kite) at the Pasir Gudang International Layang-Layang Festival, 2003.

Various types of kites in flight at the International Layang-Layang Festival in Pasir Gudang, Johor in 2001.

Kelantanese kite flyers displaying various types of *wau*.

Kite makers showing off a majestic *wau bulan* at a presentation held at the Lake Gardens in Kuala Lumpur, 1956.

Participants launching their *wau bulan* into the air during the Kelantan International Wau Festival, 2001.

Launching a kite during a competition

Launchers, gripping their kites just below the base of the wings, prepare to release them into the wind.

Handlers hold a line of string to steer and stabilize their kites once they soar into the air.

Competitors must tie their kites to a wooden bar so that the judges can determine which is the highest.

Bird singing

For centuries, the zebra dove, better known in Malaysia as the **merbok**, *has been prized for its voice. These birds are bred and trained to sing complex melodies in order to participate in contests.* **Merbok**-*singing competitions have been a fixture on the local and regional festive calendars since the 1960s, and champion-calibre birds can earn trophies and other prizes.*

Spectators watch and listen to *merbok* singing during a competition in Selangor, 1969.

Valuable voices

In Malaysia, there are a number of bird species prized and kept for the beauty and musicality of their voices. The bulbul, spotted dove, shama, magpie, white eye, *hwamei* and zebra dove are all celebrated for their cooing and singing. The most popular singing bird, the zebra dove (*Geopelia striata*), is known locally as the *merbok* or *ketitir*. The species, the smallest of the dove family, is indigenous to the lowlands of Southeast Asia.

In the wild, *merbok* feed on grass seeds or *padi*. They typically live alone and are only seen in pairs during the mating season from February to August. They are very shy and rapidly fly away upon encountering any impending danger. *Merbok* sing throughout the year except on rainy days and during moulting, although they tend to sing more during the mating season. Those birds bred in cages typically sing more during the daylight hours.

Male *merbok* are renowned for their innate vocal abilities, and are able to carry sophisticated melodies. To the untrained ear, *merbok* calls may all sound similar. To a serious enthusiast, each bird possesses a unique and distinguishable voice signature.

Proud owners stand with their winning birds and trophies after a *merbok* singing contest held in Ipoh, 1971.

Participants and spectators at the annual Putrajaya Bird-Singing Competition, 2006.

Origins of bird singing competitions

As early as the 16th century, *padi* planters in Kelantan relaxed by listening to the melodic songs of the *merbok* in the trees. They soon began to domesticate *merbok*, keeping them in captivity by placing the birds in bamboo cages pulled up by ropes onto bamboo poles some 4-metres tall to simulate the birds' natural environment and entice them to sing. While listening, the farmers casually compared the songs of one bird to another. Thus began the first informal *merbok*-singing competitions.

In the 19th century, royalty from the Kelantan and Pattani sultanates often received *merbok* as gifts from commoners and also exchanged them as royal gifts. The mixing of bloodlines through breeding started from these exchanges and from obtaining *merbok* from different localities known for having birds with superior quality voices. In the late 1800s, the first formal *merbok*-singing competition was organized within the palace grounds in Kota Bharu.

Bird-singing contests became increasingly popular in Malaysia and Thailand, and commoners began to organize their own competitions. With the establishment of the Persatuan Seni Suara Burung Ketitir Kelantan (Merbok-Singing Association of Kelantan) in 1967, the standard—and now universally accepted—criteria for assessing the voices of *merbok* was promulgated.

By the late 1960s, *merbok*-singing competitions had spread throughout Malaysia as well as to Singapore and Indonesia. As of 2008, there are approximately 10,000 *merbok* enthusiasts in Malaysia, who keep the birds either for competitive purposes or just for the sheer pleasure of listening to their serenades.

The competitive bird-singing circuit

As Persatuan Seni Suara Burung Ketitir Kelantan is the only bird-singing association registered with the Federal Government, Kelantan is the nexus of bird-singing events in the country. Apart from monthly competitions which are organized by the association, individuals also conduct informal contests three times a week. The state also hosts two annual international-level competitions, which attract hundreds of competitors from the Southeast Asian region, in honour of the Sultan of Kelantan's birthday and Independence day. Besides the *merbok*, other species of birds (such as the spotted dove, shama and hill mynah) take part in these grand events, occupying their own separate sections within the same grounds.

Contests are held monthly on a rotational basis in Kuala Lumpur, Selangor, Johor, Kedah, Perlis, Penang, Melaka and Perak. Putrajaya organized international competitions in 2002 and 2005.

Merbok breeding as an industry

There are *merbok* breeders in all of the states of Malaysia, especially in Kelantan due to its close proximity to southern Thailand, the international hub of *merbok* breeding. The prices paid for *merbok* vary considerably, and enthusiasts must pay a hefty sum for champion-calibre birds. In 2002, for example, a champion bird was sold for RM180,000. Prices of RM50,000 to RM100,000 are standard for champions.

Called zebra doves because of the black stripes which appear on their bodies, merbok are typically between 20 and 23 centimetres in length and have a wingspan of 24 to 26 centimetres.

Such high-priced birds are bought not only for competition but also for breeding, as their untrained offspring can also fetch sizeable sums.

As the result of generations of breeding, the singing voice of the *merbok* has advanced to the stage where the voice of their wild forefathers has been rendered useless for competitive purposes.

When selecting competitive-quality birds, experts base their choice on the same set of criteria that is used to judge *merbok* during competitions. The objective of breeding is to improve the singing voice of *merbok* offspring. The only way to achieve this is to select a suitable female with a voice that possesses what is lacking in the male voice.

Merbok training

A young *merbok* begins to show the potential of its voice at two and a half months. By three months, it has to be taken out to the competition grounds to accustom it to singing on the poles there. At eight months, the *merbok* is ready to formally compete, although its voice only develops fully at the age of two years. A *merbok* has a singing life span of about seven years, but a few champion birds—like Kubang Buaya of Kelantan, Sri Besut of Terengganu and Anak Boay of Johor, who all competed in the 1970s and 1980s—were competitive for over ten years. Other than getting the bird accustomed to singing on a pole, trainers are not able to influence the inherent quality of a bird's voice or its singing.

Bird cages
The prices of cages can range from a mere RM100 up to RM5000, depending on the workmanship and material used. The body of the cage is usually crafted from a hard species of bamboo, the perch and head are fashioned from hardwoods, and the hooks are made of corrugated metal. Cups containing water, padi, sand and grass seed are placed on both ends of the perch and on the floor of the cage.

Structure of the competition

For competitive purposes, *merbok* are classified into three groups based on the tone of their voices: class A for birds with low, bass tones, class B for birds with intermediate tones between bass and treble and class C for birds with high-pitched, treble tones.

The various classes of *merbok* are grouped separately during competitions and, at the conclusion of the contest, a bird is crowned champion in each of the respective classes. The birds sing to their individual capabilities and those that sing the closest to the required criteria are selected as the winners. Ten birds are chosen as as the winners and the rest receive consolation prizes.

The competitions are divided into four 45-minute segments—three segments in which the *merbok* sing and the judges listen and assess the birds' performances, and a final segment during which the judges confer and select the winners based on their markings.

Competitions are held on a flat surface in open areas. Four-metre poles are fixed into the ground in rows at even intervals. Small semi-circular metal pipes are welded to the tops of the poles, and ropes are passed through these pipes to raise up the bird cages.

In the early morning, the appointed judges take their position and the competition begins. Each judge moves around the grounds repeatedly, listening to the singing birds in a specific class and awarding marks accordingly.

The voices of *merbok* are evaluated according to a standard set of criteria, and a total of up to 85 marks are awarded by judges for four aspects of the song: the *seru* or *angkatan* or beginning of the song (17 marks), the *jalan* or middle of the song (17 marks), the *air-suara* or the quality and fullness of their voice (17 marks) and the *kong* or ending of the song (34 marks). Although it carries no marks, the overall melody is used to determine the winner in the event that two competing birds finish with the same score.

A score sheet contains the pole numbers, which serve to identify the competitors, four columns for the standard set of criteria and a remarks column. A bird must be heard by a majority of judges in all four segments. *Merbok* that are unable to sing or sing fewer than ten calls in a stretch in any segment are automatically

disqualified. A *merbok* usually sings more than 30 calls at a time before it stops for breath or food and drink and then commences singing again.

Competitors raising their cages at the start of a bird-singing competition in Ipoh, 2007.

Judges tabulating the results of a bird-singing competition in Kelantan, 2004. The competition attracted over 1000 participants from Southeast Asia.

Silat

With a history dating back over 2000 years, silat is the traditional martial art of the Malay race. Silat comprises several different aspects: self-defence, mental and spiritual development, art and culture, and sport. It can be practised as a means of cultivating character and conviction, protecting oneself against imminent danger, participating in ancient customs and traditions and competing against opponents.

Combatant throwing his opponent during a silat festival in Penang, 2005.

Performer, accompanied by music on traditional instruments, showcasing silat dance movements.

The *semenanjung kris* is the most honoured of the silat weapons, traditionally being the close-range weapon of choice of royalty and commoners alike. A silat exponent is expected to be able to skilfully wield all of the weapons that were included in the traditional warrior's arsenal.

History of silat

The Malay word 'silat' derives from the combination of *si*, a prefix used to denote an individual who is involved in a certain occupation, and *elat*, which means to confuse or deceive. Silat has come to refer to the Malay art of fighting by using self–defence, often involving the use of complex strategy and trickery.

The origins of silat are lost to antiquity. There is no definitive evidence as to who first developed it or what area of the Malay Archipelago gave birth to it. Archaeologists have unearthed evidence—a copper kris dating back 2000 years—which suggests that silat existed in Malay society before the presence of external influences.

By the 7th century CE, warriors were employing silat tactics to protect and defend the Srivijaya empire. Silat flourished and eventually spread throughout the entire Srivijaya empire, including the Malay Peninsula and Java Island. It grew to become a versatile method of self-defence, encompassing such diverse fields as applied diplomacy, psychology, medicine and weaponry.

With the introduction of Islam to Southeast Asia in the 13th century, the religion's tenets and teachings were incorporated into the principles and rituals of silat. The fighting art is repeatedly referenced in the Malay Annals (*Sejarah Melayu*) and the seminal literary epic *Hikayat Hang Tuah*, both compiled in the 17th century. These two works feature the story of Hang Tuah, a 15th-century admiral from Melaka who has come to represent the prototypical silat warrior.

From the Melaka sultanate of the 15th century through the Portuguese, Dutch, British and Japanese colonizations, Malay warriors used silat to defend themselves against attack and oppression, and as a unifying element to channel and promote the spirit of patriotism among their ethnic group.

Exponents taking part in a combat demonstration. Silat techniques can take the form of complex punches, arm locks or throws, and can be applied to an opponent irrespective of size or strength.

PESAKA logo.

Silat styles

To promote silat locally, the National Silat Federation of Malaysia (Persekutuan Silat Kebangsaan Malaysia or PESAKA) was established in 1983 by the founding masters of the four main styles: Datuk Meor Abdul Rahman Meor Hashim of Silat Seni Gayong, Hanafi Haji Ahmad of Seni Silat Cekak, Datuk Omardin Mauju of Seni Silat Lincah and Anuar Abdul Wahab of Seni Gayung Fatani. Although these styles have led PESAKA since its inception, more than 400 different silat styles are practised in Malaysia. These styles can be broadly classified into three categories: Silat Melayu, which adheres to the indigenous traditional form; Pencak Silat, which originated in Indonesia and emphasizes

Silat training rituals and routines

1. Silat Gayong students perform feats such as jumping through a ring of fire during training.

2. Students from the Seni Silat Pusaka Gayong school performing their routines.

3. Teacher from the Seni Silat Gayung Fatani school giving his students a bath in lime water to mark the completion of their training.

4. Members of the Seni Silat Gayung Fatani group reciting a prayer after their training.

self-defence; and eclectic styles which incorporate elements of foreign martial arts.

Silat is also linked to other aspects of Malay culture. A silat exponent will often cultivate an interest in fields such as metalwork, woodcraft, traditional dancing, Malay dress, medicine and music. A master of silat is referred to as a *pendekar*, derived from the words *pandai akal* which mean 'someone who has mastered intelligence'. In 2006, the Federal Government recognized silat as the official Malaysian art of self-defence and listed it under the National Heritage Act.

Silat as a sport

After Independence, silat grew to become an organized and officially-recognized martial art throughout Southeast Asia. In 1980, umbrella bodies representing silat schools in Malaysia, Indonesia, Brunei and Singapore convened in Jakarta and formed the International Pencak Silat Federation (Persekutuan Pencak Silat Antarabangsa or PERSILAT). PERSILAT has made extensive efforts to promote silat both as a sport and recreational activity at the international level. The federation has expanded to encompass member associations from 49 countries including the United States, Germany, Australia and Denmark. The goal of PERSILAT is to make silat an Olympic sport.

At the 1979 SEA Games in Jakarta, silat debuted as a competitive sport. Pencak Silat World Championships were subsequently organized in Singapore in 1980 and in Jakarta in 1981 and 1982. The first championship tournament outside Asia took place in Austria in 1986. Silat was also introduced as an exhibition sport at the 2002 Asian Games in Korea.

In the late 1980s and early 1990s, Ruzaidi Abdul Rahman, Ahmad Fauzi Othman, Ahmad Khushairi, Ahmad Wardi Salim and Mohd Khairi rose to the highest level of the sport by winning events at the Pencak Silat World Championships. In the 2000s, Zakri Ibrahim, Azrin Abdul Malek and Ahmad Shahril Zailudin all reached the pinnacle of the sport. At the 2007 Pencak Silat World Championships in Pahang, the Malaysian team won seven gold, five silver and eight bronze medals.

Silat competitions

Silat tanding

Silat tanding is a full-contact fight between two competitors from the same weight class. The match is contested on a ring measuring 10 metres in length and width. The two exponents, wearing body protection, position themselves in different corners. A referee, called a *wasit*, oversees the proceedings. The match consists of three rounds, each with a duration of two minutes and a break of one minute in between.

The winner is the fighter who accumulates the most points. Points are decided by a jury of five people who are stationed at designated positions around the ring. Punches and kicks are allowed to the chest, stomach, ribs and back, but strikes to the groin, spine and head are not permitted.

ABOVE LEFT: National competitor Ismail Darus (right) blocking a kick from his Thai opponent during the Pencak World Silat Championships in Penang, 2002.

FAR LEFT: Malaysia's Norazian Anuar (left) kicking her opponent during the 1997 Pencak World Silat Championships in Kuala Lumpur.

LEFT: Malaysian gold medallists (from left) Mohd Arif Kamis, Ahmad Sharil Zailudin and Ahmad Faisal Omar at the 2002 Pencak World Silat Championships in Penang.

Silat seni

A *silat seni* (art of silat) competition at the international level is divided into three categories: *jurus tunggal* (a sequence of movements with one exponent), *jurus ganda* (a sequence of movements with two exponents) and *jurus regu* (a sequence of movements with three exponents).

Jurus tunggal

A single competitor performs a predetermined set of 100 movements, comprising an unarmed section, a section armed with a machete and a third section armed with a staff. The entire performance must be completed in exactly 3 minutes, and points are awarded according to the exponent's skill and precision in executing the sequence. Developed by PERSILAT, the *jurus tunggal* routine incorporates techniques from many different *silat* styles.

Jurus ganda

Two exponents from the same team showcase their skills by performing a freestyle 3-minute fighting sequence which is specially choreographed by their team. The routine must contain attack and defence components, and can be performed either empty-handed or with traditional weapons. Points are awarded not only for the skill and precision of the movements, but also for the overall cohesion and originality of the sequence.

Jurus regu

Three competitors from the same team execute a predetermined 3-minute sequence of movements. The routine, which contains elements of various schools and styles of silat, was created by PERSILAT to exhibit the exponents' capabilities. Points are awarded based on the team's ability to accurately perform the routine while synchronizing their movements.

Orang Asli recreation

The indigenous Orang Asli have their own variety of recreational activities ranging from simple children's games to marriage-eligibility games and complex puzzle games. Many of these games are based on agricultural activities, have social or spiritual significance and have been passed down from one generation to the next.

Contestants race each other to grate the most coconuts in the shortest period of time during an Orang Asli festival in Perak, 1976.

Orang Asli boys taking part in a spear-throwing contest.

Farmer participating in a wood chopping competition at an Orang Asli settlement in Kuala Lumpur in 1979.

Orang Asli men competing in a pole climbing competition in Kelantan, 1990.

A vanishing tradition

The various ethnic groups or sub-groups of the Orang Asli each have their own games, some of which are common among other sub-groups, while others belong solely to a specific ethnic group. These games, however, are usually not considered as games, but as either forms of play or as part of socio-cultural activities. Most Orang Asli games have not been developed into conventional sports with the exception of spearing (javelin), bow and arrows (archery) and blowpipes.

As a result of the introduction of various non-indigenous games, most of the Orang Asli games are no longer played or have simply vanished from local knowledge and socio-cultural practices.

Children's games

A popular game played by Semai children is *bebatak*, which is based on a myth of the Batak people of Sumatra who were traditionally perceived to be cannibals. According to Semai mythology, Batak people supposedly came from the moon. A banyan tree on the moon fell over and the edge of its trunk reached the earth, thus bridging the moon and earth. The Batak walked through the fallen tree and occupied the earth for many years until the trunk began to rot, thus driving them back to the moon before their bridge collapsed. During their stay on the earth, the Batak captured and ate the Semai people.

Based on this myth, children play a version of the game of catch. In the game, one of the participating children takes on the role of the Batak while the rest play the roles of the Semai. The child playing the role of the Batak has to chase and try to capture the other players. A Semai who is touched by the Batak is considered 'dead' and has to take over as the Batak. A similar game is also played by Semai children while swimming in the river.

Another variation of this game is called *batak berencheeb*, which is a game of hide and seek. In *batak berencheeb*, the person selected as the Batak has to search for the other children who are hiding. The first person found by the Batak will in turn assume the latter's role.

Games which represent marriageability

A number of games played by older youths involve *padi* planting activities. Often the purpose of these games is to showcase one's skill and ability. In *padi* pounding, for example, synchronous pounding by groups of five or six people requires great skill, experience and coordination.

ABOVE: Orang Asli youths demonstrating how to husk *padi* using a tray.

RIGHT: Orang Asli women pounding *padi*.

Each member has to know precisely when to pound and when to remove the pounding stick from the pounding block. If the timing is not exactly right, the pounding sticks will 'crash' in the pounder, resulting in the *padi* spilling over and going to waste. Besides being an essential food staple, *padi* has spiritual and sacred significance for the Orang Asli. The person who causes the *padi* to spill over is considered the loser of the game, and will bring embarrassment to his or her group. For Semai youths, such games often function as a means of assessing and meeting potential marriage partners.

Women have their own unique games which highlight their skills and eligibility for marriage. One such game demonstrates how skilled a woman is at removing the *padi* from its husk using a tray. Not everyone can remove the husk quickly and cleanly, and women who can achieve this are recognized by their communities. The recognition comes in the form of invitations to help out at major events and ceremonies held at private households. Being invited to participate in such events raises the status and prestige of a woman, thereby enhancing her chances of getting married.

Games based on social activities

Other Orang Asli games demonstrate the capabilities of men in activities such as hunting, fishing, trapping, using weapons such as blowpipes, spears, archery and felling trees during the clearing season. Orang Asli males strive to be recognized and respected by members of their community for their prowess in performing particular tasks.

Orang Asli women showcase their abilities by serving their families and participating in their communities. They constantly work toward improving their skills in daily activities such as weaving and cooking while also partaking in ritualistic activities such as singing and dancing.

For both unmarried men and women, social activities are extremely important opportunities to attract potential spouses, as well as prove their worthiness to potential parents-in-law. At weddings, for example, men and women have separate roles and activities. For women, one of their tasks is to grate coconuts for cooking. In this activity, they attempt to grate as many coconuts as possible in the shortest amount of time. After this contest of speed, the men will follow up with a contest of strength, breaking coconut shells with their elbows. The winner, by manifesting his strength, raises his stature within the community. Women also try to distinguish themselves at weddings in informal cooking competitions during which they each try to display their culinary skills.

Among the lowland Semai, there is a rarely played rice-eating competition. In this game, the participants compete to see who can consume the most rice. If a person manages to eat a massive amount of rice without stopping, this indicates that he possesses remarkable strength and capacity.

Games of physical prowess

The Temuan partake in many of their own traditional games. In one of these games, held at the end of the harvest season, two men holding a *padi* pounding stick stand facing each other within an area which is marked by two lines drawn behind them. Each of them has to push his opponent out from his territory. The man who still remains in the marked area is declared the winner.

Another game played by the Temuan people is known as *main lesung*. This game involves three male players. Two of the players join their hands together tightly and the third player tries to unlock the hands and get into the circle. If the third player manages to unlock the hands, he wins.

The Temuan also play a game called *gunjai*, a race using walking sticks. In this game, competitors have to race a certain distance without falling. Those who fall are eliminated. *Gunjai* is usually held during welcoming ceremonies and other festive celebrations.

ABOVE AND RIGHT: Orang Asli boys from the Semai group attempting to solve puzzles.

BELOW RIGHT: The *cheek riknuij* puzzle.

Puzzle games

The Semai have developed puzzle games that test the intellectual ability and patience of the participants. One such game is called *cheek riknuij*, which literally translates as 'things that make you lost'. The puzzle is made of five lengths of rattan. One length is 'the pillar' of the frame while the rest function as side frames. The side frames are divided into two sets, each of which has two lengths of rattan of a different size. Each set of the side frames is bent into a 'U' shape with both its edges tied up together with the edge of the pillar. When the frame is assembled, one string is tied loosely around the pillar, which is located in the middle of the frame. The aim of this game is to release the string from the pillar. When this is done, the second task is to put the string back around the pillar.

The origin of *cheek riknuij* is based on a legend about a hunter who got lost in the jungle, grew tired and decided to rest under a big tree. A ghost, however, resided in that tree and intended to eat the man later at night. The hunter, weary from wandering, soon fell asleep and dreamed of a wise old man who taught him a game. The hunter woke up and cut five pieces of rattan and tied them into the *cheek riknuij* puzzle. He lit a fire and commenced playing the game. When the ghost came, it was so intrigued by the game that it spent the entire night trying to release the string from the pillar. The ghost was so obsessed with solving the puzzle that it forgot about eating the hunter and thus he managed to save himself. When the sun rose, the ghost had no choice but to leave.

In addition to the Semai, other sub-groups of Orang Asli such as the Jakun, Mah Meri, Jah Hut and Semelai also have their own game puzzles which require mental ability and patience to solve.

Modern interpretations

In the past, weapons such as bows and arrows, blowpipes and spears were used exclusively as hunting tools and not for sport. Orang Asli weapons were often strengthened and enhanced by the use of charms and magic spells. Consequently, many of them were considered taboo and dangerous. These weapons, however, are now commonly used as sporting equipment and can be found at both local and international events.

Orang Asli men taking part in a blowpipe-shooting competition as children look on.

Traditional recreation of Sabah

Sabah's traditional games vary from simple children's pastimes to organized adult sports which function as entertainment at village gatherings. Equipment is skilfully made from materials found in the natural environment or discarded from the household. Games are a vibrant and essential component of the social and cultural life of the people of Sabah.

Bajau and Iranun horsemen at the annual Tamu Besar festival in Kota Belud in 2006.

Participants racing to the finish line in a stilt-walking competition during the Kiulu 4M Challenge.

Bamboo pop-gun or *bakakuk*.

Children's games

The recreational activities of Sabah children may be individual or collective, and many are precursors to adult games. Girls often pass time by playing 'cat's cradle' (*laba-laba*) in which a loop of thread or string is stretched between their hands and manipulated into various shapes including animals, flowers and stars. Using smooth pebbles or rubber seeds, groups of girls play *main batu* or 'five stones' during which each player throws one stone up, grabs the others and catches the falling stone without dropping any of them (see 'Malay children's games: Challenging body and mind'). The girl who gathers the most stones is the winner. Variations of this game are played with seven stones. *Gapur* is a variant of *main batu* played by Iranun girls which utilizes thin bamboo sticks instead of stones. Each girl tosses up 31 sticks and tries to catch them on the back of her hand. Those who catch an even number of sticks drop out of the game, while those who catch an odd number continue until a winner is declared.

Kadazandusun boys, in particular, make catapults (*lositik*) from forked pieces of smooth wood and strips of rubber or elastic to shoot (*momolositik*) stones or rubber seeds at birds, fruits and other objects. They also create bamboo pop-guns (*bakakuk*) by pushing a stick up a thin bamboo tube to launch rubber seeds or pebbles. Sometimes the projectile is tied to the bamboo to prevent it from actually hitting the target or being lost. Other favourite pastimes are sliding (Kadazandusun *rumuhus*, to slide), during which a child is dragged along on a piece of palm bark or frond by others (see 'Malay children's games: Lyrical and natural variations'); hopscotch (*tinting*) and marbles (*main guli*) (see 'Malay children's games: Challenging body and mind'); and stilt-walking, known in Kadazandusun as *minsurukud* from *sukud* or stilt, or *rampanau* meaning 'long-walking'. The Bajau of Semporna call this *kaldang* or 'stilts'. Bajau Laut children use these when mooring their boats in shallow coastal waters (see 'Traditional water sports').

Gala-gala (Kadazandusun) or *main gala* (Iranun and Brunei) is played at night by two teams of children. A large square of string, comprising four smaller equal squares, is tied to twigs about a metre off the ground. After flipping a coin to determine who starts, the first team proceeds into the squares. If they touch either the strings or sticks, they lose and the opposing team takes a turn. Iranun youths traditionally play *main gala* on the beach at night when the moon is full. It requires great agility to move through the spaces between the strings in the dark.

Datu-datuan, another Iranun game, features six boys against six girls. The boys' team leader is called a *datu* and the girls' leader is a *baih* (both of which are traditional Iranun aristocratic titles). The two teams face each other with the boys' row behind the *baih*, and the girls behind the *datu*. One of the boys whispers to the *baih* that he wants to capture a girl of a certain name. One of the girls then tells the *datu* her name. If it is the same as that whispered by the boy, the *baih* beats a small gong and the girl enters the boys' team. This process continues until only one girl remains. If the *baih* is captured, she and the other girls free themselves by singing a poetic *bayuk* called *Ira-Ira*.

Adult recreation

Many forms of adult recreation, such as *gala-gala*, *rampanau*, tug-of-war (Kadazandusun *migayat do hukud*) and top spinning are derived from children's games. Wooden spinning-tops have many shapes, each around 5 centimetres high with spiked bases. Top spinning, known as *bosing* (Kadazandusun), *mbedtig* (Iranun) or *main gasing* (Brunei and Kadayan), is a popular men's sport. In the Iranun version, each player activates his top with a string, then scoops it onto a coconut-bark 'spoon' as it spins. Teams use various

Traditional Iranun games

1. Women compete at making *piusu* for rice cakes, the equivalent of the Malay *ketupat*.

2. A man playing the game called *kuba* in which he bends backwards to drop his coconut shell on top

of another in a motion called *ulug-ulug*.

3. A group of men taking part in a game of *sepak manggis*.

4. A man spins his top on a palm bark scoop using a technique known as *dtimbanga*.

Puzzles and board games

Inuog dazang is a puzzle of the Rungus community of Kudat and Pitas. It consists of a twisted rattan knot interspersed with a string loop. Great ingenuity is needed to extricate the string from the knot. There are many kinds of *inuog dazang*. The simplest is the man's puzzle or *inuog dazang kusai* which has two rattan loops intertwined around a central stem. The woman's puzzle, *inuog dazang tondu*, is more complicated with four or more intertwined rattan loops, because the Rungus believe women are better intellectually equipped to solve complicated puzzles than men.

Sukian is a traditional Iranun board game similar to chess or draughts played by two or three participants using a square patterned board and sets of 120 pieces. The Brunei and Kadayan communities play a similar game called *pasang*.

*LEFT: A Rungus man trying to solve the *inuog dazang kusai* puzzle by removing it from the knot without untying it, and then reinserting it. In the past, the parents of an eligible daughter would test the mental prowess of a prospective son-in-law by seeing how quickly he could solve the puzzle.*

*ABOVE: Iranun playing a traditional board game called *sukian*.*

Kadazandusun wrestling and martial arts

Various traditional martial arts or *kuntau* are practised in Sabah with different communities adopting their own unique styles.

The Kadazandusun *migogol* is a wrestling match between two fully-clothed barefooted men who try to topple each other using their arms and legs. Each grabs his opponent under the armpits or around the back, and attempts to lift and subsequently throw him down. The competitors are not allowed to use their hands below their opponent's waist or above his shoulders.

Contestants challenging each other to a match of (1) body wrestling or *migogol* (2) finger wrestling or *mipadsa* and (3) arm wrestling or *mipulos*.

The legs can be used to pull down an opponent's legs, but kicking and foot stomping are forbidden. In order to win, a competitor must knock his opponent flat on the back.

In leg wrestling or *mibinti*, two opponents try to topple each other by kicking with the tops of their feet while their hands are held behind their backs.

Kadazandusun arm wrestling or *mipulos* involves two men facing each other across a high ledge or table. Each rests his right elbow on the table and grasps his opponent's right palm. His elbow must not be lifted from the table. He supports himself with his left hand, but his chest, legs and feet must not touch the table. The winner is the competitor who pulls his opponent's hand to his chest and maintains this position for three counts.

During finger wrestling or *mipadsa*, two men stand with the two middle fingers of their right hands interlaced, and their other hands behind their backs. They cannot move their bodies or push and pull their opponent's hands. The objective of the game is to twist the opponent's hand and hold it for a count of three.

techniques to maintain the motion of their tops and the winners are those whose tops spin for the longest period of time. Since 2004, the Brunei and Kadayan communities of Sipitang have held an annual *gasing* competition. Iranun women play *gapur* as a diversion to ward off boredom or sleep while drying *padi*.

Some adult games evolved from work-related activities. The blowpipe (Kadazandusun *sosopuk*) is traditionally an indigenous hunting weapon used by men to blow darts (*monopuk*) at fixed targets as a competitive village sport. While harvesting *padi*, adults and children compete to collect misshapen rice stalks. Iranun women compete to see who is fastest at weaving small square palm-frond containers or *piusu* for rice cakes. Other adult games, such as the Iranun *kuba* in which men throw coconut shells according to various rules and postures, are intended to develop physical strength and prowess.

Sepak manggis is a ball game played by two teams of men during festive occasions such as weddings. The *manggis*, a colourfully decorated container of sweets and other small prizes, is suspended about 20 metres above the ground from a long bamboo pole. The teams take turns kicking a cane ball at each other. The winning team is that which kicks the ball to hit the *manggis*, thereby releasing its prizes. *Sepak manggis* originated in South America, from where it was taken by the Spaniards to the Maranao of Mindanao in the Philippines, who introduced it to the Iranun. It is played by both the Iranun and Bajau communities in Kota Belud.

Sports involving animals

Water buffalo have functioned as beasts of burden, bridewealth components and ritual sacrifices in many indigenous cultures. Buffalo racing (*milumba karabau*) serves as entertainment during festive social gatherings for the Kadazandusun.

Skilled horsemanship has traditionally been a part of Iranun culture. Horses were transported on barges from Mindanao to Lahad Datu and traded into east coast Iranun communities. During the 1890s, the Royal Turf Club was established at Tanjung Aru in Jesselton (now Kota Kinabalu) where pony racing was introduced by the British. As a result of acculturation between the Iranun and Bajau along the west coast,

the Bajau of Kota Belud have become adept at riding horses. Bajau horse trainers bring their horses from Kota Belud to compete in weekend races.

Traditional cockfighting (Kadazandusun *mitutuk* or *misabung do tandaa*) involved aggressive, prize cockerels that fought each other in a circular pen, while male spectators bet on the outcome. Officially banned because it engendered gambling and animal cruelty, cockfighting has almost disappeared from interior communities but occasionally occurs in Tuaran and Kota Belud.

Kota Belud 'cowboys' participating in a buffalo race during the annual Tamu Besar Festival, 2005.

Traditional recreation of Sarawak

The recreational activities of Sarawak originated primarily from agricultural ceremonies and practices. Besides testing individual abilities, games serve as a means of bringing communities together and celebrating festivities. Both young and old partake in a variety of activities which reflect the richness of the culture of Sarawak.

Iban men preparing for a cockfight, c. 1900.

Iban men competing in a traditional wrestling match.

Early beginnings

In 19th century rural Sarawak, boys spent most of their time swimming, running and playing boisterous games, while girls were more likely to stay indoors and help their mothers with household chores. As there was no formal educational system, children acquired life skills from their elders. For example, from the age of five or six, boys accompanied men on their jungle excursions and in the *padi* fields where they were expected to make themselves useful by chasing away birds and other pests.

Traditionally, many of the outdoor games played by young boys were trials of strength and the endurance of pain, and functioned as practice for hunting and warfare. Traditional wrestling was a popular activity during which two young men grasped each other's loincloth and attempted to lift and floor the opponent by strength and skill. Mothers occasionally tried to stop their sons from wrestling, but usually to no avail as the young wrestlers would fear being teased by their friends if they showed any sign of cowardice.

In 1854, English naturalist A.R. Wallace observed a group of Bidayuh boys playing in an open space between a river and a longhouse at Tebakang. They were 'playing at a game something like prisoners' base, their ornaments of beads and brass wire and their gay-coloured kerchiefs and waist-cloths forming a very pleasing sight'.

Children's games

Male children in Sarawak are exposed to the rites and practice of combat at an early age. At the beginning of the harvest, young boys are allowed to carry wooden swords and shields. Older boys engage in mock battles by shooting clay pellets from blowpipes. Such a pellet, shot at close range, can inflict considerable pain and the combatants may sustain injuries. An important part of the game, however, is not to show any sign of weakness.

Young boys spend a lot of time in the river, taking part in friendly swimming races and playing ducks and drakes, which involves skimming a flat stone over the water's surface and counting how many times it bounces before it sinks.

Tibau

Swinging or *tibau* is a popular pastime among the Melanau people of the Rajang delta during the annual Kaul festival (a thanksgiving festival held by fisherman in honour of the gods of the sea). *Tibau* originated as a religious ritual during which daring young men swung together on a rattan rope, 6–9 metres long, singing songs in praise of their orchards in an effort to ensure good harvests. The songs were performed in an archaic dialect, which subsequently disappeared from common usage.

The *tibau* swing consists of a rope (**1**) which is suspended from the apex of a bipod stand (**2**), usually buttressed with struts. A ladder-like structure is positioned about 6–9 metres from the stand (**3**).

The first participant holds the end of the rope and climbs up the ladder. He proceeds to swing on the rope while singing about the flowers of a chosen fruit tree. As he swings back, the second player leaps onto his back and sings about the ripening of the fruits of the same tree. Thus, the rope swings back and forth, and a new player leaps on each time it comes back to the ladder. The third person sings in praise of the fruits getting rounder and larger, the fourth about their changing colour, the fifth about the fruits expanding and tasting sour and the sixth celebrates the sweet smell of the fruits. The final person sings about the monkeys coming to eat the fruits; his verse is supposed to be witty so as to earn laughter and applause from the audience and his fellow participants (**4**).

When a team leaps off at the end of their turn, another team commences swinging on the *tibau* and singing in praise of another type of fruit. While there is no formal scoring system, the audience applauds adept rhyming and singing as well as skilful leaping and swinging. At the end of the competition, the winning team usually becomes apparent by the amount of cheering and acclaim it receives.

When a *tibau* has been built, small boys play on it early in the morning to gain experience, while the older boys and men usually showcase their skills later in the day.

Tibau players jumping and swinging during the Kaul festival in 2003.

Other popular children's pastimes in Sarawak are 'onc-wheeler' and *main telong*. The former utilizes a large milk powder tin lid that is perforated in the centre and nailed to the end of a stick so that it can rotate. A child then runs around the village, pushing this vehicle ahead of himself and making motorbike engine noises. In *main telong*, a tin is inverted over a firm post which is about 50 centimetres high. The objective of the game is to throw a short stick and dislodge the tin from the post.

Common forms of recreation

Among the traditional games played throughout Sarawak are *tibau*, top spinning (see 'Top spinning'), racing, wrestling, cockfighting and kite flying (see 'Kite flying').

Gender-based games

Males in Sarawak compete in a test of strength in which two men sit on the ground with the soles of their feet against each other while grasping a thick

stick with both hands. Each then tries to yank his adversary from the ground. This may be done by brute strength, or by a quick, unexpected jerk. Sometimes a man may test his strength against two or three boys in the same way.

In another game, two men stand, each holding one of his ankles. One of the players positions

Contestants taking part in a traditional wrestling competition at a folk games demonstration held in conjunction with the Kaul festival, 2005.

himself as firmly as he can, while the other swings himself around on one leg, striking his opponent's free leg in an effort to topple him. This hopping and tumbling game affords considerable amusement to its spectators.

Females in Sarawak do not roam the villages in groups the way their male counterparts do, and consequently their leisure is mainly confined to indoor activities. The harvest festivities, however, provide an opportunity for women to partake in an array of outdoor activities. In Central Borneo, females take part in a water squirting competition using bamboo syringes. Females also perform a dance at harvest time by leaping between two hardwood pestles rhythmically manoeuvred by two of their group. The dancer jumps in and out of the constantly opening and closing gap between the pestles; the rhythm picks up as the game proceeds. One false step can result in a painful blow to the ankle which inevitably leads to screams of laughter and delight from fellow participants and the crowd.

BELOW: Woman demonstrating a traditional harvest dance.

BOTTOM: *Bek alok*, a traditional race in which participants must carry a rice-pounding stick, is a popular pastime of the Orang Ulu.

Traditional water sports

Malaysians have a natural affinity for water-based recreation. Traditional water sports comprise a wide spectrum of games and activities which are played throughout the country by people of all ages. Numerous events, competitions and festivals are held to showcase the beauty and excitement of traditional water sports.

Longboat paddlers racing on the Sarawak River during the Regatta Sarawak in 2005.

Contestants in a slippery pole climbing competition during a water festival in Port Dickson, Negeri Sembilan in 2006.

An evolving tradition

Water sports are traditionally practised in Malaysia as a form of celebration, a showcase of the local community's skills and athletic prowess and an expression of appreciation for the vital role of waterways in their lives.

Malaysia's traditional water sports are constantly changing and evolving. While most originated as leisure activities, many water-based recreational activities later developed into competitive games and some have now even become internationally-recognized sports. Others have evolved within local communities to encompass unique water sports festivals and special events. However, some traditional Malaysian water sports have remained true to their humble roots, and their great popularity during festive occasions is evidence of their enduring appeal.

Traditional water-based recreation

In Sabah, bamboo stilts called *rampanau* are used by children to cross rivers and other bodies of water. To make these stilts, holes are cut into light, sturdy bamboo poles according to a desired height, and separate pieces of bamboo are then fashioned and fitted into the holes as foot stands. Walking using *rampanau* is still a favourite recreational pastime, but has also been incorporated into a modern extreme

Racing on the water

The Semporna Regatta features contestants vying for the title of 'Most Beautiful *Lepa*'. Dancers and musicians on board these ancient sea craft seek to entertain the spectators and impress the judges.

Competitors in the Kiulu 4M Challenge paddling through rocky waters on bamboo rafts.

The Semporna Regatta

Regatta Lepa or Semporna Regatta is a recreational event which is held annually in April to celebrate the *lepa*, a single mast sailing boat used by the east coast Bajau community in Semporna, Sabah. The festival is an opportunity for the Bajau to show off their elaborately carved boats and compete to determine which one is the most beautiful. The colourfully decorated *lepa* are lined up on the port, decked with dancers, musicians and family members who sing and cheer on the performers. Another interesting aspect of the Regatta Lepa is the boat tug-of-war. Participants tug at the ropes from their boats in the water. The team that successfully pulls their rival's boat past a designated marker is declared the winner of the contest.

The Kiulu 4M Challenge and the Regatta Sarawak

The Kiulu 4M Challenge is an extreme sports event that tests the physical and mental endurance of its participants. It is the only freshwater event in Sabah which incorporates the traditional pastimes of Sabah's native communities. Held annually in the scenic Kiulu valley, the Kiulu 4M Challenge requires its participants to complete a sequence of traditional water-based activities that include *manangkus* (running), *mamangkar* (bamboo rafting), *manampatau* (swimming with a bamboo pole) and *mamarampanau* (walking or running on bamboo stilts). The simplicity of the activities belies the difficulty of the gruelling Kiulu 4M Challenge course. Participants are divided into categories according to their number and their various levels of ability.

The Regatta Sarawak has been held annually since 1872 as an event to mark the beginning of the new year. It is a grand cultural affair, consisting of traditional longboat races, dragon boat races and other activities such as climbing greasy poles, duck catching competitions and pillow fights. The traditional longboat races, instituted by the Brooke government (1841–1941), commemorate ancient customs during which fierce warriors in huge war canoes competed against each other as a means to settle local rivalries without resorting to war and headhunting. Modern events, like powerboat and jet ski racing competitions, have also been incorporated into the Regatta Sarawak programme to add excitement and variety.

Dragon boat racing

Dragon boat festivals in Malaysia, also known as *tuan wu*, trace their origins back to China in the 4th century BCE. The most exhilarating part of these traditional festivals involves the dragon boat races, which are held in commemoration of the life and death of Chu Yuan, a legendary Chinese poet and patriot who lived during the Chou dynasty. Dragon boat races water sports competition in Sabah. Stilt-walking, known as *kaldang* by the Bajau Laut of Semporna, is a popular form of recreation among Bajau Laut (Sea Bajau) children.

In the game of duck catching, ducks are released into a pond or open body of water, and participants are required to jump into the water and try to catch them. The winner is the individual who is able to grab the most ducks within a certain time limit or the fastest person to catch a duck and return to the jetty. The antics of the contestants are often hilarious to behold and the event is a staple of water events and festivals in Malaysia.

Diving for plates is another popular activity in which plates are dropped from the jetty into the water and participants must dive down to retrieve them. It is a widely practised traditional sport among the seafaring communities, particularly those living on the islands and coastlines of Sabah.

The game of *pukul bantal* or pillow fighting is a water-based game involving two contestants who fight each other with pillows while balancing on a greasy pole suspended horizontally over the water. The objective is to knock the opponent into the water below. The victor remains on the pole until he is defeated by another contestant.

ABOVE: Bajau divers in Sabah holding up porcelain plates that they retrieved from the seabed, 2003. Whoever garners the most plates within a predetermined period of time is declared the winner of the contest. It is believed that the game originated from the practice of salvaging pieces of porcelain from sunken ships.

ABOVE LEFT: Participants in a pukul bantal (pillow fighting) contest during a festival in Port Dickson, Negeri Sembilan in 2006.

LEFT: Competitors in a duck catching contest held in Sarawak, 1977.

The 25th annual dragon boat race organized by the Malacca Dragon Boat Association on the Melaka River, 2007. A total of 17 teams took part in the competition.

were introduced to Malaysia by migrating clans from mainland China, who eventually settled in Borneo and the former Malayan states. Outside China, Malaya became one of the first countries to formally recognize dragon boat racing as a sporting activity in 1934. Dragon boat races have now become annual events, particularly in the states of Penang, Sabah and Sarawak.

The state of Penang held the first official dragon boat race in 1956 and since then dragon boat racing has become one of the most popular water-based competitions in Malaysia. Dragon boats are long, narrow vessels with a flat base. Modern competitive dragon boats are made from fibre glass material.

The thrill of watching a dragon boat race is heightened by the roar of the spectators and the pounding of large drums mounted on the front of each boat. Success in dragon boat racing depends on a team's ability to strategize and coordinate.

In Malaysia, dragon boat racing has attracted international competition, with teams from China, Macau, Japan, Singapore, Australia, Indonesia, USA, Norway, Germany, New Zealand and Brunei participating in various events. Under the auspices of the International Dragon Boat Federation (IDBF) in Beijing, teams take part in a worldwide racing circuit which runs throughout the year. In 2008, the IDBF world championships will be held in Penang.

A **dragon's tail** is attached at the **stern** of the boat.

The **helmsman**, manning the stern, steers the boat and keeps it on course.

In a traditional race, 12 to 20 **rowers** sit in rows of two to propel the craft forward through the water over distances between 200 and 2000 metres.

The **drum beater**, who sits at the bow, plays a crucial role in motivating the members of his team and determining the pace of the boat. The rowers use the rhythmic beats of the drum to time and synchronize their strokes.

Elaborately carved and vibrantly painted replicas of a **dragon's head** and neck are fixed at the **prow** of each boat.

Traditional Chinese recreation

Some Chinese recreational activities emphasize health by attaining a balance in body, mind and spirit, a principle embodied in taiji quan *and* qigong *exercises. The importance of cultivating a person's mental agility and strategic thinking is reflected by the Chinese community's interest in games such as* xiangi, weiqi *and* mahjong. *Chinese children in Malaysia still take part in numerous pastimes that originated in ancient China.*

Over 1500 exponents from 40 *taiji quan* groups gathered in Merdeka Square in Kuala Lumpur to conduct a demonstration of their exercises, 1991.

Stamps showing four species of Siamese fighting fish (*ikan pelaga*) which are native to Malaysia and Thailand.

Total balance

The concept of total balance in body, mind and spirit is the basis for many of the traditional recreational activities practised by the Chinese community in Malaysia. This holistic perspective drives the Chinese to partake in psychologically and spiritually beneficial recreation such as *taiji quan* and *qigong*.

Mental fitness

The Chinese prize mental fitness in young and old alike and use board games as a means of sharpening observation and of developing strategic thinking skills. *Xiangqi*, *weiqi* and *mahjong* are all played not only as a source of diversion, but also as a means of intellectual enrichment.

Elderly Chinese performing their daily *taiji quan* exercises at the Lake Garden in Kuala Lumpur.

Exponents of the Soaring Crane *qigong* school performing a routine in Kuala Lumpur, 2004. Soaring Crane is one of the most popular *qigong* exercises in the world, practised by approximately 30 million people in over 80 countries.

Taiji quan and qigong

In the mornings and evenings, people from all walks of life congregate at parks, fields, courts and playgrounds in Malaysia to take part in *taiji quan* and *qigong*, forms of traditional Chinese exercise which promote health maintenance.

Translated from Mandarin as 'supreme ultimate fist', *taiji quan* is a soft-style Chinese martial art distinctive for its muscle-skeletal relaxation approach. *Taiji quan* traces its origins to a 12th century Taoist monk in China, who combined the Wu Tang Shan Taoist monastery's breathing exercises with martial arts learnt from the Shaolin Buddhist monastery. *Taiji quan* has evolved though the ages with the development of five major classical styles which differ, not in philosophy, but in their various training approaches. The most popular style is the Yang style, which was established in 1820. *Taiji quan* involves solo routines and exercises, duet routines or pushing hands and acupressure-related manipulations (see 'Wushu').

An important facet of *taiji quan* is *qigong*, a traditional form of Chinese medicine which has developed into a comprehensive exercise system in its own right. Made up of the characters *qi* and *gong*, which mean breath or life force and work respectively, *qigong* is the practice of accumulating life force through breathing exercises along with physical postures and movements.

Children's games

The early Chinese settlers in Malaya brought with them a cultural enjoyment of animal fights. Chinese boys, particularly in rural areas, carry on this tradition by staging fights between fish and between insects. Siamese fighting fish, locally known as *ikan pelaga*, remain a popular choice as combatants. A fish fight involves introducing a male fighting fish into a jar containing another male fighting fish. The fish start biting at each other's fins or mouths and usually fight to the death. Other types of animal fighting contests involve grasshoppers, crickets, ants or spiders. These creatures are caught by children and pitted against one another in an enclosed area.

Playing with the *jian zi* (shuttlecock) and *chi lin* (diabolo) are also common Chinese children's pastimes. *Jian zi*, which has existed since the Han Dynasty in the 5th century BCE, requires players to hit the shuttlecock with their bodies and prevent it from touching the ground. A *chi lin* is a dumbbell–shaped yo-yo– like object with a groove in the middle in which

Boys playing with *chi lin* during the Chinese New Year festivities in Melaka, 2006. This spinning activity was first documented in the annals of the Ming dynasty (1386–1644 CE). By the 18th century, it had spread throughout Asia and to Europe.

to place a string connected to two sticks. The *chi lin* is spun and moves rapidly on the string, producing a howling sound. Because it is not bound by the string, the *chi lin* can be tossed as high as the player desires and, as with the conventional yo-yo, there are many tricks and techniques which can be executed. Previously made of wood, *chi lin* are now fashioned from plastic and are aerodynamically designed.

Chinese youths also commonly play 'house', a hopscotch game similar to *teng-teng*, and *kalitoi*, a variation of *galah panjang* (see 'Malay children's games: Challenging body and mind').

Board games

Weiqi (go)

Commonly known as 'go', *weiqi* is one of the oldest board games in the world, tracing its origins to China before 500 BCE. *Weiqi* can be translated from Mandarin as 'encirclement chess' which accurately describes the main objectives of the game: maximizing one's controlled territory by enclosing and capturing the opponent's stones as well as protecting one's own stones from capture.

Weiqi is a highly intellectual game that hones observational and tactical skills. Two players alternate to place either black or white stones on a board of 19 horizontal and vertical lines. Holding the stone between the tips of their outstretched index and middle fingers, the players strike the board firmly to create a sharp click. The board is usually made from solid hardwood, the white stones from clamshell and the black stones from slate.

Due to the strategic nature of the board game, *weiqi* has been frequently compared to combat. In Sun Tzu's *The Art of War*, written in the 6th century BCE, *weiqi* strategies were used in formulating military tactics. A game of *weiqi* can only end when a consensus has been reached between the two parties to end the game or when neither of the players can make further moves and decide to pass on their turns consecutively. Only after that can the scores be counted by adding the number of empty points and the number of points occupied by the player's stones. During a competition, matches will typically last 1–3 hours.

In countries where *weiqi* is popular, a ranking system is employed to indicate a player's skill or strength. In Malaysia, *weiqi* is played both at home and in friendly tournaments organized by the Malaysia Weiqi Association. The association is led by its founding president, K.S. Tiong. In 2006, it had a membership of 80 individuals throughout the country. Teng Boon Ping was crowned the champion of the Malaysia Weiqi Tournament in 2007 and was Malaysia's representative at the 28th World Amateur Go Championship in 2007 in Japan. The world championships are organized by the International Go Federation (IGF), of which the Malaysia Weiqi Association is a member. *Weiqi* has also been introduced to students of all ages in Chinese schools. In 2006, the Malaysia Weiqi Association organized the first inter-secondary school tournament.

Weiqi was included as a demonstration sport at the 2007 SEA Games in Korat and will be included as an official event at the 2010 Asian Games in Guangzhou.

Weiqi teams from Malaysia and Japan taking part in a competition in Kuala Lumpur, 2006.

Mahjong

A widely played pastime in Malaysia, particularly among elderly Chinese, *mahjong* originated in China in the mid-1800s. It arrived in Malaya in the 19th century with the influx of Chinese migrant workers who played *mahjong* for amusement and to sharpen their cognitive skills.

Points are scored by selecting and discarding tiles to form similar groups or runs. The element of chance comes into play during the shuffling and drawing of tiles to form a player's hand, an exercise referred to as 'building the wall'.

There are four players, each occupying a side of the *mahjong* table. A *mahjong* set is made up of 144 wooden or ivory tiles, three dice and chips to denote the points of the players. The tiles are divided io three categories: suits, honour and flowers. Every round begins with the shuffling of the tiles in the centre of the table. The objective of the game is to obtain complete suits (usually in groups of three) from either 13 or 16 tiles. Hence, to win the game, either the 14th or 17th tile needs to complete the hand.

LEFT: Mahjong charity tournament taking place at Admiralty House in Kuala Lumpur, 1951.

BELOW RIGHT: During each turn, a player draws a tile from the pile and discards a tile onto the table.

BELOW LEFT: It is widely believed that the three-player variation of *mahjong* originated in Malaysia.

Xiangqi (Chinese chess)

Xiangqi, which means representational chess, is also known as Chinese chess and originates from the same family of strategic board games as Western chess, Japanese *shogi* and Korean *janggi*. Played in China since the 4th century BCE, *xiangqi* has developed a following throughout the world. With 16 pieces to a side, almost all of *xiangqi's* pieces have Western equivalents, some with exactly the same movements and others with vastly different movements. The objective of *xiangqi* is to checkmate the opponent's general, the equivalent of a king in Western chess. A general is considered to be in check when it is threatened by the opponent's piece. When a player's general is unable to escape check during his move, it is checkmated and the player loses the game.

Xiangqi is a popular board game especially in Asia and Europe, where there are governing leagues and clubs set up to oversee the development of the sport. In Malaysia, the nationwide league governing *xiangqi* is the Malaysia Chinese Chess Association under the auspices of the

Two players face off during a three-day Chinese chess competition in Ipoh, 2006.

Malaysian Chinese Association (MCA). Presided over by Lau Chiak Tuan as at 2007, the league is responsible for organizing local tournaments and the development of local players for regional and international tournaments. In the past years, Malaysian Chinese chess players have represented the country in regional competitions including annual friendly tournaments such as the Singapore–Malaysia–Thailand Friendship Tournament in 2005.

Traditional Indian recreation

The Indian community of Malaysia takes part in a wide variety of traditional games and recreational activities, many of which originated centuries ago in India. Indian traditional games are enjoyed by people of all ages, genders and levels of ability, and many are played in conjunction with religious and cultural festivals.

Uri adithal
A popular event during temple functions, *uri adithal*, also known as *kuri paichal* or *manjal satti*, requires participants to be blindfolded and, with a wooden stick, attempt to hit a clay pot containing a yellow cloth tied to a post and lifted up and down. An individual's coordination and aim are tested and substantial prize money awaits the winner who is able to break the clay pot.

An enduring tradition

Most Malaysian Indian traditional games trace their roots back to India. Some games, however, were created among the Indian migrant communities that came to Southeast Asia as early as the 1st century CE. There are striking similarities between many traditional Indian games and other indigenous games from countries in Southeast Asia, indicating a high degree of cross-cultural influence. Many internationally popular games such as chess, dice throwing and badminton are also said to have originated in India. Over the course of the last millennium, Indian games have changed to suit the social, cultural and religious functions of the communities in which they have been played.

The Malaysian Indian community, made up primarily of Tamils from South India, have preserved their traditional games, some of which are not commonly played in India. Traditional Indian recreation in Malaysia comprises indoor and outdoor activities which can be classified into groups according to the gender, age, and intellectual, emotional and physical capabilities of participants. Some forms of traditional Indian recreation are enjoyed as everyday pastimes, while other activities are specially organized during cultural and religious celebrations.

Children's recreation

Malaysian Indian children play an array of traditional games which test their intellectual and physical abilities and allow them to have fun. They also play their own versions of popular local traditional games such as *batu seremban*, *teng-teng*, *kunda kundi* and *galah panjang* (see 'Malay children's games: Challenging body and mind').

Aadu-puli attam, a game of 'goats versus tigers', is believed to have been invented long ago by shepherds who wanted to train their youths to be more vigilant. It is played by two players, one representing the tiger and the other 15 goats, on the floor or on a board. The tiger, typically represented by a tamarind seed, tries to win the game by capturing the goats, represented by pebbles or saga seeds. The goats attempt to achieve victory by evading capture and surrounding and entrapping the tiger.

Uppu-mootai is a race game in which a player must carry another team member, called the *uppu-mootai* or salt bag, on his back to the finish line. If the salt bag falls off, the team must start over again.

In *nondi*, the player who acts as the *nondi*, or crippled person, has to tie one leg with a cloth. He then attempts to catch the other players by limping and jumping on the other leg. When another player is caught, he in turn becomes the *nondi*.

Gender-based recreation

Indian women's recreation affords females the opportunity to showcase their intellectual and artistic abilities. Men's recreation is intended to test the physical and mental strength of young males. Games such as kabaddi, silambam (see 'Silambam') and *uri adithal* give young men a chance to display their fortitude and stamina.

Above: Mother and daughter putting the finishing touches on their winning entry in a *kolam*-making competition in Penang, 2006. Made from five colours of grated coconut, their *kolam* used doves and flowers to symbolize peace and harmony.

Below: Participants taking part in a *kolam*-making competition organized in conjunction with the Deepavali festivities in Melaka, 2007.

Young women taking part in a friendly game of *pallangkuli* during an Indian traditional games festival in Petaling Jaya, 2006.

Pallangkuli, which originated from Tamil Nadu in India, is a popular game among Indian women. It is similar to the game of *congkak*, which is commonly played in the Malay community (see 'Congkak'). Traditionally, a *pallangkuli* board is made of solid wood carved into a rectangular shape with smooth edges and 14 holes. Tamarind seeds, pebbles or cowry shells can function as chips. Although the rules and methods of play may vary, the overall objective of the game is to capture the most chips. Two women compete to see whose strategic and calculative skills are superior.

Indian women take pride in designing *kolam*, floor designs usually made with rice flour which can be beautiful and complicated works of art. Tying and weaving together flowers into a garland, called *poo pinnuthal*, can also be considered an art form as it requires incredible patience and skill. During festivals, competitions are often conducted, judged by skilful veterans, to see who can craft the most intricate and elaborate *kolam* or garland.

The Indian version of wrestling, *payalwan*, is a very manly game which was initially started as a means of determining the 'king' of strength in a particular area. The object is to pin the opponent on the ground. Sometimes competitors apply coconut oil to their bodies to better evade their opponent's grip.

Sarukkal, played by young men during temple or village celebrations, entertains spectators but may be dangerous for participants. A palm or coconut tree is greased in order to make it slippery. A cash reward, usually a sizeable sum, is tied in a cloth bundle and suspended from the top of the tree. The competitors must race to climb the tree to obtain the reward. Most of the participants, however, end up falling down the slippery tree, adding humour to the proceedings.

Originally staged in the state of Tamil Nadu in India, *jallikattu kalai* or bull fighting requires the participants to tame a bull without using weapons, by grabbing it by horns. The bull is released into an open space and several men individually try to control it with only their bare hands. *Jallikattu kalai*

can be dangerous, even fatal, but it remains popular, particularly among rural men, as a means of proving their manliness.

General recreation

Thayam or *pandi* is a dice game that has many variants. The aim of the game is for a player to move his chips on a board according to the number which he rolls with the dice.

Chathurangam is the most intellectually challenging game invented by the Indians. Although the rules of the game are essentially identical to Western chess, which evolved out of the Indian game, some of the pieces in the Indian variation, such as the elephant piece, are different from their Western counterparts.

Parama-patham is similar to the game of 'snakes and ladders'. Indians connect this game to their overall philosophy of life in which an individual encounters both good and bad luck.

Thoranam, traditional decorations made with coconut or mango leaves, are crafted as a form of recreation to get young men to participate in Indian festivals and temple events. Contests are often organized to determine who can make the finest and most creative decorations.

During festivals, saffron or coloured powder is mixed with water and youths engage in playful splashing fights, called *manjal nirattu vizhat* or *holi*, thus creating a joyful atmosphere.

ABOVE: Tying together coconut leaves to make *thoranam* during Deepavali in Penang, 2003.

BELOW: Girl screaming with glee after getting splashed by water mixed with saffron during a festival at the Laksmi Narayan Temple in Kuala Lumpur, 2007.

Kabaddi

Origins

Kabaddi evolved from the story of an epic battle between Abhimanyu and seven warriors. In the Indian epic the *Mahabharata*, the seven warriors defended themselves by forming a barricade as Abhimanyu charged them. Although Abhimanyu penetrated the barricade, he was encircled by the seven warriors. Unable to escape the chain formation, Abhimanyu was eventually captured and killed.

The game of kabaddi was conceived around 2000 BCE as a method of honing soldiers' self-defence skills and counterattack reflexes.

KAM logo.

Local development

Kabaddi came to Malaya with the Indian workers brought into the country by the British to work on rubber plantations in the late 19th century. It was commonly played as a pastime in the rubber estates, and was especially popular during Indian festivals such as Ponggal and New Year.

The Kabaddi Association of Malaysia (KAM) was formed in 2000, and became a member of the Asian Kabaddi Federation the same year. In 2002, Malaysia's kabaddi team participated at the Asian Games in Busan. The country hosted the Asian Championship in 2003 and the Malaysian team emerged as runners-up.

The KAM organizes an annual interstate tournament, while individual states organize their own championships.

Players from the Seivasangkari team (in stripes) attacking a Perak player during the finals of the KAM–NSC Kabaddi Circuit in Kuala Lumpur, 2001.

Game play

Two teams alternate in sending a raider onto the opponent's side of the court. The raider's aim is to break through the barricade formed by the opposing players, tag the opposing players and return to his own court in one breath while continuously chanting the word 'kabaddi'. For each successful touch and return, he is awarded a point. The opposing players touched by the raider are considered out. The aim of the opposing side is to hold the raider and stop him from returning to his own court until after he takes another breath (or, in the modern variation, a period of 20 seconds). If the raider cannot return to his own court in the same breath while chanting 'kabaddi', he is declared out and the opposing side scores a point. A player is also out if he steps out of the boundaries of the field during the course of play unless he oversteps the boundaries in the course of a struggle with an opposing player.

A player can be brought back into the game when an opposing player is tagged out. An 'iona' (bonus of two points) is awarded to a team when the entire opposition is declared out. The game then proceeds with the reinstatement of all players on both sides. When time runs out, the team which has accumulated the most points wins the game.

- Kabaddi is played over two halves of 20 minutes in men's and junior boys' games and two halves of 15 minutes each in women's and junior girls' competitions, with a five-minute interval in between.
- Each team comprises 12 players (seven on the field and five substitutes).
- Kabaddi is typically played on grass courts lined with lime powder and on rubber foam mats in halls.

Player trying to break through the barricade formed by the opposing team. In order to earn points, he must touch the players from the opposing team and return to his team's side of the court in one breath (or 20 seconds). The opposing teams tries to prevent him from entering their side of the court and returning to his own side.

22.9 metres

24.4 metres

Malay children's games: Challenging body and mind

Many Malay traditional games promote the development of children's physical and intellectual abilities. These games help to foster proficiency in areas such as balance, concentration, speed and accuracy. The common denominator for children, however, is having fun, and traditional Malay children's games have survived because of the amusement they afford.

Stamp issued in 2000 depicting children playing a game of *baling tin*.

Children in Kuala Lumpur enjoying a game of *guli*.

Games that test accuracy

Kunda kundi, baling tin, baling botol and *main guli* are examples of traditional Malay games which demand and cultivate the ability to aim with precision. *Baling tin* (hit the tins) and *baling botol* (hit the bottles) are raucous outdoor games that require accuracy, speed and stamina. The objective is to use a ball to topple a stack of tins or a row of bottles. Boys and girls mix together to form two teams, one team acting as attackers and the other as defenders. An attacker throws the ball at the tins or bottles and tries to knock them down, then quickly attempts to retrieve the ball as the defenders rearrange the tins or bottles. The attackers try to prevent the defenders from getting control of the ball. The defenders frantically pursue the individual holding the ball, but the ball can be passed by an attacker to a fellow team-mate. If the ball is intercepted, the defenders assume the role of the attackers. The team that upends the most tins or bottles within a given period of time is the winner.

Students taking part in a game of *harimau dengan kambing*, in which a 'tiger' (right) must try to break through a 'fence' formed by other players to touch and thereby capture a 'goat'.

Schoolchildren enjoying a game of *teng-teng* in Kuala Lumpur.

Main guli (playing marbles), perhaps the most popular game of accuracy in Malaysia, has many variations. In the most common version of *main guli*, a circle and a line are drawn on the ground about 1.5 metres apart. The player who rolls his marble closest to the circle without getting it inside starts the game. Each player places a similar number of his marbles within the circle. Using a larger marble, players attempt to knock the other players' marbles out of the circle in order to capture them. The objective of the game is to acquire as many of the opponents' marbles as possible. Players alternate and continue their turn from the point where their larger marble ends up after hitting the other marbles.

Another variation of *main guli* involves using breakable white chalk marbles. Each player is allotted one such marble and the aim is to prevent other players from hitting and cracking one's marble with their own marbles. If a player's marble breaks, he must withdraw from the game.

Games of concentration

Requiring only a few pebbles and a flat surface, *batu seremban* or *selambut* is a widely popular pastime among Malay girls, and helps to develop a keen sense of focus and coordination. In one fluid motion, participants

Batu seremban

Batu seremban or *selambut* can be played by two or more players both indoors and outdoors. This game requires five or seven pebbles or small cloth bags filled with either sand or saga seeds. The game begins with each player placing her pebbles in the palm of her hand, throwing them into the air and catching them as they come down with the same hand. The player who catches the most stones begins the game. Before each player's turn, the pebbles are randomly scattered. Points are awarded to the players when they complete each successive round.

Girls playing *batu seremban* at a cultural festival in Kuala Lumpur.

Game play

- **First round:** The player throws a pebble in the air (1) and quickly picks up another pebble (2) before catching the first pebble with the same hand (3). This is done three more times to gather the remaining pebbles.
- **Second round:** The player must pick up two pebbles each time the other pebble is thrown and caught.
- **Third round:** The player must pick up one and then three pebbles while throwing and catching the other pebble.
- **Fourth round:** The player must pick up all four of the pebbles while throwing and catching the other pebble.
- **Fifth round:** The player must throw a pebble up, pick up the four scattered pebbles with one hand and transfer them all to the other hand before catching the thrown pebble.
- **Extra round:** After the fifth sequence, it is up to the player's ingenuity to create and execute new sequences.

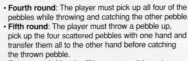

Player kicking a *capteh* or shuttlecock with the side of his foot in an effort to keep it in the air.

must toss a pebble in the air, collect other pebbles from the ground and catch the airborne pebble before it falls.

Sepak bulu ayam, which translates as 'kicking the chicken feathers', is frequently played by boys in open spaces and has many similarities to *sepak raga* or *sepak takraw* (see 'Sepak takraw'). Players are separated into teams of equal number. The aim of the game is to keep a *capteh* (a shuttlecock made from three chicken feathers attached by a nail to a round rubber or plastic base) in the air for as long as possible. Teams count the number of times they kick or hit the *capteh* with their feet, knees, shoulders and head before it falls to the ground. Every kick or hit is worth one point, and the team that accumulates the most points is the winner.

Games that require agility and speed

Kaki hantu is a favourite pastime among boys, who carve footholds on bamboo poles and use them as stilts to move around and race each other.

Teng-teng (hopscotch) is a popular balancing game played primarily by girls on a variety of shapes, such as squares and crosses, drawn onto the ground with chalk. Adeptly hopping forwards and backwards into various boxes, a player must complete an entire sequence, for which she receives a point. If she makes a mistake by stepping on the line or failing to follow the correct order, she has to wait for her turn again to go through the whole sequence from the beginning.

Galah panjang or *tui* is a game that involves between four and ten players divided into two teams. One team tries to prevent the other team from crossing into predetermined areas by tagging them. The defending team members are only allowed to move along specific lines that are drawn on the ground before the start of the game. If one of the attacking team manages to avoid being tagged and crosses over into the guarded area and back, his entire team receives a point and gets to have another chance to attack their opponents. If, however, a member of the defending team tags one of the attackers, the teams switch positions and the game is restarted. *Galah panjang* is often played on a badminton court, utilizing the various lines on the court to signify the guarded areas in the game.

Another game which requires speed is *harimau dengan kambing* in which one player assumes the role of the tiger while the other players become goats or act as a fence encircling the goats. The tiger tries to break into the circle by moving swiftly while the players who are forming the fence strive to stop him from doing so. If the tiger manages to touch a goat, that player in turn becomes the next tiger.

In *ram ram rip,* one player outstretches his open palm while the other players place their index fingers in the middle of it. The player with the open palm then shouts out '*ram ram rip*' and rapidly closes his palm in an effort to ensnare a player, who must then take his place.

Boys playing *kunda kundi* at a Petaling Jaya school.

Kunda kundi

An outdoor game played by teams of two to eight children, *kunda kundi* requires a short stick of approximately 15 centimetres in length and a long stick about 30 centimetres long. A 16-centimetre by 8-centimetre oval-shaped hole is dug into the ground. The game begins with one team standing around the hole while the other team positions themselves a distance away, spread out from each other and facing the hole.

Stage 1: A player puts the short stick across the hole and then flicks it using the longer stick, thereby making it fly as high and as far as possible. Members of the defending team attempt to catch the short stick before it lands. If one of them catches it in mid-air, the player is considered 'dead' and must be replaced by another team member. If it is caught with one hand, the entire attacking team is 'dead' and the teams reverse roles. If the short stick is not caught before it touches the ground, a member of the defending team picks it up and attempts to throw it either into the hole or to hit the long stick laid over the hole. If this is achieved, the player who hit the short stick is 'dead' and must be replaced.

Stage 2: If the defending team fails to either hit the long stick or get the short stick into the hole, the player goes again, this time using one hand to throw the short stick and the other hand holding the long stick with which he bats the short stick as far as possible. Again, the defending team tries to either catch the stick or, if it falls to the ground, throw it back towards the hole. This time, however, the player with the long stick acts as a batsman and attempts to hit the short stick as it is tossed towards the hole. From the place where it lands, the distance of the short stick from the hole is measured using the long stick, with each length counting as a point for the attacking team.

Stage 3: During the next stage, termed *patuk ayam* (chicken peck), the small stick is placed into the hole and its edge is hit with the long stick, causing it to fly upwards. It is then hit again with the long stick as far as possible. Once again, the defending team either tries to catch it or toss it back into the hole while a player from the attacking team tries to bat it away. However, the distance from the small stick to the hole is now measured using the small stick, with each length being equivalent to a point. The points are then added to points obtained earlier. An attacking player is also 'dead' if the short stick's distance from the hole is less than one length of the long stick. Teams alternate after all the members of the attacking team have had their turn.

Students playing *galah panjang* at a school in Kuala Lumpur.

Malay children's games: Lyrical and natural variations

Numerous Malay children's games include rhyming verses orally passed down from one generation to the next, adding a sense of amusement to the proceedings. These poetic exchanges also help Malay youths get a firm grasp of their language and heritage. Children creatively make use of plants such as palm fronds and bamboo to play other traditional games.

Children playing *jala itik*, a game which involves the singing of poetic verses.

Games which incorporate pantun verses

Cap kelipik

In *cap kelipik*, two or more players sit down either facing each other or in a circle, putting their left hands flat on the floor in front of them. One player starts the game by touching each hand using her right hand or a short stick. This action is accompanied by a song such as:

Cap kelipik kelepuk kelepak
Buah berangan longkah kulit
Angkat cerana tak ada tembakau
Mari sama kita balik

Toop, tup, toop, tup
Chestnuts shelled with ease
Alas, no tobacco with the betel leaves
Let's then go home as we please.

The player whose hand is the last to be touched when the song ends has to stretch out her left hand, clench it and place it in the middle of the circle. The game proceeds in the same way and the next player whose hand is last touched has to place her clenched left fist on the previous player's and so on until all the players' left fists are stacked together. The player whose hand is at the bottom of the pile then brings it to the top and the following player follows suit while all the players sing:

Tom tom bak ayam didik
Telur langit telur bulan
Bertemu lalu pecah sebiji.

Clucking like the hen in the pen
One egg from the moon, one from the sky
One gets broken as they meet when down they fly.

One of the variations of *cap kelipik* is *injit-injit semut*. Players pinch the hand under theirs while their own hand is pinched by the one above them. Each time the pinching is repeated, children repeatedly sing the following verse:

Injit–injit semut siapa sakit naik atas!

Bite, ants, bite! Go ye up, if ye feel the bite!

Jala itik

In *jala itik*, two players serve as team leaders while the other players form a line. The leaders hold hands and raise their arms to make an arch, under which the other players walk while the leaders sing:

Jan–jan jala
Jala itik jala ayam
Berapa lubang kecil
Seratus lima puluh
Singgah Cik Dayang singgah
Makan sirih mulut merah.

Net and netting
Nets for ducks and nets for chickens
How many little holes can there be?
A hundred and fifty
Come little miss, come to me
chewing the betel leaves, red the lips will be.

When the song ends, the leaders, hands still joined, ensnare the player who is between them. The ensnared player is asked in a whisper to choose one of the two teams and then stands behind the leader of that team. After all players have been caught this way, the players form a chain behind their leaders and hold on to the waist of the player in front of them. The two leaders, hands still joined, then proceed to tug at each other. The team that is pulled across a designated line between the leaders loses.

Games involving the creative use of plants

1. *Tarik upih* (Pulling the base of the frond) is a racing game that is enjoyed by children and sometimes adults. Using an old *pinang* frond, one person will sit at its base while the other end is pulled by other participants. *Tarik upih* is usually played between neighbouring villages during festivals and celebrations.

2. *Gelungsuran* is a popular pastime among boys. It involves placing a coconut frond (or sometimes a cardboard box) atop a grassy hill, where the child sits on the frond and slides downhill.

3. *Bedil buluh* or ***letup-letup*** requires a 'gun' made out of a length of bamboo up to 38 centimetres long with a diameter of 1.3 centimetres. Another length of bamboo, small enough to go through the hollow part of the 'gun', is used as a piston. Small seeds from the *cermai* or *senduduk* trees or pieces of paper are soaked in water until they soften and then are moulded into round balls. These pellets are pushed into the bamboo pipe and shot out its other end, often producing a loud bang, in an effort to hit opponents.

Congkak

The ancient game of mancala, *likely brought by merchants to the Malay Peninsula during the 16th century, has evolved into* congkak, *a local variant of the game and a familiar sight in the traditional Malay kampong. Playing* congkak *requires a high level of concentration, mathematical acumen, perseverance and a little luck. The game remains an enduring form of recreation for Malaysians of all ages and ethnicities.*

Youths participating in a *congkak* competition organized at a school in Kuala Lumpur, 2005.

Ancient origins

Although many Malaysians assume that *congkak* is a indigenous pastime, it is, in fact, only one of many versions of *mancala*, an ancient game of wits. *Mancala* is commonly played throughout Africa, Asia, the Caribbean and the Middle East. Although the origins of *mancala* are uncertain, there is a broad consensus that it originated in Africa. *Mancala* boards dating back to around the 6th century have been discovered in Ethiopia, but many experts believe that the history of the game goes back even further.

By the Middle Ages, references to *mancala* were made in Islamic religious texts. This has given rise to speculation that the game was brought to various parts of Asia by Arab traders travelling eastward. Melaka, on the Malay Peninsula, would have been one of the primary destinations of these traders, as it had already been established as a main port in Southeast Asia by the 16th century. It is likely that this was how *mancala*, the original form of *congkak*, was first introduced locally.

Mancala, which means 'to move things about' in Arabic, is not a familiar term in Malaysia. The Malay word *congkak* refers to cowrie shells, that were traditionally used by locals to play the game. The name may also have been derived from another Malay word, *congak*, which means 'to count mentally'.

A local tradition

The playing of *congkak* has long been a local cultural tradition and is widespread among the Malay community. Nevertheless, Malaysians of other ethnic backgrounds have come to appreciate the game. In the past, *congkak* was not only a leisure activity, but also served as a platform for social interaction. Despite the spread of more modern diversions, *congkak* continually commands a large following in Malaysia, especially among people in rural areas. Overall, the game appears to be more popular among women and girls compared to their male counterparts. It would be rare to find a Malay girl in a kampong who has never played *congkak*.

While a major *congkak* championship or competition has yet to be organized in Malaysia, it is common to find adults and teenagers taking part in friendly *congkak* matches during local cultural events or exhibitions. Although the game can involve complex strategies and high levels of concentration, *congkak* is still considered to be more of an enjoyable pastime to be played with friends and neighbours.

Playing congkak

Equipment

Although there are numerous variations of the game, *congkak* is usually played on a board with two rows of seven hollowed-out bowls. The two rows of holes on a *congkak* board are located between two larger holes, one at each end of the board. These larger holes are known as the stores or *rumah* (houses).

The two players face each other with the *congkak* board between them. Each player's store is located on his left, and he controls the seven holes on his side of the board known as the kampong. Before the game begins, seven counter pieces or seeds are distributed into each of the 14 holes, while the stores are left empty. Thus, *congkak* is conventionally played with a total of 98 seeds.

Congkak game play

The objective of *congkak* is to accumulate as many seeds as possible in one's store. The game ends when there are no more seeds in both of the players' kampong. In a typical game turn, a player can continue sowing, or moving the seeds, repeatedly. The more times she sows during his turn, the faster she accumulates seeds in her store. The challenge is to avoid dropping the last seed into an empty hole, thereby ending the player's turn.

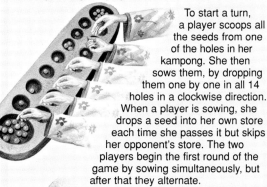

To start a turn, a player scoops all the seeds from one of the holes in her kampong. She then sows them, by dropping them one by one in all 14 holes in a clockwise direction. When a player is sowing, she drops a seed into her own store each time she passes it but skips her opponent's store. The two players begin the first round of the game by sowing simultaneously, but after that they alternate.

If the last seed in a player's hand falls into an occupied hole, she then scoops up all the seeds in that hole and continues sowing.

If the last seed in a player's hand falls into her store, she gets to sow again from another hole in her kampong.

If the last seed in a player's hand falls into an empty hole, her turn is over and the other player commences sowing.

ABOVE: 'Malaysian Unity' stamp released in 2002 depicting children and a woman of various ethnicities engrossed in a game of *congkak*.

ABOVE RIGHT: The *congkak* board is featured on the back of a 10-sen Malaysian coin, underscoring its importance as a traditional pastime.

Traditional *congkak* board of unknown antiquity which features 12 holes, as opposed to the more popular 16-hole version, from the collection of Muzium Negara Malaysia in Kuala Lumpur.

Modern interpretation of the *congkak* board by Syarikat Permainan Malaysia (SPM) which won a Product Excellence Award, given by the Ministry of International Trade and Industry, in 1998.

1. Participants playing on the world's largest Monopoly board in the 'Nokia Presents Monopoly Championship' in Petaling Jaya, 2005.

2. Youths playing online games during the 2006 TM Net Broadband Fiesta in Kuantan.

3. Players competing in the Johor Open Carrom Championship, 2000.

4. Demonstration of the traditional Malay board game of *dam aji*, a local variation of draughts, on Balok beach in Kuantan, 2006.

5. Players of all ages attempting *sudoku* number puzzles. Introduced in 1984 in Japan, *sudoku* has become widely popular among Malaysians.

6. Students taking part in the 2003 Penang Schools Sports Council's Chess Championship, which attracted over 300 participants.

MIND GAMES

Mind games demand great intellectual agility, fortitude and perseverance. Malaysians have a deep and enduring passion for a wide range of mind games, and take part in them both recreationally and competitively. Many traditional mind games, such as *congkak* (see 'Congkak'), *mahjong*, *xiangqi* and *weiqi* (see 'Traditional Chinese recreation'), *cheek riknuij* (see 'Orang Asli recreation'), *thayam* and *aadu-puli attam* (see 'Traditional Indian recreation') and *sukian* (see 'Traditional recreation of Sabah'), still continue to be played locally.

Mind games appeal to Malaysians of all ethnicities, genders and ages, and serve as a source of both diversion and enrichment.

Chess has been organized on a competitive basis in the country for quite some time. The first local chess club was established in the 19th century and national chess championships have been held since 1949.

Chess set manufactured in Malaysia by Royal Selangor, the world's largest pewter maker.

The Malaysian Chess Federation (MCF), initially founded in 1960, has been the driving force behind the local development of the game, and has played host to international chess events such as the Asian Team Championship and Selangor Open as well as numerous national competitions. Malaysian chess exponents have proven themselves to be worthy opponents on the international circuit and, as of 2008, the country boasts three FIDE international masters: Jimmy Liew, Mas Hafizulhelmi Agus Rahman and Wong Zi Jing.

Malaysians also play a range of other board and card games. Commonly considered to be merely leisure activities, these games are taken quite seriously by many in the country. Indeed, local players have formed their own associations, such as the Malaysian Scrabble Association (MSA) and Malaysian Contract Bridge Association (MCBA), and have risen to the top of international rankings in several games. The release of Malaysian editions of Monopoly and Scrabble was met with widespread enthusiasm.

In the mid-1990s, cyber cafés began to appear throughout the country and online games (video games played through the internet or a computer network) emerged as a new form of recreation for Malaysia's youth. Playing online games has become a legitimate competitive endeavour, and local cyber-athletes participate in a variety of tournaments in Malaysia and abroad.

Dignitaries, including Tun Siti Hasmah Mohd Ali (third from right), officiating the opening ceremony of the 'Giant and Longest Saidina Gameplay' at Multimedia University in Putrajaya, 2006.

Chess

Chess is one of the world's premier board games with its roots in India around 1500 years ago. Modern day chess, which developed in Europe during the 15th century, came to the Malayan Archipelago in the 19th century with the establishment of a chess club in Singapore. The first Malayan Championship was held just after World War II. By competing regularly in local and international chess competitions, Malaysian players have gained experience and recognition.

More than 500 junior players took part in the 2006 Malaysian National Age-Group Chess Championship at the OCM's Indoor Stadium in Kuala Lumpur. The tournament has been held since 1990.

TOP: Deputy Prime Minister Dato' Sri Najib Tun Razak (right) with current and founding MCF president Dato' Tan Chin Nam at the launch of the 3rd Malaysian Chess Festival in Kuala Lumpur, 2006.

ABOVE: Malaysian international masters Jimmy Liew (background, left) and Mas Hafizulhelmi Agus Rahman (foreground, left) in action against Iranian players at the World Chess Olympiad held in Yerevan, Armenia in 1996.

Chess history

A primitive form of chess dates back to 500 CE in India. In the 9th and 10th centuries, chess flourished as an art in the Muslim world. Modern day or 'Western' chess only originated in southern Europe during the last quarter of the 15th century. As of 2006, there were approximately 400 million chess players around the globe.

The *Fédération Internationale des Échecs* (FIDE) is the governing body of world chess. Founded in 1924, the FIDE administers a version of the world championship and conducts the World Chess Olympiad every two years. It awards such titles as, in ascending order, FIDE master (FM), international master (IM) and grandmaster (GM).

Chess in Malaya

In 1925, Yugoslavian Grandmaster Boris Kostich became the first titled player to visit Southeast Asia and compete against local players. World champion Alexander Alekhine toured Asia in 1933, playing exhibition games in Singapore as part of his itinerary. Eugene Ernest Colman, a renowned chess master who came to Malaya in 1902 and who rose to become solicitor-general of Singapore, won nearly every tournament held locally for over 30 years.

During World War II, however, the game was almost non-existent in the Malay Peninsula. It was only in 1949 that the first-ever Malayan Chess Championship was held, and was won by Patrick Aherne, a British actor. In 1958, Choo Min Wang became the first Malaysian to win this tournament. Choo later became Malaysia's first international-level player, competing in the 1963 Djakarta zonal tournament and finishing in fourth place.

Chess governance

The founding father of modern Malaysian chess was Dr Foo Lum Choon, who served as president of the Chess Association of Malaya (CAM) from its founding in 1960 until 1973, when the organization was deregistered. It was renamed the Malaysian Chess Federation (MCF) and re-registered in 1975. Dato' Tan Chin Nam served as MCF president from 1974 to 1986. He was succeeded by Tan Sri Sabaruddin Chik, who

held the office until 2001. In 2006, Dato' Tan Chin Nam resumed his role as MCF president.

Chess competitions

For many years the two most significant tournaments in Malaysia were the National Closed Chess Championship and the Selangor Open, both founded as annual events in 1974. Choo Min Wang won the first Closed Championship held in Kuala Lumpur. The Selangor Open, held in several locations in Kuala Lumpur, attracted many strong masters from abroad, and was a foreign preserve until 1981, when Jimmy Liew, one of Malaysia's three international masters, won the seventh edition of this event.

In 1981, the MCF held the first Merdeka Team Chess Championship in Kuala Lumpur. This tournament has become a national chess festival with many other associated events, including the annual Dato' Arthur Tan Malaysia Open, which debuted in 2004. This annual 1000-player festival typically gathers grandmasters and international masters from 20 or more countries. Thousands of participants compete in chess events in local schools and state-level tournaments.

Malaysians in the international arena

Malaysian masters began competing internationally in the early 1970s, but they did not gain solid practice until Dato' Tan Chin Nam established the Asian Masters Circuit, a series of tournaments from 1980 to 1984.

A Malaysian has yet to earn the grandmaster title, but there are three international masters: Jimmy Liew, Mas Hafizulhelmi Agus Rahman and Wong Zi Jing. Malaysians typically occupy respectable mid-table positions in regional team tournaments as well as in the World Chess Olympiad, the premier biennial gathering of the world chess community. Malaysia's chess Olympiad debut was in Yugoslavia in 1972, finishing 59th among 63 teams. At the Dubai Olympiad in 1986, the national team finished 42nd among 108 nations for its best-ever result.

Nur Shazwani Zulkafi (right) representing Malaysia in a match against the Philippines during the SEA Games in Vietnam, 2003. The Malaysian team captured three bronze medals.

Ng Ek Leong won a gold medal for his performance as the second reserve board. In 16 Olympiad appearances, Malaysian players have won 306, lost 393 and drawn 253 games.

Jimmy's masterly victory

International Master Jimmy Liew's kingside demolition of former Filipino world-title candidate Grandmaster Eugenio Torre at the Sixth Asian Team Championship in Dubai in 1986 featured a rare opening, original middle-game strategy and a powerful attack.

ABOVE RIGHT: Diagram of Jimmy Liew's winning move in his match against Eugenio Torre, 1986.
ABOVE LEFT: International Master Jimmy Liew.

Online games

In the 1990s, online gaming rapidly became a widespread activity among Malaysian youth. Cyber cafés created an ideal environment for people to collectively participate in multiplayer online gaming. In 2008, it is not uncommon to see young adults of all backgrounds playing online games as a social activity, and Malaysian cyber-athletes participate regularly in local and international competitions.

Online games and cyber cafes

Malaysians were not exposed to online games until JARING (Joint Advanced Research Integrated Networking project), the first internet service provider (ISP), brought online access to the country in 1992. At that time, however, few people owned personal computers (PCs), and fewer still had online access. The emergence of cyber cafés in Malaysia during the mid-1990s fostered an increase in PC and internet usage. As such cafés contain numerous PCs that are networked together and typically have more stable internet connections with greater bandwidth than home PCs, cyber cafés have become online gaming centres frequented by scores of young adults.

Types of online games

Online games comprise all video games that are played over the internet or some form of computer network which allows players to connect together. There are essentially three types of online games: browser-based games, single-player games with network multiplayer capabilities (multiplayer games) and massively multiplayer online games (MMOGs).

Some single-player games have multiplayer modes that allow two or more players to participate in the same game session. Players can create or join these games over a local area network (LAN),

Tournaments and local cyber-athletes

There are many minor tournaments, informally organized by local cyber cafés, for multiplayer games such as Counter Strike, Warcraft III and DotA. These events can carry rewards of cash or prizes worth thousands of Ringgit. Local MMOG publishers also organize tournaments to promote interest in their games. Perhaps the most well-known tournament of this kind is the Ragnarok World Championships. Two Malaysian teams, Tengtilei and Kaos, captured third and fourth place respectively in the 2004 tournament finals held in Seoul.

On a larger scale, the World Cyber Games (WCG), an international electronic sports event, is organized by the Korean company International Cyber Marketing. Malaysia has been sending its own gamers or cyber-athletes every year since 2001, and the 2004 and the 2006 WCG events were held in Kuala Lumpur.

Team Kaos battling it out during the final round of the Malaysian leg of the Ragnarok World Championships in 2004.

or through the internet if they are located in different geographical areas.

Quake and Doom, Starcraft, Red Alert, Warcraft, Diablo, Defence of the Ancients (DotA) and the FIFA World Cup series are all multiplayer games that have been popular locally. But the most widely played multiplayer game in Malaysia, as well as in the world, is Counter-Strike (CS). CS has been dominating local cyber cafés since the late 1990s. Many CS players have formed their own clans to partake in various CS tournaments organized locally.

MMOGs involve persistent virtual worlds, in which thousands of 'avatars' or game characters live and interact with each other. The most common sub-genre of MMOGs is the role-playing variation (MMORPGs). Graphic-based MMOGs were introduced in the late 1980s, but it wasn't until the mid-1990s that Malaysians were first exposed to them. In early 2002, TIME dotNet published the first Malaysian MMORPG, Legends of Dark Ages.

In 2003, Game Flier Sdn Bhd brought the country a Malay-language version of the role playing online game Ragnarok. Early local MMORPGs focused heavily on player versus player combat and had violent, dark and serious themes. Some other games published in Malaysia that follow this trend include Dragon Raja, Fung Wan Online, Risk Your Life and Knight Online.

Since 2004, there has been a shift by publishers towards MMORPGs that present a more light-hearted approach. These games are usually designed to be colourful and cartoonish and, though competitive, rarely contain battle elements that promote killing among the players' characters. Examples of this new style of MMORPGs include Maple Story, Audition and Pangya.

Societies, guilds and clans

Due to the great diversity of games, official online gaming associations, societies or clubs have not been established in Malaysia. Instead, gamers usually form communities that are unique and specific to one particular online game. Online games of the multiplayer and MMOG varieties usually have features that allow players to create guilds or clans in the gameworld itself. Communities where these players meet in real life (or IRL, a term used to refer to actual reality outside the game world) usually stem from in-game connections.

Top: Participants playing Counter-Strike at the World Cyber Games 2004 held in Kuala Lumpur.

Above: Representatives of the sponsors of the world's first Mobile Massively Multiplayer Online Game (3MOG) opening an event in Kuala Lumpur, 2006.

Below: Tan Soon Hua, champion of the Starcraft: Broodwar event at the World Cyber Games 2006 in Kuala Lumpur.

Bottom: The World Cyber Games 2006 held in Kuala Lumpur met with a large and enthusiastic crowd of gamers and enthusiasts.

Other board and card games

Malaysians play a wide range of recreational board and card games, many of which have been popularized overseas but can be purchased readily in the local market. Some of these board and card games have also become competitive endeavours with exponents forming national associations to streamline and promote the development of these games to international standards.

Participants in a draughts competition during a cultural festival in Penang, 2006.

Scrabble

Some of the 168 students from 19 schools who participated in the fourth National Junior Scrabble Championship in Petaling Jaya, 2005.

Popularizing Scrabble

In the 1980s, a handful of Malaysians such as Mohd Ali Ismail, Haji Abdul Majid, Mohd Idrus Ismail and Raja Fuadin began to take note of Scrabble events held overseas. They started organizing weekly Scrabble competitive meets in Kampung Baru and at the Kuala Lumpur YMCA. By the 1990s, Scrabble had become so popular that *The Star* newspaper started a Scrabble column which included the latest news on the game.

A similar game to Scrabble, Sahibba, was created in the mid-1970s. The initial version was in Malay and was followed by a bilingual version, the latter can be played in both languages at the same time, making it the world's first bilingual crossword board game.

Competitive game play

The first national Scrabble tournament in Malaysia was held at the Bukit Bintang shopping complex in 1991. The Malaysian National Championship has since then been a benchmark used to select champions to compete in the World Scrabble Championships (WSC). Other annual championships were soon organized throughout Malaysia.

Many Scrabble players, such as Brother Michael Wong and Dr Salahudin bin Mohamed, organized workshops and competitions at the novice level. An intensive campaign to introduce Scrabble into over 100 local schools was started in 2003.

Formal organization

The Malaysian Scrabble Association (MSA) was founded by Mohd Ali Ismail in 1994. Dato' Dr Abdullah Fadzil Che Wan was elected as the first president of the MSA at the first annual general meeting in 1995. In 1997, Brother Michael Wong became the second president of the MSA, a position he still held in 2007.

Famous scrabblers

Mohd Ali Ismail was Malaysia's first national champion, and the first Malaysian representative to the WSC in 1991. Tan Teong Chuan burst onto the Scrabble scene when he emerged as the champion in the 1995 Malaysian National Championships and represented Malaysia in the 1995 WSC in London. He placed 31st out of a field of 64 world-class players, and the organizers were so impressed by his performance that they awarded two places to Malaysia for the 1997 WSC in Washington. As at 2007, Ganesh Asirvatham had been the Malaysian national champion since 2001. He has won almost every major Malaysian Scrabble tournament as well as several foreign ones. Ganesh has represented Malaysia at the WSC multiple times and earned a second place result at the 2007 event in Mumbai. He created a new world record at the event by playing 25 opponents simultaneously and defeating 21 of them.

Scrabble wizard Ganesh Asirvatham places a word.

Bridge

Origins of bridge

Bridge is a member of the whist family of card games, which can be traced to written references as far back as 1529 in England. It has since evolved into one of the most popular card games in the world. The present, universally-played form of bridge, called 'contract bridge', was first played in 1925 by American philanthropist Harold Vanderbilt and a group of friends while sailing through the Panama Canal. Vanderbilt promoted the game extensively, amended existing rules and formulated new ones that have remained virtually unchanged.

Early bridge sessions

It is uncertain exactly when bridge first came to Malaysia, but it was introduced by the expatriate European community and has been played in the card rooms of various clubs throughout the country and private homes since before World War II. In the early 1950s, bridge was organized and played in competitions at the Selangor Club (now known as the Royal Selangor Club). It is the only club which has had a regular weekly bridge session for the past 50 years and, since 1962, an annual interport match against the Royal Bangkok Sports Club.

Local and foreign women playing bridge at the Royal Selangor Club in Kuala Lumpur, 1971.

In 1961, the Selangor Club was invited to send a team to represent Malaya in the Far East Bridge Federation Championships in Bangkok. It was necessary to form a national bridge association so that the selected team would be a truly national team. In September 1961, a group of dedicated players formed the Malayan Contract Bridge Association, which is now known as the Malaysian Contract Bridge Association (MCBA). The founding president was Dr F.R. Bhupalan. The MCBA is the governing authority for bridge in Malaysia, and a member of the Olympic Council of Malaysia, World Bridge Federation and Pacific Asia Bridge Federation. Branches of the association were established in Penang, Perak, Melaka and Sabah, although in 2006 the only active branches were in Penang and Selangor.

Contemporary bridge scene

Regular weekly matches are held at various clubs in Kuala Lumpur and Penang such as the Royal Selangor Club, Royal Lake Club, Royal Selangor Golf Club, Japan Club and the Penang Turf Club. The MCBA has organized annual tournaments since the association's inception. It also hosts an Open and a Mixed Congress, and invites visitors from neighbouring countries to increase the level of competition. On the international circuit, Malaysia participates in the ASEAN Bridge Club Championships and the Pacific Asia Bridge Federation (formerly the Far East Bridge Federation) Championships. Since 1988, Malaysia has also sent a team to the World Bridge Team Olympiad which is held every four years under the auspices of the World Bridge Federation. The Malaysian ladies team won the Far East Bridge Federation Ladies team event in 1965 and a ladies pair from Malaysia became the first ladies pair to win the Far East Open Pairs in 1975.

Monopoly

Economic success

In terms of overall sales, Monopoly is one of the most successful board games ever invented. Monopoly, a property trading game that has sold in excess of 200 million units, is named after the concept in economics of a single seller dominating the market. The players use play money to acquire wealth by purchasing, renting and trading properties.

Local editions

In addition to the many versions of Monopoly in various languages, the game itself has been adapted for the needs of various localities. Although the game originally featured Atlantic City addresses, there are editions based on many other major cities. Monopoly players in Malaysia are most familiar with the London edition. In fact, it is through this edition that many Malaysians learned about the famous streets and sites in the English capital. In 1995, an official Malaysian edition was released to the delight of local players.

Metallic *wau* (kite) token specially made for the Malaysian edition of Monopoly.

Local spin-offs

The success of Monopoly has spawned many unofficial variants and copies of the game with rules that can be similar or different. The most noteworthy of these in Malaysia is the bilingual Saidina, which was released in 1978.

Championships

National level competitions have been conducted to select representatives for the World Monopoly Championship. The first of these was held in Subang Jaya in 2000.

Ting Sie Bing, inventor of Saidina, with his creation. He intended the game to be used by schoolchildren as a tool for learning the basics of economics and commerce.

The winner, Teoh Kah Yong, went on to compete with other national champions at the world event in Toronto.

Three years later, a larger event took place in Genting Highlands, following several state-level competitions in Selangor, Penang and Melaka. The winner of the Malaysian Monopoly Championship 2003, Kumarendra Chandra, walked away with a cash prize of RM10,000. The Malaysian representative to the World Monopoly Championship in Tokyo, Andyputra Zachardyutama bin Muhamad Kaddyran, was selected from another national competition in 2004. In a performance, he was placed seventh overall at the event.

The Malaysian edition of Monopoly. The game features properties such as Putrajaya (the most expensive property on the board with a value of RM4000), Petaling Street and the PETRONAS Twin Towers.

Trading card games

A popular pursuit

Trading card games (popularly referred to as TCGs) are a popular pursuit among both children and adults in Malaysia's major urban centres. Games involving illustrated trading cards are played in fast food restaurants, comic shops and shopping centres. A trading card game involves collectible cards played using a set of rules. Each player's deck of cards can be changed within the confines of the game's rules, and are bought, sold and traded frequently. The most popular trading card game in Malaysia and internationally is Magic: The Gathering manufactured by Wizards of the Coast. Other popular games include Pokémon, Legend of the Five Rings and Yu-Gi-Oh. All of these trading card games are produced outside Malaysia and imported by local distributors.

A typical Saturday afternoon for trading card game enthusiasts at Comics Corner in Damansara Jaya. The game laid out on the table is Legend of the Five Rings.

Playing mechanics

Each trading card game has rules determining the objectives and system of play and setting parameters for constructing playing decks. Individual card text often breaks the preset rules. Players build decks beforehand by selecting cards from various pools. During play, each player takes turns running through a fixed turn sequence.

The local scene

Trading card games in Malaysia are played on a casual as well as a competitive basis. Magic: The Gathering, for example, has a large following due to the number of local tournaments run by Malaysians. Magic: The Gathering tournaments are supported by the sponsorship of Wizards of the Coast, with prize money and products being used as incentives. In 2006, the game's world championship, the Magic Grand Prix, was held at the Kuala Lumpur Convention Centre.

Famous players

Since 2000, numerous Malaysians have earned top honours in regional and international tournaments in both individual and team events.

Terry Soh won the 2005 edition of one of Magic: The Gathering's international marquee events, the Magic Invitational. Soh is considered one of the most accomplished and dedicated Malaysian enthusiasts of the game. Along with several other Malaysians, he travels abroad on a regular basis to participate in tournaments. Soh's first major achievement came at the 2002 Grand Prix Singapore, where he finished second. He also finished in the top eight in both the 2001 and 2002 World Championships and in the top four at the 2005 Pro Tour Nagoya. At the 2005 Magic Invitational tournament at the Las Vegas E3 Gadget and Games Exposition, he emerged as champion. Soh is one of only a handful of players to be given the honour of designing a Magic card (and having the artist draw the illustration with his own face on it) and having a special edition 'famous players' biography card inserted into selected packets of Magic cards that are sold at retail outlets around the world.

Terry Soh's Magic: The Gathering playing card, which he designed after his likeness, and his 'famous players' biography card.

1. Cricket match being played between the York Nondescripts and the Federal Territory team in Kuala Lumpur, 1978.

2. Teams competing in the HMS Malaya Cup tournament, the annual inter-state rugby championship, on the *padang* in Kuala Lumpur, 1961.

3. Players taking part in the final match of the Excel Cup Futsal Championship in Petaling Jaya, 2002. Futsal, a five-a-side indoor variation of football, is widely popular in the country.

4. Teams from Perak (left) and Selangor met in Malaya Cup final at Stadium Merdeka in Kuala Lumpur, 1957. Perak emerged victorious over the defending champions by a score of 3–2.

5. Teams from PETRONAS (left) and Majlis Perbandaran Shah Alam (MPSA) competing in the semi-final of the Malaysian Volleyball League, 1997.

6. Poon Fook Loke (second from right) diving and shooting at the goal during a hockey match against the Soviet Union in Kuala Lumpur, 1981.

TEAM SPORTS

Besides being very important aspects of the sports scene, team sports have helped nation building and fostered national integration. Football is one of the most popular team sports. In the years before Independence, the climax of the football season was the Malaya Cup final, a fiercely fought competition between state teams which was dominated by Selangor and Singapore. The Merdeka Tournament, inaugurated in 1957 in conjunction with the celebration of the country's Independence, was the region's premier football event, and Malaya and South Korea were perennial champions. Malaysia's highest football achievement was qualifying for the 1972 and 1980 Olympic Games. The Football Association of Malaysia (FAM) launched semi- and fully-professional leagues in 1989 and 1994 respectively, and established various football programmes, training centres and schools.

Malaysia's Mohd Azman (right) blocks a spike by his opponent from South Korea during the sepak takraw semi-final match at the Asian Games, 2002. Malaysia won 3–0.

Hockey is popular in Malaysia as both a spectator and participatory sport. Local tournaments, including quadrangular and triangular matches among the states, the North versus South Classic, and the FMS versus the Colony, were organized in the early 1900s. Since Independence, hockey has flourished in the country under the auspices of the Malaysian Hockey Federation (MHF) which organizes the national league, national junior league, the Razak Cup as well as various age-group tournaments. As of 2008, the men's national team hovers just outside the top 10 in the International Hockey Federation world rankings. Since 1932, the national side has played in international competitions, including numerous Olympic Games and World Cups. Malaysia's greatest accomplishment was finishing fourth in the 1975 World Cup held in Kuala Lumpur.

Sepak takraw, a variation of an ancient Malay game, emerged in the mid-1900s as a competitive sport. A combination of football and volleyball, sepak takraw is a visually stunning spectacle. Immensely popular in Southeast Asia, where Malaysia and Thailand tend to dominate international tournaments, sepak takraw is catching on in other countries around the world.

Rugby and cricket were brought to Malaya by the British in the late 19th century and, although neither sport is widely played, a core of committed exponents and enthusiasts keep interest in them alive. Introduced to the country by school teachers in the 1930s and 1970s respectively, volleyball and handball have evolved into popular and organized sports. Basketball is well established locally, particularly among Chinese youths, due to the efforts of the Malaysian Amateur Basketball Association (MABA), which conducts a busy calendar of events nationwide. Netball, a version of basketball played primarily by women, is also very popular in the country. Baseball is a young sport in the country, with the Baseball Federation of Malaysia being founded in 1996 and only two states and a handful of clubs playing the game. Softball has grown steadily since the 1960s and now has teams from nine states, the police and universities partici-pating in leagues conducted by the Softball Association of Malaysia (SAM).

Sepak takraw

Sepak raga is an ancient game which has been played on the Malay Peninsula for over 500 years. The word sepak *means 'to kick' while* raga *refers to 'a rattan ball'. The rules and method of playing* sepak raga *have changed markedly over time, and sepak takraw, a modern variation, has emerged as a competitive sport. Sepak takraw is a fast-paced sport that demands physical and mental strength and dexterity. Malaysia's national teams have achieved great success in international competitions.*

Group of men enjoying a game of *sepak raga* in Terengganu.

Sepak raga jaring players demonstrating the sport in Kuala Lumpur, 1960.

Royal origins

Written evidence suggests that *sepak raga* was played in Melaka as far back as the 15th century; it is mentioned in the *Sejarah Melayu* (Malay Annals). *Sepak raga* was traditionally played by Malays throughout the Peninsula and was a popular form of recreation in the royal court of Melaka.

It is still possible to see *sepak raga* being played in rural areas and towns in Malaysia, especially in areas with a sizeable Malay population. *Sepak raga* also has a large following in other Southeast Asian countries such as Thailand, Indonesia, Myanmar, Cambodia, Laos and the Philippines, but is played in various different forms.

Sepak Takraw Federation of Malaysia logo.

In the local variation, a group of players form a circle approximately 15 metres in diameter. They try to hit a rattan ball and keep it in the air by propelling it with any part of their bodies except their hands. Teams compete against each other by counting the number of times the ball makes contact with their players before it touches the ground, and thereby determine their scores.

The evolution of the game

The popularity of *sepak raga* increased significantly in the 19th century. During that period, it was not uncommon to see diverse groups of people coming together to play the game. By the mid-1930s, however, *sepak raga* had evolved from being a simple game played in a circle to a competitive sport comprising two opposing teams playing on two sides of a net. Furthermore, this new form of playing the game incorporated the rules and procedures used in the game of badminton. This adaptation of the game of *sepak raga* was called *sepak raga jaring* (*jaring* meaning 'net') and was played officially for the first time in 1935 in Negeri Sembilan in conjunction with the Silver Jubilee celebration in honour of King George V.

Several sources have laid claim to the invention of *sepak raga jaring*, and the question of who originated the game is still a matter of speculation. Groups from a number of states in Peninsular Malaysia as well as Singapore and Thailand maintain that they were the first to start playing this version of the game.

BELOW: Mohd Khir Johari (left), first president of the Sepak Raga Association of Malaya, shaking hands with players from Selangor at the opening of the Tunku Abdul Rahman Cup tournament in Kuala Lumpur, 1968.

BOTTOM: Datuk Ahmad Ismail (in yellow), President of the Sepaktakraw Association of Malaysia as at 2008, with the national team.

According to one theory, *sepak raga jaring* was invented in Penang by a group of local fishermen, who wanted to engage in a game of *sepak raga*, but felt bored with the traditional way of playing. Consequently, they incorporated a broken fishing net and started to play a variant of the game fashioned after badminton.

The making of a sport

Through the efforts of veteran players such as Hashim Mydin, Yaacob Syed and Abdul Rahman Mohamad, an initial set of rules and regulations for *sepak raga jaring* was drawn up in 1946. *Sepak raga jaring* was demonstrated as an exhibition sport in 1946 for an audience at a veterinary hospital in Penang. Due to the burgeoning popularity of the sport, other states in Peninsular Malaysia began organizing competitive matches and tournaments.

The determination of officials from various groups and organizations, most notably the Penang Sepak Raga Association, led to the establishment of the Sepak Raga Association of Malaya in 1960. Representatives from Singapore, Selangor, Kedah and Penang met, drafted the official rules and regulations of the game, and unanimously agreed to create a national governing body. The Sepak Raga Association of Malaya was officially formed on 25 June 1960 in Penang. Mohd Khir Johari was elected as the association's first president.

Following the founding of a national governing body, several other associations were established throughout Peninsular Malaysia and Singapore. The government also assisted in promoting the game by organizing matches between various states.

In 1962, the first national *sepak raga jaring* competition was held. The Penang team emerged as champion and was awarded the first Khir Johari Gold Cup, while Singapore finished as the runner-up. The competition has been held annually since 1962. Other events have also been organized—the Tunku Abdul Rahman Cup, the Tun Abdul Razak Cup, the Datuk Haji Ali Haji Ahmad Cup and the Tan Sri Samad Idris Cup.

Becoming an international sport

The name 'sepak takraw' was born on 19 November 1965, just before the start of the third Southeast Asian Peninsular (SEAP) Games in Kuala Lumpur.

There was a heated discussion among the participating countries regarding the name of the sport. Malaysia and Singapore wanted to maintain the name of *sepak raga jaring* while Thailand and Laos insisted on *takraw*, the Thai word for ball. In the spirit of cooperation, they agreed to adopt the name of sepak takraw and, with several amendments, accept the rules and regulations of the sport as previously set forth by the Sepak Raga Association of Malaya. One significant change was the agreement to use the Thai rattan ball, a larger and heavier version, for game play. The countries also formed the Asian Sepak Takraw Federation, paving the way for international competitions.

Sepak takraw was included as one of the events in the SEAP games in 1965, and the Malaysian team won the gold medal by defeating their Thai counterparts. In the same year, the Sepak Raga Association of Malaya was renamed the Sepaktakraw Association of Malaysia.

During the 1970s and 1980s, many private sector institutions, such as Malaysian Airline System (MAS), Utusan Malaysia and Radio Televisyen Malaysia (RTM), came forward to sponsor championships and thereby promote the popularity of sepak takraw. In 1985, 1987, 1988 and 1990, the Sepak Takraw

World Championships were held in Kuala Lumpur. Popularity soared internationally and by 1990, 15 countries including the USA, Australia, Japan, Germany, Korea and China took part in the Sepak Takraw World Championships. The International Sepak Takraw Federation (ISTAF), the global governing body, boasts a membership of over 20 countries.

Malaysia has established itself, along with Thailand, as a perennial powerhouse in the sport. The Malaysian team emerged as the inaugural champions of the King's Cup World Sepak Takraw Championships, considered by most to be the sport's most prestigious event, in Thailand in 1985, and went on to repeat as champions in 1988. Sepak takraw was introduced as an event in 1990 at the Asian Games in Beijing, and the Malaysian team captured two gold medals. At the 1994 Asian Games in Hiroshima, Malaysia clinched another gold medal in the sepak takraw competition. Since the sport was introduced in the SEA Games programme in 1965, Malaysia has won 13 sepak takraw gold medals, most recently at the 2005 games in Manila.

TOP: Player from Kuala Lumpur (left) attacking while his opponent from Terengganu attempts to block the shot during the final of the Khir Johari Gold Cup in Kedah, 2007.

ABOVE: Malaysian team posing after winning the silver medal in the team event at the 2006 Asian Games in Doha. The team won a total of two silver medals and one bronze medal.

How the game is played

Sepak takraw is played by two teams comprising three players each. The first team to capture two 21-point sets or one 21-point set and the third, deciding 15-point set is declared the winner of the game.

A team scores a point if the ball lands in the court of play on the opponent's side of the net, if the ball drops outside the court of play on the team's side of the net, if the ball touches an opponent's hands or arms, if an opponent touches the net or steps on the half-court line, or if the opposing team hits the ball more than three times.

Generally, the rules of volleyball apply to sepak takraw with three major exceptions:
- Players are not allowed to use their hands or arms.
- A player or team can touch the ball no more than three times successively.
- Players do not have to rotate their positions on defence.

LEFT: Malaysia's N. Abdul Ghani passing the ball to his team-mate during the Asian Games, 1998.

FAR LEFT: National player Ahmad Ezzat Mohd (left) leaps into the air and acrobatically kicks the ball in the Asian Games final against Thailand, 1998. Malaysia lost the match and took home the silver medal.

Malaysian player preparing to feed the ball to his team-mate who will serve it into play during the 2006 Asian Games in Doha. The ball, weighing approximately 250 grams, is typically made from rattan or plastic.

1.52 metres

13.4 metres

6.1 metres

Tekong

Left-inside

Right-inside

Tekong circle

The service
At the beginning of each point, one player from serving team, called the '*tekong*', positions himself with one foot in the *tekong* circle. The two remaining players, referred to as the 'left-inside' and 'right-inside', stand in the quarter circles near the half-court line, and one of them throws the ball to the *tekong* who in turn kicks it over the net into the opponent's half of the court.

Football: Origins and the domestic game

From its earliest recorded appearance in the Malay Peninsula in the late 19th century, football rapidly became popular among the local population, as well as the British. It did not take long for the sport to become formally organized. Expanding from its original administrative base in Selangor, and boosted by the close involvement of both the nation's first prime minister and the fifth Sultan of Pahang, the sport continues to be one of the most popular and widely played in the country.

The North (right) and South teams at the Raffle Range Stadium in Kuala Lumpur, 1952.

TOP: Football match being played in Kuala Lumpur, 1903.

ABOVE: Teams from Selangor (right) and Singapore that played in the 1927 H.M.S. Malaya Cup final in Kuala Lumpur comprising (bottom row, from left) Wan Puteh, Un Sun, Abdul Fatteh, Yong Liang, B. de Souza, J.E. King, T. Doig, T.D. Welsh, (middle row, from left) Loo Beng, Kemat, Chee Lim, Roy Smith, H.W. Thomson (President of the Malaya Cup Committee), C.C. Perdiau, (top row, from left) Lin Teck Seng (linesman), J.J. Sheehan and R.H. Gale. Selangor emerged victorious, winning 8–1.

Souvenir programme for the 26th H.M.S. Malaya Cup final between teams from Penang and Singapore held in Ipoh, 1952.

Origins

There is some debate about who invented the game of football, but none about when it took on the content and character of an organized sport. Football burgeoned in the public schools of mid-19th century England. Since those schools trained the civil servants of the British Empire, it was no surprise that they fostered its growth in the Malay States in the last three decades of that century when British rule was consolidated.

The indigenous Malays of the Malay Peninsula took readily to the sport, for they found it an exciting variant of a native recreation: *sepak raga*, a game in which a rattan ball is juggled by two teams of three players using any body part other than the arms (see 'Sepak takraw'). Indeed, the Malay word for football, *bola sepak*, was formed by combining the words *bola* (ball) and *sepak* (kick). The term gained currency as the sport's popularity spread throughout the Malay States.

The immigrant Chinese and Indians, who mainly worked in the tin mines and on the rubber plantations, were also exponents of the sport for they had seen and played versions of it in the countries from which they came. Indeed, when a structure for the staging of the sport on a competitive basis began to take shape in the early 20th century, the driving force was members of the Indian and Chinese communities, including those employed in the lower echelons of the civil service and in commercial houses established by the British, as well as those who were rubber estate or mine owners.

Early organization

In 1905, the Selangor Amateur Football League was launched featuring two types of football clubs: those comprising British players and those constituting local or Asian players, such as Selangor Recreation Club (SRC). The SRC was particularly successful in the early years, winning the Watson Shield in 1907 and 1909. The shield was named after R.G. Watson, a member of the Malayan Civil Service, who donated the trophy.

In 1910, the Tamil Union Association Football League was organized with teams competing for the Valupillai Shield, named in recognition of rubber estate owner C.A. Valupillai, an ardent fan of the game. The league spawned a club, Tamil Union, that made its debut in the multi-racial Selangor league in 1911, having found that playing in an intra-Indian league did little to spur improvement.

The state of Selangor became the focal point of football activity, largely because its capital at that time, Kuala Lumpur, had become the administrative and business centre of the British colonial administration. Clubs sprouted and competitions multiplied, so that by 1926 there was a strong impetus to form a governing body. The Selangor Football Association was founded in that same year.

Inter-state competition

Even before football competitions became structured under a controlling body in Selangor, the visit of the battleship H.M.S. *Malaya* to the Malay Peninsula in 1921 became the launching pad for another event: the H.M.S. Malaya Cup. The officers and men of the H.M.S. *Malaya*, to commemorate their visit—during which they played rugby and football matches against club teams—donated a trophy to inaugurate rugby and football competitions in the Malay Peninsula.

The Malaysia Cup trophy.

The Selangor Club (now known as the Royal Selangor Club), one of the oldest and most prestigious clubs in the country, formed a committee to oversee the H.M.S. Malaya Cup football competition. The states along the west coast of Peninsular Malaya—Selangor, Perak, Negeri Sembilan, Johor, Melaka—and Singapore all formed associations in their respective states and fielded teams in this competition which began in 1921. Between 1921 and 1932, the H.M.S. Malaya Cup was the premier annual football competition in the country, conferring prestige on its winners and providing a focal point for the growing numbers of fans of the sport. Standout players during this period included A.L. Henry, Abu Hanifah, Pang Siang Hock, Sharif Awang, Sheikh Mustapha, Dollah Don and Khoo Bin Keng.

In 1940, control of the Football Association of Malaya (FAM), which had been officially founded in

Organization

Officially established as the national governing body for football in 1933, the Football Association of Malaysia (FAM) has spearheaded the growth of the sport locally. The first president of the FAM was Sir Andrew Caldecott. In its early days, FAM promoted football by organizing leagues and tournaments such as the H.M.S. Malaya Cup.

FAM founding president Sir Andrew Caldecott.

In 1951, Tunku Abdul Rahman Putra was elected president of the FAM and, under his leadership, the association experienced significant growth and change. The Asian Football Confederation (AFC) was formed in 1954 with the FAM as one of its 14 founding members. Two years later, the FAM was inducted as a member of the Fédération Internationale de Football Association (FIFA). After the construction of Stadium Merdeka and the staging of the first Merdeka Tournament in 1957, football's popularity reached new heights in Malaya and the country became a prominent player in the international arena.

Football Association of Malaysia logo.

FAM president from 1976 to 1984 Tan Sri Hamzah Abu Samah.

FAM president as at 2008 Sultan Ahmad Shah.

Malaysia's second Prime Minister, Tun Abdul Razak, assumed the role of the FAM President in 1974, but served for only one year. Tan Sri Hamzah Abu Samah presided over the FAM from 1976 to 1984, and led the national team to new heights in international competitions.

In 1984, Sultan Ahmad Shah of Pahang, an avid fan of the sport, was elected president of the FAM, a position which he still holds. Under his leadership, the FAM was transformed into a dynamic organization lauded by FIFA in the early 1990s as one of the best organized national associations in Asia.

In 1989, the FAM kicked-off the semi-professional football league, after 30 senior officials of the association visited several countries in Europe to study their professional structures. Malaysia was the only country at that time in which the national league was played between states or regions and not between clubs. Teams from 16 state football associations of Malaysia along with Singapore and Brunei were divided into two divisions with teams playing a home-and-away league and prize money awarded to the top three in each division. The top six teams of the first division and the top two teams of the second division would then move into the Malaysia Cup competition.

The football competitions in Malaysia have subsequently been restructured. At the summit is the Super League, which is contested by 14 teams, followed by the Premier League, the Malaysia Cup, the FA Cup, the FAM Cup and the President's Cup. The Charity Shield match, between the Malaysia Cup champions and the league champions, is also held each season.

Singapore (in white) and Selangor squaring off in the Malaysia Cup final at Stadium Merdeka, 1978. Selangor won 4–2.

The transition of Malaysian football from amateur to professional status was not without its problems. In the 1980s, allegations of match-fixing began to taint the national league. The FAM felt obliged to take drastic action in 1994, and a total of 84 national and first-team club players were banned. Since 1989, foreign players from other parts of Asia, Africa, Australia and Europe have been allowed to play in local competitions.

The FAM has introduced a development scheme through which 14 academies and 65 centres nationwide come under the auspices of the Ministry of Youth and Sports.

The FAM oversees the development of women's football and Futsal, an indoor five-a-side variation of football. Malaysia hosted the KL World Fives Futsal Championship in 2003 and 2008.

The Majlis Perbandaran Petaling Jaya (MPPJ) goalkeeper tries to foil a Negeri Sembilan striker during the Super League playoffs, 2003.

The Tunku (right), then FAM president, standing next to the trophy at the Merdeka Tournament in Kuala Lumpur, 1971.

1933 by the states that took part in the H.M.S. Malaya Cup, shifted from Singapore to Malaya. Between 1941 and 1945, the Japanese invasion and Occupation of Malaya caused an interruption to local football activity. After the war, the FAM was revived and played a vital role in re-launching the H.M.S. Malaya Cup in 1948. The competition expanded that same year to encompass the east coast states of Terengganu, Kelantan and Pahang, hitherto outside the ambit of direct British rule; all three states fielded teams in the annual event in 1948.

Football flourishes

The end of World War II brought the winds of change to the Malay Peninsula. As their aspirations for independence from British rule stirred, Asians began to take control of football's governing bodies. Tunku Abdul Rahman Putra was elected president of the Selangor Football Association in 1949. A great fan of the game, the Tunku had won renown by developing the Kedah state team, which had reached the 1940 H.M.S. Malaya Cup final match against Singapore.

Based on his many achievements, the Tunku put his growing stature as leader of the Malayan nation's quest for independence to great use in the football arena. He became president of the FAM in 1951 and

when he was appointed chief minister of the Federation of Malaya the following year, he pushed for the building of a football stadium in the capital Kuala Lumpur. It was a huge project that critics warned would be a liability. But when Malaya eventually gained its independence in 1957, with the Tunku as its first prime minister, part of the celebration was the hosting of the world's first international invitational football tournament, the Merdeka Tournament, by the FAM.

The Tunku's confidence in the Malayan people's interest and support for the game was vindicated when the inaugural event was a financial success in that the gate receipts covered the costs. Sir Stanley Rous, then president of the Fédération Internationale de Football Association (FIFA), the world governing body for football, was amazed that such a young nation could organize an all-expenses–paid tournament for Asian countries without losing money. The Tunku's triumph garnered him much prestige, and he was unanimously voted president of the Asian Football Confederation (AFC) in 1958. In his new role, the Tunku established an Asian youth tournament for the Rahman gold trophy, which began in 1959 in Kuala Lumpur. Under his leadership, the AFC evolved into a driving force on the international football scene.

Dollah Don (right) attempting to head the ball into the goal during a match against South China, 1947.

Teams from Malaya (in stripes) and Burma during the first Merdeka Tournament at Stadium Merdeka in 1957.

Football: International achievements

In terms of performance in international competitions, Malaysian football peaked in the 1970s and early 1980s. The national team qualified twice for the Olympic Games during that period, and made their mark in various regional tournaments. The following decades witnessed a decline in the overall competitiveness of the Malaysian team. The national side, however, has experienced a resurgence of late. In 2007, Malaysia emerged victorious from the Merdeka Tournament held in conjunction with the 50th anniversary of the country's Independence.

Merdeka Tournament Championship Team, 1958

The Malayan team that won the 1958 Merdeka Tournament comprising (first row, from left) Mok Wai Hong, Wong Kim Seng, Robert Choe, Ng Boon Bee, (second row, from left) Ahmad Nazari, Jalil Che Din, Rahim Omar, Chan Tuck Choy, Tunku Abdul Rahman Putra (President of the Football Association of Malaya), Abdul Ghani Minhat, Sexton Lourdes, M. Govindasamy, Lim Kee Siong, (back row, from left) Kwok Kin Keng, Lim Ah Lek, Boey Chong Lian, Zainal Abidin, Kwong Chong Yin, Woo Ah Wah, Choo Seng Quee, Yusof Bakar, M. Joseph, Edwin Dutton, Boey Ban Chuan and Wong Yuen Ching.

Yang di-Pertuan Agong Tuanku Syed Putra Jamalullail (left) presenting Malayan team captain Edwin Dutton with the Merdeka Tournament trophy, 1960.

Malaysia's heyday and beyond

For nearly two decades following its inception in 1957, the Merdeka Tournament was Asia's premier football event, and the national team regularly won the annual competition. Although Hong Kong triumphed in the inaugural edition, Malaya went on to win the Merdeka Tournament in 1958, 1959 and 1968, and shared the title with South Korea in 1960.

With its bronze medal performance in the 1962 Asian Games in Jakarta, Malaya firmly established itself on the international football scene. The national team won the 18th Merdeka Tournament in 1974 after beating South Korea 1–0. At the 1974 Asian Games in Tehran, they overwhelmed North Korea 2–1 to earn the bronze medal.

The national squad had looked forward to the final round of the Asian Football Confederation (AFC) Asian Cup in Tehran in 1976. However, several key players were unavailable for the competition because they had suffered injuries in various Malaysia Cup matches. Having had only

four days of preparation, the team lost 2–1 to Kuwait and held China to a 1–1 draw.

The Malaysians won the Merdeka title in 1976 by defeating Japan 2–0. In the 1980 AFC Asian Cup, the national team beat the UAE 2–0, fought South Korea and Qatar to 1–1 draws, and lost to Kuwait 1–3.

Decline and revival

From the 1980s onwards, the growing number of invitational tournaments in Asia and the steadily rising importance of the qualifying tournaments for the quadrennial triplicity of the FIFA World Cup, the Olympic Games and the AFC Asian Cup, reduced the perceived value and utility of the Merdeka event. The tournament eventually diminished in prestige due to the lack of Asian invitees fielding their first teams. Correspondingly, Malaysia faded as a football force in Asia.

After qualifying for the Olympic Games in 1972 in Munich, and for the 1980 competition in Moscow (although the Malaysian team did not participate that year as the nation joined the American-led boycott of the event), Malaysian football went into decline. The national team did, however, capture the Merdeka Tournament trophy in 1986 and 1993, and the SEA Games gold medal in 1989.

To arrest and reverse the gradual descent in the national team's performance, a revamp in the administration of Malaysian football was undertaken. Under the leadership of Sultan Ahmad Shah, the Football Association of Malaysia (FAM) oversaw the transition of Malaysian football from amateur to semi-professional status and, after 1994, to a fully professional basis (see 'Football: Origins and the domestic game').

In August 2007, Malaysia hosted the 39th Merdeka Tournament in conjunction with the celebration of the 50th anniversary of the nation's Independence. After defeating Laos, Lesotho and Singapore, the national under-23 team overwhelmed Myanmar 3–1 in the final before a crowd of 40,000 people at the Shah Alam Stadium to win the tournament.

1. Malaysian team making a victory lap around Stadium Merdeka with the trophy after defeating Japan to win the Merdeka Tournament, 1976.

2. Malaysian players (right) on the attack during the final of the Merdeka Tournament held in conjunction with the 50th anniversary of Independence in 2007 at the Shah Alam Stadium. Malaysia defeated Myanmar 3–1.

3. Malaysian team captain Mohd Shukor Adan lifting the Merdeka Tournament trophy after his team defeated Myanmar to capture the title after a lapse of 14 years, 2007.

Malaysia in Olympic football: 1971–72 and 1980

1971–72

In 1971, Malaysia emerged from a qualifying series with an impeccable four-win record, without conceding a single goal, to earn the right to represent East Asia at the Olympic Games in Munich.

Coached by Scotsman Dave McLaren, who had distinguished himself as a goal-keeper on the Penang team two decades earlier when he was doing national service for Britain, Malaysia overcame opposition from Taiwan and the Philippines and upset Japan—the Olympic bronze medallists in 1968—and South Korea.

Malaysian team members (from left) M. Chandran, Namat Abdullah, Soh Chin Aun and Wong Choon Wah carrying the flag upon their triumphant return to the Kuala Lumpur airport, 1971.

To the Malaysian captain, M. Chandran, the victory against South Korea on the chilly evening of 25 September 1971 at the Seoul Stadium stands out as his team's most memorable match. Despite the driving rain and the crowd, the Malaysians were determined not to allow external factors to influence their performance. Chandran recalled, 'What gave me immense satisfaction was the manner in which the team kept their composure against the tremendous rally by the Koreans. After we took the lead in the 54th minute through striker Syed Ahmad Abu Bakar, the Koreans retaliated with waves of menacing raids'. During the heavy bombardment by the Koreans, Chandran and his team-mates displayed immense patience and resilience, and walked off the pitch at the final whistle with their one goal still intact. In the final match of the five-nation qualifying tournament, the Malaysians possessed too much power for the Filipinos, beating them by a score of 5–0.

The adulation heaped on the heroes when they returned from Seoul was tremendous. Thousands of fans lined up all the way from the airport to the residence of Datuk Harun Idris, the Chief Minister of Selangor, who was also team manager.

The Munich Olympics, however, were a whole new experience for the Malaysians. Chandran recollected that, 'Though I was 28 years old, the oldest and the most experienced player in the squad, I was still nervous. In fact, all of us were awed by the occasion. Facing the Germans in the opening match did not help either. We started nervously against them but did exceptionally well by keeping the score sheet clean by the end of the first half. The Germans finally triumphed 3–0, but it wasn't because we played badly. It was because they were technically superior. Yes, we lost 3–0, but it was still our best display.'

The national team proceeded to face the United States, and emerged victorious, winning 3–0. But in their final first round match, the Malaysian team's Olympic run was ended by the hounding tactics of the Moroccans who won 6–0.

Syed Ahmad Abu Bakar (in white) heading in the winning goal in Malaysia's 1–0 win over South Korea in a pre-liminary Olympic match in Seoul, 1971.

Bakri Ibni (right) takes a fall after a tackle by a South Korean defender during the Olympic qualifying final in 1980. Bakri scored the first goal of Malaysia's 2–1 victory.

1980

In 1980, Malaysia mounted their campaign for a berth at the Moscow Olympic Games with vigour—beating Indonesia 6–1, South Korea 3–0 and Brunei 3–1, drawing with Japan 1–1 and thrashing the Philippines 8–1.

Despite losing to the Malaysians, the South Koreans won the rest of their matches and were cruising towards a showdown with the local team. In the all-important final encounter at Stadium Merdeka, the Koreans battled with characteristic tenacity. Malaysia's Bakri Ibni scored the first goal. The Koreans stormed back, and after pounding the Malaysian defence, equalized in the 58th minute. However, James Wong, on receiving a square pass from his team-mate Hassan Sani, penetrated the Korean penalty box, and drew the goalkeeper out before neatly tucking in the winner. The Yang di-Pertuan Agong Sultan Ahmad Shah was unable to contain his joy and

Yang di-Pertuan Agong Sultan Ahmad Shah (right), current president of FAM, congratulating team captain Soh Chin Aun after Malaysia's victory over Korea.

went down to the pitch to personally congratulate every member of the team for their stirring performance instead of waiting for the captain, Soh Chin Aun, to come up to the royal box after the game.

Shortly thereafter, the United States Olympic Council decided to boycott the Moscow Olympics in response to the Soviet Union's invasion of Afghanistan. Malaysia responded to the call by the United States for a worldwide boycott of the Olympic Games, and consequently the football team did not take part in the 1980 competition. Since then, the Malaysian football team has not qualified for participation in the Olympic Games.

1. Abdul Ghani Minhat's dazzling dribbling and shooting skills earned him the moniker of *Raja Bola* or King of Football. He was the star of the Malayan team which emerged victorious in the Merdeka Tournaments of 1958, 1959 and 1960.

2. Mokhtar Dahari (centre), commonly known as 'Supermokh', possessed tremendous speed, a thunderous kick and an unerring eye for goals. Mokhtar played for Malaysia from 1972 to 1985, earning his first cap when he was only 19. In his 167 games for the country, scored 125 goals.

3. Team captain M. Chandran receiving a hero's welcome upon his return from the Malaysian team's success at the Pre-Olympic qualifying tournament at Seoul, 1971. Highly respected as a defender and team leader, Chandran went on to coach the national team after his retirement in 1974.

4. Malaysian fans nicknamed Soh Chin Aun (right) the 'Towkay', loosely translated as the 'boss', because of his commanding play as a defender. Soh is the most capped player in local football history, having turned out in national colours 252 times from 1971 to 1983.

Hockey: Origins and the domestic game

The sport of hockey—also called 'field hockey' to distinguish it from a similar but faster variation played on ice (see 'Ice sports')—has been played in Malaysia since the late 19th century. Numerous domestic and international tournaments have been held locally, and have been well attended by the public, particularly in the 1960s and 1970s.

Teams from Selangor (in white) and Perak playing in a match on the Selangor Club *padang* in Kuala Lumpur, 1948.

Origins of the sport

It is difficult to state with any certainty when or where hockey was first played. There is, however, evidence that a game resembling modern hockey was played some 4000 years ago in Egypt. On the wall of a tomb built about 2000 BCE in the Nile Valley, there is a drawing which shows two people in a 'bully off', the ritual which accompanied the start of a modern hockey game before the rules were changed in the 1960s.

The game travelled to Greece and was later taken up by the Romans. Evidence that a game similar to hockey was played in ancient Greece was discovered in Athens in 1922. A carving on a wall built by Themistocles in 500 BCE shows six people playing a game resembling hockey with two players bent over a ball in a 'bully-off' stance.

The birth of modern hockey occurred in 1886, when the British Hockey Association was established. The then Prince of Wales, King Edward VII, was the first president of the association. Hundreds of hockey clubs, which had already sprung up all over England, became members of the British Hockey Association. The first international match was played in 1907

Badges worn by members of the Perak Hockey Association before (left) and after World War II.

between England and France and this was followed by a number of similar competitions among several European countries.

Hockey was played as an exhibition event at the 2nd Olympic Games in Paris in 1900, but it was only included as a competitive sport at the 4th Olympic Games in London in 1908. It was then dropped from the programme until the 1920 Games in Antwerp, but was not included in the Paris games four years later because of limited support.

In response to this omission from the Olympics in 1924, a world hockey association was established in Paris that same year. Representatives of seven European countries collectively set up the Fédération Internationale de Hockey sur Gazon (FIH) which became the world body governing the game. The success of the FIH in structuring the sport led to the reinstatement of hockey as an Olympic sport in 1928. As of 2008, the FIH is headquartered in Switzerland and has a membership of 116 associations.

Top: Teams from Perak and the Armed Forces facing off in a match in Kuala Lumpur, 1967.

Above: Perak Hockey centre forward Raja Azlan Shah (left) with team captain Abdul Hamid Aroop, 1949.

Organization

The Malayan Hockey Council was the first Pan-Malayan organization formed in 1948 to administer and develop the game in the country. The Malayan Hockey Council became the Malayan Hockey Federation and later, in 1963, was renamed the Malaysian Hockey Federation (MHF). The council's first president was Sir George Oehlers. Subsequent presidents comprise E.B. David (1950–53), Herman de Souza (1953–57), Tun Abdul Razak (1957–76), Tun Hussein Onn (1977–81), Sultan Azlan Shah (1981–2004), Raja Muda Perak Raja Dr Nazrin Shah (2004–07) and Admiral Tan Sri Dato' Sri Mohd Anwar Mohd Nor (2007–present).

In 2005, the Malaysian Hockey Confederation (MHC) was established. This joint body between the MHF and the Malaysian Women's Hockey Association (MWHA) was formed as a single body to represent the country internationally.

Sultan Azlan Shah (right), MHF president from 1981 to 2004, presenting a trophy to Maybank captain Wallace Tan after his team triumphed over UAB in the Malaysia Hockey League final, 1988.

Malayan Hockey Council founding president Sir George Oehlers (left), MHF president from 2004 to 2007 Raja Muda Perak Dr Nazrin Shah (middle) and MHF president as at 2008 Admiral Tan Sri Dato' Sri Mohd Anwar Mohd Nor.

Logos of the Malayan Hockey Council (left), the MHF (middle) and the MWHA.

Prime Minister and MHF President Tun Abdul Razak (left) officiating the opening of the East Asian Regional Championship at Stadium Merdeka, 1973.

Game play

Hockey, or field hockey as it is known in some parts of the world, is a stick and ball game that was originally played on grass but now, especially in international competitions, is held on synthetic surfaces. A regulation length hockey match lasts 70 minutes, broken into two halves comprising 35 minutes each.

Two teams of 11 players compete against each other using their 'hooked' sticks to hit, push, pass and dribble a small, hard ball. The objective of the game is to score by getting the ball into the opponents' goal which is protected by a goalkeeper. The other 10 players play as attackers, defenders and midfielders, depending on the team's strategy.

A goal can be scored from a field goal, a penalty corner or a penalty stroke. A field goal is a goal scored from open play, but the ball has to be struck from a semi-circular area in front of the opponents' goal called the shooting circle. If an attacker hits the ball from outside the shooting circle and it goes directly into the goal or is only touched by a defender on the way, it does not count as a goal.

If a defending team breaks certain rules in the shooting circle, the other team may be awarded a penalty corner. To take a penalty corner, play is stopped to allow the teams to take their positions on attack and defence. The ball is then put in play by one attacker who passes the ball to his team-mates whose feet and sticks should be outside the shooting circle before taking a shot at goal. A penalty stroke, awarded for serious fouls, is a push, scoop or flick taken at goal by a chosen player and defended only by the goalkeeper.

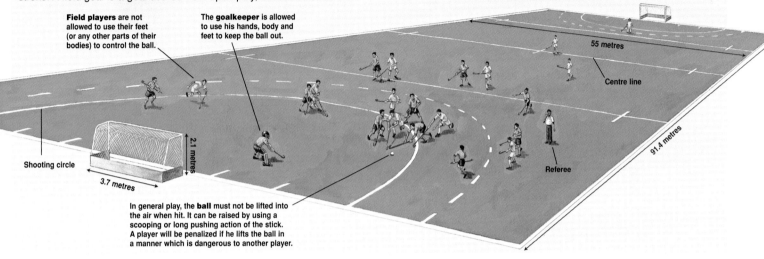

Field players are not allowed to use their feet (or any other parts of their bodies) to control the ball.

The **goalkeeper** is allowed to use his hands, body and feet to keep the ball out.

55 metres

Centre line

91.4 metres

Shooting circle

2.1 metres

3.7 metres

Referee

In general play, the **ball** must not be lifted into the air when hit. It can be raised by using a scooping or long pushing action of the stick. A player will be penalized if he lifts the ball in a manner which is dangerous to another player.

Hockey in Malaysia

Competitive hockey was introduced to the Malay Peninsula by the Royal Engineers of the British Army and was first played in the Malay States as early as 1892. Inter-state games between Singapore and Selangor were played as early as 1904. Although in the early days the game was the exclusive preserve of Europeans and their clubs, Malayans too began to take to hockey, leading to the establishment of state hockey associations and inter-state matches that began in the 1920s. The North versus South Classic and the Federated Malay States (FMS) versus the Colony Test match were fixtures on the local hockey calendar.

Among the outstanding pre-war players were Baharom, Osman Basir, N.C. Caleb, David Navarednam, Abdul Hamid Aroop, Aladad Khan, Tajuddin and Sheikh Mustapha.

League hockey was organized for the first time in Taiping, Perak, in 1946. This encouraged other districts of Perak to start league competitions of their own, a concept that soon spread to other states and led to an overall improvement of standards in the sport.

Starting in 1949, the Malayan Hockey Council conducted quadrangular and triangular tournaments among the states, including Singapore, which proved to be a success in terms of public interest.

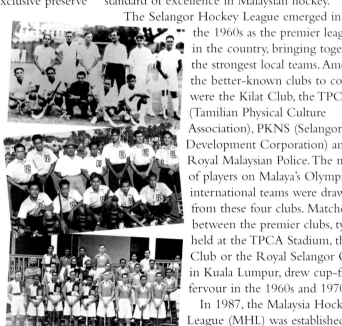

In the 1963–64 season, the inter-state Razak Cup was first played. It was the championship of Malaysian hockey and the symbol of local hockey supremacy. The first team to win the cup was Singapore, with Negeri Sembilan the victors the following year. The Razak Cup still remains the standard of excellence in Malaysian hockey.

The Selangor Hockey League emerged in the 1960s as the premier league in the country, bringing together the strongest local teams. Among the better-known clubs to compete were the Kilat Club, the TPCA (Tamilian Physical Culture Association), PKNS (Selangor State Development Corporation) and the Royal Malaysian Police. The majority of players on Malaya's Olympic and international teams were drawn from these four clubs. Matches between the premier clubs, typically held at the TPCA Stadium, the Kilat Club or the Royal Selangor Club in Kuala Lumpur, drew cup-final fervour in the 1960s and 1970s.

In 1987, the Malaysia Hockey League (MHL) was established and competitions were organized between employer clubs. As of 2008, the MHL remains the premier league and is one of the main factors in the revival of Malaysian hockey. State- and national-level competitions ultimately lead to a championship tournament.

LEFT TOP: FMS team which defeated the Colony in the 12th, and last, hockey Test in Kuala Lumpur, 1938.

LEFT MIDDLE: Perak Hockey Team prior to a match against Negeri Sembilan in Singapore, 1949.

LEFT BOTTOM: An inter-state match between Negeri Sembilan and Melaka.

BELOW: Players from the Armed Forces team advancing on goal in a match against Negeri Sembilan during the Razak Cup tournament in Johor, 2006.

Hockey: International achievements

Malaysian teams have competed internationally since the 1930s, and have continually achieved success on the world stage. The high point of Malaysian hockey was the 3rd Hockey World Cup held in Kuala Lumpur in 1975, when hockey-fever gripped the nation and national players became household names. Malaysians continue to distinguish themselves in international competitions such as the 2006 Commonwealth Games and the 2007 Asia Cup in which the national team won bronze medals.

First Malaysian Olympic Games hockey team, 1956

Seated from left: T. Nadarajah, Philip Sankey, Wilfred Vias (vice captain), V.T. Duray (umpire), Herman de Souza (chef de mission), K. Aryaduray (manager), S. Selvanayagam (captain), Chua Eng Cheng and Gerald D. Toff. Standing from left: S. Devendran, Aminullah Karim, Noel Arul, Peter Van Huizen, Tommy Lawrence, M. Shanmuganathan, Gian Singh, P. Alagendra, Mike Shepherdson, Hamzah Shamsuddin, Sheikh Ali and Chuah Eng Kim.

Malaysian hockey performances at the Olympic Games

1956	Melbourne	9th
1964	Tokyo	9th
1968	Mexico City	15th
1972	Munich	8th
1976	Montreal	8th
1984	Los Angeles	11th
1992	Barcelona	9th
1996	Atlanta	11th
2000	Sydney	11th

Early international experience

In 1932, the Malayan Hockey Council (see 'Hockey: Origins and the domestic game'), for the first time, invited a foreign national team to tour Malaya. India, the invited team, had been world champions since 1928. Malaya played its first international match abroad against the Indian Olympic team in Singapore in 1932. India won 7–1. Four years later, the Malayan team made its first international tour by visiting Hong Kong. The dominant Indian team returned for another month-long tour of Malaya in 1954. The Indians won all of their 15 matches, with a goal-tally of 121 for and seven against. The visit of the Indian team and the appointment of a coach from India from 1954 to 1955 was a useful prelude to the visit of another of the world's best teams, the Pakistani national team in 1955.

The experience gained from playing the Indians and Pakistanis served the Malayan team well in its maiden Olympic Games appearance at Melbourne in 1956—the team finished ninth overall. The national hockey team has since made appearances in eight other Olympic Games.

World Cup campaigns

Malaysia first participated in the World Cup of Hockey in 1973 in Amsterdam, and they came in 11th place out of 12 teams. The Malaysians subsequently finished fourth in the 1975 competition in Kuala Lumpur. However, at the 1978 and 1982 World Cups in Argentina and India respectively, the national team finished in 10th place. At the 1998 competition in Germany, Malaysia finished 11th, while in the 2002 World Cup in Kuala Lumpur, they finished in eighth place.

Commonwealth Games highlights

At the 1998 Kuala Lumpur Commonwealth Games, the national team emerged as runners-up to Australia, losing 0–4 after upsetting India 1–0 in the semi-finals. At the 2006 games in Melbourne, Malaysia won the bronze medal by defeating England 2–0 after losing to Australia in the semi-finals.

Miniature sheet issued in conjunction with Malaysia's hosting of the World Cup in 2002.

International events hosted by Malaysia

Of the two World Cups (1975 and 2002), two Junior World Cups (1982 and 1989) and many other international and regional tournaments held locally such as the SEA Games and East Asia Regionals, the 1975 World Cup in Kuala Lumpur was the finest both in terms of organization and the success of the national team. Since 1983, Malaysia has hosted the annual Sultan Azlan Shah Cup Tournament, one of the premier international hockey events. In 2007, the national team defeated Canada, South Korea and India and drew with Pakistan to qualify, after a lapse of 22 years, for the final of the event. Olympic champions Australia, however, clinched the 2007 Sultan Azlan Shah Cup after beating the home team 3–1.

1. National team player Mohd Shahrun Nabil Abdullah (second from right) celebrating his goal against Japan during the Asian Games in Doha, 2006.

2. Goalkeeper from Bangladesh diving to stop a shot by Azlan Misron of Malaysia (second from right) during the Asian Games in Korea, 2002. The Malaysian team took home the bronze medal.

3. Malaysia's Norfarah Hashim (left) vying for control of the ball with a player from India during the Indira Gandhi International Gold Cup in New Delhi, 2005.

Drama at the 1975 World Cup

The 3rd World Cup in Kuala Lumpur in March 1975 was a resounding success in terms of its organization and the Malaysian team's performance. For two weeks, hockey gripped the nation, pushing politics from the front pages of newspapers and providing several captivating hours of primetime television coverage.

Malaysia dethroned defending champions Holland in their last group match at the Kilat Club ground in Pantai, Kuala Lumpur on the wet morning of 11 March. Supported by a partisan crowd of several thousand cascading down the slopes surrounding the clubhouse, Malaysia ended Holland's Cup defence with a sensational 2–1 victory on the stroke of fulltime. Poon Fook Loke gave Malaysia the lead with a field goal in the 14th minute. Team captain N. Sri Shanmuganathan and his teammates maintained their lead into the second half until Ties Kruize scored with a penalty stroke for Holland in the 63rd minute. As time was running out, Malaysia put the Dutch goal under siege. In injury time, Malaysia's M. Mahendran was checked in his stride during a goalmouth foray. Frenchman Alain Renaud, who umpired the match with compatriot Louis Gillet, awarded Malaysia a short corner which N. Sri Shanmuganathan converted in the closing seconds of the match.

Malaysia's subsequent 3–2 semi-final loss to India was another hotly contested affair. Watched by a record crowd of 60,000, the largest ever assembled for a single event at Stadium Merdeka, Malaysia came within a whisker of defeating India, leading 2–1 with only a few minutes left. The Indians, however, managed to level the score before grabbing a late winner in extra-time. India then went on to beat Pakistan in the final. In a final classification match for third place, Malaysia lost 0–4 to West Germany.

LEFT: National men's hockey team marching at the opening ceremony of the 3rd Hockey World Cup at Merdeka Stadium in Kuala Lumpur in 1975.

BELOW: Malaysian players (from left in white strips) N. Palanisamy, K. Balasingam, Wong Choon Hin and A. Francis battling against India in the semi-final match. The game was interrupted by torrential rain after 7 minutes, and had to be postponed until the morning of the day before the final.

1. M. Mahendran (left) in action during the World Cup, 1975. A skilful forward who is remembered for his awesome dribbling skills and prolific goal scoring, Mahendran remains hockey's only winner of the NSC Sportsman of the Year award which he received in 1972.

2. Ho Koh Chye (right) making a save against the Australian Olympic team during a Test match which ended in a 1–1 draw, 1960. Ho was named national coach in 1970, and led Malaysia to a fourth place finish in the 1975 World Cup.

3. M. Shanmuganathan played as a defender for the national team in two Olympic Games, Melbourne in 1956 and Tokyo in 1964, and bagged five goals.

4. N. Sri Shanmuganathan (right) captained the national hockey team at the 1970 Asian Games as well as at the Olympic Games in 1972 and 1976 and the World Cups in 1973 and 1975. After his retirement, Sri Shan was the national coach from 1987 to 1988.

5. The most capped player in local hockey history, forward Nor Saiful Zaini Nasiruddin turned out in national colours a record 328 times from 1985 to 2000, competing in three Olympic Games and three Asian Games as well as a World Cup.

6. Forward Mirnawan Nawawi played for the national side from 1989 to 2002, participating in three Olympic Games, three Asian Games and two World Cups. Mirnawan is best remembered for his winning goal against India in the semi-final match of the 1998 Commonwealth Games in Kuala Lumpur which catapulted the Malaysian team to the final and ultimately a silver medal.

Cricket

Brought to Malaya by the British in the late 19th century, cricket rapidly became an organized, competitive sport in the country. After World War II, the Malayan Cricket Association (MCA) was established, and local players began to shine in international competitions. Cricket was officially included as one of the sports played during the Merdeka celebrations in 1957. Malaysia has hosted a number of major international tournaments, and included cricket as an event in the Commonwealth Games in Kuala Lumpur in 1998.

Cricket match being played on the *padang* in front of the Royal Selangor Club, 1991.

The Australian and Malayan cricket teams posing for a picture together, 1927. Malaya shocked the cricket world by defeating Australia. One observer remarked that, 'no one, except the actual spectators believed the news. It was against the order of nature'.

Origins of the sport

Although the exact origins of cricket remain unknown, a nascent form of the sport can be traced back to a children's game played in England in the 13th century. During the 17th century, cricket emerged as an organized, competitive sport in England, culminating in a 'great cricket match' in Sussex in 1697. The 18th century saw the spread of cricket within England and to other parts of the globe and the formal establishment of the laws of the game in 1744. The global governing body, the International Cricket Council, was founded in 1909, and currently comprises associations from 97 member countries.

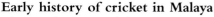

Cricket: A Malaysian Experience by Dr Alex Delilkan was first published in 1970.

Early history of cricket in Malaya

The Royal Selangor Club was the home of cricket from the late 19th century until 1987. Founded by a group of British planters in 1884, the club and its *padang* have been the venue for many of the significant cricket matches played locally.

It is widely believed that cricket was first played in Malaya between 1884 and 1886, when the acting resident of Selangor sought to improve the quality of the *padang* and construct a proper cricket pitch. The first formal match was organized between Selangor and Melaka in 1887. Two years later, the Perak–Selangor series was conceived, followed by the Selangor–Singapore series in 1891.

The first century scored on the *padang* was in 1899 when C. Glassford registered 101 for the Lake Club. The following year brought the first double century: an unbeaten 212 by Dr Lucy in a friendly match. The country's most historic victory occurred more than twenty years later, on 6 June 1927, when Malaya achieved the seemingly impossible feat of beating Australia by 39 runs. *The Cricketer* magazine, dated 23 July 1927, declared with pride, 'The home side's fielding was excellent, and N.J.A. Foster's management of his team left nothing to be desired. It was the greatest day in Malayan cricket history.'

Rules of the game

Cricket is played between two teams of 11 players on a grass pitch surrounded by a roughly circular field.

At any time the batting side must have two batsmen at opposite ends of the pitch. The striking batsman faces the opposing fielding team's bowler. One 'over' comprises six balls delivered by the bowler. At the end of each over, another bowler operates from the opposite end.

Each time a batsman strikes the ball and runs to the opposite end, it is considered one run. If the ball crosses the marking around the edge of the field, known as the 'boundary', four runs are credited to the batsman. When the batsman hits the ball over the 'boundary' without it touching the ground, six runs are scored. The team that scores more runs is declared the winner.

Traditionally, cricket was played either over three days or five days. 'Test' international matches were played over five days, at the end of which the two teams could end up in a stalemate. However, a draw is a non-option in limited-over cricket which restricts each side to 50 overs.

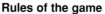

Wicket keeper fielding the ball during a game at the Bayu Emas cricket oval in Klang.

Dismissal

There are five forms of 'dismissal' which result in a batsman being declared 'out':

- **Bowled**: When the ball strikes the stumps or dislodges the bails.

- **Caught**: When the batsman lofts the ball and one of the fielders catches it before it touches the ground.

- **LBW**: When the ball raps the batsman's pads, and in response to an appeal by the fielders, the umpire decides that the ball would have hit the stumps had it not been blocked by the pads. If the appeal is upheld by the umpire, the batsman is considered out 'leg before wicket' ('LBW').

- **Run out**: When the batsman fails to get to the opposite end before a fielder or the wicketkeeper dislodges the stumps.

- **Stumped**: When the batsman, in attempting to strike the ball, misses, and the wicketkeeper whips off the bails, while the batsman's foot or feet are still out off the batting crease.

Fielding positions

Besides the wicket-keeper and bowler, the nine other players of the fielding team station themselves at various positions on the field. Fielding positions are not fixed, and players move themselves according to tactical decisions made by their team captain.

The field of play

Area shown in artwork on the right.

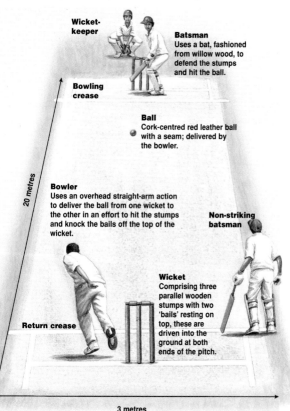

Wicket-keeper

Batsman
Uses a bat, fashioned from willow wood, to defend the stumps and hit the ball.

Bowling crease

Ball
Cork-centred red leather ball with a seam; delivered by the bowler.

Bowler
Uses an overhead straight-arm action to deliver the ball from one wicket to the other in an effort to hit the stumps and knock the bails off the top of the wicket.

Non-striking batsman

20 metres

Return crease

Wicket
Comprising three parallel wooden stumps with two 'bails' resting on top, these are driven into the ground at both ends of the pitch.

3 metres

Prior to World War II, cricket activities were conducted by the leading clubs in each individual state or colony, and the Singapore Cricket Club oversaw the general administration of the sport. The war brought sports in Malaya to a grinding halt. After the surrender of the Japanese, the country rapidly recovered, and cricket associations started mushrooming up all over the country in the late 1940s. Selangor, Negeri Sembilan and Pahang had established active associations by the end of the 1947 season, and Singapore and Johor were in the process of forming their own bodies. At the North versus South match, Selangor promulgated a proposal to form the Malayan Cricket Association (MCA, now known as the Malaysian Cricket Association). An interim committee was appointed and Selangor was assigned to draft the constitution. In 1948, the MCA was founded to structure and develop the sport of cricket in the country.

The Hong Kong cricket contingent were the first visitors after the war in 1948. The 'All-Malaya' team, in turn, toured Hong Kong in 1955 and 1959, and, representing Malaysia, in 1963 and 1971. In the late 1950s and 1960s, the country hosted clubs from New Zealand, Ceylon, England, Australia, Hong Kong and Pakistan as well as several Commonwealth teams.

Local cricket standouts
Among the household names just after World War II who had a profound influence on the next generation of cricket players were Lall Singh, Eu Cheow Teik, 'Poppy' Williams, the Labrooy brothers, Joe Andres, Appuni and Hayati Meah. The next generation of post-war players included Mike and Christie Shepherdson, Alex Delilkan, Chua Eng Cheng, Gurucharan Singh, M.C. Kailasapathy, Alwi Zahaman, T. Sivagnanam, Khoo Bing Keng and Ranjit Singh.

Recent developments
In 1967, Malaysia became an associate member of the International Cricket Council (ICC) and played in the inaugural ICC Trophy competition in 1979. The national team has appeared in every ICC Trophy since then, with the exception of the 2005 tournament for which they failed to qualify. Malaysia is also an associate member of the Asian Cricket Council (ACC), and has competed in every ACC trophy tournament.

The retirement of the excellent crop of cricketers who dominated the game in the 1950s, 1960s and 1970s left a vacuum. The 1980s witnessed a decline in the popularity of cricket, and many laterite pitches were converted to football and hockey fields.

In the 1990s, however, cricket experienced a revival in the country, led by standout players such as Banergee Nain. The Malaysian team took part in the Plate competition of the ICC Trophy tournament in 1990 and 1994. Malaysia then made history by

Stamp issued during the 1997 ICC Trophy tournament in Kuala Lumpur.

introducing cricket as an event at the Commonwealth Games in Kuala Lumpur in 1998. The MCA has played host to numerous international events including the ICC Trophy in 1997 and the ACC Trophy and DLF Cup Triangular Series in 2006, and has organized numerous local leagues and competitions. Under the leadership of current MCA president Tunku Tan Sri Imran Tuanku Ja'afar, the association has sought to promote cricket in Malaysia and develop local coaches and players. A Malaysian women's national cricket team has been formed and competed in one match against Singapore in 2006, winning by 58 runs. The overall goal of the MCA is to see Malaysia get Test status by the year 2020.

Supporting the development of cricket in Malaysia is the Malay Cricket Association of Malaysia. The organization has as its home the Bayuemas Oval and the Tuanku Ja'afar Cricket Academy. It runs many competitions, especially for youths, and regularly supplies MCA with talent to represent the country.

Notable cricketers

Mike Shepherdson was the most accomplished batsman in the country. Against Hong Kong in the Interport series in 1955, 1961, 1963 and 1965, he scored 83, 132, 107 and 70 respectively. His timing and footwork enabled him to play his shots with smooth elegance and great composure.

Mike Shepherdson (right) driving the ball for Selangor during the MCA Interstate League final, 1962.

Gurucharan Singh was a natural leg-spinner, marvellous close-in fielder and an explosive batsman. One of his many brilliant performances was a magnificent 62 in 20 minutes in the 1959 Interport match against Hong Kong. In a Saudara Cup competition against Singapore in 1971, Gurucharan finished with a career-best score of 152.

Gurucharan Singh (left), captain of the Selangor team, receiving a trophy after his team defeated Singapore to win the MCA Interstate Championship, 1967.

Dr Alex Delilkan was selected to play for his school, St Joseph's Institution, when he was only 11 years old. He was a fourth-year medical student when he made his debut for Malaya against Hong Kong in 1957. In that match, he made 50 out of 145 in Malaya's first innings and scored an unbeaten 22 out of 118. Against the Commonwealth team in 1962, Delilkan bagged 6 for 79 in the first innings and 4 for 101 in the second. But the high point of his career was bowling the legendary Sir Gary Sobers with his first ball–the first time the West Indian maestro had suffered this indignity–when the Commonwealth team played in Kuala Lumpur in 1964. A true all-rounder, Delilkan captained the national side from 1959 until 1973, maintaining his medical and cricket careers simultaneously.

Dr Alex Delilkan (centre) starting a run during a test match between Malaysia and Singapore, 1971. He was run out for 88. Malaysia won the cup by an innings.

Lall Singh, a brilliant fielder and batsman, became the first and only local-born Test-cricketer. When Singh was invited to attend trials in India by the Indian Cricket Board in 1931, a group of Indians in Malaya set up a fund to finance his travels. Singh went on to play for India in a Test series against England before returning to Malaya to work as a grounds-keeper. In 2004, he became the first and only cricketer inducted into the OCM Hall of Fame.

Lall Singh preparing to play a match at Lord's, the famous English cricket ground, c. 1930s.

The Bayuemas Oval in Klang and (inset) the logo of the Malay Cricket Association of Malaysia.

MALAYSIA CRICKET

ABOVE LEFT: MCA President as at 2008 Tunku Tan Sri Imran Tuanku Ja'afar.

ABOVE RIGHT: Logo of the Malaysia Cricket Association.

Rugby

From its origins in England, the intensely physical sport of rugby spread to the Malay Peninsula before the end of the 19th century. Initially, rugby was mainly played by Europeans, who dominated the H.M.S. Malaya Cup for decades. Locals formed their own tournament, the All Blues Cup, in 1934, and the sport remained mainly segregated between Asians and Europeans until the early 1960s. That did not stop the emergence of well-supported Malaysian rugby competitions, a tradition which has grown to include the hosting of several international events.

Kedah beat the Armed Forces by a score of 18–9 in the championship match of the last H.M.S. Malaya Cup during the 1982–83 season. By that time, the H.M.S. Malaya Cup had already become a junior tournament, having lost its status as the nation's premier rugby tournament in 1975 to the MRU Cup.

TOP: Selangor versus Singapore in the inaugural H.M.S. Malaya Cup final, 1922.

MIDDLE: H.M.S. Malaya Cup final being played on the Selangor Club padang in 1959.

ABOVE: Player from the King Edward VII school catching a throw-in during a match, 2006. King Edward VII of Taiping was one the earliest schools to have played rugby in the country. It was introduced there by T.J. Thomas in 1923.

The origins of rugby and its introduction to Malaya

Rugby was first played at Rugby School in Warwickshire, England in 1823 when William Ellis Webb, a schoolboy, picked up the ball and ran with it during a football game. The earliest mention of the game being played in Malaya was in the *Selangor Journal* of 1893. The precise date when rugby was introduced in the country, however, remains unclear.

By the end of the 19th century, rugby had become a popular pastime of the British in Malaya, with makeshift teams dominated by the planters who then formed a sizeable community. Occasionally there were matches between a team of players from a particular nation and a composite team of various nationalities, such as the Scotland versus the Rest of the World match held every Saint Andrew's Day (30 November) until the late 1950s. British educators and the Irish La Salle Brothers introduced rugby to their respective schools in the country.

Early tournaments

Rugby experienced a boost following the maiden visit to Malaya of the British battleship H.M.S. *Malaya* on 17 January 1921. As a token of appreciation for the country which had paid for its construction, the ship's officers and crew donated the H.M.S. Malaya Cup for an annual inter-state rugby competition.

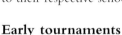

The programme for the 1934 North vs. South Annual Classic organized by the MRU.

The competition was launched later that year with six teams taking part: Selangor, Perak, Penang, Negeri Sembilan, Melaka and Singapore. Selangor beat Singapore 5–3 in the inaugural final. The tournament was conducted under the auspices of a joint committee comprising representatives from the participating teams. Apart from the war years, the only other break in the H.M.S. Malaya Cup tournament, until it ended in 1983, was in 1948 due to the outbreak of the Emergency in Malaya. Coincidentally, this was the same year that the battleship H.M.S. *Malaya* was scrapped.

In response to the H.M.S. Malaya Cup being an exclusive expatriate preserve, a group of Asians formed the Negeri Sembilan All Blues Rugby Association in 1925 to promote and encourage rugby in the local community. The association donated a trophy and launched the All Blues Cup tournament, for Asians only, in 1934. Initially three teams (Perak, Negeri Sembilan and Melaka) took part, but subsequently more teams joined the competition and formed their own respective All Blues committees.

Rugby after Independence

By 1963, Asians had taken greater control of the various state rugby unions from the Europeans. By this time, the All Blues Cup had become redundant as the H.M.S. Malaya Cup had already begun to attract increasing numbers of Asian players. The various All Blues state committees were dissolved, and the Malayan Rugby Union (MRU), that had been established in 1927, became the sport's sole governing body.

During the Emergency (1948–60), numerous British and Commonwealth military units were deployed in Malaya. Some stayed until the mid-1960s. Their presence further boosted local rugby as many of these units had their own renowned rugby teams, the most notable being from the 1st Fiji Regiment, the 1st Royal New Zealand Infantry Regiment and the

Organization

The Malayan Rugby Union (MRU) was formed in 1927 with J.C.M. Bell as president. It assumed responsibility for the HMS Malaya Cup tournament in 1935. At first, only expatriate clubs were voting members; local clubs were affiliates

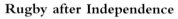

MRU logo.

MRU president as at 2008 Dato' Muhammad Muhiyuddin Abdullah.

with no voting rights. Later, club membership was abolished and all state rugby unions—then controlled by Europeans—became affiliates of the MRU. In 1964, the Malayan Rugby Union was renamed the Malaysian Rugby Union. As of 2008, the MRU has 16 affiliates comprising each of the states, the Federal Territory of Kuala Lumpur and the Sports Councils of the Royal Malaysian Police and the Malaysian Armed Forces.

The game

Rugby requires not only skills in handling, passing and kicking an oval-shaped ball but also tackling ability. The game is played between two teams usually of 15 players each, though there are abbreviated versions such as 'sevens' and 'tens'. In rugby, rules are known as laws.

The object of the game is to score as many points as possible by carrying, passing, kicking and grounding the ball. A player may run with the ball and is allowed to kick it in any direction, but he must not pass or knock it forward with his hand. A try is scored when a player grounds the ball in his opponents' in-goal area. The scoring team has the right to take a kick at goal, known as a conversion kick, that can be taken by either a place kick or a drop kick. If the kick goes over the crossbar of the goal, a score is made. A penalty try is awarded between the goal posts if a player would have probably scored if not for foul play by the opposing team; a conversion kick also applies in this case. A dropped goal occurs in general play when a player drops the ball from his hands and kicks it over the crossbar upon its rebound. A penalty goal is scored by a kick over the crossbar from a penalty spot.

Unlike most other sports, a rugby referee will not blow his whistle to indicate the end of full-time if the ball is still being played. He will do so only if the ball is deemed to be dead, that is when a breakdown in play occurs or the ball is out of the field of play. Another difference from many other sports is that the referee must also consult a team on its option to restart the game after its opponents have committed certain infringements.

Scoring system	
• Try	5 points
• Penalty try	5 points
• Conversion kick	2 points
• Dropped goal	3 points
• Penalty goal	3 points

Malaysian player diving for a try during a match against Thailand, 2006.

Competitions in the new millennium

In 2003, two new cup competitions began, the new-look MRU Cup and the President's Cup. Participation in the Agong's Cup has since been open exclusively to teams that have qualified from these cups. The stronger teams play in the MRU Cup, with the top four teams qualifying for the Agong's Cup competition. Only the top two teams can qualify from the President's Cup.

A two-tier national inter-club rugby championship was implemented in 2004. The upper tier, known as the Super League Cup, is for the stronger clubs. The lower tier is called the National Inter-Club Championship.

Over the years, there has been an increase in the number of tournaments at both state and club levels, such as the Negeri Sembilan Royal Sevens, the Alor Star International Sevens and the Perak Tens. The more established competitions are the Penang Tens, the Royal Selangor Club's Jonah Jones and the Cobra International Tens, the last of which showcases foreign teams with World Cup players.

International participation

The Malaysian team has competed regularly in the Asian Rugby Football Union (ARFU) tournament since 1970. Starting in 1976, the national team participated in the Hong Kong Sevens for many years. The MRU has been involved in the Asian qualifying rounds for the World Cup. However, the MRU's foreign endeavours have met with scant success.

The MRU's other regional competition is with Thailand for the Vajiralongkorn Trophy, a biennial contest that was established in 1955. The annual international with Singapore, initiated in 1966 when the Singapore Rugby Union broke away from the MRU, was scrapped in 1977.

4th Queen's Own Hussars. In addition, the British garrison at Singapore assembled a powerful team that played in the H.M.S. Malaya Cup under various banners over the years. But the Joint Services was the most stellar team, winning five titles in a row from 1965 to 1969. Apart from strengthening many state teams in the H.M.S. Malaya Cup, these servicemen players also helped raise the standard of the various local club competitions with their regular participation.

In 1979, the MRU launched the MRU Open Invitational in an attempt to attract foreign participation. It also saw the compulsory shift of three major teams (Singapore Civilians, New Zealand Forces and Australian Forces) from the MRU Cup competition, which had been started in 1975, to the MRU Open. The MRU Cup was left with only four teams.

The inception of the Agong's Cup (which replaced the H.M.S. Malaya Cup) in 1983, the final of which was graced by the presence of the Yang di-Pertuan Agong, contributed to the demise of the MRU Cup in 1984. The Agong's Cup became the nation's premier tournament a year after its establishment, a status that it has since maintained. The MRU Open Invitational was discontinued in 1989 due to a lack of regional support.

The H.M.S. Malaya Cup was the symbol of Malaysian rugby supremacy for more than five decades. The trophy is shown here with a rugby ball in front of its plinth.

Teams competing in the Cobra International Tens tournament, 2006.

ABOVE: Ng Peng Kong's book entitled *Rugby: A Malaysian Chapter* was first published in 2003. It traces the history of the sport in the country.

BELOW: Players pouncing on a loose ball in a match during the Alor Star International Sevens tournament, 2005.

BOTTOM: The 2007 national rugby team. The Malaysian team was ranked 70th out of 95 national squads in 2007 according to the International Rugby Board ranking system.

Basketball

Introduced to Malaya in the 1920s by China through regular exhibition matches played by visiting university teams, basketball has developed into a highly competitive sport with Malaysian national teams regularly taking part in major international events. With the recent introduction of various grassroot level programmes, the game is set to soar to new heights.

Malaysia taking on the Philippines during the Southeast Asian Peninsular (SEAP) Games in 1965.

Top: Malaysian national women's team playing a game against Indonesia during the 7th Asian Basketball Championship in Kuala Lumpur, 1978.

Above: Participants in the PETRONAS 3-on-3 Basketball Challenge in Johor, 2005. A total of 98 teams competed in the event.

Origins of the game

In 1891, basketball was invented by Dr James Naismith, a teacher at a YMCA training school in the United States, and the first game was played with a soccer ball and two raised peach baskets used as goals. The Fédération Internationale de Basketball (FIBA) was founded in Geneva in 1932, and the sport was included for the first time as an event in the 1936 Berlin Olympic Games.

Basketball arrives in Malaya

Basketball was introduced to Chinese schools in Malaya in the early 1920s by teachers from China. The game was first played on outdoor gravel courts and later spread to Chinese sports clubs. University and club teams visiting from China and Hong Kong helped propagate the sport throughout Malaya in the 1930s, and books containing the official rules of the game printed in Chinese were imported from Shanghai. Since then, the game has become one of the most popular sports among the local Chinese community.

Malaysia's Ooi Ban Sin in action against the Saudi Arabian team during the Asian Basketball Championships, 2005.

In 1934, the first inter-state tournament for Malayan Chinese was organized. In 1956, FIBA rule books were printed locally in Chinese and English.

Local development

In 1958, the inaugural Agong's Cup National Basketball Championship was held in Kuala Lumpur. It has since grown to become the most significant basketball tournament in Malaysia for both men and women, with state teams competing every year to determine the national champion. In 1965, the first Malaysian Youth Basketball Championship, exclusively for junior players, was held in Penang.

Malaya was among the seven teams that participated in the inaugural Asian Basketball Confederation (ABC) Championship held in Manila in 1960. The first major basketball tournament in Malaysia, the 1965 ABC Championship in Kuala Lumpur, helped to promote the game in the country.

A league was organized by the Malaysian Amateur Basketball Association (MABA) in 1984 and 1985, but was subsequently stopped due to financial constraints.

In 1994, MABA signed a sponsorship deal with PETRONAS, the national petroleum company, to enlist its financial support until 2010. The funds provided by PETRONAS are utilized in various basketball-related projects in Malaysia including the 'Tall Talents' programme, which helps to form the backbone of the national team, and the National Basketball Academy, which was established in 1997. PETRONAS '3 on 3 Streetball Challenge' events are organized throughout the year at various locations in order to promote the game at the grassroots level. In 2006, the MABA-sanctioned AND1 Streetball Challenge, comprising seven legs held throughout the country, was organized to get more youths involved in the game.

Major achievements

Since 1965, the Malaysian women's team has won the gold medal at the biennial SEA Games 11 times, clinching five consecutive gold medals between 1977 and 1985, and, most recently, winning the gold medal at the 2007 games in Thailand. The national men's team, which has won five SEA Games gold medals, achieved a milestone by qualifying for the sixth world championship in Spain in 1986.

National player Goh Koon Gee received the National Sportswoman of the Year award in 1968. National centre Wong Tai Ong was selected to represent the FIBA Asia All Stars in Korea in 1997.

MABA logo.

MABA president since 1990 Dato' Loke Yuen Yow.

The Malaysian Amateur Basketball Association

The Malaya Amateur Basketball Association (MABA, later renamed the Malaysian Amateur Basketball Association) was formed in 1958 as the national governing body for basketball with Quek Kai Dong as its first president. The national association became affiliated to the Asian Basketball Confederation (ABC) (now known as FIBA Asia) in 1960, paving the way for the national team to participate in international competitions. As of 2008, MABA comprises 13 state basketball associations as well as teams from the Royal Malaysia Police and the Armed Forces.

Yang di-Pertuan Agong Tuanku Ismail Nasiruddin Shah (left) being greeted by Quek Kai Dong, the first president of MABA, at the opening of the 1965 ABC Championship at Stadium Negara in Kuala Lumpur.

Netball

Netball has been a popular sport for girls and women since it was first introduced in the 1940s. The Malaysian Schools Sports Council and the Malaysian Netball Association have been instrumental in pioneering the growth of the sport. Since 1983, Malaysia has organized and taken part in numerous international events.

Girls playing netball during physical education class at Saint Anne's school in Kedah, 1959.

Women's basketball

Netball, a version of basketball which required less physical strength and was more suited to women, was first played in England in 1895. The game spread throughout the British colonies in the first half of the 20th century primarily through British teachers and nuns.

Netball was initially played on grass courts divided into three sections with goals consisting of poles with a hoop and net at the top. A set of rules was formulated in 1957, paving the way for the establishment of the International Federation of Women's Basketball and Netball in 1960.

Local development

In the 1940s, netball was introduced and played in English-medium schools in Malaya by expatriate teachers and nuns. The game was then popularized by local teachers in subsequent decades. In the 1970s and 1980s, netball spread widely across the country and was played competitively among girls and women in schools, government departments and clubs.

The Malaysian Netball Association (MNA) was formed in 1978. The first Malaysian National Netball Meet was held in 1979 at Stadium Negara and won by the Royal Malaysia Police team. By the 1980s, the MNA had 17 affiliates, comprising 14 state teams along with the Malaysian Armed Forces, the Royal Malaysia Police and the National Electricity Board.

Netball events

The Malaysian National Netball Meet for schools, organized by the Malaysian Schools Sports Council, is held annually, as are tournaments for university students, teachers and government servants.

Under the auspices of the MNA, many other national and international netball events have been held. The MNA has conducted the National Netball Championship since 1979 and the National Youth Championships since 1984. The MNA also organized the first Asian Netball Championship in Kuala Lumpur in 1985, which Malaysia won.
At the 1998

MNA logo.

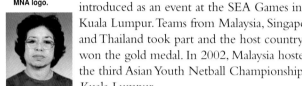

MNA founding president Hajah Norminshah Sabirin.

MNA president as at 2008 Tengku Datin Seri Noor Hazah Al'Hajah Tengku Abd. Aziz Shah.

Commonwealth Games in Kuala Lumpur, 12 countries, including Malaysia, took part in the inaugural netball event. In 2001, netball was introduced as an event at the SEA Games in Kuala Lumpur. Teams from Malaysia, Singapore and Thailand took part and the host country won the gold medal. In 2002, Malaysia hosted the third Asian Youth Netball Championship in Kuala Lumpur.

International achievements

In 1983, Malaysia participated for the first time in the World Netball Championships held in Singapore. The country's most significant international achievements have been securing 16th and 19th positions at the 1995 and 1999 world championships respectively. At the World Youth Championships, Malaysia finished eighth in 2000 and 14th in 2005. In the Asian Open Championships, the national team emerged victorious in the 1985 event held in Malaysia and finished as runner-up three times, in 1990, 1997 and 2005. The Malaysian team won the Asian Youth Netball Championships in 2004 and 2006.

TOP: Malaysian players (in yellow) watching their shot fall into the goal during the final match of the Asian Youth Netball Championships against Singapore, 2002. Malaysia won 44–42.

ABOVE: Malaysian players celebrating after their victory in the championship match against Singapore during the SEA Games in Kuala Lumpur, 2001.

Rules of netball

Netball is a team sport played by two teams of seven players. Goals are scored from within the shooting circle by throwing the ball into a ring attached to a high post. The team with the most goals at the end of four 15-minute quarters is declared the winner.

The court is divided into three equal parts with players restricted to their respective playing areas. A player is deemed offside if she enters any area other than the playing area for her designated position.

A player in possession of the ball with one or both hands may pass the ball in any manner except by rolling it. The ball must be caught or touched in each third of the court and cannot be hurled from one end of the court to the other. When handling the ball, players can only move one step in any direction.

Only the goal attack (GA) and the goal shooter (GS) can score a goal. A shot at goal is only counted when the shooter is wholly inside the shooting circle.

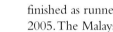

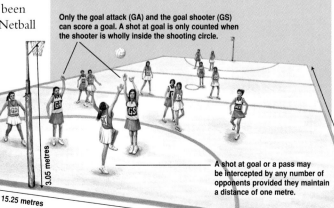

3.05 metres

15.25 metres

30.5 metres

A shot at goal or a pass may be intercepted by any number of opponents provided they maintain a distance of one metre.

Girls enjoying a game of beach netball during a festival on Pulau Langkawi, 2005. Beach netball involves teams of three or five players and only a single net post.

Handball

Introduced to Malaysia in the 1970s, handball has steadily grown in popularity. This proliferation has been especially visible among school children, thanks to the inclusion of the game in the national curriculum in the early 1980s. The number of local tournaments and leagues continues to grow, thereby ensuring the sport's ongoing development.

A women's handball demonstration at Universiti Malaya to promote the game among tertiary-level students.

KL Star player (centre) trying to wrest control of the ball from his opponents from the Kinta team during the Malaysia Handball Clubs League, 2006.

The origins of handball

Handball was invented in Europe soon after World War I, and initially played as an off-season game on football pitches with 11 players per team. In 1938, due to unfavourable weather in Europe, the game of handball was moved indoors. The number of players was reduced to seven per team and the size of the playing area was truncated. The International Handball Federation (IHF) was formed in 1946 in Switzerland.

In 2008, handball is played by approximately five million people across 171 countries. It is contested at the Olympic Games, Asian Games and SEA Games.

The game in Malaysia

Handball made a relatively late entrance into Malaysia. It was introduced in 1976 by Lim Hock Han, the head of Universiti Malaya's Sports Unit. He also taught the game to groups of school teachers and students in several schools in Selangor. The game was gradually spread, mainly by teachers, throughout Malaysia. In the 1980s, as handball had rapidly developed a following among school children, the government decided to form a task force to popularize the game in schools.

The nation's first handball association, the Selangor and Federal Territory Handball Association, was formed in 1981. In 1984, the Malaysian Handball Federation (MAHF) was formed with

MAHF president as at 2008 Dato' Suhaimi Yacob.

Cheah Hai Su as its founding president. In 1994, the MAHF became a member of the IHF. Since the 1990s, handball's growth has depended on the initiatives of the MAHF and its affiliated state associations as well as school sports councils.

MAHF logo.

Achievements and events

Malaysia's highest international achievement was winning the bronze medal in the men's event at the 2003 SEA Games in Vietnam and in the men's and women's events at the 2007 SEA Games in Thailand.

Within Malaysia, the MAHF National Championship is held annually, as are various tournaments organized by the respective state handball associations. For the under-12, 15 and 18 age groups, tournaments are conducted each year at the district, state and national levels.

How the game is played

- Handball is played by teams of seven per side.
- The game is divided into two 30-minute halves.
- The objective is for a team to score as many points as possible by throwing the ball into an opposing team's goal.

  Players may not take more than three steps or hold the ball for more than three seconds when they have possession of it. In order to maintain possession of a ball after three seconds, a player may dribble it, akin to basketball, pass it to a fellow team member, or shoot it at the opposing team's goal. In contrast to football, players may use their hands as well as any other part of their body above the knee to touch the ball.

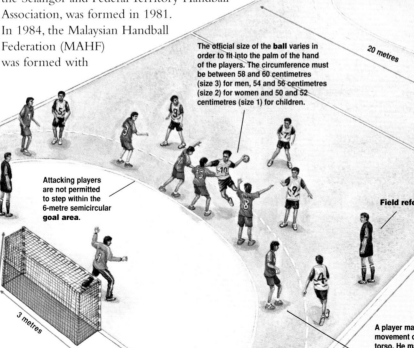

The **goalkeeper** may touch and stop the ball with his legs or any other part of his body.

The official size of the **ball** varies in order to fit into the palm of the hand of the players. The circumference must be between 58 and 60 centimetres (size 3) for men, 54 and 56 centimetres (size 2) for women and 50 and 52 centimetres (size 1) for children.

20 metres

40 metres

Goal referee.

Attacking players are not permitted to step within the 6-metre semicircular **goal area.**

Field referee.

2 metres

3 metres

A player may attempt to impede the movement of an opponent by using his torso. He may not attempt to hold, trip or block the opponent's movement with either his arms or legs. He is also not allowed to charge or hit his opponent.

Volleyball

Volleyball has grown to become a popular sport in Malaysia, particularly among Chinese youth. The game was introduced to Chinese schools and associations in the country by exponents from Hong Kong and China. The establishment of the Malaysia Volleyball Association (MAVA) in 1959 led to the development of numerous leagues and events. Beach volleyball, as both a form of recreation and a competitive sport, is played on many beaches throughout Malaysia.

Two Thai opponents try to block a Malaysian player's spike during the Southeast Asia Junior Men's Volleyball Championship in Pahang, 2005.

Birth of the 'YMCA game'

Volleyball was invented in 1895 by the director of physical education at a YMCA in Massachusetts. In the early 20th century, the YMCA and American military personnel were largely responsible for the propagation of the game throughout the world. The Fédération Internationale de Volleyball (FIVB) was formed in 1947, and the first world championships were held in 1949 for men and 1952 for women.

Volleyball arrives in Malaya

In the early 1930s, university volleyball teams from Hong Kong and China began making visits to Singapore, Kuala Lumpur and Penang where they played friendly matches, organized by state Chinese athletics associations, against local teams.

Chinese school teachers had a crucial role in boosting public interest in volleyball among their students as well as in local associations. Competitions were initially conducted as friendly matches between volleyball teams within particular states, but interstate volleyball tournaments were subsequently organized.

Events and achievements

Following the establishment of the Malaya Amateur Volleyball Association (MAVA) in 1959, the first annual National Volleyball Championship was held in Penang in 1960. The 'Far-East' system, in which nine players on each side took part, was initially utilized for the tournament. The international system, with only six players to a side, was adopted at the first Malaysian National Volleyball Championships held in Singapore in 1965. Only men could participate in the national championships until the second tournament in Pahang in 1966, at which a women's event was introduced. The inaugural National Youth Volleyball Championship took place in Penang in 1968.

Malaysia made its debut in international volleyball competition when it took part in the third Asian Games in Jakarta in 1962. MAVA organized its first international competition when Malaysia hosted the third SEAP Games in 1965. Other notable international championships held in Malaysia include the Women's World Volleyball Grand Prix in 1993, 1999 and 2000 and Men's Junior World Volleyball Championship in 1995.

The Malaysian men's team captured silver medals in the beach volleyball competition at the 1997 SEA Games in Jakarta and in the men's indoor volleyball event at the 2001 SEA Games in Kuala Lumpur. Mohd Nasiruddin Mohd Hashim was a member of both medal-winning teams. The national women's beach volleyball team won a bronze medal at the 2007 SEA Games in Thailand.

Beach volleyball

Introduced to Malaysia in the early 1990s, beach volleyball is played on many beaches throughout the country. A national circuit has been conducted since 1997 and several international tournaments have been held locally. Beach volleyball is played on a 16-metre by 8-metre sand court with teams comprising two players each.

Malaysian player going for a spike during the Sports Toto-Morib Beach Volleyball Carnival, 2005.

Organization

In 1959, volleyball in Malaya took a great leap forward when representatives convened to form the Malaya Amateur Volleyball Association in Penang. Ong Keng Seng was appointed as the first president of this new body, which would oversee the development of the sport in the country. The federation was subsequently renamed as the Malaysian Amateur Volleyball Association (MAVA) and Malaysia Volleyball Association in 1965 and 1992 respectively.

MAVA has affiliate members from 13 states as well as from the Federal Territories of Kuala Lumpur and Labuan, the Malaysian Armed Forces and the Royal Malaysia Police. MAVA's annual local tournaments include the Under-14 and Under-16 Youth Championships, the Under-20 Junior Championship and the national championship as well as numerous national beach volleyball events each year.

MAVA founding president Ong Keng Seng.

MAVA president as at 2008 Dato' Lee Jin Xian.

MAVA logo.

Rules of volleyball

Volleyball is played by two teams of six players each on an 18-metre by 9-metre court divided by a 2.43-metre high net (2.24 metres for women). The objective of the game is to send a ball over the net and hit the ground on the opposing team's half of the court, and to prevent the same effort by the opposing team. Each team has three hits to return the ball over the net and onto the opponents' side. The ball is put in play with a service hit over the net by a designated player. The rally continues until the ball is grounded on the playing court, goes out of play or a team fails to return it properly. The team which wins the rally scores a point. When the receiving team wins a rally, it gains a point and the right to serve, and its players rotate one position clockwise. The first team to score 25 points wins the set and the first team to capture three sets wins the match.

Common volleyball shots include (from left) the overhand serve, the spike, the underhand serve and the forearm pass.

Baseball

Introduced to Malaysia by Japanese and American expatriates in the 1960s, baseball has seen a sudden surge of interest manifested by the formation of state associations and clubs all over the country. The Baseball Federation of Malaysia, formed in 2004, has launched a 5-year development programme to further promote the sport locally.

Player sliding into home plate during the President Cup tournament, 2005.

ABOVE: Pitcher throwing the ball while the batter prepares to swing during Selangor league competition, 2001.

BELOW: The President Cup is awarded to the team that wins the national championship.

International development

Baseball has been played in both England and America since at least the early 19th century. The first basic rules of the modern game were drawn up in 1845, and in that same year the Knickerbocker Baseball Club of New York, the first professional baseball team, was formed. The following years saw the creation of many more clubs. In 1871, the National Association of Professional Baseball Players was established in the United States where baseball has since grown to become a national pastime.

In Asia, a baseball league was established in Japan in 1936. The post-World War II years saw the rapid development of the sport as a result of the American influence in East Asian countries including the Philippines. The popularity of baseball increased in Asia after the Japanese team beat the United States in the final at the Olympic Games in Los Angeles in 1984, when baseball was introduced as a demonstration sport.

Introduction of baseball to Malaysia

As a result of the influence of the Japanese and Americans during the late 1960s, baseball began to be played in Malaysia. As industrialization and foreign investment increased in the Klang Valley and Penang,

Logo of the Baseball Federation of Malaysia.

Founding and current president of the Baseball Federation of Malaysia Dato' Noh Abdullah.

a number of Japanese and American companies as well as foreign banks formed their own baseball clubs and local employees were encouraged to take up the game. Initially, baseball was played together with softball, and a number of states established softball and baseball associations. But inter-state and club baseball competitions were not organized until 1994.

A pro-tem committee was formed in 1994 to pave the way for the establishment of the Amateur Baseball Association of Malaysia in 1996 under the Societies Act 1966. It was subsequently renamed the Baseball Federation of Malaysia (BFM) in 2004. The BFM is a member of the International Baseball Federation (IBAF), the Baseball Federation of Asia (BFA) and Olympic Council of Malaysia (OCM).

Under the BFM's Constitution, membership is open to all state sports councils and clubs registerable under the Sports Commission as well as the sports councils of institutions of higher learning. As of 2008, six state associations are affiliated to the federation. Baseball clubs in Malaysia include the Kuala Lumpur All-Stars Baseball Club, Stars Baseball Club and Aces Baseball and Softball Club.

Development programmes and events

The federation has embarked on a 5-year development programme from 2005 to 2009, focusing primarily on schools and institutions of higher learning. However, to keep abreast of regional developments in the sport, a national team was developed for Malaysia's maiden participation at the 2005 SEA Games in the Philippines, paving the way for future participation in international events. In 2007, Malaysia's baseball team participated in the 24th SEA Games in Thailand.

In the inaugural national championship held in 2005, six teams vied for the President Cup. Selangor 'A' emerged as the champions. The 2007 championship saw the participation of 10 teams with the Kuala Lumpur All-Stars Baseball Club finishing as champions.

Malaysian youths (in blue shirts) greeting their opponents from Japan before a friendly game during the World Children's Baseball Fair, 2005. Malaysia has taken part in the annual event, which promotes friendship and the love of baseball among nations, seven times since 1995.

Game play

- Baseball is played between two teams of nine players.
- Each game comprises nine segments called innings in which both teams are given the chance to bat and score runs.
- The game centres around the contest between the pitcher, who hurls a small, leather-covered ball in the direction of a batter from the opposing team.
- The batter tries to hit the ball with a cylindrical bat, typically made of wood, and score runs by advancing himself and his team-mates around four bases placed at the corners of a diamond-shaped field.
- A 'home run' occurs when, after hitting the ball, the batter is able to circle all of the bases and score a run himself. This feat is normally achieved by the batter hitting the ball over the outfield fence.

Pitcher

The pitcher's throwing motion.

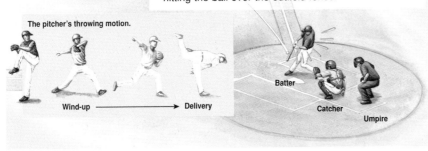

Wind-up → Delivery

Batter

Catcher

Umpire

Softball

Originally an indoor sport, softball has grown to become a popular pastime across the globe. In Malaysia, softball came to prominence in the 1960s after being introduced in the local school system. The Softball Association of Malaysia (SAM) has played a pivotal role in the promotion of the sport in the country.

Malaysian captain Isa Mohd Nor swinging at the ball in a game against Thailand during the ASEAN Softball Championship, 1976. Malaysia won the game 12–0.

History of the game

Softball was invented in Chicago in 1887 as an indoor sport. The International Softball Federation (ISF) was founded in 1952 with the aim of promoting the game outside the United States. There are two variants of the sport: fast pitch and slow pitch. Fast pitch competitions, in which the pitcher delivers the ball at maximum velocity with little or no arc, are the most common. The first world championships in fast pitch softball were held for women in Melbourne in 1965 and for men in Mexico City in 1966. Slow pitch championships only began in 1987. Women's fast pitch softball debuted as a medal sport at the 1996 Olympic Games in Atlanta. As of 2008, softball is played by more than 20 million people globally, and the ISF boasts 128 member organizations.

Softball in Malaysia

By the early 1960s, softball was beginning to establish a following in Malaya. As a result of this burgeoning popularity, the Methodist Boys School in Kuala Lumpur changed one its sports co-curriculum options from cricket to softball in 1962. Simultaneously, M.W. McKenzie, an American diplomat and former semi-professional player, began teaching local school-children the rudiments of the sport. Hence, the roots of softball in the country originated from the Malayan school circuit.

The first competitive softball match in Malaya was held in 1963, when the crew of the United States Seventh Fleet flagship, USS *Providence*, took on a local team, Carriers Coolers, at Stadium Merdeka. In 1970, three Singaporean teams, including their championship team the Pirates, played a friendly tournament against the seven Malaysian teams during the Pesta Pulau Pinang softball carnival. At the end of the tournament, the Pirates emerged as the overall champions.

In 1972, representatives from Penang, Perak and Selangor gathered at the Perak Chief Minister's residence to initiate the formation of the Softball Association of Malaysia (SAM). This association was officially registered in 1974 and the pro-tem committee was headed by the then Chief Minister of Perak, Dato' Sri Kamaruddin Mat Isa.

Competitions

The first Malaysian Open Softball Championship was organized in Ipoh in 1974. The Eagles team from Singapore won the first championship, while the Malaysian team clinched the title in 1975. The National Under-21 Championship was inaugurated in 1976.

In 1987, the SAM introduced the National Under-15 Championship as part of its continual efforts to improve the standard and popularity of softball among Malaysian youths. As of 2008, the SAM conducts the Malaysian Open Men's and Women's Softball Championships on an annual basis.

Malaysia's first international exposure came when the SAM proposed the formation of the ASEAN Softball Federation and hosted the first ASEAN Championship in Kuala Lumpur in 1976. Both men's and women's softball were included in the SEA Games programme for the first time at the 1979 event in Indonesia and the Malaysian men's team took the bronze medal.

The SAM also sent teams to participate in the Women's World Softball Championship in Taiwan in 1982 and the Asian Men's Softball Championship in Japan in 1985. Men's and women's softball were included in the 2005 and 2007 SEA Games in the Philippines and Thailand respectively, although the Malaysian teams did not capture any medals.

Organization

The SAM currently has nine state affiliate members as well as two associate members, the Royal Malaysia Police Sports Council and the Malaysian Universities Sports Council. The executive committee of the SAM is elected by the general council which comprises representatives of all affiliate members.

Logo of the Softball Association of Malaysia (SAM).

Low Beng Choo, SAM president as at 2008.

Top: Penang player (right) tries to run to third base while his opponent from Perak waits for his team to throw him the ball during the National Softball Championship, 1999.

Above: Catcher fielding a pitch during the 2003 Negeri Sembilan school softball championships.

Game play

A game of softball is played in seven segments or innings in which each team has the opportunity to bat and, by advancing its players around the bases, score runs. The rules of softball are similar to those of baseball. The primary differences between the sports are the size of the ball (a softball has a 30-centimetre circumference, while a baseball is only 23 centimetres) and the dimensions of the field of play (a softball field is markedly smaller than a baseball field).

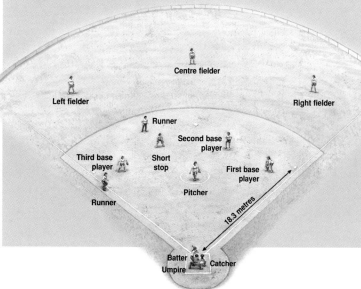

Centre fielder

Left fielder

Right fielder

Runner

Second base player

Third base player

Short stop

First base player

Pitcher

Runner

18.3 metres

Batter

Umpire

Catcher

Team from Perak, winners of the 33rd National Softball Championship held in Selangor, 2007.

1. The Thomas Cup competition being played at Stadium Negara, 1970.

2. World champion Nicol David (left) returns the ball to Natalie Grinham of Australia during the 2006 World Women's Squash Championship in Belfast. Nicol went on to win the match and defend her title.

3. Players from Malaysia and China taking part in a friendly table tennis match at Stadium Merdeka, 1973.

4. Badminton Association of Malaysia President Tan Sri Mohd Khir Johari (centre) and members of the Malaysian team triumphantly holding the Thomas Cup upon their return from Jakarta, 1967.

5. Koo Kien Keat (left) and Tan Boon Heong playing in the semi-finals of the 2007 All England Open Championships. The Malaysian pair won the tournament and claimed the title.

6. S.A. Azman playing against India in the Davis Cup in Kuala Lumpur, 1963.

7. Prime Minister Tun Abdul Razak (left) presenting Tunku Imran Tuanku Ja'afar with a trophy after his victory in Malaysia's inaugural national squash championship held in 1973.

8. Malaysian badminton team celebrating their victory in the Thomas Cup competition in Kuala Lumpur, 1992.

RACQUET SPORTS

Of all the racquet sports in Malaysia, badminton has had the longest tradition of success, and it is one of the most popular sports in the country in terms of interest and participation. From villages in rural areas to city back-lanes and housing estates, it is not unusual to see children and adults playing the game. Most schools and public recreation centres have badminton courts and numerous private training centres have been set up.

Badminton is also an exciting spectator sport featuring lightning fast exchanges, an array of movements, spectacular smashes and retrievals. Prestigious tournaments held in Malaysia, such as the Thomas Cup which pits national teams against each other for the title of the top badminton nation in the world, draw huge crowds. The country has been on the world badminton stage since the 1950s when stars like Ooi Teik Hock, Wong Peng Soon and Eddy Choong dominated the prestigious All England Open Championships. Since then, there has been a long string of Malaysian champions in both the singles and doubles events. Recent successes in the All England championships were achieved by Mohd Hafiz Hashim, who won the singles crown in 2003, and Koo Kien Keat and Tan Boon Heong who brought the doubles title back to Malaysia in 2007 after 25 years. Malaya won the first three Thomas Cup titles in 1949, 1952 and 1955. The country has been a formidable contender since then, capturing the cup again in 1967. Malaysia last won the cup in 1992 and was runner-up in 2002.

All of Malaysia's Olympic medals have come from badminton. In Barcelona in 1992, Razif and Jalani Sidek took the men's doubles bronze. The men's doubles pair of Cheah Soon Kit and Yap Kim Hock won the silver in Atlanta in 1996, while Rashid Sidek returned with the men's singles bronze.

Squash has also had a long and illustrious history in the country. Members of the British armed forces played squash in military camps in Malaya in the 1800s, and the game was maintained in private clubs and played primarily for recreation. Squash started to take off as a competitive sport in the country in the late 1970s. The Squash Racquets Association of Malaysia (SRAM) was formed in 1973, and stars like Jerry Loo and S. Maniam began shining at the international level. Good management by SRAM saw a steady stream of world class players emerging. Malaysia is now Asia's top squash nation, having won the Asian championships several times in recent years. Malaysia's most successful player is Nicol David, who took the Asian Games gold medal in 1998 and the women's world title in 2005 and has been ranked world number one ever since. Still in her early 20s, Nicol has already carved her name into the annals of the sport.

Tennis courts were initially available only in private clubs for the wealthier strata of society and it was only in the mid-1970s that public courts became available. The sport is widely popular and numerous local and international tournaments have been organized in Malaysia.

Table tennis has been played in the country on an organized basis since 1952. Over the years, Malaysia has achieved some success internationally, notably at the SEA Games.

Badminton: Origins and the domestic game

Played in the country since the early 19th century, badminton is one of the most popular sports locally and Malaysia's international achievements, beginning with victory in the Thomas Cup in 1949, have made it one of the top badminton nations in the world. The Badminton Association of Malaysia (BAM), formed in 1934, has spearheaded the growth and development of local players, coaches and infrastructure.

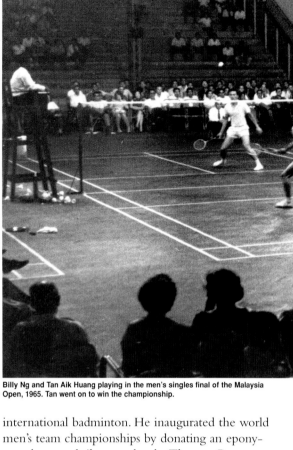

Billy Ng and Tan Aik Huang playing in the men's singles final of the Malaysia Open, 1965. Tan went on to win the championship.

TOP: BAM President Tan Sri Elyas Omar (centre) embracing players after the team's victory in the Thomas Cup competition, 1992.

ABOVE LEFT: BAM logo.

ABOVE RIGHT: BAM President as at 2008 Dato' Mohd Nadzmi Mohd Salleh.

The game of badminton

The origin of badminton is a subject of great debate. The sport is said to have begun in early 19th-century India when British soldiers played a similar local traditional game called 'poona'. However, another form, known as 'battledore', had been played in Europe since the Middle Ages.

Badminton received its name in 1873 from the Duke of Beaufort. During a garden party at his country mansion, called Badminton House, the game of 'poona' was demonstrated. The Duke renamed it 'the Game of Badminton', and it has since grown to become a popular racquet sport.

In 1877, the Bath Badminton Club in England, in an effort to make the game more uniform, set forth a set of basic rules. The popularity of badminton grew rapidly in England and this prompted the formation of an association to govern the sport. In 1893, the Badminton Association of England (BAE) was formed by 14 clubs and a formalized set of regulations was promulgated.

In 1899, the BAE organized the inaugural All England Open Badminton Championships, which functioned as the unofficial world championships until 1977.

International organization

The International Badminton Federation (IBF) was the brainchild of multiple All England winner Sir George Alan Thomas from England who founded the association with nine affiliates in 1934 and was appointed as its first president. Sir George Alan Thomas remained at the helm for 21 years until 1955 and played a major role in the early development of

TOP: The Malayan shutters beat Denmark 8–1 to win the inaugural Thomas Cup event in 1949.

ABOVE: Abdullah Piruz (picture) and Ismail Marjan became the first Malay players to compete in the Thomas Cup competition in 1952.

RIGHT: Ismail Marjan (left) and Ong Poh Lim playing for Malaya, c. 1950s.

international badminton. He inaugurated the world men's team championships by donating an eponymously named silver trophy, the Thomas Cup, in 1939. Due to World War II, the first competition was held only in 1948 and finished in February 1949 with Malaya emerging as the inaugural champions by beating Denmark 8–1 at Queen's Hall in Preston, England.

The Uber Cup, the women's world team championships, was named after Betty Uber, a leading English player in the 1950s and the donor of the trophy in 1956. At the inaugural event in 1957, the United States defeated Denmark 6–1 at Lytham St Anne's in England.

A milestone for badminton was achieved in 1992 in Barcelona when the sport was included in the Olympic Games for the first time as a medal sport.

The IBF was renamed the Badminton World Federation (BWF) in 2006. Headquartered in Kuala Lumpur since 2005, it is one of the most active world sports associations with a membership of 156 affiliates.

Badminton in Malaysia

Badminton is widely believed to have been brought to Penang by the East India Company in 1809, and was said to be favourite pastime at Suffolk House, the residence of Captain Francis Light.

Sir George Alan Thomas visited Penang between 1920 and 1923 and suggested, in light of the popularity of badminton on the island, that an association to govern the sport be formed. The Penang Badminton Association was founded in

1. Rashid Sidek standing on the podium, holding his trophy and mock cheque, after winning the Malaysia Open men's singles event, 1991.

2. Lee Chong Wei in action at the Malaysia Open, 2006. He went on to capture the men's singles championship. As at January 2008, Lee is ranked second in the world by the Badminton World Federation (BWF) ranking system.

3. Wong Mew Choo captured the women's singles gold medal in the 2003 SEA Games, becoming the first Malaysian woman to win with a SEA Games gold since 1977. In 2007, she reached the final of the Malaysia Open and won the China Open in Guangzhou. As at January 2008, she is ranked 8th in the world by the BWF ranking system.

4. A.S. Samuel, winner of the inaugural Malaya Open in 1937.

1925 and Selangor established an association of its own in 1928. The Perak Badminton Association was formed through the efforts of John Lowe Woods in 1931. Woods went on to form the Badminton Association of Malaya (BAM) on 11 November 1934 and became its first president. The sport was introduced in missionary schools around the country, and in the first half of the 20th century there were more than 50 badminton clubs in Malaya and Singapore.

Initially, Malaya was unknown in the global badminton scene. With the exception of H.S. Ong, who reached the semi-finals in 1927, there were no Malayan players competing in the All England Championships. All that changed in 1936 when five-time All England champion J.F. Devlin of Ireland arrived to promote the game locally and held friendly matches with some of the top players in Malaya. After Devlin was convincingly beaten by Singapore champion Leow Kim Fatt (who coached Malaya to the 1955 Thomas Cup), Foo Lum Choon of Selangor, Tan Cheng Phor of Perak, and Thung Ghim Huat of Penang, the world began to realize that there was a new badminton powerhouse.

The years between 1949 and 1957 are considered as the golden era of Malayan badminton as local players brought home three Thomas Cups in 1949, 1952 and 1955 and dominated the All England Championships. Indonesia took up the mantle after that and China joined the fray in 1982 after winning the Thomas Cup on their first attempt.

In 1985, under the leadership of Tan Sri Elyas Omar, the BAM took stock of the challengers and decided to employ

Local badminton events

In 1937, the Foong Seong Cup, the men's inter-state championships, became the first official tournament held by the BAM. This was followed by the first Malaya Open (called the Malaysia Open since 1963) later the same year. In 1955, the Heah Joo Seang Cup, the women's inter-state championship, was inaugurated; it was later renamed the BAM–Milo Cup in 1988. Of these, only the Malaysia Open has survived and remains the most prestigious tournament in the country. It is considered a major international competition on the badminton circuit and is utilized as one of the tournaments to determine overall BWF player ranking.

The National Grand Prix circuit was inaugurated in 1980, and Misbun Sidek won the first of his six titles that year. His brothers Razif and Jalani Sidek remain the most successful doubles team to have participated in this event, winning a record ten straight titles from 1981 to 1990. Limited exclusively to Malaysians, the National Grand Prix circuit enables top local players to showcase their skills.

The BAM oversees all the official badminton competitions in the country, including the Asian and world level tournaments the BWF has designated Malaysia to host for that particular year. Over the years, Malaysia has been the venue for major international tournaments such as the Thomas and Uber Cup finals, the World Badminton championships, the World Grand Prix finals, the Asian Badminton championships and the Asian Junior championships.

Malaysia Open men's singles champions

Year	Champion	Country
1937	A.S. Samuel	Malaya
1938	Tan Choong Tee	Malaya
1939	Seah Eng Hee	Malaya
1940–41	Wong Peng Soon	Malaya
1942–46	No competition	
1947	Wong Peng Soon	Malaya
1948	Ooi Teck Hock	Malaya
1949–53	Wong Peng Soon	Malaya
1954	Ong Poh Lim	Malaya
1955	Ferry Sonneville	Indonesia
1956	Ong Poh Lim	Malaya
1957	Eddie Choong	Malaya
1958–59	Charoen Watanasin	Thailand
1960	Eddy Choong	Malaya
1961	Jim Poole	USA
1962	Charoen Watanasin	Thailand
1963	Yew Cheng Hoe	Malaysia
1964	Billy Ng	Malaysia
1965–66	Tan Aik Huang	Malaysia
1967–82	No competition	
1983	Liem Swie King	Indonesia
1984	Icuk Sugiarto	Indonesia
1985	Morten Frost	Denmark
1986	Zhao Jian Hua	China
1987	Yang Yang	China
1988–89	Xiong Guobao	China
1990–92	Rashid Sidek	Malaysia
1993	Ardy Wiranata	Indonesia
1994	Joko Suprianto	Indonesia
1995	Alan Budi Kusuma	Indonesia
1996	Ong Ewe Hock	Malaysia
1997	Hermawan Susanto	Indonesia
1998	Peter Gade	Denmark
1999	Lu Yigang	China
2000	Taufik Hidayat	Indonesia
2001	Ong Ewe Hock	Malaysia
2002	James Chua	Malaysia
2003	Chen Hong	China
2004–06	Lee Chong Wei	Malaysia
2007	Peter Gade	Denmark
2008	Lee Chong Wei	Malaysia

foreign coaches to boost Malaysia's performance. Fang Kaixiang of China became the first chief coach of the 1986–88 Thomas Cup 'Project Squad'. The cup was eventually recaptured in 1992 with a 3–2 victory over Indonesia, much to the joy of Malaysian fans.

The BAM further promoted badminton activity in the country when it launched the Malaysian Badminton Academy (MBA). Specially selected national players were housed in a facility which had a training arena with 10 badminton courts. In 2001, the MBA was renamed the National Training Centre and moved to a new facility with 18 courts.

National shuttlers in their first training session at the 18-court National Training Centre at the Juara Stadium in Bukit Kiara when it opened in 2001.

Artwork of the 1992 Thomas Cup champions by the cartoonist Zoy that appeared in the *New Straits Times*.

Badminton: International achievements

Malaysia rose to prominence on the international badminton scene in the early 1950s and has since established itself as a perennial powerhouse. By virtue of their efforts in major individual and team competitions, Malaysian badminton players have forged a tradition of excellence in the sport. Malaysia's only three Olympic Games medals were won on the badminton court.

ABOVE: Cheah Soon Kit (left) and Soo Beng Kiang celebrate after scoring the winning point against Indonesia to secure Malaysia's Thomas Cup win, 1992.

RIGHT: Miniature sheet issued in 1992 showing the Malaysian Thomas Cup championship team.

TOP: A runner-up in the All England championships in 1949, Ooi Teik Hock was also a member of the Malayan Thomas Cup winning teams in 1949, 1952 and 1955.

ABOVE: Malaysian team members triumphantly carrying the Thomas Cup during a parade in Kuala Lumpur, 1967.

All England Championships

In the 1950s, Malaya established itself as a world badminton powerhouse through its players' performances in the All England Open Badminton Championships. The men dominated the All England scene, starting with Ooi Teik Hock who finished as runner-up in 1949, followed by Wong Peng Soon and Eddy Choong who collectively won the singles event from 1950 to 1957. Ooi Teik Hock and Teoh Seng Khoon won the men's doubles event in 1949, followed by the Choong brothers, Eddy and David, who went on to capture the doubles title for three consecutive years from 1951 to 1953 and were runners-up to Ooi Teik Hock and Ong Poh Lim in 1954 and again in 1955.

Teh Kew San and Lim Say Hup won the doubles competition in 1959, followed by Ng Boon Bee and Tan Yee Khan in 1965 and 1966, and later Ng Boon Bee and Punch Gunalan in 1971.

Razif and Jalani Sidek emerged as doubles champions in 1982, and later as runners-up in 1986 and 1988. Cheah Soon Kit and Yap Kim Hock finished as runners-up in 1996.

After a lapse of more than a quarter of a century since Tan Aik Huang won the 1966 All England singles event, Mohd Hafiz Hashim won the singles crown in 2003. In 2007, Koo Kien Keat and Tan Boon Heong claimed the doubles championship, bringing the title back to Malaysia after 25 years.

Thomas Cup

The IBF introduced the Thomas Cup in 1948 and Malaya emerged victorious in the first three series in 1948–49, 1951–52 and 1954–55. The country finished as runners-up in the 1957–59 series, and then won again in 1967. Malaysia was placed second again in 1988 and 1990 before winning the title again in 1992. In 2002, Malaysia finished second.

Recent standout players

1. Malaysian team captain Wong Choong Hann competing in a singles match during the 2007 Malaysia Open in Kuala Lumpur.

2. Cheah Soon Kit (left) and Yap Kim Hock in action during the Commonwealth Games in Kuala Lumpur, 1998. The pair clinched a silver medal at the 1996 Olympic Games in Atlanta, Malaysia's highest achievement to date in Olympic competition.

3. Chin Eci Hui (left) returning a shot while her partner Wong Pei Tty looks on during the Commonwealth Games, 2006. They went on to win the women's doubles gold medal.

4. Mohd Roslin Hashim playing in the men's singles competition at the Olympic Games in Athens, 2004.

5. Mohd Hafiz Hashim competing in the 2007 Malaysia Open in Kuala Lumpur.

6. Tan Boon Heong (left) and Koo Kien Keat triumphantly holding up their All England trophies, 2007. After capturing the gold in the Asian Games in late 2006, the pair went on to claim the All England doubles title.

Badminton greats

In the 1940s and 1950s, **Eddy Choong** won 75 International Badminton Championships in 14 different countries. In the All England Open Badminton Championships, Choong triumphed in the singles event four times in 1953, 1954, 1956 and 1957 and, with his brother David as a partner, he captured the doubles crown in 1951, 1952 and 1953.

Ng Boon Bee (left) and **Tan Yee Khan** were the country's first Asian Games gold medallists in badminton in 1962. This pair proceeded to win the 1966 Asian Games men's doubles title and the 1965 and 1966 All England doubles titles.

Teh Kew San (right) and **Lim Say Hup** won the 1959 All England doubles title and finished as runners-up in 1960. As partners, they won numerous international events including the Canadian Open in 1959 and 1960 and the Malayan Open in 1957, 1959 and 1960. Both players were members of Malaysia's 1958 Thomas Cup squad, and Teh Kew San went on to captain the 1967 Thomas Cup team to victory.

Punch Gunalan emerged as All England doubles champion in 1971, a Commonwealth Games gold medallist in the doubles event and singles event in 1970 and 1974 respectively and an Asian Games gold medallist in the singles and doubles events in 1970.

Tan Aik Huang in action during the Thomas Cup competition, 1967, from which Malaysia emerged victorious. Tan made history in 1966 by clinching the All England Open Badminton Championships singles title as well as two gold medals at the inaugural badminton competition at the Jamaica Commonwealth Games.

Wong Peng Soon was the first Asian to win the All England Open Badminton Championships, capturing the singles title in 1950, 1951, 1952 and 1955. He was also a member of the Malayan teams that won the Thomas Cup in 1949, 1952, and served as the captain of the 1955 team which again brought home the Thomas Cup.

In 1978, **Sylvia Ng** became the first Malaysian woman to win a Commonwealth Games gold medal when she won the women's singles event at the competition in Canada. Partnering with Rosalind Singha Ang, Sylvia captured a bronze medal in the women's doubles event at the 1974 Commonwealth Games in New Zealand.

1. At the age of 18, **Misbun Sidek** was selected as a member of the 1978 Thomas Cup squad. He went on to establish himself on the international scene, winning a host of events including the German, Swedish and Canadian Opens, and finished as runner-up in the All England singles competition.

2. **Razif Sidek** (left) and **Jalani Sidek** won the All England men's doubles title in 1982 and created history by becoming the first Malaysian medallists at

the Olympic Games, clinching a bronze in the doubles competition in Barcelona in 1992. The pair set the record for winning the most National Grand Prix doubles events in Malaysian badminton history.

3. **Rashid Sidek** in his bronze-medal performance at the Olympic Games in 1996. Rashid and his brothers Razif, Jalani and Rahman were members of the Malaysian team which clinched the Thomas Cup in 1992.

Commonwealth Games

Malaysia has a long and illustrious tradition of excellence in badminton at the Commonwealth Games. In the inaugural badminton competition in 1966, Tan Aik Huang took the men's singles title and, along with his partner Yew Cheng Hoe, captured the doubles crown. Four years later in Edinburgh, Punch Gunalan and Ng Boon Bee teamed up to win the men's doubles gold medal. Punch went on to bag the men's singles gold at the 1974 Commonwealth Games in Christchurch. In 1978, it was the women's turn to bring home the gold with Sylvia Ng winning the singles title.

The Sidek brothers shone in the Commonwealth Games competition in the 1980s and 1990s. Razif Sidek won the men's doubles gold with Ong Beng Teong in 1982, and with his brother Jalani in 1990. Rashid Sidek took the men's singles title in 1990 and 1994. Cheah Soon Kit and Soo Beng Kiang also won a gold in the men's doubles event in 1994.

At the 1998 Commonwealth Games in Kuala Lumpur, the hosts won three gold medals: Wong Choong Hann in the men's singles event, Choong

Tan Fook and Lee Wan Wah in the men's doubles and the men's team event. At the 2002 games in Manchester, Malaysia took three gold medals by virtue of the performances of singles player Mohd Hafiz Hashim, the men's doubles pair of Chan Chong Ming and Chew Choon Eng and the women's team of Lim Pek Siah and Ang Li Peng.

The 2006 Commonwealth Games in Melbourne was the country's best showing in the competition's history. Malaysia grabbed four of the six gold medals at stake. Lee Chong Wei triumphed in the men's singles event, Koo Kien Keat and Chan Chong Ming won the men's doubles event, Wong Pei Tty and Chin Eei Hui grabbed the women's doubles title and Malaysia won the mixed team event.

Olympic Games

Badminton debuted as an Olympic sport in Barcelona in 1992. In the inaugural competition, Razif and Jalani Sidek captured the bronze medal in the men's doubles event. The partnership of Cheah Soon Kit and Yap Kim Hock won the silver medal at the Olympic Games in Atlanta in 1996 and Rashid Sidek returned with the singles bronze.

Squash

Since the late 1970s, squash has grown in prominence in Malaysia with international success providing evidence of the attention it has received from exponents of the sport. Already established as Asia's top squash nation, Malaysia witnessed one of its own, Nicol David, rise in the international ranks to become ladies' world champion in 2005. Squash has been selected by the government as one of the eight core sports, signalling a commitment to the development of future champions.

Match being played during the 2007 CIMB Malaysian Open Squash Championships at The Curve shopping centre in Selangor.

Above Left: Founding president of SRAM Dato' Dr Hisham AlBakri.

Above Right: SRAM president as at 2008 Dato' A. Sani Karim.

SRAM logo.

Origins

Squash began in the early 18th century when inmates in Fleet prison in England, an institution for debtors, threw balls at the prison walls for fun. They then took to hitting the balls with racquets and thus the sport was born. The students of Harrow, a public school outside London, picked up the sport around the early 1830s. Instead of the wool and cloth ball used by the prisoners, the students employed balls made of rubber, which 'squashed' when they hit the wall, thus spawning a new name for the sport. The sport subsequently spread to much of England and the United States.

Above Left: Tuanku Ja'afar Tuanku Abdul Rahman with his trophy from the first official squash competition in the country at The Malay College Kuala Kangsar in 1939.

Above Right: First national champion Tunku Imran Tuanku Ja'afar.

The first governing bodies to be formed were the United States Squash Racquets Association and the Canadian Squash Racquets Association, both in the early 1900s. It was only in 1966 that representatives from Australia, Germany, Britain, India, New Zealand, Pakistan, South Africa, the United States, Canada and Egypt met to form a world body, the International Squash Racquets Federation. In 1992, the name of the federation was changed to the World Squash Federation (WSF).

Despite more than 170 years of history and worldwide popularity, squash has not been admitted into the Olympic programme. In 2005, after seven rounds of voting by International Olympic Committee (IOC) members, squash emerged as one of two sports to be placed on a final ballot, but was unable to garner the two-thirds majority necessary to gain Olympic status.

Early squash

Before World War II, members of the British armed forces played squash in military camps while others played in private members-only clubs. Only a handful of locals, largely those who had returned from abroad, played it in Malaysia. The first organized squash competition was held in 1939 at The Malay College Kuala Kangsar. Tuanku Ja'afar

Students of The Malay College Kuala Kangsar playing a game of 'fives'. A predecessor to squash, 'fives' was introduced to Malaya in the early 20th century but never became popular.

Tuanku Abdul Rahman of Negeri Sembilan (later Yang di-Pertuan Agong, 1994–99) beat Abdul Razak (later prime minister, 1970–75) in the final; both were students in the college at the time.

The sport flourished in Malaysia only from the late 1970s. The first batch of players who really got the game going included Tuanku Ja'afar's son, Tunku Imran, the first national champion, who beat Hood Salleh in Malaysia's inaugural national championship in 1973. Women pioneers in the sport included Anna Kronenberg and Sandra Liew.

Tunku Imran went on to become the founding secretary of the Squash Rackets Association of Malaysia (SRAM), which in 2006 changed its name to the Squash Racquets Association of Malaysia. It was formed on 25 June 1973, largely by former students from universities abroad. Its founding president was Dato' Dr Hisham AlBakri. Tunku Imran succeeded him and initiated the highly successful 'Catch 'em young' programme in 1982. Dato' A. Sani Karim has been president of the association since 2004.

Breakthrough players

The 1980s saw the rise of star squash players such as Jerry Loo, S. Maniam, and K.L. Tan, but there were no prominent women players during

Above Left: K.L. Tan (left) reaching down to make a shot during the final of the national championships in Subang, 1986. He went on to defeat Chong Sow Loong and win the title.

Above Right: S. Maniam in action, 1990.

this era. With a more structured programme and stronger financial backing in the 1990s, players such as Tan Tian Huat, Lim Kim Jim and Kenneth Low made big strides, and women players including Mary Lee, Sandra Wu and Kuan Choy Lin became dominant figures in the Malaysian women's game.

In 2008, players such as Ong Beng Hee, Mohd Azlan Iskandar and Nicol David are household names in Malaysia due to their success. Born in 1983, Nicol David's talent was discovered at a very young age, and she won the Scottish Open Under-12 title in 1994 and the British Open Under-14 title in 1996. She won the world junior title in 1999 and 2001. Nicol became the first person to win in every age-group of the British Open, and eventually landed the senior title in 2005. Along with many others, Nicol was supported by the junior development programmes of the National Sports Council in the mid-1980s and the Rakan Sukan programme, initiated in 1996. Rakan Sukan promotes sporting excellence among youth by enlisting local private companies for sports sponsorships.

International achievements

Squash was first introduced in the 1991 SEA Games in Singapore but Malaysia did not participate. At that time, Singapore and the Philippines dominated the sport. At the 1995 SEA Games in Chiang Mai, Kenneth Low became the first Malaysian men's singles champion. At the 1997, 1999 and 2001 editions of the SEA Games, Malaysia swept all four gold medals (men's and women's singles and men's and women's doubles) in the squash competition.

Squash was introduced in the Asian Games in Bangkok in 1998, and Nicol David affirmed her status as the best in the region by winning the women's singles gold at the event. At the next Asian Games in Busan in 2002, Ong Beng Hee took the men's singles gold medal, and Nicol finished as runner-up in the women's singles. This disappointment marked a turning point in Nicol's career. After an eight-month break, she came back stronger than ever and went on to be crowned world champion in 2005.

Malaysia's rise to prominence on the Asian regional squash scene took place in 2000. The Malaysian men defeated Pakistan for the first time to emerge as the Asian champions while Ong Beng Hee became the individual's winner. Nicol also captured the individual crown, but Hong Kong triumphed over the women's team for the gold medal. The performance was stellar and established Malaysia as an Asian powerhouse in squash. From that time through 2006, Malaysia remained undefeated as a team in Asian championship tournaments.

Ong Beng Hee became the world junior champion at the World Junior Men's Championship in New Jersey in 1998. A year later, Nicol captured

Nicol David: World squash champion

Born in Penang in 1983, Nicol David displayed her prodigious talent in squash at an early age, becoming the first player ever to win the World Junior Championship at the age of 16 and then proceeding to capture the title again at the next biennial event in 2001. Her quick rise in the Women's International Squash Players Association (WISPA) rankings saw her, after clinching the World Squash Open title in December 2005, become the number one ladies' squash player in January 2006. After briefly losing her number one ranking in April 2006, Nicol reclaimed the top spot in August 2006 and has not relinquished it since then. She went on to hold an unprecedented 14-month, 51-match winning streak in 2006–07, including victories in the British Squash Open and World Squash Open in 2006. Nicol won eight tournaments out of the 11 she competed in on the World Tour Circuit in 2007.

Nicol kissing the championship trophy after her victory in the final over Rachael Grinham at the 2005 World Squash Open.

Nicol David reaching for the ball during the women's squash final of the Asian Games in Doha, 2006. She went on to win the match and capture the gold medal.

the crown at the World Junior Women's Championship in Antwerp. In 2000, Malaysia decided to focus on training and developing new professional players. Ong Beng Hee became one of the pioneers in professional squash, giving up university studies in order to concentrate on the sport. He did well in several major tournaments and was ranked seventh in the world in 2001—the highest rank ever achieved by a Malaysian men's player under the Professional Squash Association (PSA). However, it was Nicol David who made history for Malaysian squash. She turned professional in 2000 and became the first Malaysian woman to win a world title and the first Malaysian squash player to be ranked first in the world under the Women's International Squash Players Association (WISPA) in December 2005 and January 2006 respectively. After suffering an upset in the 2006 Melbourne Commonwealth Games in March when she finished the women's singles event in fourth place, Nicol went on to establish an unbeaten record for the remainder of 2006, earning titles in six successive WISPA World Tour events and retaining her number one ranking.

Future prospects

Squash is included in the Malaysian government's core sports programme, initiated in 2004, through which eight sports are specially selected for intensive development. A host of young players are being moulded for the future, among them Mohd Azlan Iskandar, who became the national men's number one in 2006 and Low Wee Wern, who captured the Under-19 Asian junior title in Singapore in 2006.

BELOW: World junior champion hopeful Low Wee Wern en route to winning her first Asian junior title in Singapore in 2006.

BOTTOM: Ong Beng Hee (left) battling Mohd Azlan Iskandar in the men's singles squash final at the 2006 Asian Games in Doha. Ong Beng Hee went on to win the match and capture the gold medal.

Table tennis

From its invention in the late 19th century, table tennis or 'ping pong' has evolved into a sport that is played competitively by some 40 million players worldwide and by many more recreationally. Table tennis contests have been organized in Malaysia since 1952. The country has hosted numerous world-class tournaments and Malaysian players have achieved notable success at the international level.

Players taking part in the 4th Asian Table Tennis Championships in Kuala Lumpur, 1978.

T.T.A.M.
Logo of the Table Tennis Association of Malaysia (TTAM).

ABOVE LEFT: Founding TTAM president Tay Boon Seng.

ABOVE RIGHT: TTAM president as at 2007 Dato' Sri Chan Kong Choy.

International history

A descendant of the ancient medieval game of tennis, table tennis was first played as a social diversion with improvised equipment in England during the late 19th century. Between 1905 and 1910, national associations started to form around the world and the process of standardizing rules began. In 1926, the International Table Tennis Federation (ITTF) was founded and the first world championship held in Berlin.

Local development of the sport

The history of table tennis in Malaysia dates back to the formation of the Selangor, Perak and Penang table tennis associations in the early 1950s. In the same period, various Chinese recreation clubs and

Top ranked players Mohd Shakirin Ibrahim (left) and Chan Koon Wah competing in a men's doubles match, 2006. In 2006, Mohd Shakirin Ibrahim became the first non-Chinese player to win a national men's singles title.

associations in these three states were also actively involved in promoting the game. A national association was established in 1958 with Heah Joo Seng as its president. The Table Tennis Association of Malaysia (TTAM) was formed in 1963 and comprised the associations of Peninsular Malaysia, Singapore, Sabah and Sarawak. Singapore withdrew from the TTAM in 1965.

Common styles of gripping

Shakehand grip
Also known as the 'Western' or 'tennis' grip, the shakehand grip resembles the way in which a handshake is performed. The primary advantage of using the shakehand grip is that it enables a player to easily perform both forehand and backhand strokes.

Penhold grip
Popular with players throughout Asia, the penhold grip derives its name from its similarity to the manner in which a writing instrument is held. Players who employ the penhold grip typically hit the ball with only one side of the racquet.

Table tennis events

The first Malayan Table Tennis Championships were held in Penang in 1959 and thereafter annually until 1963. The inaugural Malaysian Table Tennis Championships took place in Kedah in 1964 and have since then been organized annually by various states.

The first official international table tennis competition held in Malaysia was the third SEAP Games in 1965. Malaysia has since hosted many international table tennis championships including the SEA Games, the Asian Table Tennis Championships and the Commonwealth Table Tennis Championships.

Malaysia has also organized many table tennis tournaments and championships sanctioned by the ITTF such as the ITTF World Cup, the ITTF World Circuit and the ITTF Pro-Tour. The most significant world event hosted by Malaysia was the 45th World Table Tennis Championships in 2000.

Since 1959, the country has participated in the Asian, Commonwealth and Southeast Asian table tennis championships. Malaysia took part in the World Table Tennis Championships for the first time in 1971 and has regularly played in this event since then. In the first ever Olympic Games to feature table tennis in 1988, Malaysia was represented by Leong Mee Wan and Lau Wai Cheng.

Miniature sheet issued in conjunction with the 2000 World Table Tennis Championships.

Notable achievements

1970 TTFA Asian Table Tennis Championships: 3rd position for the men's team of Hor Yoon Chuan, Soong Poh Wah, Lim Hee Ping and Loong Peng Sum.

1985 SEA Games: Gold medal won by the men's team comprising Peong Tah Seng, Kok Chong Fatt, Tay Kee and Lim Chin Leong.

1987 SEA Games: Gold medal won by the women's team comprising Leong Mee Wan and Lau Wai Cheng.

1989 SEA Games: Gold medal won by Lim Chin Leong in the men's singles event.

1989 SEA Games: Gold medal won by Leong Mee Wan in the women's singles event.

1991 SEA Games: Gold medal won by the women's team comprising Chong Choi Thing and Phua Bee Sim.

2001 World Table Tennis Championships: 18th position for the women's team comprising Yao Linjing, Beh Lee Wei, Beh Lee Fong and Ng Sock Khim.

2003 ATTU Asian Table Tennis Championships: 5th position for the women's team comprising Yao Linjing, Beh Lee Wei, Beh Lee Fong and Ng Sock Khim.

Yao Linjing (left) and Liu Jun Hui competing at the Asian Table Tennis Championships in Japan, 1998.

Ng Sock Khim (right) prepares to return the service of her opponent from England during the 2002 Commonwealth Games in England.

Tennis

Introduced to Malaya by the British in the late 1800s, tennis was initially played only by members of elite clubs. With the subsequent establishment of public courts and local competitions, however, the sport became a popular pastime. The Lawn Tennis Association of Malaysia (LTAM) has spearheaded the development of tennis in the country.

Malaysian players returning a shot during a Davis Cup match against India in Kuala Lumpur, 1963.

The origins of tennis

The game of tennis was first played in royal circles in 13th-century France by hitting a ball with the palm of the hand. By the time tennis appeared at the Royal Tennis Court inside the Hampton Court Palace in England, racquets had superseded the hand gloves used in earlier variants of the game. Tennis was played indoors until the 18th century when it was taken outdoors in England onto the lawns of houses. With the introduction of other court surfaces (clay, cement and carpet), most tennis matches no longer take place on grass courts.

Local development of the sport

Tennis was introduced to Malaya by the British. In the late 1800s, the expatriate community began establishing social clubs such as the Lake Club and the Royal Selangor Club in Kuala Lumpur, which typically contained tennis courts.

In 1921, Lawn Tennis of Malaya (LTM), the national tennis association, was founded with Justice James McCabe Reay as president. The inaugural Malayan championship in 1921 featured a men's singles event. Top players convened at the Singapore Cricket Club to compete for a cup presented by L.E. Gaunt. The first two competitions were won by Japanese expatriates, but a local Chinese, Khoo Hooi Hye, captured four of the next five competitions and became the first Malayan to compete in the Wimbledon tournament in England in 1936.

Many individual states also conducted their own lawn tennis state championships. Early competitions were the exclusive preserve of tennis club members. The first tournament open to all players took place in 1926. By the mid-1930s, tennis was played year round throughout Malaya and enjoyed greater popularity than any other sport. However, at that time tennis was primarily a club sport. Only a few schools were fortunate enough to have tennis courts like those of The Malay College Kuala Kangsar, where sons of royalty and prominent government administrators were educated.

Facilities for players who were not members of clubs were available only from the mid-1970s when public courts were built by local government authorities. The LTM organized annual tennis championships beginning with the Chua Choon Long Cup (later renamed the LTAM Cup). Since the mid-1980s, the most anticipated tournament has been the Malaysian Open. Played annually on the grass courts of the Royal Selangor Club, the event has attracted first-class players from around the globe. In the 1980s, the International Tennis Federation Men's Satellite Circuit and Association of Tennis Professionals (ATP) challengers were regularly held in the country.

The Lawn Tennis Association of Malaysia (LTAM) was revitalized by new management in the early 2000s. Junior development programmes were instituted as a means of cultivating future prospects. Malaysian players continue to take part in Davis Cup and Fed Cup competitions as well as other international events such as the Asian Games and SEA Games.

Participants in the All-Malaya Malay Tennis Tournament at the Suleiman Club in Kuala Lumpur, 1938.

LTAM logo.

TOP: LTAM president from 1984 to 1999 Tun Ghafar Baba.

ABOVE LEFT: LTAM president from 1999 to 2005 Tan Sri Sallehuddin Mohamad.

ABOVE RIGHT: LTAM president as at 2008 Datuk Abdul Razak Latiff.

1. V. Selvam (right) and Azwan Hizan playing in a Davis Cup match against Indonesia in Kuala Lumpur, 2000.

2. Si Yew Ming competing in a mixed doubles match at the SEA Games in Vietnam, 2003. Along with partner Khoo Chin Bee, Si won the bronze medal.

3. Adam Malik competing in a Davis Cup match, 1992. He became the youngest player ever to take part in the Davis Cup competition when he represented Malaysia in 1982 at the age of 14.

Achievements

In SEAP Games competition, S.A. Azman won silver medals in the men's doubles event with Tan Song Kean in 1961, and in the mixed doubles events with Katherine Leong in 1959 and Claire Chan in 1961. Radhika Menon and Lim Kheo Suan won a gold medal in the women's doubles competition at the SEAP games in 1973, and Radhika Menon captured the women's singles silver medal at the 1975 event. Khoo Chin Bee won a silver medal in the women's singles event at the 1995 SEA Games. Most recently, the women's team brought home a bronze medal from the 2007 SEA Games in Thailand.

V. Selvam has been the top ranked Malaysian tennis player since 1986. He has won four bronze medals in the men's singles event at the SEA Games, and achieved the ranking of 290th in the world, the highest ever by a Malaysian.

Raja Permaisuri Agong Tuanku Intan Zaharah (right) awarding the Malaysian Open trophy to S.A. Azman, winner of the men's singles event, at the Selangor Club, 1967.

Organization

Lawn Tennis of Malaya was renamed the Lawn Tennis Association of Malaysia (LTAM) after the formation of Malaysia in 1963, and it became a full member of the ITF in the same year. The LTAM is the controlling body of tennis in the country, and consists of the tennis associations of the various states of Malaysia and the Armed Forces Sports Council. The LTAM oversees the organization of the sport of tennis in Malaysia and is dedicated to the development of local players, coaches and officials.

1. **National bowlers** (from left) Stanley Tai, Allan Lee and Richard Phua at the Asian Games in South Korea, 1986. The Malaysian bowling team returned with one silver and two bronze medals.

2. **Malaysian snooker and billiards players** (from left) Simon Sim, Moh Loon Hong, Ng Ann Seng, Sam Chong, Ibrahim Amir, Alan Tam and Patrick Ooi preparing for the Asian Games in South Korea, 2002.

3. **V. Nellan** participated in the 1976 and 1977 World Cup events. In the latter event, he and partner Bobby Lim finished 11th out of 52 teams. Nellan won the 1987 Malaysian PGA Championship.

4. **Woodball player** putting during the National Woodball Championship held at the Lanjut Golf and Beach Resort in Pahang, 2004.

5. **Siti Zalina Ahmad** making a shot during the women's singles lawn bowls final at the Commonwealth Games in Melbourne, 2006. She triumphed over her opponent from Wales, and created history by emerging as the women's singles champion at two consecutive Commonwealth Games in 2002 and 2006.

6. **Malaysia's Che Ibrahim Fairuz Hanishah** (third from left) aiming her arrow at the target during the archery competition at the Asian Games in Korea, 2002.

7. **National pétanque player** Saiful Bahari Musmin competing in the men's shooting event at the 2007 SEA Games in Thailand. He won the bronze medal in the competition.

8. **National shooter Hasli Izwan Amir Hassan** competing in the 25-metre rapid fire pistol event at the Ally Ong Trophy championships in Subang, 2006. He won the event and set a new national record in the process.

PRECISION SPORTS

Precision sports emphasize mental ability and accuracy. Malaysians have achieved a great deal of success in the international arena, reaching world-class status in lawn bowls and tenpin bowling and distinguishing themselves at the Asian level in archery, shooting and snooker and billiards.

Malaysia's women's lawn bowls triples team comprising (from left) Nor Hashimah Ismail, Azlina Arshad and Nor Iryani Azmi celebrating after receiving their gold medals at the Commonwealth Games in Melbourne, 2006.

Golf has been played in Malaysia since the late 19th century, starting with a handful of exclusive, private clubs. In the late 1960s, a burgeoning class of local professionals created a huge new market for the game, and over the following two decades, over 200 golf courses were developed all over the country.

Lawn bowls has forged a tradition of excellence. The game has been played in private clubs in the country since the late 19th century, but it was not until the Malaysia Lawn Bowls Federation (MLBF) was formed in 1997 that the development of the sport accelerated. At the 1998 Commonwealth Games in Kuala Lumpur, the hosts captured two silver medals. Since then, Malaysia has consistently achieved success in international events. As at November 2007, four Malaysian lawn bowlers were ranked in the top 20 by the World Bowls Board.

Although cue sports were introduced by the British, it was only with the formation of the Malaysian Snooker and Billiards Federation (MSBF) in 1986 that Malaysia began participating in international tournaments. In 1990, Sam Chong became the first Malaysian to win the Asian Snooker Championships, paving the way for other local players to shine in Asian-level competitions.

Malaysia's first bowling alley opened in Penang in 1961 as a business venture. Bowling has since built up a strong local following, and bowling centres are common in cities and large towns throughout the country. Under the stellar administration of the Malaysian Tenpin Bowling Congress (MTBC), formed in 1974, international achievements have been substantial. Gold medals in the five-man team event at the 1978 Asian Games and the three-man team event at 1979 FIQ World Championships established Malaysia firmly on the world stage. Youth development programmes, created by the National Sports Council in the 1980s, have paid dividends, producing world championship calibre bowlers.

The National Archery Association of Malaysia (NAAM), formed in 1975, has steadily developed the sport. Malaysia has had strong showings at the SEA Games and is ranked as the top country in Southeast Asia.

Shooting was established as a sport in the country on an organized basis in 1949 with the formation of the National Shooting Association of Malaysia (NSAM). In the last twenty years, Malaysians have shot their way to glory in international competitions such as the Commonwealth and Asian Games.

Pétanque was brought to Malaysia by the Ministry of Youth and Sports in 1987 as a sport for the masses. Woodball, invented in Taiwan in 1990, was introduced to Malaysia in 1995. The relative ease with which both sports can be picked up has led them to develop a strong local following.

Golf: Origins and the domestic game

Golf clubs were first established in Malaya by the British in the late 19th century. Since the 1970s, the number and variety of golfing facilities in the country have greatly increased, and Malaysia is now home to 207 golf courses. Golf is governed locally by five organizations, each of which oversees a different aspect of the sport.

Prime Minister Tunku Abdul Rahman Putra, a pioneer of golf in Malaysia, in action.

Origins of the game

Historians generally concur that the Scots taught the world to play golf, but who actually invented the game is subject to debate. Besides the Scots, the Dutch, French and Belgians have also claimed to be the originators of the sport.

According to written records, a game called, variously, 'goff', 'gowf' or 'golf' was being played as early as 1457 in Scotland. A proclamation of that date by James II of Scotland forbade by Royal Decree the playing of the widely popular games of 'futeball' and 'gowf' because they interfered with archery, which was a much more important sport as skilled archers were vital to national defence.

The first instructional pamphlet on how to play the game was written by Thomas Kincaid in Edinburgh in 1687. The first golf club was founded in 1744 by the Honourable Company of Edinburgh. Around the same time, the first Rules of Golf—13 in all—were drawn up for the inaugural competition. In 1754, the first golf club, the Society of St. Andrews Golfers (known as the Royal and Ancient Golf Club of St. Andrews since 1834), was formed. The oldest golf club in England, the Royal Blackheath Golf Club, came into existence in 1766.

Introduction of golf to Malaya

The British introduced golf to Malaya at the end of the 19th century, and formed the first local golf clubs. The clubs were modelled on the traditional British facilities which typically featured well-defined and carefully tended courses accompanied by premises for golfers to change their clothes and store their equipment. The first local club, established in 1876, was the Sarawak Club. The Perak Golf Club (later known as the New Club, Taiping) became the first golf club in the Malay Peninsula in 1885, and was affiliated to the Royal and Ancient Golf Club of St. Andrews. The Selangor Golf Club (now known as the Royal Selangor Golf Club) was founded in 1893. The club celebrated its centenary in 1993, graced by the presence of the Captain of the Royal and Ancient Golf Club of St. Andrews, the Right Honourable Johnny Lindesay-Bethune.

At the beginning of 2008, Malaysia had 207 golf courses, some of which were designed by golf course architects Robert Trent Jones and Ronald Fream, and legendary golfers including Jack Nicklaus, Arnold Palmer, Gary Player and Greg Norman.

A meeting of the members of the Malaya Golfing Society at the Ham Manor Golf Club in England, 1961.

The Malaya Golfing Society

From the early 1900s until shortly after the country's independence in 1957, golf championships at the federal, state and club levels were dominated by expatriate Europeans. The Malaya Golfing Society was formed in the United Kingdom by golfers on leave or retired from Malaya. The required qualifications were one-time residence in Malaya, and an interest in the game of golf. The society organized many competitions in the United Kingdom, including for the Selangor Cup and the Sir John Hay Challenge Bowl.

Sir John Hay presenting his Challenge Bowl to its first winner, Mrs Johnson, 1962.

Prominent golf clubs in Malaysia

Ariff Tuah Ahmad Sarji (left), winner of the Royal Selangor Golf Club centenary championship in 1993, with the Right Honourable Johnny Lindesay-Bethune, Captain of the Royal and Ancient Golf Club of St. Andrews.

1. The Selangor Golf Club (now known as the Royal Selangor Golf Club) clubhouse and course in the 1940s. Established in 1893, the club played host to the inaugural Putra Cup and Malaysian Open in 1961 and 1962 respectively. Initially named the Selangor Golf Club, it was given its 'royal' designation in 1963 by the Yang di-Pertuan Agong Tuanku Syed Putra Syed Hassan Jamallulail.

2. The New Club in Taiping, 1895. The first club in the Malay Peninsula. It was initially known as the Perak Golf Club.

3. A round of golf being played at the New Club in Taiping. Membership in the club was only made available to locals after World War II, and the first Malaysian president of the club was elected in 1967.

4. Petaling Hill, the original home of the Selangor Golf Club, c. 1895. The club was established on 21 August 1893 by 30 founding members. It was subsequently relocated to a new site in 1918 to make way for a public park.

5. Opened in 1986, the Saujana Golf and Country Club in Petaling Jaya is among the premier golf facilities in the country. With state-of-the-art courses designed by Ronald Fream, the club has hosted seven Malaysian Opens, three Kosaido Malaysian Ladies Opens and the 2002 World Amateur Golf Team Championships.

6. Commemorative stamps featuring the Royal Selangor Golf Club specially issued in 1993 in conjunction with the club's centenary.

7. Established in 1991, the Kuala Lumpur Golf and Country Club (KLGCC) is located at Bukit Kiara. The course, comprising two 18-hole layouts, was the site of the 2006 Malaysian Open and is the host of the annual Sime Darby Masters-KL Amateur Open.

Golf organizations

MGA president from 1988 to 2007 Dato' Thomas Lee (left) and MGA president as at 2008 Tunku Abdul Majid Iskandar. Lee received the Sports Leadership Award in 2006.

Malaysian Golf Association (MGA)

The MGA was formed in 1929. In 2007, the MGA had 176 members including golf clubs in Sabah, Sarawak and Labuan. It is affiliated to the Royal and Ancient Golf Club of Saint Andrews, Scotland, and is a member of the International Golf Federation, the Asia-Pacific Golf Confederation and the United States Golf Association. It is registered under the Sports Development Act 1997, which recognizes the association as the national governing body of amateur golf.

SGSM founding president C.H.W. Cochrane (left) and president as at 2008 Tan Sri Sallehuddin Mohamad.

Professional Golfers Tour Malaysia (PGTM) Sdn Bhd

Registered on 8 August 2007, PGTM comprises 72 top Malaysian professionals, the first 50 members being made shareholders of the company. Their objective is to organize a well-developed and lucrative domestic circuit.

Malaysian Ladies Golf Association (MALGA)

The MALGA, formed in 1983, organizes amateur tournaments for ladies and is also in charge of the

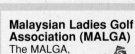

ladies national team.

MALGA president as at 2008 Tunku Puteri Jawahir Tuanku Jaafar.

Malaysian Professional Golfers' Association (MPGA)

The MPGA was established in 1975. It is recognized as the governing body for professional golfers in the country.

Senior Golfers' Society of Malaysia (SGSM)

The SGSM was formed in 1931 with C.H.W. Cochrane as its first president. The purpose of the society is to maintain and support golfers above the age of 55.

Golf: International events and achievements

Local enthusiasm for the sport of golf has grown steadily since its introduction to the country in the late 19th century. Malaysia has played host to numerous major international golf events including the World Amateur Team Championship and the World Cup of Golf. Malaysian golfers have distinguished themselves on the international professional golf circuit.

A 1962 photo of former Malayan Amateur Open Golf Championship winners George Halliday (left) and W.J. Gibb.

The Malaysian Open

The Malayan Open made its debut in the Far East Golf Circuit in 1962, thanks to the efforts of H.C. Clarke, the President of the Federation of Malaya Golf Association, and the patronage of Prime Minister Tunku Abdul Rahman Putra. Many world golfing greats have participated in this event (now called the Malaysian Open Golf Championship) including Peter Thomson, Kel Nagle, Bob Charles, Orville Moody, Payne Stewart, Tony Jacklin, Isao Aoki, David Graham, Graham Marsh, Ian Woosnam, Colin Montgomery, Vijay Singh, Lee Westwood, Michael Campbell and Padrig Harrington. The Malaysian Open

The Seagram Cup.

The first all-Asian team to represent Malaya at the World Amateur Golf Team Championship for the Eisenhower Trophy in 1960 comprising (from left) E.S. Choong, T.S. Leong, Pat Lim and H.Y. Loh.

has been sanctioned by the European Tour since 1999, and is a part of the Asian Tour.

As of 2008, no Malaysian has won the Malaysian Open Golf Championship. Local golfer M. Ramayah finished third in 1983. In 1994, Malaysian golfer P. Gunasegaran tied with Sweden's Joachim Haeggman and New Zealand's Frank Nobilo, and the three players were engaged in a playoff from which Joachim Haeggman emerged victorious.

Putra Cup

Tunku Abdul Rahman Putra is regarded by some as the 'Father of Malaysian Golf'. In 1961, the Tunku founded the Subang National Golf Club and, in the same year, donated the Tunku Abdul Rahman Putra Cup trophy for amateur golfers in Southeast Asia to foster friendship among sportsmen in the region.

A major annual amateur event, this championship is now known as the Southeast Asia Amateur Golf Team Championship. Malaysia has produced winning teams that have included players such as Suffian Tan, Saad Yusof, P. Segaran, N. Ravichanthiran, Bobby Lim, Shahabuddin Yusof, Sulaiman Bluah, Darwis Deran, Zainal Abidin Yusof, Danny Chia, R. Nachimuthu, Rahizam Ramli, Wong Hung Nung, Zaki Sulaiman, John Eu and K. Bathumalai.

The Putra Cup.

Winners of the Malaysian Open

1962	Frank Phillips	1974	Graham Marsh	1986	Stewart Ginn	1997	Lee Westwood
1963	Bill Dunk	1975	Graham Marsh	1987	Terry Gale	1998	Ed Frayatt
1964	Tommo Ishii	1976	Hsu Sheng San	1988	Tray Tyner	1999	Gerry Norquist
1965	Tommo Ishii	1977	Stewart Ginn	1989	Jeff Maggert	2000	Wei-Tze Yeh
1966	Harold Henning	1978	Brian Jones	1990	Glen Day	2001	Vijay Singh
1967	Ireneo Legaspi	1979	Lu His Chuen	1991	Rick Gibson	2002	Alastair Forsyth
1968	Kenji Hosoishi	1980	Mark McNulty	1992	Vijay Singh	2003	Arjun Atwal
1969	Takaaki Kono	1981	Lu His Chuen	1993	Gerry Norquist	2004	Thongchai Jaidee
1970	Ben Arda	1982	Denny Hepler	1994	Joakim	2005	Thongchai Jaidee
1971	Takaaki Kono	1983	Terry Gale		Haeggman	2006	Charlie Wi
1972	Yakashi Murakami	1984	Lu His Chuen	1995	Clay Devers	2007	Peter Hedblom
1973	Hideyo Sugimoto	1985	Terry Gale	1996	Steve Flesch		

Winners of the Malaysian Amateur Open Golf Championship

1894	D.A.M. Brown	1923	E.P. Kyle	1952	B.J. Newey	1980	Peter Chong
1895	D.A.M. Brown	1924	J. Crabb Watt	1953	R.B. Lauriston	1981	Gooi Liong Kee
1896	D.A.M. Brown	1925	L.D. Hardie	1954	C.H. Beamish	1982	Barie Bluah
1897	D.A.M. Brown	1926	W.J. Gibb	1955	C.H. Beamish	1983	John Williamson
1898	P. Fowlie	1927	W.J. Gibb	1956	B. Lauriston	1984	P. Segaran
1899	C.G. Glassford	1928	E.P. Kyle	1957	N.A. Harvey	1985	Suffian Tan
1900	C. MacBain	1929	R. Craik	1958	D.W. McMullan	1986	Buari Sumaat
1901	C.G. Glassford	1930	E.P. Kyle	1959	R.C.W. Stokes	1987	Lester Peterson
1902	A.B. Stephens	1931	W.H. Elkins	1960	F.H. Turner	1988	Nandasena
1903	F. Ferguson	1932	M.M. Paterson	1961	S.C. Beaty		Pereira
1904	T.R. Longmuir	1933	M.M. Paterson	1962	J.L.O. Sullivan	1989	Stuart Bouvier
1905	R.A. Campbell	1934	W.J. Gibb	1963	Darwis Deran	1990	Robert Allenby
1906	R.A. Campbell	1935	R. Craik	1964	J.H. Mitchell	1991	Shane Tait
1907	Captain J.	1936	W.H. Elkins	1965	Darwis Deran	1992	Stephen Leaney
	Kirkwood	1937	M.M. Paterson	1966	Phua Tin Kiay	1993	Chang Tse-Peng
1908	D.A.M. Brown	1938	C.A.R. Bateman	1967	Zainal Abidin	1994	Mardan Mamat
1909	C.V. Miles	1939	E. Laidlaw		Yusof	1995	Marcus
1910	G.R.K. Mugliston		Thomson	1968	Jalal Deran		Wheelhouse
1911	C.T. Durward	1940	George Halliday	1969	Jalal Deran	1996	Jarrod Moseley
1912	J.L. Humphreys	1941	No competition	1970	A.J. Malcolm I	1997	R. Nachimuthu
1913	J. Crabb Watt	1942	No competition	1971	James Stewart I	1998	Cameron Percy
1914	C.J. Foot	1943	No competition	1972	Hassan Ali	1999	Anura Rohana
1915	R.T. Reid	1944	No competition	1973	Brian Marks	2000	Shiv Kapur
1916	J. Crabb Watt	1945	No competition	1974	Tan Yee Khan	2001	Kao Bo Song
1917	No competition	1946	No competition	1975	Nazamuddin	2002	Eddy Lee
1918	No competition	1947	No competition		Yusof	2003	Luke Hickmott
1919	J.L. Humphreys	1948	R.B. Lauriston	1976	Eshak Bluah	2004	Doug Holloway
1920	G. Gibson	1949	W.J. Gibb	1977	Eshak Bluah	2005	Juvic Pangunsan
1921	E.P. Kyle	1950	D.A.O. Davies	1978	Chen Tse-Ming	2006	Andrew Dott
1922	E.P. Kyle	1951	R.R. Jackson	1979	Sumano	2007	Goh Kun Yang

Malaysian Amateur Open Golf Championship

The most important event on the pre-Independence golf calendar was the annual amateur championship, inaugurated in 1894 by Major General Sir Charles Warren, who presented the Warren Shield to the winner of the competition. Initially referred to as the Straits Championship, and the event was subsequently called the Federated Malay States and Straits Settlement Championship in 1921. After the formation of the Malayan Golf Association in 1929, the championship was renamed the Malayan Golf Championship. The mode of play was stroke play from 1894 to 1919, match play from 1920 to 1965, and back to stroke play after 1966. The championship is now known as the Malaysian Amateur Open Golf Championship.

From 1894 to 1960, the Malayan Amateur Open Golf Championship was dominated by European golfers residing in the country. Darwis Deran became the first local to win the championship in 1963. Three sets of Malaysian

Malaysian Amateur Open Golf Championship trophy.

brothers—Jalal and Darwis Deran, Sulaiman, Eshak and Barie Bluah, and Zainal Abidin, Nazamuddin and Shahabuddin Yusof—emerged as standout players through their performances in the Malayan Amateur Open Golf Championship as well as other events including the Putra Cup, Eisenhower Trophy and World Cup.

Other international events

The inaugural World Cup was played in Montreal in 1953. The annual event was initially known as the Canada Cup, as it was the brainchild of Canadian industrialist John Jay Hopkins, but was subsequently renamed the World Cup in 1967 and the World Cup of Golf in 1993. It is regarded as the 'Olympics of Golf' and is contested by teams of two men from participating countries around the world.

Malaysia first qualified to play in the World Cup in 1969, and sent a team comprising K.C. Choo and Jalal Deran to Singapore to take part in the event. As of 2008, the country has competed in 22 World Cup competitions, and has been represented by local golfers including Zainal Abidin Yusof, Bobby Lim, Danny Chia, Nazamuddin Yusof, V. Nellan, Eshak Bluah, Indra Mohd Yusof, M. Ramayah, P. Gunasegaran, Rashid Ismail, Shahabuddin Yusof, Barie Bluah, Iain Steel and Mohd Ali Kadir.

Malaysia's best performance in the World Cup of Golf was in 1994 in Puerto Rico when M. Ramayah and P. Gunasegaran placed ninth out of 32 teams in the competition, and M. Ramayah finished sixth in the individual standings.

Malaysia hosted the 45th World Cup of Golf in 1999 at the Mines Golf and Country Club in Selangor. Thirty-two nations participated, and Malaysia was represented by M. Ramayah and P. Gunasegaran. Approximately 600 million people around the globe watched the event from which the American team of Tiger Woods and Mark O'Meara emerged victorious.

The World Amateur Golf Team Championship for the Eisenhower Trophy was first played in St. Andrews in 1958. As there was not much time to organize a local team, Malaya fielded four Europeans on leave in the United Kingdom at the time. In 1960, Malaya was represented by Pat Lim, T.S. Leong, E.S. Choong and

H.Y. Loh. The country has competed in subsequent World Amateur Golf Team Championships, and those who have done national duty include Suffian Tan, Saad Yusof, Rashid Mallal, N. Ravichanthiran, P. Segaran, K.C. Choo, Jalal Deran, S. Siva Chandhran, Lim Eng Seng and Hussin Mohd Shaaban.

In 2002, Malaysia organized the World Amateur Team Championship at the Saujana Golf and Country Club in Selangor. In the men's competition for the Eisenhower Trophy, 63 countries took part, while the women's competition for the Esperito Santo Trophy saw the participation of teams from 39 nations.

Malaysian golfers also have also participated in other team events such as the Nomura Cup, the Asian Amateur Team Championship Games, the Asian and SEA Games.

International achievements

Several Malaysian professional golfers have achieved great distinction in international competitions. M. Ramayah won the Marcos Invitational Golf Championship in 1980, beating a star-studded field which included Orville Moody, David Graham, Gary Player, Sandy Lyle and Bernard Langer. Danny Chia created history by winning the Taiwan Open in 2002, thereby becoming the first Malaysian to capture a European Tour-sanctioned event on the Asian Circuit. Airil Rizman Zahari emerged victorious in the Pakistan Open in 2007, another European Tour-sanctioned tournament on the Asian circuit. Malaysia's first lady golfer to play on the Ladies Professional Golfers' Association Tour was Lim Siew Ai.

1. Darwis Deran and Zainal Abidin Yusof
2. Bobby Lim
3. Nazamuddin Yusoff
4. Rashid Ismail
5. Tan Yee Khan
6. V. Nellan
7. Shahabuddin Yusof
8. Suffian Tan
9. P. Gunasegaran
10. R. Nachimuthu
11. M. Ramayah
12. Eshak Bluah
13. Jalal Deran
14. P. Segaran

ABOVE: Malaysian teams at the 2002 World Amateur Team Championship at the Saujana Golf and Country Club.

LEFT: Tiger Woods (left) and Mark O'Meara (right) receiving the World Cup from the Yang-di Pertuan Agong Sultan Salahuddin Abdul Aziz Shah after winning the event held at the Mines Resort City in Kuala Lumpur, 1999.

1. Iain Steel putting during the SK Telecom Open in Seoul, 2006.

2. Airil Rizman Zahari holding the trophy after winning the 2007 Pakistan Open Golf Tournament.

3. Lim Siew Ai, who began her rookie year in the 2005 LPGA Tour, hitting from a sandtrap during the US Women's Open in Kansas.

4. Danny Chia clearing the ball from the bunker at the 18th hole of the Malaysian Open, 2003.

Lawn bowls

Bowls has been played in the country since the late 19th century. The sport declined locally in the 1970s, but was revived in the late 1990s with the support and encouragement of the government. Malaysia first distinguished itself in the lawn bowling event at the 16th Commonwealth Games in 1998 in Kuala Lumpur. Under the Malaysia Lawn Bowls Federation (MLBF), Malaysia is now one of the leading countries in the sport of bowls.

The roots of the game

Lawn bowls is believed to have originated from a game played in ancient Egypt which was similar to skittles, but incorporated the use of round stones. This early form of the sport subsequently spread across Europe, taking on a variety of forms and names; it was referred to as *bocce* in Italy, *boules* in France and *bolla* by the Saxons.

The game had become entrenched in Britain by the 13th century. The oldest lawn bowls club in the world, the Southampton Old Bowling Green Club, was established in 1299. The game's popularity spread still wider with its introduction to various parts of the British empire, from Australia and New Zealand to South Africa, Hong Kong and Canada. In Polynesia, the sport is known as *ula miaka*.

Local development of the sport

The earliest written record of lawn bowls being played in Malaya was during the visit of Prince Alfred, Duke of Edinburgh, to the Penang Club in December 1869. In the early 1900s, lawn bowls was also being played on the lawn belonging to the Penang Cricket Club.

The Esplanade in Penang in 1890. It functioned as a lawn bowling green during the British colonial period in Malaya.

Tan Sri Dato' Seri Ahmad Sarji Abdul Hamid (left) with Deputy Prime Minister Dato' Sri Najib Tun Razak at the launch of *Lawn Bowls in Malaysia: The President's Memoir* written by Tan Sri Ahmad Sarji, 2005.

World ranking

Four Malaysian lawn bowlers are ranked among the top 20 in the world by the World Bowls Board as at November 2007: (clockwise from top left) Nor Hashimah Ismail (10th in the women's rankings), Siti Zalina Ahmad (third in the women's rankings), Safuan Said (first in the men's rankings) and Nor Iryani Azmi (ninth in the women's rankings).

In Kuala Lumpur, lawn bowling competitions were held at the Lake Club which was established in 1890. This club operated a lawn bowls green until 1973 when it was converted into a croquet ground. Lawn bowls was also played at the Selangor Golf Club's bowling green in the 1930s. The Singapore Cricket Club competed against Penang in 1937 for a trophy.

More recently, Australian soldiers stationed in the country became exponents of the sport. They formed a club known as the Sergeant's Mess Bowls Club in Butterworth, Penang and constructed a lawn bowling green in 1970.

How the game is played

The objective of lawn bowls is for a player to bowl his or her bowls as close as possible to the jack. The jack may be placed at a distance of 23–35 metres. It is imperative for a player to gauge the curvature needed to place the bowls near the jack, especially when the opponents have their bowls guarding it.

The singles game starts with the jack being rolled—by the bowler who wins a coin toss—from the delivery mat to the opposite end of the rink. The bowlers then bowl each of their four bowls in turn, using either a forehand or backhand style to deliver their bowls. When all of the bowls have been bowled, an end is completed. The result of the end is then tallied: a shot is counted for each player's bowl that is closer to the jack than the opponent's. The player that has the majority of shots is declared the winner of the end and then the ensuing end begins.

The team with the most winning ends wins the game. Play typically continues until one of the players (in a singles game) or teams (in pairs, threes or fours) achieves 21 shots. In the event of a draw, a tie-breaker end or ends are bowled until the winners are determined.

Several variants of the game exist: pairs, triples and fours. In the pairs games, as in the singles game, each player has four bowls, in triples it is three per player and in fours, two bowls per player.

An end of a pairs game being played. Players from both teams alternate until they have each delivered four bowls.

34–40 metres

5 metres

National Lawn Bowls Complex, Bukit Kiara, Kuala Lumpur.

Lawn bowling can be played indoors or outdoors. Outdoor surfaces are usually grass, but marl (a sand-clay mixture) is sometimes used as an alternative. Indoor matches are normally played on a flat carpeted surface.

Lawns are divided into six rectangular sections called rinks. The green is surrounded by a ditch and a bank and the corners are fixed with white wooden pegs.

Bowls and a jack.

Balls (Bowls)

Bowls are biased, purposely designed to travel in a curved path. They are made deliberately lopsided so that when bowled they curve towards their flat side as they slow down. Bowls are also called woods because they are usually made of *lignum vitae*, a heavy and hard wood, but may alternatively be made of rubber. Bowls are 120–146 millimetres in diameter with a maximum weight of 1.5 kilograms and are usually brown or black.

Jack

The jack is a small, white or yellow ball weighing between 200 and 300 grams and with a diameter of 63–64 millimetres.

International achievements by Malaysia

World Bowls Championships			
Christchurch, 2008	1	-	4

World Champion of Champions
Christchurch, 2005 Women's singles champion–Nor Iryani Azmi
Warilla, 2007 Women's singles runner-up–Siti Zalina Ahmad

World Cup			
Warilla, 2006	-	1	1

World Junior Cup			
Hong Kong, 2005	1	1	-

Commonwealth Games			
Kuala Lumpur, 1998	-	1	2
Manchester, 2002	1	-	1
Melbourne, 2006	2	-	-

Asia Pacific Bowls Championship			
Dunedin, 1995	-	-	2
Warilla, 1997	-	-	1
Kuala Lumpur, 1999	-	2	3
Moama, 2001	-	-	3
Brisbane, 2003*	2	2	4
Darebin, 2005	1	2	-
Christchurch, 2007	1	1	3

Asian Lawn Bowls Championship			
Hong Kong, 2001*	5	3	-
Manila, 2002*	7	-	1
Kuala Lumpur, 2003*	7	1	0
Kuala Lumpur, 2005*	5	1	2
Brunei, 2006*	5	1	1
Kuala Lumpur, 2007*	6		

SEA Games			
Brunei, 1999*	4	1	1
Kuala Lumpur, 2001*	5	1	-
Manila, 2005*	3	2	1
Bangkok, 2007*	4	1	1

*Malaysia was overall champion

ABOVE RIGHT: Siti Zalina Ahmad, a gold medallist at two consecutive Commonwealth Games in 2002 and 2006, became the first Asian bowler to win the Australian Open in 2007. She also emerged as Asia's Singles Champion for the sixth time in 2007.

ABOVE LEFT: At the age of 20, Nur Fidrah Noh won the women's singles event at the 2007 New Zealand National Open Championships, becoming the first Asian and youngest bowler to capture a singles title in the competition.

Organization

The Malaysia Lawn Bowls Federation (MLBF) was registered in March 1997 under the Sports Development Act 1997.

The federation is a member of the World Bowls Limited, World Indoor Bowls Council and an affiliated member of the Olympic Council of Malaysia. Members of the federation comprise state lawn bowls associations as well as the sports councils of the Royal Malaysian Police and Malaysian Armed Forces. Members of the MLBF may also include clubs which are registered for the purpose of lawn bowling. The MLBF is the controlling body of the sport of lawn bowls in Malaysia, including indoor bowls, and promotes the development of the sport.

MLBF logo.

MLBF president as at 2008 Tan Sri Dato' Seri Ahmad Sarji Abdul Hamid (above) and his certificate of praise for excellence in sports leadership given by the National Sports Council in 2006.

Malaysian events and achievements

At the national level, the MLBF and the state lawn bowls associations have organized events such as the President's Cup, Prestige Cup, Bowls Malaysia Cup, the national singles, pairs, triples and fours and the youth championships. The first international competition hosted by Malaysia in recent times was the Malaysian Wira Six Nation Tournament organized by the MLBF in 1998 in preparation for the Commonwealth Games in Kuala Lumpur later that year.

Other international events include the Malaysia–Singapore Test Series which led to the establishment of the Tan Sri Ahmad Sarji Cup Championship, held in Johor Bahru in 1998 and Singapore in 1999 with the added participation of Brunei. Malaysia won the championships on both occasions. In 2000, the Tan Sri Ahmad Sarji Cup Championship was held in Brunei. The participating nations agreed to convert the championship into the Asian Lawn Bowls Championships the following year. Malaysia has dominated the Asian Lawn Bowls Championship since then.

At the 16th Commonwealth Games in Kuala Lumpur in 1998, lawn bowling contributed one silver medal and two bronze medals to the nation's medal tally. Siti Zalina Ahmad won the women's singles event at the Manchester Commonwealth Games in 2002 and successfully defended her title four years later at the Melbourne Commonwealth Games.

Malaysia organized the 8th Asia Pacific Lawn Bowls Championship in 1999, which drew participants from 15 nations, and emerged from the competition with five medals. Malaysia became the Asia Pacific champion team at the championship held in Australia in 2003.

In 2001, Malaysia hosted the 21st SEA Games in Kuala Lumpur and the national team distinguished itself by becoming the overall champion.

In 2006, the Bayuemas Indoor Bowls Stadium, one of the world's largest indoor lawn bowls facilities, was opened. The RM6-million complex hosted the Asia Pacific Singles and Mixed Pairs Bowls Championship in 2006 and the World Indoor Bowls Under-25 Championship in 2007.

In 2005, Nor Iryani Azmi emerged as the winner of the women's singles event at the World Champion of Champions tournament in New Zealand. World Bowls introduced a ranking system in 2005, and ranked Nor Iryani Azmi number three in the world for that year. As at February 2008, Safuan Said is ranked first and Siti Zalina Ahmad is ranked second in the world.

At the 2008 World Bowls Championships in Christchurch, Safuan Said emerged as the men's singles champion and the Malaysian team finished third in the overall standings behind New Zealand and Australia.

TOP: The Malaysian team at the 6th Asian Lawn Bowls Championship held in Kuala Lumpur, 2007.

ABOVE: Bayuemas Indoor Bowls Stadium in Port Klang.

LEFT: Saedah Abdul Rahim in action during the finals of the women's singles event at the Commonwealth Games in Kuala Lumpur, 1998. She won a silver medal for Malaysia.

Snooker and billiards

Snooker and billiards are games that require steady mental focus and a commitment to training. Inspired by Malaysian pioneers such as Sam Chong and Moh Loon Hong, many young players have taken to the games in a serious and professional manner. With the many recreational centres offering snooker and billiards games, Malaysia has a continuously expanding base of aspiring professionals.

Snooker centre in Johor, 1987.

Tan Kim Song, a Malayan snooker and billiards pioneer, lining up a shot during a tournament, 1953.

Early history of cue games

The earliest recorded reference to billiards dates back to 1574 when French monarch Henry III had a custom-made, polished stone slab table with a wooden frame and legs installed in his castle. By the end of the 17th century, the game was prevalent among the royal courts of Europe, due primarily to the efforts of French King Louis XIV, an avid player and exponent of the game. The earliest versions of the game were played with two ivory balls and various obstacles such as miniature gates, arches, pins and chess pieces on the table.

The Americans modified the game of English billiards by adding two coloured balls and thereby creating four-ball billiards, which gave the sport even more variety. This game in turn evolved into 15-ball pool played with balls numbered to determine the number of points players accumulated. The word 'pool' means a collective bet, and is actually a shortening of 'pool billiards'. In the early 1900s, eight-ball pool was developed from the 15-ball version and around 1920, nine-ball pool appeared for the first time. Eight-ball pool derives its name from the fact that either player has to pocket the black number eight ball in a legal manner to win. In the nine-ball variation, the winner is the player who legally pockets the number nine ball. Eight- and nine-ball pool are the most commonly played versions of the game around the globe.

In 1875, in Jubbulpore, India, British Colonel Sir Neville Chamberlain suggested adding coloured balls to a billiards game, hence creating the game of snooker. After its introduction in England, snooker quickly eclipsed billiards in popularity. The first world snooker championships took place in Nottingham, England in 1927 and the event has been held at the Crucible Theatre in Sheffield since 1977.

Local development of snooker

Introduced to the country by the British, cue sports were not particularly popular in Malaysia prior to the 1980s, and were played primarily in exclusive clubs. In 1984, in conjunction with the formation of the Asian Billiards and Snooker Federation, the inaugural Asian snooker championship was held in Bangkok and Malaysia took part. Peter Chin from Sabah participated, but did not get past the group qualifying stages. In 1984–85, the game gained local recognition when prominent names from the United Kingdom, including world champion Steve Davis, embarked on a promotional tour of the Far East, stopping in Malaysia to compete in the Camus Invitational Masters at Putra World Trade Centre in Kuala Lumpur.

Formed in 1986, the Malaysian Snooker and Billiards Federation (MSBF) organizes annual national championships. The inaugural tournament was held in 1986 in Kuala Lumpur, and Peter Chin emerged as the winner. Over the years, the national championships have attracted an average of 90 participants each year. Sam Chong captured a record five national titles between 1989 and 1999, and is the most successful player in the history of the championship. The MSBF also conducts the annual national under-21 championships to help discover and develop new talent. Many promising talents, such as Moh Keen Ho, have emerged from this competition.

Malaysia hosted the fourth Asian Snooker Championship in Kuala Lumpur in 1987, the Far East leg of the 1996 World Cup qualifiers at Genting Highlands and the 2004 Asian Junior Championship in Kuala Lumpur. In 2003, the MSBF initiated a tour series in which

Organization

The Malaysian Snooker and Billiards Federation (MSBF) was formed by office bearers from the Federal Territory Snooker and Billiards Association (FTSBA) in 1986. The MSBF was accepted in 1987 as an affiliate of the OCM, paving the way for the country's participation in both snooker and billiards in the Jakarta SEA Games. In 1989, the Registrar of Societies endorsed MSBF as the sole body for the promotion and development of the games in the country. The MSBF operates the Academy of Snooker at the NSC complex in Bukit Jalil, Kuala Lumpur.

Logo of the Malaysian Snooker and Billiards Federation.

MSBF president as at 2008 Professor Dato' W.Y. Chin.

Peter Chin playing at the fourth Asian Snooker Championships, 1987.

Snooker maestros

Ooi Chin Kay preparing to shoot during the final round of the ASEAN Cup tournament against Hong Kong, 2001.

The most accomplished snooker player in Malaysia is Sam Chong. In 1991, after sustained success on the Asian tour, Chong became the first Malaysian to play on the professional circuit in the United Kingdom. At his peak, Chong was ranked 89th in the world. In 1990, he became the first Malaysian to win the coveted Asian Snooker Championship. In recognition of his achievements, Chong was given the National Sportsman of the Year Award in 1995 and named Olympian of the Year in 1995 by the Olympic Council of Malaysia (OCM). Chong is the current coach of the national team, training a new generation of snooker players to succeed in the sport.

Another Malaysian snooker standout is Ooi Chin Kay who, having started as an underdog, became the 1994 Asian Snooker Champion. He then teamed up with Chong to win the doubles gold medal at the 1998 Asian Games in Bangkok, in which Chong also grabbed the silver in the individual event.

Moh Keen Ho, a rising star of Malaysian snooker, became the Asian under-21 champion in 2005, thus automatically qualifying for the World Snooker Association's Professional Main Tour in 2005–06. With his success, Moh was sent to the United Kingdom Snooker Academy for four months in 2005 by the National Sports Council to gain tournament exposure.

ABOVE: Malaysian snooker players (from left) Moh Loon Hong, Frank Koh, Ng Ann Seng, Sam Chong, Elvin Cheah and Liew Kit Fatt.

RIGHT: Sam Chong lining up his cue during the final round of the Snooker ASEAN Cup tournament against Hong Kong, 2001.

The eldest son of billiards champion Moh Loon Hong, Moh Keen Ho showed great promise to become the Asian under-21 champion in 2005.

numerous tournaments are staged all over the country, culminating in the grand finals at the XZ Club in Petaling Jaya.

Billiards in Malaysia

Tunku Abdul Rahman Putra, the first prime minister of Malaysia, was known to occasionally play billiards in the 1960s and was highly supportive of local competitions. Starting in 1980, the Malaysian Open Billiards Masters, the first inter-regional billiards competition, took place for five consecutive years as part of the Penang Pesta Sukan Meet. The top billiards players from Thailand, Malaysia and Singapore participated in the competition, which was divided into three-ball and four-ball categories. Moh Loon Hong was crowned the overall masters champion by virtue of winning both three- and four-ball events. In 1984, the tournament was discontinued due to a lack of popular interest.

The MSBF staged Malaysia's first National Billiards Championship at the Gold Dash snooker centre in Kuala Lumpur in 1991, with Moh Loon Hong capturing the inaugural title. Moh also won the next two National Championships at the Marco Polo Snooker Centre in Kuala Lumpur, before the event was discontinued.

International achievements

The Malaysian SEA Games squad consisting of Sam Chong, Ng Ann Seng and Ooi Chin Kay won the nine-ball billiards team gold medal in Singapore in 1993. This led to their masterly performance in the Chiangmai SEA Games in 1995 when Sam Chong, Liew Kit Fatt, John Yong, Ng Ann Seng and Moh Loon Hong collectively won six gold medals.

Malaysia captured three silver medals at the 2003 SEA Games in Vietnam in the men's snooker doubles, snooker team and the billiards eight-ball singles events.

Five bronze medals were secured in the 2005 SEA Games in Manila in the men's billiards nine-ball singles, billiards 15-ball doubles, men's snooker singles, snooker doubles and billiards doubles. Suhana Dewi Sabtu won the silver in the women's billiards nine-ball singles, becoming the first Malaysian woman to win a medal in an international billiards competition.

Ibrahim Amir, Alan Tan and Patrick Ooi represented Malaysia at the billiards World Nine-ball Pool Championships held in Taipei in 2004 and 2005. Ooi advanced to the final 32 before losing to Taiwan's most famous pool player, Chao Fung Fung.

At the Asian Games in Qatar in 2006, Esther Kwan Suet Yee captured the silver medal in the nine-ball singles event.

At the 2007 SEA Games in Korat, Moh Keen Ho won the gold medal in the men's snooker singles event as well as a silver medal in the men's snooker doubles event with partner Yong Kein Foot. Malaysia also won silver medals in the men's snooker team and men's English billiards doubles events, and bronze medals in the men's nine-ball pool doubles and men's eight-ball pool singles competitions.

ABOVE LEFT: Suhana Dewi Sabtu in her silver medal winning performance in the nine-ball singles event at the 2005 SEA Games in Manila.

ABOVE: Members of the Malaysian snooker team (from left) Lai Chee Wei, Thor Chuan Leong, Moh Keen Ho, Patrick Ooi, Esther Kwan Suet Yee and Suhana Dewi Sabtu, 2006.

LEFT: Esther Kwan Suet Yee was the only Malaysian to win a medal in a cue sport event at the Asian Games in Qatar, 2006.

Tenpin bowling

Tenpin bowling boasts over 100 million participants in 90 countries spanning six continents. As a result of the support of several key institutions and the success of youth development programmes, tenpin bowling has become one of the most popular and prominent sports in Malaysia and local bowlers have risen to remarkable heights in international competitions. In 2003 and 2007, the women's team emerged as world champions after striking gold at the FIQ World Championships.

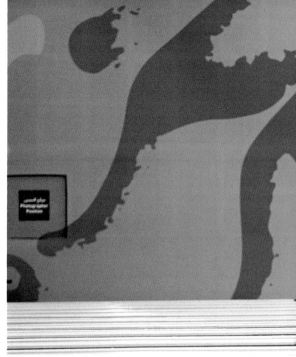

Esther Cheah, 2005 FIQ world champion, throwing a ball during the 2006 Asian Games in Doha. She went on to win the women's singles gold medal.

TOP: Bowler participating in a tournament at the Federal Bowl in Kuala Lumpur, 1968.

ABOVE: Players and spectators at an event held at the 48-lane Sunway Pyramid bowling centre, 2005.

MTBC logo.

Dato' Dr P.S. Nathan (right) receiving the 2005 National Sports Leadership Award from Minister of Youth and Sports Dato' Sri Azalina Othman Said.

Origins of bowling

The sport of bowling is believed to be at least 5200 years old. In the 1930s, a British anthropologist discovered artefacts in an ancient grave of a child in Egypt that resembled the ball and pins used in a bowling game. Other scholars posit that bowling originated between 300 and 400 CE.

Bowling games of many varieties have been created and played widely around the world. In Germany, bowling was used in a religious ceremony to determine the morality of the participants. Parishioners rolled or threw stones at pins. Those who knocked down pins were thought to possess good character, while others who were less skilled had to perform penance. Martin Luther, an eminent German theologian, has been credited with the writing of the formal playing rules of ninepin bowling.

Tenpin bowling evolved out of the game of ninepin bowling or 'skittles'. British, Dutch and German immigrants took ninepin bowling with them when they migrated to the United States. As ninepin bowling grew in popularity, betting on the game became widespread. In an attempt to eradicate gambling, the state of Connecticut passed a law outlawing ninepin bowling in 1841. To circumvent the law, proprietors simply added a tenth pin, thereby creating the game of tenpin bowling. Over the next 50 years, tenpin bowling spread throughout the country but did not possess standardized rules for scoring or equipment. Tenpin bowling was officially recognized as a sport in 1895 in New York City, when the American Bowling Congress was formed. Representatives determined rules such as the length of the lane (18.3 metres) and the distance between pins (0.3 metre) as well as the highest score (300).

In 1952, the Fédération Internationale des Quilleurs (FIQ) was founded in Germany to administer and serve the sports of ninepin and tenpin bowling. Starting in 1952, World Championships were held every four years. In 2006, they began to be held annually.

Under the auspices of the FIQ, the World Tenpin Bowling Association (WTBA) was founded as the world governing body of tenpin bowling. International bowling, under the WTBA, is organized into three regional zones: Asian, European and American. Each zone hosts annual championships and has established a scoring system to select the bowlers who qualify for the World Ranking Masters.

Dato' Dr P.S. Nathan

In 1984, Dato' Dr P.S. Nathan, the founding and current president of the Malaysian Tenpin Bowling Congress (MTBC), was elected president of the Asian Bowling Federation. Three years later, he became the first Malaysian to head a world sports governing body when he became president of the WTBA, a position which he held until 2003. In 1991, Nathan was given the Golden Pin Award by the WTBA in recognition of his contribution to the sport.

Tenpin bowling in Malaysia

Bowling first arrived in Malaysia in 1961 with the opening of International Bowl in Penang. By 1965, two additional centres in Selangor and one in Perak had been built. The sport of tenpin bowling spread and

1979 FIQ world champions (from left) Edward Lim, Koo Boon Jin and Allan Hooi.

evolved rapidly in the 1960s, leading to the development of an organizational structure within the country as well as achievements on the international stage in the 1970s.

In the early 1970s, Malaysia established itself as a regional bowling power. At the 1970 Asian FIQ Championships in Hong Kong, Johnny Kim, Allan Lee, Allan Hooi, O.B. Lim, Patrick Soh and Y.K. Thong represented Malaysia and earned eight of nine possible gold medals. In the following two years, Allan Hooi captured consecutive titles at the Asian Masters, demonstrating Malaysia's increasing prominence on the international bowling circuit.

In 1974, the Malaysian Tenpin Bowling Congress (MTBC) was formed. The first MTBC president, Dato' Dr P.S. Nathan, still retains the position as

place at the World Cup. Alex Liew earned five international titles in 2005. In 2006, the youth team captured eight medals, including four gold medals at the World Youth Championships in Germany. In September, the men's team won two medals at the FIQ-WTBA World Championships in Korea. At the Asian Games in December in Doha, the men's and women's teams earned three gold and three silver medals. After her performance in the Asian Games, Esther Cheah was named 2006 female Olympian of the Year by the Olympic Council of Malaysia. At the 2007 FIQ-WTBA World Championships in Mexico, the Malaysian women's team defeated the United States by seven pins to clinch the gold medal in the team event.

Each January, the MTBC hosts the national championship and the interstate tournament, pitting the country's top adult and youth bowlers against each other. In support of youth development, a junior circuit is also conducted. In 2008, there are more than 10 stops around the country, culminating in the Grand Prix finals. Malaysia also plays host to several international tournaments that attract bowlers from around the world. In 2007, the Sunway Pyramid was the site of the 30th annual Malaysian Open tournament with a first prize of US$25,000.

ABOVE: Alex Liew in action during the Asian Games in Doha, 2006. Liew garnered an impressive five international titles in 2005.

BELOW RIGHT: The men's and women's teams both emerged as champions at the World Tenpin Team Cup in Denmark, 2003. The women's team went on to win the 2003 FIQ-WTBA World Championships, marking the first time a nation had ever won both events in the same year.

BELOW LEFT: The women's team celebrating their victory in the team event at the FIQ-WTBA World Championships in Mexico, 2007. The five-women team posted a combined total of 6323 pinfalls to defeat their opponents from the United States and surpass the previous world record—which they set en route to winning the gold medal in the 2003—by 43 pins.

of 2008. One year after the formation of the MTBC, President Dato' Dr. P.S. Nathan captured a gold medal in the singles event at the SEA Games. Malaysia enjoyed further success at the 1978 Asian Games, winning gold with a team comprising Dato' Dr P.S. Nathan, Edward Lim, Koo Boon Jin, Allan Hooi, Hubert Lee and Holloway Cheah. In 1979, Malaysia firmly established itself on the international scene when Allan Hooi, Edward Lim and Koo Boon Jin won a gold medal in the three-man team event at the 1979 FIQ World Championships in Manila. In 1983, Michael Chuah finished as runner-up at the World Cup in Mexico.

Establishing a tradition of excellence
In 1988, the National Sports Council (NSC) began funding a national youth development programme which soon starting paying dividends. Shalin Zulkifli, a future national bowling sensation, was one of the students in the initial youth development programme in Shah Alam. In 1991, Lisa Kwan earned a silver medal at the FIQ World Championships. Two years later, the national team captured six gold and six silver medals at the SEA

Ben Heng celebrating after delivering the winning strike during the 2003 World Tenpin Team Cup in Denmark.

Games in Singapore. In 2003, the women's and men's national teams won the World Tenpin Team Cup after the women garnered the team gold medal at the FIQ-WTBA World Championships.

Recent developments
Youth development programmes continue to bring forth champions. Both 2005 and 2006 were landmark years for Malaysian bowlers in international bowling competitions. Esther Cheah earned a gold medal in the singles event at the 2005 FIQ-WTBA World Championships and Wendy Chai finished in third

Shalin Zulkifli
After progressing through the youth development programme, Shalin Zulkifli quickly became an international bowling phenomenon, earning the World Bowling Writers Association award for Bowler of the Year in 1994. That year, as a 16-year-old, Shalin represented Malaysia at the Asian Games in Hiroshima and won a gold medal in the Masters event. Since that remarkable victory, she has been the face of Malaysian bowling and become a household name around the country. Shalin's accomplishments, including the Asian Games Masters Gold (2002), World Tenpin Masters Champion (2001) and runner-up at the prestigious World Ranking Masters (2004), have been a contributing factor to the growing popularity of tenpin bowling in Malaysia and around Asia. Shalin won six international titles in 2006.

The Shalin Cup bowling tournament was introduced in 2002 to encourage the development of young talent. In 2006, 191 bowlers under the age of 14 participated in the event.

ABOVE LEFT: Shalin Zulkifli holding up the World Tenpin Masters trophy after beating Norway's Tore Togersen in England, 2001. Her victory marked the first time a woman ever defeated a man in a major world bowling final.

ABOVE RIGHT: Shalin Zulkifli in the middle of her approach during a tournament in Penang, 2001.

Archery

It was only in the 1970s that competitive archery was introduced locally by Malaysians who had travelled to Europe and America and developed an interest in the sport. Ever since a Malaysian qualified for the archery event in the 2004 Olympic Games, the sport has been receiving more attention locally.

Mon Redee Sut Txi (left) preparing to release her arrow during the finals of the 2003 SEA Games in Vietnam. In 2004, Mon Redee became the first Malaysian archer to qualify for the Olympic Games.

TOP: The Malaysian Armed Forces Archery Tournament in Kuala Lumpur, 1978. At that time, regulations compelled archers to dress in white uniforms.

ABOVE: Junior archers aiming for the targets during the National Sports Council (NSC) Junior Archery Championships held at the NSC Sports Complex in Kuala Lumpur, 2002.

NAAM founding president Tan Sri Arshad Ayub.

NAAM president as at 2008 Tan Sri Abdul Halil Abdul Mutalib.

NAAM logo.

Mohd Marbawi Sulaiman being carried by fellow archers after winning two gold medals at the SEA Games in Vietnam, 2003.

An enduring tradition

Throughout the ancient world, bows and arrows were commonly used in hunting and combat. The first known organized archery competition was held in England in 1583 and involved 3000 participants. By the 17th century, gunfire had rendered the bow obsolete as a weapon and archery began to be practised solely as a form of recreation.

Archery has since developed into a competitive sport and was included in the first modern Olympic Games in 1896. The international governing body, Fédération Internationale de Tir à l'Arc (FITA), was formed in 1931.

Local archery

During the 1970s, the sport of archery was brought to Malaysia by individuals who had been exposed to it while they were living overseas in America or Europe. Upon their return, they started archery clubs and competitions among themselves.

The Malaysian Armed Forces Cricket Ground in Kuala Lumpur, the Penang Botanical Gardens and the Chinese Recreation Club in Penang functioned as the first archery fields in the country.

The National Archery Association of Malaysia (NAAM), formed in 1975 by members of the Selangor Bowman Club and the Armed Forces Archery Association, oversees the organization and development of the sport in the country. Originally there were only six organizations registered under the NAAM, but the association has grown to encompass 21 organizations. Youth archers are registered with the Malaysian Schools Sports Council, which conducts archery programmes and competitions for students.

Since 1987, the NAAM has conducted annual archery championships which have functioned as the platform through which the best archers are chosen to represent the country at the international level.

International marks

Archery was introduced as an event at the 1977 SEA Games in Kuala Lumpur. Malaysian Cheng Jun won three silver medals. Malaysia took part in archery at the Asian Games for the first time in Bangkok in 1978 and Malaysian archer Remy Yap won a silver medal in the 30-metre

event. At the 2003 SEA Games in Vietnam, Mohd Marbawi Sulaiman and Mon Redee Sut Txi captured two gold medals and two silver medals respectively in the individual and team events. Mon Redee Sut Txi qualified for the Olympic Games in Athens in 2004, becoming the first Malaysian archer to reach the pinnacle of the sport.

At the 2005 SEA Games in Manila, Lang Hon Keong and Ting Leong Fan won one gold and one silver medal respectively and the men's team won the gold in the inaugural compound event. Wan Mohd Khalmizan Wan Abdul Aziz bagged a silver medal in the recurve competition. At the 2007 SEA Games in Thailand, Cheng Chu Sian and Wan Mohd Khalmizan Wan Abdul Aziz won a gold and silver respectively in the men's recurve and Malaysia won a gold, silver and a bronze in the men's recurve, women's recurve and men's compound events respectively. Three Malaysian archers—Cheng Chu Sian, Mohd Marbawi Sulaiman and Wan Mohd Khalmizan Wan Abdul Aziz—have qualified for the 2008 Olympic Games.

Outdoor target archery

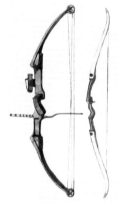

The compound bow, (left) which utilizes a more complex system of levers and cables, is permitted in some Paralympic Games. The recurve bow (right) is the only bow allowed in the Olympic Games.

Individual competition

During the qualification round, arrows are shot in bunches or ends of three to six from distances ranging from 30 to 90 metres at 80- and 122-centimetre diameter target faces. The top archers advance to the elimination round in which the only distance is 70 metres for both men and women and the face of the target is 122 centimetres. Competitors are allotted a set time in which to shoot each end.

Team competition

Teams of three shoot at a 122-centimetre target placed 70 metres away for both men and women. One match consists of three ends of nine arrows. Each team member shoots three arrows per end and all three archers are required to finish shooting before the prescribed time limit of three minutes.

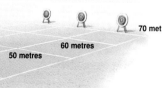

70 met
60 metres
50 metres
30 metres

Shooting

Initially limited to police and military personnel in the early 1900s, the sport of shooting gradually found its way into the public domain through plantation owners and hunters. Local shooters actively compete in the sport at various local and international competitions.

Nurul Hudda Baharin, winner of a Commonwealth Games gold medal in 1998, participating in a shooting competition at the Subang shooting range in 2003.

Establishing a tradition

Shooting competitions date back to the 11th century in Europe, but the modern practice of sport shooting began in the 19th century with the development of shooting equipment and the formation of many national shooting federations. At the first Olympic Games in 1896 in Athens, shooting had the highest number of participants of any sport. The first shooting world championship was held the following year in France.

Formed in 1907, the International Shooting Sport Federation (ISSF), the world governing body, comprises 157 national federations from 137 affiliated countries.

NSAM founding president Tan Sri S.M. Yong.

NSAM president as at 2008 Ally T.H. Ong.

NSAM logo.

Taking the sport public

Among the earliest recorded shooting competitions in Malaya were the Hannigan and Warren Shields, held in the early 1900s. However, only police personnel were eligible to participate in these contests. Shooting was introduced to civilians only in 1925 when the Penang Free School's cadets were allowed to try out the sport after being given proper training. As shooting grew in popularity, enthusiasts, especially police personnel, felt that there was a need to organize inter-state competitions. Thus, the Osborne Shield, the unofficial national competition, was created in 1930 and continued until the Japanese Occupation of Malaya from 1941 to 1945. After the occupation, British military

personnel and plantation owners along with local hunters revived sport shooting with impromptu competitions, but it was regarded more as a hobby than a sport.

Popular interest in shooting led to the construction of a makeshift shooting range at the Wardieburn Camp in Kuala Lumpur where some British units were stationed in the late 1940s and 1950s. In 1948, a group of local licensed gun owners, led by former Chief Justice of Malaya Tan Sri S.M. Yong, formed the Selangor Shooting Association (SSA). In 1949, Yong became the founding president of the National Shooting Association of Malaya (NSAM), which initially shared the same shooting range with the SSA.

The association's name was changed to the Federation of Malaya Shooting Association, but with the formation of Malaysia in 1963 it was renamed the National Shooting Association of Malaysia.

In 1965, the NSAM's range in Kuala Lumpur was relocated to Subang while, in the same year, Tun Tan Siew Sin, the then finance minister of Malaysia, took over as the president of the NSAM.

The NSAM has regularly organized national competitions at both senior and junior levels as well as international shooting championships including the SEA Games, Asian Shooting Championships and Commonwealth Games.

TOP: Shooting team from the 1939 Warren Shield rifle competition at the Johor police training centre.

ABOVE: Tun Tan Siew Sin, finance minister and president of the National Shooting Association of Malaysia, showcasing his shooting skills at the Seremban shooting range, 1966.

International achievements

Since 1959, Malaysian shooters have consistently brought back medals from the SEA Games, Asian Games and Commonwealth Games. The highest international achievement by a Malaysian shooter was by Nurul Hudda Baharin who won a gold medal in the women's air rifle event at the 1998 Commonwealth Games in Kuala Lumpur. Prior to this, trap shooter Peter Lim won an individual silver medal at the Asian Games in Seoul in 1986. In other competitions, Abdul Mutalib Abdul Razak and Jasni Shaari won gold medals at the Second Commonwealth Shooting Federation Championships held in Langkawi in 1997 in the three positions pairs event. Mohd Emran Zakaria captured an individual gold medal in the air rifle men's event at the Third Commonwealth Shooting Federation Championships in Auckland in 1999.

1. Irina Maharani showing off the two gold medals she won in the women's 10-metre air pistol event at the SEA Games in Kuala Lumpur, 2001.

2. Trap shooters Bernard Yeoh (left) and Charles Chen preparing to compete at the 2006 Commonwealth Games.

3. Mohd Hameleay Abdul Mutalib firing his air rifle during the Asian Games in 2006.

Olympic shooting events

Trap, double trap and skeet (shotgun)

300-metre and 50-metre free rifle

10-metre air rifle

25-metre rapid fire pistol

50-metre free pistol

10-metre air pistol

Pétanque

An open space, a small wooden jack, metal boules and a couple of companions is all that one needs to begin playing pétanque. This French game is a variation of English bowls and Italian bocce and can be enjoyed by children and adults alike. Initially only popular in Europe, pétanque has spread to other parts of the world and is now played both as a recreational pastime and competitive sport.

National pétanque team players practising the throwing motion, 2003.

Dato' Sri Najib Tun Razak (right) and Royal Professor Ungku A. Aziz at the launch of pétanque in Malaysia in Petaling Jaya, 1990.

BELOW LEFT: President of the Pétanque Federation of Malaysia (PFM) as at 2008 Dato' Seri Shahidan Kassim.

BELOW RIGHT: PFM logo.

BOTTOM: National pétanque team member Mohd Firdaus Adli Mohd Bakri training for the SEA Games in Vietnam, 2003.

Early history

Pétanque was developed in the early 1900s in southern France from *jeu provençal,* the local game of bowls, which involved taking a two-step run-up before releasing the ball. But pétanque was invented after Jules LeNoir, a keen *jeu provençal* player, was involved in an accident and confined to a wheelchair. His caring fellow villagers decided to modify the rules of the game so that no run-up was required and the length of the pitch was shortened. The player's feet had to be placed together in a circle, a position described as *pieds tanqués* (stuck feet). The international pétanque body, Fédération Internationale de Pétanque et Jeu Provençal, was founded in 1958 in Marseille and the first world championships were organized in 1959 in Belgium.

A new sport for the masses

Pétanque was introduced to Malaysia in 1987. In 1989, Royal Professor Ungku A. Aziz, president of ANGKASA (the National Apex Co-operative of Malaysia), promoted the game among cooperative societies in several states and schools. In 1990, pétanque was officially declared a sport by the Minister of Youth and Sports, and in 1991 ANGKASA started to organize tournaments and programmes. In 1993, the Ministry of Youth and Sports declared pétanque a new mass sport under the 'Sport for All' campaign. The Pétanque Federation of Malaysia (PFM) was formed in 1996 to ensure that the sport developed widespread appeal in Malaysia.

Pétanque was first introduced as an event at the SEA Games in 2001 in Kuala Lumpur. Malaysian pétanque players have won two silver medals and seven bronze medals in SEA Games competitions since then. In 2002, Malaysia played host to the Asian Pétanque Championships.

Pétanque is gaining popularity locally as a way of promoting a healthy lifestyle. In 2005, over 1600 adult cooperative members took part in the annual pétanque competition and more than 2500 students participated in pétanque contests. As at January 2006, a total of 38,222 individuals nationwide had attended ANGKASA pétanque workshops.

Pétanque game play

Participants competing in a pétanque tournament in Penang, 2004.

The court

Competition standards require a marked terrain of 4 metres by 15 metres as the minimum dimension for game play. Players may double the court size to make the game more challenging.

Equipment

Pétanque is played with two main pieces of equipment: metal *boules* and a jack or *cochonnet* ('piglet'). According to the official specifications, *boules* are each fashioned from metal with a diameter of 7–8 centimetres and a weight of between 0.65–0.80 kilograms. The jack is a light wooden ball measuring 25–35 millimetres in diameter.

Wooden jack surrounded by metal *boules*.

Game play

Pétanque is played by two teams, ranging from one to three players a side. Players are each allotted three *boules*, except in the triples game, when each player is given only two *boules*.

The starting position for a game is determined by first drawing a circle 0.5 metre in diameter on the playing field. The first player tosses the jack from within this circle to a distance of about 6–10 metres away. Both feet must be in the circle and on the ground while throwing the jack. The same player or a team-mate then throws the first *boule*. This is followed by a player from the opposite team. The next player is decided based on whose *boule* is furthest from the jack.

Players may attempt to hit and displace their opponent's *boule* with their own so that their teammates have a better chance of scoring a point. The aim of the game is to throw the *boule* as close as possible to the jack. This is done by placing the *boule* in such a position, or by knocking away the opponent's *boule*. The end continues until all *boules* have been thrown. The team with the closest *boule* or *boules* to the jack wins that end. For every *boule* closest to the jack, the winning team earns one point. The game proceeds until one of the teams scores 13 points.

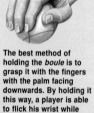

The best method of holding the *boule* is to grasp it with the fingers with the palm facing downwards. By holding it this way, a player is able to flick his wrist while throwing and impart a backspin to the *boule* so that it stops quickly upon landing.

The distance between the jack and the *boule* is measured to determine the winner.

Woodball

A simple and affordable game, woodball has managed to attract players of all ages and even families to play it together. Mastery of the game has led Malaysian players to compete in various tournaments both within the country and on the international stage.

Ariffin Mamat, the men's singles champion, preparing to strike the ball with his mallet during the Malaysian Woodball International Open Championships at the Lanjut Golf and Beach Resort in Pahang, 2003.

A new sport

Since its invention in 1990 in Taiwan, woodball has grown from a recreational game into a major competitive sport played in 22 countries around the world. In 1999, great strides were achieved with the establishment of the Asian Woodball Federation, the European Woodball Federation and the International Woodball Federation, the world governing body of the sport. The same year also saw the game recognized as a legitimate sporting event by the Asian Olympic Council.

The establishment of the local game

Woodball made its way to Malaysia in 1995 through the efforts of Thomas Kok, an avid player, who promoted the game in the country. Public response was so enthusiastic that in 1996 Malaysia's first woodball course, the 24-gate OUG Woodball Garden course, was built in Kuala Lumpur. The Association of Woodball Recreation, Kuala Lumpur was established in 1995. However, as the game continued attracting players from all over the country, the need for a national governing body became evident. Consequently, the name of the association was changed to the Malaysia Woodball Association in 1999.

As of 2008, there are a total of 13 woodball courses in Malaysia, the majority of which are concentrated in Pahang. These include a world-class course, the 24-gate Lanjut Beach Resort Woodball Course in Pahang, which has been the venue of numerous local and international tournaments.

Malaysia was given the honour of hosting the inaugural Asian Woodball Championship in 1999 and the Second World Cup Woodball Championship Woodball World Cup in 2006. The Malaysian Woodball International Open Championships have been held annually since 1997, and Malaysian woodballers have captured the gold medal in the men's category every year.

Above left: Founding president of the Malaysia Woodball Association Thomas Kok.

Above right: President of the Malaysia Woodball Association as at 2008 Yee Teng Lai.

Logo of the Malaysia Woodball Association.

Woodball equipment

Woodball must be played on an even, smooth surface, either clay or a turfed area such as in a public park or garden. Natural objects on the course such as trees, groves or mounds can be used as obstacles or boundary lines and spectators are to stand behind these boundary lines. The other boundaries of the playing area, including gates, a tee box, fairway and a green, must also be marked.

There are only three inexpensive pieces of equipment required to play woodball:

Ball   A 9.5-cm sphere made of natural wood weighing between 290 and 360 grams.

Mallet   A T-shaped club that has a long wooden shaft as its handle and is attached to a bottle shaped head with a rubber-capped striking surface.

Gate   The E-shaped gate comprises a wooden cup-shaped object suspended between two pegged wooden 'bottles' by a rotating steel shaft. The lowest part of the cup must be 7 centimetres above the ground.

In order to complete a game, a player must hit or putt a ball through a 16-centimetre wide gate.

How to play woodball

Players have to hit a solid wooden ball with a mallet or a T-shaped club from a 'tee box' towards the scoring gate which is placed on the green. Any ball that rolls outside the boundary line is referred to as 'out of bounds' and is assessed a penalty by adding one stroke to the player's score. The player completes each gate by hitting the ball through the scoring gate. Each strike of the ball is considered a stroke and, like golf, the objective of the game is to take the lowest number of strokes to complete a gate.

The woodball course

A woodball course comprises 12 fairways which can be rectilinear or in a curviform shape according to the features of the land. At least four of the fairways must be curved, two to the right and two to the left. The width of the fairway should not be narrower than 3 metres or wider than 10 metres at the turn of the fairway. Generally, fairway distances are between 40 metres and 130 metres depending on the par rating of the gate. Par is calculated based on the number of strokes it takes for a professional level player to complete the gate from the tee, through the fairway and finishing at the green. There should be at least two long-distance and two short-distance fairways.

At the start of every fairway, a horizontal line marks the 2-metre starting line, at the ends of which a 3-metre line is drawn backwards to form a rectangular starting area called the 'tee box'. With the gate in the centre, the gate area at the end of a fairway is marked off in a circle 5 metres in diameter. A buffer zone of 2 metres lies between the circumference of the gate area and the fairway boundary. Standard woodball courses are made up of 12 gates.

South China Sea

PENINSULAR MALAYSIA

Pahang

Strait of Melaka

Lanjut Golf and Beach Resort •

N

0   100 km

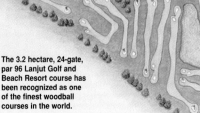

The 3.2 hectare, 24-gate, par 96 Lanjut Golf and Beach Resort course has been recognized as one of the finest woodball courses in the world.

1. Watson Nyambek (second from right), Malaysian 100-metre record holder, competing in the Asian Athletic Championships in Jakarta, 2000.

2. Zaiton Othman taking off during a heptathlon high jump competition, 1983.

3. Wong Tee Kue in his gold medal performance in the hammer event at the 1999 SEA Games in Brunei.

4. Nur Herman Majid (right) clearing a hurdle on his way to a gold medal at the 1999 SEA Games in Brunei.

5. Marina Chin (foreground), 1976 and 1977 National Sportswoman of the Year, won gold medals in the 100-metre hurdles and 4x100 relay events at the 1979 SEA Games. In 2007, she was appointed as the principal of the Bukit Jalil Sports School.

6. Nashatar Singh, winner of the 1966 Asian Games javelin gold medal, taking part in the Selangor Police Athletics Meeting at Stadium Merdeka, 1964.

7. Participants in the International Penang Bridge Run, 2001.

8. Competitors run into the water at the start of the swimming leg of the 2007 Port Dickson triathlon.

9. M. Jegathesan (second from left) showing his three Asian Games gold medals to some young fans upon his return from the competition in Bangkok, 1966.

10. Tan Sri Ghazali Shafie, president of the Malaysian Amateur Athletics Union, holding his award for excellence in sports leadership, 1979.

ATHLETICS

Athletics remains the simplest and purest form of sport, testing and pushing the limits of human physical capacities. Track and field events are multi-faceted spectacles that demand peak performances on the part of their participants. These events were an important component of Malaya's pre-Independence social fabric, and were perceived by the British as a means of instilling national pride and unity. Ipoh, Perak is where the seeds of track and field in Malaya were first planted with the staging of a formal meet in 1906. Competitions were conducted primarily at the school level in subsequent decades, producing a large crop of local athletes. In the first half of the 20th century, L.D.E. Cullen, Poh Kim Seng, Alam Sher, Alladad Khan, Lee Fun, N. Manickavasagam, Tai Swee Kee, Kee Yong Chin and Sidique Ali Merican grabbed the limelight and set the standard for athletics in the country.

Rahim Ahmad's bronze medal in the 400-metre event at the 1958 Asian Games in Tokyo was a breakthrough performance, heralding Malaya's entry into the international athletics arena. In 1966, M. Jegathesan, M. Rajamani and Nashatar Singh established Malaysia as an Asian athletics powerhouse, winning five Asian Games gold medals between them. By virtue of his victory in the 100-metre race, Jegathesan claimed the title of 'the fastest man in Asia' in 1966 and went on to compete with distinction in three consecutive Olympic Games. In subsequent decades, athletes such as Ishtiaq Mobarak, Saik Oik Cum, Rabuan Pit, Marina Chin and Watson Nyambek have carried on this tradition of success.

Hare and Hounds style chases have been around for centuries in one form or another. The original concept was to mimic the sport of hunting sport when sporting game was sparse and substitute the hounds with runners. In 1938, a Malayan version of the Hare and Hounds, called hashing, was created by a group of British expatriates. This home-grown game persevered through World War II and the Emergency and has grown to encompass 2500 chapters globally.

Roslinda Samsu competing in the women's pole vault final at the 2006 Asian Games in Doha. She took home the silver medal.

In terms of equipment, running requires little more than a pair of shoes, which may explain the enthusiasm with which Malaysians sign up for marathons and walks. The *Malay Mail* Big Walk, dating back to 1960, is the oldest active event in Malaysia, while the annual Kuala Lumpur International Marathon attracts runners from all over the world.

Triathlons have also garnered a significant following since their debut in Penang in 1989, making the three-discipline events, as well as marathons, the foremost sports tourism attractions in Malaysia. The Ironman Malaysia Triathlon, held annually in Langkawi since 2000, is rated internationally as one of the toughest Ironman challenges and attracts the sport's top competitors.

Track and field

Introduced to Malaya by the British in the early 1900s, athletics has maintained a prominent place in local sports culture. The Malaysian Amateur Althletics Union (MAAU), initially formed in 1920, has spearheaded the growth of the sport locally. The 1960s marked the highpoint of Malaysian athletics when athletes were conspicuous in their presence in society and distinguished in their performances on the track and field. Subsequent generations have carried on this tradition of athletic excellence, capturing medals in numerous international competitions.

ABOVE LEFT: M. Rajamani crossing the finish line to win the 800-metre gold medal at the 1968 SEAP Games in Bangkok.

ABOVE RIGHT: Rabuan Pit running the final leg of the 4x100-metre relay during the ASEAN Athletic Championships at Stadium Merdeka, 1980.

Participant in a long-jump competition during an athletic meet in Perak in the early 1900s.

TOP: MAAU logo.

ABOVE LEFT: MAAU founding president E.M. MacDonald.

ABOVE RIGHT: MAAU president as at 2008 Dato' Seri Shahidan Kassim.

Origins

The term 'athletics' is derived from the Greek word *athlos*, which means contest, and has come to refer to competitions involving physical strength, skill and endurance. Many athletic events have ancient origins and were organized in competitive form by the ancient Greeks. Running, jumping and throwing contests had been conducted on an informal basis in most cultures but gained worldwide prominence when they were included in the first modern Olympic Games in 1896.

The British legacy

Athletics was formally established in Malaya in the early 1900s by the British, who regarded the sport as a stimulus to nationhood. Organized meets involving Europeans, uniformed units and servicemen were a prominent feature at that time. In 1906, the first local athletics body, the Ipoh Athletic Association, was formed and the first meet was held that same year in Ipoh. Competitions were confined to various European sports clubs in Perak, Selangor, Negeri Sembilan and Pahang and continued until the outbreak of World War I.

In 1920, the first inter-state championship meeting was held in Kuala Lumpur, open to all amateur athletes, irrespective of nationality, who resided in the Federated Malay States (FMS) and Straits Settlements. The Amateur Athletics Association of British Malaya (AAABM) was formed in 1920 in Kuala Lumpur, and its task was to organize these inter-state competitions. The founding president of AAABM was Oliver Marks, and as a reflection of the primacy of athletics in society, the presidency was subsequently held by various Chief Secretaries, among them Sir W. George Maxwell (1922–26), Sir William Peel (1927–29), Sir Andrew Caldecott (1931–32) and Malcolm Bond Shelley (1933–34). During Caldecott's tenure, AAABM was renamed the Amateur Athletics Association of Malaya (AAAM).

In 1949, athletics activities, which had ceased during World War II, were restarted and AAAM was re-designated as the Federation of Malaya Amateur Athletic Union (FMAAU) in 1953. FMAAU was dissolved in 1963 to make way for the Malaysian Amateur Athletics Union (MAAU) following the formation of Malaysia. From 1963 to 1988, Tan Sri Ghazali Shafie served as MAAU president.

M. Jegathesan

LEFT: M. Jegathesan (third from left) winning the 200-metre event during the Asian Games in Jakarta, 1962.

BELOW: M. Jegathesan standing on the podium after receiving his gold medal, 1962.

The centre stage in athletics in the 1960s belonged to three-time Olympian Dr M. Jegathesan. He won the gold medal in the 200-metre event at the 1962 Asian Games in Jakarta, and became Malaysia's first ever Olympic semi-finalist in the men's 200 metres at the 1964 Tokyo Olympic Games. At the 1966 Asian Games, Jegathesan won the men's 100-metre gold medal, thereby earning himself the title of the fastest man in Asia. He also captured the 200-metre gold and the 4x100m relay gold. Jegathesan competed in three consecutive Olympic games from 1960 to 1968. His time of 20.92 in the 200-metre race during the semi-finals at the 1968 Olympic Games in Mexico City still stands as a Malaysian record. In 1984, Jegathesan authored a book entitled *A Decade on Cinders* which chronicles his achievements on and off the track in the 1960s.

Athletics success

Rahim Ahmad's bronze medal in the 400-metre race in the 1958 Asian Games in Tokyo was the first ever Malaysian medal in the Asian Games and heralded the country's entry into the international athletics arena. Two years earlier, Rahim earned the right to compete at the Melbourne Olympic Games when he clocked 49.9 seconds in the 440-yard event in the qualifying meet, erasing Irishman L.D.E. Cullen's record that had stood for 25 years.

After capturing the 200-metre gold medal at the 1962 Asian Games in Jakarta, M. Jegathesan became an Olympic Games semi-finalist in the 200-metre event in 1964. He won three gold medals at the Asian games in Bangkok in 1966. M. Rajamani became Malaysia's first woman Asian Games gold medallist when she won the 400-metre race that same year. Both athletes went on to distinguished careers in athletics, establishing themselves and their country on the international scene.

The Asian Games in 1966 proved to be a watershed moment for Malaysian athletics, as the national team collected a total of five gold medals. In addition to the medals won by M. Jegathesan and M. Rajamani, Nashatar Singh bagged an Asian Games gold medal in the javelin event, and the men's 4x100 relay team captured the gold.

Carrying on the tradition

After winning a silver medal in the 1974 Asian games, Ishtiaq Mobarak went on to appear in the

Saik Oik Cum standing on the podium after capturing the women's 400-metre gold medal at the 1978 Asian Games in Bangkok.

semi-finals of the 110-metre hurdles at the 1976 Olympic Games in Montreal. His time in the event stood as a Malaysian record for 20 years, until it was broken by Nur Herman Majid, who finished in 13.73 seconds on his way to a bronze medal at the 1994 Asian Games in Hiroshima.

M. Rajamani's feat as Asia's top woman 400-metre runner was repeated 12 years later, when 17-year-old Saik Oik Cum covered the one-lap race in 55.09 seconds and took home the goldfrom the 1978 Asian Games in Bangkok.

Almost two decades after M. Jegathesan blazed a trail into the record books, the Asian athletics world was shocked when a Malaysian policeman, Rabuan Pit, won the 100-metre gold at the 1982 Asian Games in New Delhi.

Recent achievements

Watson Nyambek, a Sarawakian sprinter whose time of 10.30 seconds in the 100-metre dash still stands as a national record, won a silver medal at the Asian Athletics Championships in Japan in 1998.

When the Commonwealth Games were held in Kuala Lumpur in 1998, race walker G. Saravanan

The purest form of sports

Athletics is the purest form of sports, comprising an array of events that involve running, jumping and throwing. These events are the perfect representation of the Olympic motto: '*Citius, Altius, Fortius*' (Faster, Higher, Stronger). Athletes measure themselves against the clock, the bar or the distance. Athletic events remain the focal point of many multi-sports festivals, particularly the Olympic Games. In formal competitions, athletics can be split into four main categories: track events, field events, road events and combined events.

ABOVE: Stadium at Bukit Jalil which functioned as the venue for track and field events during the Commonwealth Games, 1998.

BELOW: Steeplechase event at the SEA Games in Kuala Lumpur, 2001.

Track events take place on a 400-metre outdoor track in the main stadium. Short distance events include the 100-metre, 200-metre, 400-metre, 4x100-metre relay and 4x400-metre relay races, while middle distance events comprise the 800-metre, 1500-metre and 3,000-metre contests. A steeplechase is a 3,000-metre race in which runners must negotiate barriers and water jumps. For long distance runs, common events are 5,000-metre and 10,000-metre competitions. High hurdle events consist of the 110-metre (100 metres for women) and 400-metre hurdles.

Field events, comprising throwing and jumping competitions, are tests of brute strength, speed and agility. The throwing events are shot put, hammer, javelin, discus, while high jump, pole vault, long jump and triple jump fall under the umbrella of jumping events.

Road events are long distance running or walking races that are conducted on public roads, although they often finish on the track inside the stadium. Running races include the 5-kilometre, 10-kilometre, half-marathon and marathon events, and, less commonly, the 15-kilometre, 20-kilometre, 10-mile and 20-mile contests. The most common events in race walking are the 10-kilometre, 20-kilometre and 50-kilometre races.

Combined events—the decathlon for men and heptathlon for women—feature a selection of track and field events that take place over two days and are designed to showcase the athletes with the best all-round talent. Participants' performances are judged on a point system in each event, not by the position achieved. The decathlon comprises ten track and field events which are conducted over the course of two consecutive days. The first day schedule includes the 100-metre race, long jump, shot put, high jump and 400-metre race. Day two consists of the 110-metre hurdles, discus, pole vault, javelin and the 1500-metre race. The first day of the heptathlon comprises the 100-metre hurdles, high jump, shot put and 200-metre race, while the second day includes the long jump, javelin throw and 800-metre race.

capitalized on his familiarity with the route around the Titiwangsa Lake to grab the men's 50-kilometre gold medal, Malaysia's first ever in the history of the event. Four years later, Yuan Yufang won a bronze medal in the women's 20-kilometre road walk event at the Commonwealth Games in Manchester.

After taking the bronze in the women's 400-metre hurdles in the 2000 Asian Athletics Championship, Noraseela Mohd Khalid bagged the bronze at the Doha Asian Games in 2006. One year after she set a new SEA Games women's pole vault record of 4.10 metres, Roslinda Samsu captured a silver medal at the Asian Games in Doha in 2006.

G. Saravanan celebrating with fans after his surprise victory in the men's 50-kilometre road walk event at the Commonwealth Games in Kuala Lumpur, 1998.

Ishtiaq Mobarak (left) clearing a hurdle in the final of the 110-metre race during the SEA Games at Stadium Merdeka, 1977. He won the gold medal.

National athletics records

The 1960s is often referred to as the 'golden age' of Malaysian athletics, when local athletes set the standard for track and field events in the country. Subsequent decades, however, have witnessed the emergence of outstanding athletes who have surpassed the achievements of their predecessors. Only one record from the 'golden age', M. Jegathesan's time in the 200-metre event at the 1968 Olympic Games, still stands today.

Opening ceremony of the SEAP Games at Stadium Merdeka in Kuala Lumpur, 1965.

M. Ramachandran leading the pack on his way to winning a gold medal at the SEA Games in Brunei, 1999.

■ : Men
■ : Women

EVENT	DISTANCE	NAME	LOCATION	DATE
Pole vault	5.00 metres	Teh Weng Chang	Kuala Lumpur	24/03/2002
Pole vault	4.40 metres	Roslinda Samsu	Barcelona	17/06/2006

EVENT	TIME	NAME	LOCATION	DATE
1500 metres	3:45.70s	M. Vadivellan	Korat	11/12/2007
1500 metres	4:23.49s	P. Jayanthi	New Delhi	14/09/1993
3000 metres	8:59.10s	N. Shanmuganathan	Kuala Lumpur	17/09/1998
3000 metres	9:18.42s	P. Jayanthi	Germany	14/08/1993
5000 metres	14:06.84s	M. Ramachandran	Germany	05/08/1994
5000 metres	16:18.12s	Yuan Yufang	Jakarta	13/10/1997
10,000 metres	29:30.19s	M. Ramachandran	Victoria	27/08/1994
10,000 metres	33:50.80s	P. Jayanthi	Brussels	16/07/1994

EVENT	DISTANCE	NAME	LOCATION	DATE
Shot put	16.67 metres	Mohd Nazar Abd Rahim	Penang	19/08/1995
Shot put	14.41 metres	Lee Chew Har	Kuala Lumpur	15/07/1989
Discus	49.33 metres	Ngu Kit Min	Penang	11/09/2006
Discus	42.79 metres	Yap Jeng Tzan	Penang	21/09/2006

Nazmizan Muhamad (second from right) crossing the finish line first to win the 100-metre gold medal at the SEA Games in Hanoi, 2003.

EVENT	TIME	NAME	LOCATION	DATE
110-metre hurdles	13.73s	Nur Herman Majid	Hiroshima	15/10/1994
100-metre hurdles	13.39s	Moh Siew Wei	Manila	26/05/2002
400-metre hurdles	51.83s	M. Ravinthiran	Perlis	20/08/1996
400-metre hurdles	56.02s	Noraseela Khalid	Germany	17/06/2006
3000-metre hurdles	11:43.79s	Vally Michael	Seremban	04/06/2004

EVENT	TIME	NAME	LOCATION	DATE
4x100-metre relay	39.83s	Watson Nyambek Azmi Ibrahim Nazmizan Muhamad R. Ganeshwaran	Kuala Lumpur	15/09/2001
4x100-metre relay	45.37s	Anita Ali G. Shanti Sajaratuldur Hamzah Mumtaz Jaafar	Kuala Lumpur	24/08/1989
4x400-metre relay	3:06.69s	Azhar Hashim Mohd Yazid Parlan V. Samson Nordin Jadi	Kuala Lumpur	23/10/1991
4x400-metre relay	3:35.83s	R. Shanti Josephine Mary G. Shanti Rabia Abd. Salam	Singapore	17/06/1993

ABOVE: Moh Siew Wei (second from right) on her way to winning the gold medal in the women's 100-metre hurdle event at the SEA Games in Manila, 2005.

RIGHT: Noraseela Khalid clearing the last hurdle to win the 400-metre hurdle gold at the SEA Games in Hanoi, 2003.

EVENT	POINTS	NAME	LOCATION	DATE
Decathon	6989 points	Mohd Malik Tobias	Brunei	09/08/1999
Pentathlon	2657 points	Pok Chee Sing	Kuala Lumpur	01/08/1998
Heptathlon	5175 points	Zaiton Othman	Manila	11–12/12/1981

FAR LEFT: Siti Shahida Abdullah throwing a hammer during a competition in Pahang, 2007.

LEFT: Norsham Yoon throwing a javelin, 1989.

EVENT	DISTANCE	NAME	LOCATION	DATE
Hammer	58.52 metres	Wong Tee Kue	Singapore	05/09/1993
Hammer	53.35 metres	Siti Shahida Abdullah	Manila	30/11/2005
Javelin	73.34 metres	Mohd Yazid Imran	Singapore	02/09/1995
Javelin	47.50 metres	Norsham Yoon	Kuala Lumpur	23/08/1989
High jump	2.24 metres	Loo Kum Zee	Chiang Mai	14/12/1995
High jump	1.78 metres	Shabana Khanum Jalal Din	Bangkok	05/05/2005

EVENT	TIME	NAME	LOCATION	DATE
Marathon	2:29:27s	K. Baskaran	Singapore	02/12/2001
Marathon	2:49:28s	Yuan Yufang	Kuala Lumpur	30/04/2002
10-kilometre road walk	42:36.00s	Teoh Boon Lim	Germany	11/05/1996
10-kilometre road walk	45:27.00s	Cheng Tong Lean	Prague	20/04/1997
20-kilometre road walk	1:24:50s	Narinder Singh	Prague	19/04/1997
20-kilometre road walk	1:32:25s	Yuan Yufang	Manila	23/09/2003
50-kilometre road walk	4:10:05s	G. Saravanan	Kuala Lumpur	21/09/1998
5000-metre track walk	21:30.9s	Yuan Yufang	Kuala Lumpur	08/03/1998
10,000-metre track walk	43:03.02s	R. Mogan	Seremban	10/05/1997
10,000-metre track walk	45:22.05s	Yuan Yufang	Brunei	09/08/1999
20,000-metre track walk	1:30:43s	B. Thirukumaran	Perlis	02/03/1997
20,000-metre track walk	1:39:58s	Yuan Yufang	Kuala Lumpur	04/04/1999

ABOVE LEFT: Narinder Singh (right) and Teoh Boon Lim walking during the final of the men's 20-kilometre walk at the 1999 SEA Games in Brunei. Narinder took the gold medal, while Teoh finished with a silver medal.

ABOVE RIGHT: Yuan Yufang making her way to the finish line during the women's 20-kilometre walk at the Commonwealth Games in Manchester, 2002. She took third place in the event.

Loo Kum Zee clearing the bar to win the gold medal in the men's high jump event at the 1999 SEA Games in Brunei.

EVENT	TIME	NAME	LOCATION	DATE
100 metres	10.30s	Watson Nyambek	Kuala Lumpur	15/07/1998
100 metres	11.50s	G. Shanti	Kuala Lumpur	07/05/1993
200 metres	20.92s	M. Jegathesan	Mexico City	15/10/1968
200 metres	23.37s	G. Shanti	Fukuoka	22/07/1998
400 metres	46.41s	Mohd Zaiful Zainal Abidin	Brunei	20/07/2001
400 metres	52.56s	Rabia Abdul Salam	Manila	03/12/1993
800 metres	1:47.37s	B. Rajkumar	Jakarta	26/09/1985
800 metres	2:07.44s	Josephine Mary	Seoul	30/09/1986

FAR LEFT: Mohd Zaki Sadri celebrating after winning the men's long jump event at the SEA Games in Hanoi, 1997.

LEFT: Ngew Sin Mei making an attempt during the women's triple jump event at the 2006 Asian Games in Doha.

EVENT	DISTANCE	NAME	LOCATION	DATE
Long jump	7.88 metres	Josbert Tinus	Bangkok	09/06/2007
Long jump	6.27 metres	Ngew Sin Mei	Manila	09/09/2004
Triple jump	16.29 metres	Mohd Zaki Sadri	Kuala Lumpur	21/08/1989
Triple jump	13.74 metres	Ngew Sin Mei	Kuala Lumpur	10/09/2004

ABOVE: G. Shanti (right) crossing the finish line to win the women's 200-metre final at the 1997 SEA Games in Jakarta.

RIGHT: Watson Nyambek sprinting to a new national record in the 100-metre event, 1995.

Triathlon

One of the most gruelling events in the sporting world, the triathlon pushes physical and mental abilities to the limit in a test of sporting endurance. Malaysians have risen to the triathlon challenge and have competed internationally in this three-part racing event. With a prestigious Ironman triathlon event held annually in Langkawi, Malaysia has become a popular destination for international triathletes.

Logo of Triathlon Malaysia.

ABOVE LEFT: Datuk Irene Benggon Chararuks, founding president of Triathlon Malaysia.

ABOVE RIGHT: Cheah Choon Nam, president of Triathlon Malaysia as at 2008.

A multi-discipline sport

Triathlon is a three-part sports discipline comprising swimming, cycling and running. The three sports are contested as one continuous event without cessation. Changeovers or transitions between the sports are vital to the triathlete's race strategy and success. The triathlon can be conducted as an individual or team relay event over varying distances.

Triathlon history can be traced back to the early 1970s in Mission Bay, Southern California, where a group of runners, swimmers and cyclists competed in races during training sessions. The first triathlon was held in Mission Bay in 1974 with 46 athletes participating.

Triathlon races are held over four distances: sprint, Olympic, long course and ultra. The Olympic triathlon comprises a 1.5-kilometre swim, a 40-kilometre bike ride and a 10-kilometre run.

In 1989, after several failed attempts, an international governing body for triathlon was

Malaysian triathlete Kimbeley Yap crossing the finish line and winning the gold medal at the 2007 SEA Games in Thailand. She finished 1 minute and 21 seconds ahead of her nearest competitor, clinching the SEA Games women's triathlon title for a second consecutive time.

formed. Representatives from 25 countries were present at the founding congress of the International Triathlon Union (ITU) in Avignon, France. The sport was included as an event for the first time at the 2000 Olympics in Sydney.

Since 2000, triathlon has gained inclusion in other major sporting events such as the Commonwealth Games, Asian Games and SEA Games. There are also many other triathlon competitions organized in Asia and beyond, such as the Asian Series and World Series.

Malaysia takes up the challenge

Triathlon came to Malaysia in the late 1980s. The Penang Swimming Club organized the first triathlon event in the country in 1989. Subsequently, many states including Sabah, Sarawak, Melaka, Perak, Johor, Terengganu, Negeri Sembilan, and Kedah as well as Kuala Lumpur held their own triathlon competitions. In 2000, the Sabah Tourism Board hosted the Asian Triathlon Championship in accordance with ITU standards. In an attempt to promote itself as a tourist destination, Desaru in Johor organized its first triathlon in 1995, which covered the Olympic set distance.

Triathlon Malaysia, the national governing body, was established in 1994 with Datuk Irene Benggon Chararuks as its founding president. Its president as at 2008 is Cheah Choon Nam.

Initiated in 2000, the annual Ironman Langkawi Malaysia Triathlon is the premier triathlon event in the country, attracting participants from all around the world.

Triathlon has reached the stage of popularity in Malaysia where even youths are encouraged to take up the challenge. Children as young as six years old have participated in sprint triathlon competitions.

A variation of the triathlon, the duathlon is a combination of running and biking. Duathlon competitions have been organized locally since 1986.

ABOVE RIGHT: Participants make a running start during the swimming segment of the Desaru International Triathlon in Johor, 2005.

RIGHT: Competitors cycling during the Desaru Pengerang Long Distance International Triathlon in Johor, 2000.

Ironman Langkawi Malaysia Triathlon

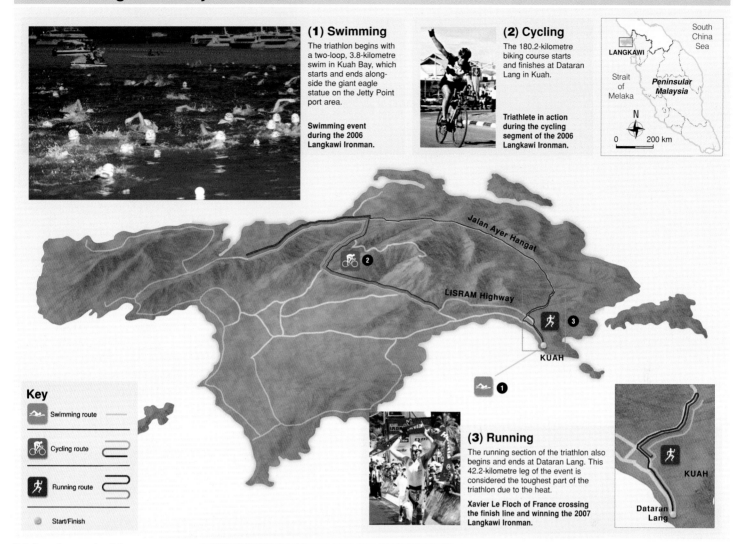

(1) Swimming

The triathlon begins with a two-loop, 3.8-kilometre swim in Kuah Bay, which starts and ends alongside the giant eagle statue on the Jetty Point port area.

Swimming event during the 2006 Langkawi Ironman.

(2) Cycling

The 180.2-kilometre biking course starts and finishes at Dataran Lang in Kuah.

Triathlete in action during the cycling segment of the 2006 Langkawi Ironman.

South China Sea

LANGKAWI

Strait of Melaka

Peninsular Malaysia

N

0   200 km

Jalan Ayer Hangat

LISRAM Highway

KUAH

Key

Swimming route

Cycling route

Running route

Start/Finish

(3) Running

The running section of the triathlon also begins and ends at Dataran Lang. This 42.2-kilometre leg of the event is considered the toughest part of the triathlon due to the heat.

Xavier Le Floch of France crossing the finish line and winning the 2007 Langkawi Ironman.

KUAH

Dataran Lang

Malaysian triathletes

Kimbeley Yap won gold medals in the women's triathlon events at the 2005 and 2007 SEA Games in the Philippines and Thailand respectively. Yap had only started her triathlon career six months prior to the 2005 event. In 2007, Yap received a scholarship from the International Triathlon Union (ITU) to train for the 2008 Olympic Games in Beijing.

In the men's triathlon, Loh Yeong Shang captured a silver medal at the Philippines SEA Games in 2005.

Eugene Chan is another prominent figure on the Malaysian triathlon scene. Trained by his father, Chan Chee Seng, Eugene has competed in numerous triathlon competitions throughout Asia, and has won many titles in the Asian Triathlon Series as well as Malaysian events.

Leading triathletes

1. Kimbeley Yap (left) cycling at the 2006 Asian Games in Doha.

2. Loh Yeong Shang (right) receiving his gold medal at the 2006 Desaru International Long Distance Triathlon.

3. Chan Chee Seng (right), one of Malaysia's most prominent triathletes, with his son Eugene, who competed in the triathlon event at the 2002 Commonwealth Games in Manchester.

4. Kimbeley Yap starting the swimming event during the 2005 SEA Games in Manila.

Hashing

Founded in the Hash House in 1938, the sport of hashing has become a global phenomenon. As at 2008, there are more than 2000 hash chapters worldwide. Its democratic nature and its emphasis on exercise and fellowship, always with a good dose of fun, have helped hashing attract people from diverse backgrounds and establish an international fraternity.

Cartoonist Lat's depiction of hashing from *Lat with a Punch*, 1988.

Participants off to a running start at the Seremban Open Hash Half Marathon, 1985.

Running the hash

The hash is sometimes referred to as a more 'civilized' form of the traditional English sport of fox hunting. The run begins with a chosen member of the group called a 'hare' laying out a trail over a long distance of varied terrain, marked with pieces of paper, chalk or flour. These trails lead to checkpoints the pack of 'harriers' must find in order to finish the run. Depending on the ingenuity of the hare, trails can be difficult to follow as there can be false or double-back trails leading the pack into circles or away from checkpoints. Trails can also be broken and dispersed up to a radius of 90 metres apart.

Hash terms

Down-Down:
The ceremony of quaffing a beverage.

Harriettes:
Female hashers.

Hazards:
Senior hashers

Knitting Circle:
Group of hashers who spend more time walking and talking than hashing.

Mismanagement:
Hash management.

On on:
On the right trail.

Receding Hareline:
List of upcoming hares.

Tradition:
Euphemism for 'rule'.

Beginnings

The sport of hashing was derived from earlier fun runs held in Malaya, called 'paper chases', organized by harrier groups. Hashing was founded in 1938 by a small group of young British expatriates who lived in the 'Hash House', a nickname given to the Selangor Club Chambers by its residents because of the supposedly poor-quality food served there.

From a fun run among friends, hashing has grown to encompass more than 2000 chapters on six continents, including Antarctica. Malaysia, as founding nation, boasts more than 170 chapters in Peninsular Malaysia, Sabah and Sarawak. The original hashing club, the Hash House Harriers in Kuala Lumpur, is affectionately known as 'Mother Hash'.

Hash events

By 1941, the Hash House Harriers had organized its 100th run and had attracted scores of members. However, the chapter would only hold another 17 runs before the Japanese invasion of Malaya. The war years caused a lapse in hash runs and the advent of the Emergency after the war was also a difficult time for hashers, who had to overcome military curfews and restrictions in order to carry out their weekly runs.

The Kuala Lumpur 1000th Post-War Run in 1966 was the first attempt at a Nash (national) Hash run in Malaysia, with all 10 of the country's hash chapters taking part.

In 1978, the first world Interhash was held in Hong Kong with around 800 participants.

The original hash house in Kuala Lumpur, 1939.

The Hash Heritage Foundation

Founded in Kuala Lumpur in 2000, the Hash Heritage Foundation aims to preserve the history and heritage of the Hash House Harriers. A non-profit organization, one of the foundation's principal aims is the rebuilding of the original hash house demolished in the mid-1960s as a centre for hash activities, an archive and museum.

This event has subsequently been organized biennially. The second Interhash was held in Kuala Lumpur in 1980 and attracted approximately 1200 hashers from around the world. Kuala Lumpur also played host to Interhash 1998, which coincided with the 60th anniversary of Mother Hash', and attracted over 6000 participants.

Over 2000 Hash House Harriers waiting for the flag off to signal the start of their race in Ipoh, 2006.

An evolving tradition

Governance of hash chapters is decentralized and they do not generally maintain any formal affiliations. Constitutions and regulations vary between chapters. As chapters were traditionally organized as male-only fraternities, the hash has had to evolve to increase its popularity. While some chapters, including Mother Hash, are men only, the majority are open to both men and women. There are also a few exclusively women's or women-managed chapters, including the Kuala Lumpur Harriettes, which was founded in 1974.

Apart from the normal hash run, chapters also organize special events like pub crawls and campouts. One of the most famous events is the 'red dress run' which originated in San Diego in 1987. Started after a new hasher arrived for a run wearing a red dress, the 'red dress run' is held annually by hash chapters all over the world and requires participants to wear an item of clothing that is red and dress-like.

Marathons, fun runs and big walks

The marathon is based on the Greek legend of Pheidippides, who in 490 BCE ran more than 40 kilometres to Athens to convey the news that the Persians had been defeated in the Battle of Marathon. Race walking is far younger, dating back to the 18th century, when aristocrats in Europe took to wagering over whose footman was fastest. Since the 1960s, Malaysia has played host to an array of marathons, fun runs and big walks for competitive, social and charitable purposes.

Runners at the starting point of the Kuala Lumpur International Marathon at Dataran Merdeka, 2003.

Modern competitions

A far cry from its ancient predecessor, the modern marathon is run on public roads or off-road trails. The men's marathon made its Olympic debut at the 1896 Olympic Games in Athens, while the women's marathon was introduced at the 1984 games in Los Angeles. In 1924, the official distance for the marathon was fixed at 42.195 kilometres.

Having emerged as a competitive endeavour in the 1800s, race walking was introduced at the Olympic Games in 1908 in London for men and in 1992 in Barcelona for women. The Olympics now includes race walks of 10 kilometres for women, and 20 kilometres and 50 kilometres for men. Race walks are also known as big walks or fun walks when they are conducted for social or charitable, as well as competitive, purposes.

Events in Malaysia

Since its inception in 1984, the Kuala Lumpur International Marathon has played a key role in popularizing marathons in Malaysia. Jointly organized by the Federal Territory AAA and Kuala Lumpur City Hall, the race is sanctioned by the Malaysian Amateur Athletics Union (MAAU).

A year younger than the Kuala Lumpur International Marathon is the Penang Bridge Run, which incorporates full-, half- and quarter-marathons as well as a fun run. Participants are required to run over the Penang Bridge and along a scenic coastal highway. Other major races include the Ipoh International Marathon and the Adidas–King of the Road.

The most significant of the many race walks in Malaysia is the *Malay Mail* Big Walk, which made its debut in 1960. More than 2800 participants walked 24 kilometres from Stadium Merdeka in Kuala Lumpur all the way to Petaling Jaya and then back to the stadium. The event was flagged off by Prime Minister Tunku Abdul Rahman Putra and Radio Malaya, the forerunner of Radio Televisyen Malaysia (RTM), gave running commentaries in Malay, English, Chinese and Tamil.

Fondly referred to as the 'Biggie', the *Malay Mail* Big Walk has attracted thousands of participants—old, young, foreign and local—and has produced championship-calibre walkers. National walker V. Subramaniam rose to prominence in the Biggie. Winning nearly every event until his retirement in 1987, Subramaniam went on to train budding big walkers at his clinics, and many of them represented Malaysia at the international level.

As the name suggests, fun walks are more of a social event in nature involving families, celebrities and organizations. They are charity-driven events which donate their proceeds to specific causes. Fun walks range in length from 5 to 80 kilometres.

Prominent fun walks in Malaysia include the Batik Fun Walk, held in conjunction with Malaysia Batik Week, and the Charity Fun Walk to raise public awareness about cancer.

Above left: Winner of the gold medal in the 20-kilometre walk at the Asian Championships in 1975, Khoo Chong Beng became the first Asian to compete in an Olympic walking event at the Montreal Olympic Games in 1976.

Above middle: V. Subramaniam was named 1978 Sportsman of the Year after his silver-medal performance in the 20-kilometre race walk at the Asian Games in Bangkok.

Above right: Maimunah Mohd Nor, 19, was the only local winner in the inaugural *Malay Mail* Big Walk in 1960.

1. Colourful participants in the 2005 Batik Fun Walk take to the streets of Kuala Lumpur.

2. Prime Minister Dato' Seri Dr Mahathir Mohamad firing a starting gun at the beginning of the Kuala Lumpur International Marathon, 1984.

3. Over 7600 runners surging across the Penang Bridge at the start of the Penang Bridge Run, 1995.

4. More than 10,000 participants walking through Dataran Merdeka during the *Malay Mail* Big Walk in 1980.

1. The Duke of Edinburgh (fourth from left) played with the Singapore Polo Club in Singapore in 1965 with (from left) Neville Clarke, Lt Col Brian Tayleur, Dr Mike Henigan and (from right) Tengku Mahmood Iskandar, Ismail Ali, Tengku Ahmad Shah and Ismail Talib.

2. Royal Selangor Polo Club President Dato' Mohamed Moiz in action at the Malaysian Open Polo Tournament, 2005.

3. Aerial view of the Selangor Turf Club, 1989. The club moved to its current location in Sungai Besi in 1993, and the old site is now home to the PETRONAS Twin Towers.

4. Horses galloping toward the finish line during a race at the Penang Turf Club in 2005.

5. Kelantan Beach Racers riding their ponies during a competition on a beach in Kota Bharu, 1997.

6. The Army team, including captain Yang di-Pertuan Agong Sultan Ahmad Shah, facing off against the Royal Pahang Polo Club, 1983.

7. Finish of the final leg of the Rothman's International 100 event held in at the Perak Turf Club, 1989. Organized horse racing in Perak began in 1896 when a turf club was established in Taiping by Lt Col Walker.

EQUINE SPORTS

Horses have long been reared in Malaysia. The *kuda padi*, a local pony, has been bred and cross-bred for centuries, especially in the east coast states of Kelantan and Terengganu. In Sabah, the Bajau are renowned for their horsemanship, which is an integral element of their culture (see 'Traditional recreation of Sabah').

Racing and polo were the first organized equine activities, introduced in 1842 and 1886 respectively, but since the 1990s the rise of Olympic-style equestrian disciplines such as showjumping, dressage, eventing and, more recently, endurance, has ignited the imagination of Malaysians.

Since the mid-1980s, the country has witnessed a dramatic increase in the number of horses, equestrian clubs, riding schools, endurance stables and private or semi-private ranches. Programmes have been implemented to introduce riding to local schoolchildren, and there are apprentice riders in the nationally funded sports school at Bukit Jalil. The Klang Valley, where previously only the Selangor Polo and Riding Club existed in Kuala Lumpur, boasts more than 30 equestrian centres and stabling facilities as of 2008. The Malaysian Equine Council, formed in 1993 to coordinate the development of equine sports in the country, has introduced the National Coaching Accreditation Scheme for Malaysians to have easy access to, and sponsorship in obtaining, internationally recognized instructors' licences.

Malaysians have competed with distinction at the SEA Games and Asian Games as well as the European Open Championships, FEI World Endurance Championships, FEI World Cup Jumping Finals and World Equestrian Games. After winning races on three continents in 2001, Datuk Kamaruddin Abdul Ghani became the world's top-ranked endurance rider. At the 2001 SEA Games, Qabil Ambak captured four gold medals, and was subsequently honoured as the Best Male Sportsman of the SEA Games and the male OCM Olympian of the Year.

The country has played host to the CSI–Star KL Grand Prix in 2003 and 2004 and the FEI World Cup Jumping Final in 2006, bringing world-class competition to the country. The Royal Malaysian Polo Association (RMPA) has established the RMPA Southeast Asian International Polo League as a regional polo fixture, while the Malayan Racing Association (MRA) organizes the Triple Crown Series.

Syed Omar and his horse, Lui 24, in flight during the jumping event at the 2006 Asian Games in Doha.

Equestrianism

Competitive equestrian events have been organized in the country for the past 150 years, although locals did not begin to participate regularly in them until after Independence. Formed in 1978, the Equestrian Association of Malaysia (EAM) has succeeded in promoting equine sports locally, and Malaysian equestrians have distinguished themselves in international competitions.

Top: Jumping competition organized in Kuala Lumpur in conjunction with the tenth anniversary of Malaysia's Independence, 1967.

ABOVE: Bajau horsemen riding their steeds through a river in Sabah.

Establishing a tradition

Equestrianism refers to the skill of riding or driving horses for practical purposes or as a recreational activity and competitive sport.

Competitive equestrianism started in Malaya with the establishment of several horse racing clubs in the 19th century, beginning with the Singapore Turf Club in 1842 (see 'Horse racing'). Polo was the next equestrian sport to be played locally; the Singapore Polo Club was founded in 1886, and other polo facilities were set up in the following years (see 'Polo'). Annual polo matches between the Selangor and Singapore Polo Clubs were a highlight of the social calendar in the early 1900s.

Horses did not specialize in particular equestrian disciplines the way they do today. During that time, 'a horse might pull a carriage in the morning, have an impromptu race in the afternoon and play polo in the evening'.

While racing, polo, gymkhana games and other equestrian activities such as showjumping, dressage and eventing were essential components of the pre-Merdeka social scene, there were not many locals who took part in equestrian sports. Equestrianism was a British dominated pastime that few Malayans could afford.

Equestrianism after Independence

After Independence, competitive equestrian standards were not high in the country. So few locals rode horses that representative teams often comprised three expatriates and one Malaysian. Regionally, Hong Kong, Singapore and Indonesia regularly won inter-Port equestrian competitions that were organized with the visitors riding the hosts' horses. This manner of competitions continued into the 1970s.

Malaysia's first Prime Minister, Tunku Abdul Rahman Putra, was an equine enthusiast. He advocated horse breeding, and spearheaded the establishment of the National Stud Farm at Tanjung Rambutan, Perak in 1969. The Tunku was a part owner of Think Big when the horse won its second Melbourne Cup in 1975.

EAM logo.

EAM founding president Tengku Abdullah Sultan Ahmad Shah.

EAM president as at 2007 Dato' Sri Dr Jamaludin Dato' Mohd Jarjis.

Action taking place during the 2006 FEI World Cup Jumping Finals held in the Putra Stadium at Bukit Jalil.

In 1978, the Equestrian Association of Malaysia (EAM) was formed with Tengku Abdullah Sultan Ahmad Shah as its first president. In the same year, the EAM became a member of the Federation Equestre Internationale (FEI), the world's governing body of Olympic-style equestrian sports.

Malaysia's campaign in the 1983 SEA Games was led by Tengku Abdullah. Under his captaincy, the polo team won the gold medal, beating the Philippines in the final. The equestrian team also won a bronze medal in the combined training event. The next time equestrian sports were included in the SEA Games was in 1995 in Thailand. Malaysia won a team show jumping gold medal in this competition.

Malaysia's equestrian renaissance

When Malaysia's fourth Prime Minister, Dato' Seri Dr Mahathir Mohamad, became a patron of equestrian

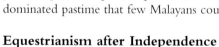

FEI-recognized equestrian sports

Jumping: Participants try to jump cleanly over a course of between 10 and 13 obstacles within a specified period of time.

Dressage: Participants must perform a series of prescribed movements in an enclosed arena to demonstrate their horses' training.

Eventing: A three-phase competition comprising dressage, cross-country (galloping over undulating ground and over 30 natural fences and obstacles) and jumping.

Endurance: A long-distance race, up to 160 kilometres, that tests the stamina of the horse over a long distance.

Reining: Contestants must guide their horses through a prescribed pattern of circles, spins and stops.

Vaulting: Often referred to as 'gymnastics on horseback', this competition requires participants to perform a series of gymnastic exercises on and off the horse's back.

Driving: Drivers must sit in a vehicle drawn by one, two or four horses and complete three events: dressage, marathon and obstacle course.

International achievements

At the 1998 Asian Games in Thailand, Malaysia won a team silver medal in dressage, and Quzier Ambak took the bronze medal in show jumping. Malaysia dominated equestrian sports at the 2001 SEA Games in Kuala Lumpur, winning five of a possible six gold medals. Qabil Ambak grabbed four gold medals: two team and two individual medals. It earned him the accolade of Best Male Sportsman of the games, and the Olympic Council of Malaysia's award for Olympian of the Year. In the same year, Datuk Kamaruddin Abdul Ghani became the top ranked endurance rider in the world. A show jumping team bronze medal at the 2002 Asian Games in Busan was followed by a silver and two bronze medals at the Doha Asian Games in 2006. Qabil Ambak surprised the dressage world in Doha by leading Malaysia to a team silver medal and capturing an individual bronze medal, while Husref Malik Jeremiah won a bronze medal in eventing. At the 2007 SEA Games in Thailand, Qabil Ambak repeated his four-gold feat, winning medals in the individual and team dressage and jumping events.

1. Yang di-Pertuan Agong Sultan Mizan Zainal Abidin participating in the Sultan Mizan Royal Foundation–PENN Horse Riding Championship in Terengganu, 2007.

2. Quzier Ambak in action during the 2005 National Horse Show held at the Selangor Turf Club Equestrian Centre.

3. At the 2005 SEA Games in Manila, Qabil Ambak won the individual show-jumping gold medal and led Malaysia to the silver medal in the team event.

4. Syed Omar jumping a fence during the 2006 FEI World Cup Jumping Finals in Kuala Lumpur.

5. Quzandria Nur performing during the dressage final of the 2002 Asian Games.

6. Datuk Kamaruddin Abdul Ghani on his way to a gold medal at the SEA Games in 2001. He won endurance races on three continents that year.

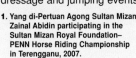

sports in the 1990s, Malaysia's equestrian renaissance began. Riding clubs sprouted up all over Malaysia, particularly in the Klang Valley, including the Bukit Kiara Equestrian and Country Resort, the Country Heights Equestrian Quarters and the Awana Ranch.

While the EAM was the local governing body of FEI-style equestrian sports, the Malaysian Equine Council (Majlis Ekuin Malaysia or MEM) was incorporated in 1993 to provide a coordinated approach in the development and promotion of equine sports and activities in Malaysia. Unlike the EAM, the council is not limited to the FEI-recognized equestrian sports. The MEM involves itself in all facets of equestrianism in Malaysia, focusing on training and education.

In 1996, the 3Q Equestrian Invitation Showjumping Challenge was held in Kuala Lumpur. Competitors flew their horses in from Indonesia, while Thai and Singaporean riders trucked theirs in. It was first time that horses crossed Southeast Asian borders to compete.

The highlight of 1997 was the inaugural Southeast Asian World Cup League season, which saw competitors from five Southeast Asian countries coming together to compete in a league of four World Cup events in Malaysia and two in Thailand. The league has been successfully held every year since then. The winner of the Southeast Asian World Cup League is invited to compete in the FEI World Cup Jumping Final.

Dr Mahathir at the reins of a horse during the opening of an equestrian centre in Kuala Lumpur, 2001.

Other equestrian events which have been organized in Malaysia include the Malaysian Open, Merdeka Masters, 3QE Classic, Malaysian Open Polo, National Horse Show, Premier Cup and Royal Selangor Horse Show.

Malaysia hosted its first ever FEI 5-Star show in 2003, the KL Grand Prix, followed by the 2006 FEI World Cup Jumping Final in Kuala Lumpur. It was the first time that the FEI World Cup Final had ever been held outside Europe or America. For four days the attention of the equestrian world was focused on Malaysia.

Sultan Mizan Zainal Abidin, the 13th Yang di-Pertuan Agong of Malaysia, is a world-ranked endurance rider who has competed at the World Equestrian Games. With his patronage, endurance riding in Malaysia is one of the fastest growing equestrian sports. The Agong's home state of Terengganu has been granted the right to host the 2008 FEI World Endurance Championships.

Horse racing

Three Malaysian turf clubs in Penang, Perak and Selangor along with the Singapore Turf Club have been organizing horse races since the 19th century. Horse racing has been heavily regulated as a result of the popularity of betting on the outcome of races. Race meetings continue to attract an immense following, and the Triple Crown Series, carrying a prize purse of RM3.5 million, is the richest sporting event in the country.

Above: Jockey Sivan astride Money Market (right) crossing the finish line at the 2004 Tunku Gold Cup race run at the Selangor Turf Club, and thereby winning a prize purse of RM500,000.

Left: The grandstand and racetrack at the Selangor Turf Club in Sungai Besi, Kuala Lumpur. The club was moved to this location in 1993 in order to ease traffic congestion in the heart of Kuala Lumpur, where it was formerly located.

Top: The first Sarawak home race in progress in Kuching, c.1880. Prized for their strength and stamina, Sulu ponies were often used in races.

Above: Queen Elizabeth II watching the Commonwealth Cup race held in her honour at the Selangor Turf Club, 1989. She is accompanied by Prince Philip (left) and Selangor Turf Club Chairman Dato' Ronald Khoo.

Origins and introduction to Malaya

Thoroughbred racing originated in England around 1660 during the reign of King Charles II who was an avid supporter of the sport and an accomplished race-rider himself. The Jockey Club was formed in England in 1752 and wielded tremendous power over horse racing activities throughout the country. Horse racing gained wider popularity with the introduction of 'classic' races in England and throughout the world.

The first known racing horses in Malaya were brought by Captain Sir Francis Light from Kolkata in 1786. The sport of horse racing was introduced to the country by the British in the early 19th century. The first recorded races were held at the Singapore Turf Club in 1843. In a two-day meeting, the first Singapore Gold Cup race was run with prize money of 150 Straits dollars awarded to the winner.

In the second half of the 19th century, racing clubs began to be established on the Malay Peninsula: the Penang Turf Club in 1864 followed by the Perak Turf Club and Selangor Turf Club in 1896. However, it was not until horses (which were previously obtained from Java, Burma and China) began to be imported from Australia in the late 19th century that horse racing took off in earnest.

MALAYAN Racing Association

Malayan Racing Association logo.

Professional racing

Horse racing in the Federated Malay States gradually changed from amateur racing and gymkhanas to professional competitions subject to a code of rules. The Straits Racing Association (known as the Malayan Racing Association since 1961) was formed in 1896 to regulate and coordinate racing at the four turf clubs. Horses usually travelled by coastal steamer and rail from one location to another to compete.

The membership of the Selangor Turf Club rose steadily in the early 1900s until the onset of World War I. In 1913, a betting ordinance was passed, signalling the start of the government's long-standing campaign against illegal bookmaking in the country. The ordinance

also provided for day members of the four turf clubs, thus opening the doors of these clubs to the general public instead of limiting entrance to registered members and horse owners.

By 1939, racing had become immensely popular and the chairman of the Selangor Turf Club was able to report a record profit of 30,400 Straits dollars. The Selangor Gold Cup (known as the Tunku Gold Cup since 1968) was inaugurated in 1939.

Due to World War II, professional horse racing was halted in Malaya from 1941 to 1943. After the war ended, horse racing resumed under the British Military Administration, but amateurs continued to ride competitively against professionals. In 1946, these informal 'Skye' meetings were discontinued.

The Malayan Amateur Racing Association (MARA) was set up in 1951 and on 31 August of that year, the Selangor Turf Club organized the first official amateur race meeting.

The Yang di-Pertuan Agong Gold Cup (renamed the Selangor Gold Cup in 1996) was introduced in 1958. The inaugural race, carrying a prize purse of 9100 Straits dollars, was won by renowned jockey Moses Lee astride a horse named Take Easy.

In the 1960s, race days were changed from Wednesday to Sunday, thus enabling more fans to attend racing events. Horse racing in Malaysia continued to flourish in the 1970s, with legendary jockeys such as Yves St Martin, Lester Piggott and Pat Eddery coming to the country to compete. In 1989, Queen Elizabeth II attended the Commonwealth Cup event held in her honour at the Selangor Turf Club.

Established in 2003, the Triple Crown Series (comprising the Tunku Gold Cup, Selangor Gold Cup and Piala Emas Sultan Selangor) carries a prize purse of RM3.5 million, making it the richest sporting event in Malaysia.

Selangor Club Chairman Tunku Dato' Seri Shahbuddin Tunku Besar Burhanuddin (sixth from left) and Deputy Chairman Datuk Richard Cham (third from left) with the Selangor Turf Club Committee members and the winning team at the 2007 Selangor Gold Cup race.

Polo

Introduced by the British, the 'sport of kings' has a long and rich tradition in Malaysia. Since the early 1900s, polo has been played competitively in the country, especially by members of the royal families who continue to play an active role in the sport.

Royal patronage

The first known game of polo took place around 600 BCE between the Turkomens and the Persians, and was won by the former. The game spread from Persia to Egypt and eastwards to India, China and Japan. In the 1850s, British tea planters became aware of a game called pulu, (meaning 'wooden ball' in Tibetan) played in Manipur, India. In 1859, they

Sultan Abu Bakar with the Royal Pahang team, c. 1930s.

formed the world's first known polo club in Silchar. From India, the British introduced the game to England, establishing the first polo club in the country in 1872.

Evolution of polo in Malaysia

Polo was brought to Malaya by the British armed forces in the late 19th century and soon attracted the attention of the Perak, Pahang and Johor royal families. Records show that the first polo club formed in British Malaya was the Singapore Polo Club in 1886. The first polo club in the Malay States, the Selangor Polo Club, was established in 1902 at Port Swettenham (now Port Klang). Polo matches between the Selangor and Singapore polo clubs began in 1903. By 1919, three other polo clubs had been founded in Butterworth, Penang and Johor.

In 1911, the Selangor Polo Club was relocated to Gurney Drive in Kuala Lumpur. From there it was subsequently moved to the Selangor Turf Club in Jalan Ampang in 1946 where the game was played at the centre of the race course, and finally onto its current location at Ampang Hilir in 1963 after being granted a lease by Prime Minister Tunku Abdul Rahman Putra.

The Iskandar Polo Club was founded in Kuala Kangsar in 1923 by Sultan Iskandar of Perak who was himself a keen player. The Sikh mounted regiment of the British army regularly participated in polo matches there. In 1972, the Iskandar Polo Club was relocated to Ipoh to the former Queen's Hussars Polo Club grounds. The Royal Pahang Polo Club was formed in 1926 and the Sabah Polo Club was founded in 1981. The Bukit Kiara Equestrian and Country Resort (now renamed Bukit Kiara Resort), which was established in 1990, uniquely features indoor polo, in which each team fields three instead of four players.

TOP: Sultan Iskandar (fourth from left) along with fellow polo players at the Iskandar Polo Club, c. 1920s.

MIDDLE: Polo match being played at the Selangor Polo Club, 2006.

ABOVE: Distinguished Malaysian polo players—including Sultan Ahmad Shah (sixth from right), Tengku Abdullah Sultan Ahmad Shah (centre), Tunku Dato' Seri Syed Amir Abidin Jamalullail (fifth from right), and Tan Sri Dato' Seri Dr M. Mahadevan (fourth from right)—before the start of a game during the Selangor Polo Club centenary celebration in 2002.

The Royal Malaysian Polo Association

The Malayan Polo Association (subsequently renamed the Royal Malaysian Polo Association or RMPA) was formed in 1922 as the governing body of polo in Malaya by the Selangor Polo Club, the Royal Pahang Polo Club, the Penang Polo Club and the Singapore Polo Club. The Royal Johor Polo Club, and the Iskandar Polo Club of Perak subsequently joined the association along with polo clubs from Jakarta and Bangkok.

RMPA logo.

As of 2008, the major polo events in the country include the Royal Pahang Classic, Malaysian Open Polo Tournament, Hookahs Polo tournament and RMPA-Royal Selangor International League Polo Tournament. In 2005, the RMPA established the RMPA Southeast Asian International Polo League, comprising four tournaments. The Royal Pahang II team captured the inaugural championship and the BRDB–Royal Pahang Polo Club emerged victorious in 2006.

Members of the BRDB–Royal Pahang Polo Club holding the trophy after winning the 2006 RMPA Southeast Asian International Polo League tournament.

Tengku Abdullah Sultan Ahmad Shah, president of the Royal Malaysian Polo Association as at 2008.

Malaysian polo standouts

As it is known as the sport of kings, it is no surprise that members of the royal families in Malaysia have become adept at polo. Among the most prominent exponents are Sultan Ahmad Shah, Tengku Abdullah Sultan Ahmad Shah and Tunku Ibrahim Ismail Sultan Iskandar. As of 2006, the highest handicapped player in the country was Shariman Sarir, now deceased, of the Royal Pahang Polo Club who played to a handicap of +6.

Malaysia won the gold medal in the polo event at the 2007 SEA Games in Thailand. The national team also took the gold medal at the SEA Games in Singapore in 1983, when polo was last contested as an event.

LEFT: Yang di-Pertuan Agong Sultan Ahmad Shah playing for Pahang in a match against Selangor in Port Dickson, 1981.

RIGHT: Shariman Sarir in action.

1. Formula One cars waiting for the green light to signal the start of the 2007 PETRONAS F1 Malaysian Grand Prix at the Sepang International Circuit.

2. Participants in the International Rainforest Challenge trying to extricate their vehicle from a river in Terengganu, 2007.

3. Karamjit Singh and Allen Oh taking part in the 2000 Malaysian Rally Championship in Klang.

4. The May–June 1962 issue of the *Malayan Sports Illustrated* featuring the first Malaysia Grand Prix on its cover.

5. Winners from the Shell and PETRONAS teams holding their trophies at the PETRONAS Sprinta AAM Malaysian Cub Prix Championship 2007 at the Sepang International Circuit.

6. Cyclists riding through the gates of the town of Kemaman during the 'Kuantan–Kuala Terengganu' stage of the Tour de Langkawi, 1999.

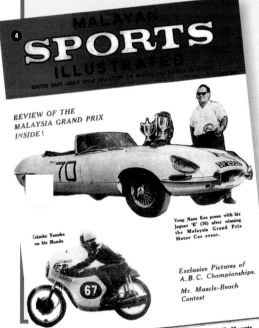

WHEEL SPORTS

Commemorative stamps marking the opening of the Sepang International Circuit in 1999.

Organized car races in Malaysia go as far back as 1940, when the first Johor Grand Prix was held to raise money for the War Fund. A second event, held in 1949, was the first formal grand prix event held in Southeast Asia. The Johor Grand Prix continued to run until 1953 and was superseded by the Johor Coronation Grand Prix in 1960.

In Kuala Lumpur, a street circuit running around Parliament House, Lake Gardens and Kenny Hill functioned as the site of racing events in the early 1960s. These events, known as the Tunku Abdul Rahman Circuit Races, were subsequently moved to Petaling Jaya and the Batu Tiga Circuit in Shah Alam.

The first Malaysia Grand Prix was held in 1962 on the Old Upper Thomson Road Circuit in Singapore. It continued to be run there until 1965, after which it was relocated to the Batu Tiga Circuit. The event was conducted annually in Shah Alam from 1968 to 1982, except for 1976, and then one more time in 1995. The opening of the Sepang International Circuit (SIC) in 1999 led to the revival of the Malaysia Grand Prix and elevated it to the heights of Formula One.

Malaysia's most successful racer is World Rally Champion Karamjit Singh, and the PETRONAS EON Racing Team is Asia's most successful rallying team. Rally races are held regularly in Malaysia, including the Felda-AAM Malaysian Rally Championship and the Malaysian Rally, which is part of the FIA Asia-Pacific Rally Championship circuit.

Car races are not the only speed events organized in Malaysia. Motorbike races conducted in the country include PETRONAS Sprinta AAM Malaysian Cub Prix Championship, SIC-AAM Malaysian Motocross Championship and PETRONAS Sprinta FIM Asian Grand Prix, while the Malaysian Motorcycle Grand Prix has been part of the FIM World Motorcycle Grand Prix Championship since 1991.

The first bicycles were introduced to Malaya by the British in the early 20th century. Since then, local cyclists have achieved international success; After his performances in 2003 and 2006, Josiah Ng becamethe only cyclist to have won the World Cup keirin event twice. Malaysia hosts the Tour de Langkawi. Held annually since 1996, the Tour de Langkawi is the biggest race on the UCI Asia Tour calendar.

Malaysia's natural terrain is a perfect venue for off-road races. 4x4 activities are regularly organized for enthusiasts who seek to pit their abilities against nature. The annual International Rainforest Challenge, considered one of the world's most demanding off-road races, was first held in 1997 and continues to attract 4x4 enthusiasts from all over the world.

Josiah Ng winning the keirin final at the 2001 SEA Games.

Formula One and motor racing

The history of organized car racing in Malaysia stretches back to the 1940s, and the Malaysia Grand Prix has been held since 1962. The opening of the state-of-the-art Sepang International Circuit in 1999 ushered in a new era for car racing in the country; Malaysia earned the right to host Formula One (F1), the most prestigious event on the international racing circuit. The country has staged the F1 PETRONAS Malaysian Grand Prix nine times, and has signed a contract to extend its hosting of the race until 2015. Malaysia also hosts and takes part in other racing competitions such as the A1 GP World Cup of Motorsports.

Start/finish line: Since the inception of the F1 PETRONAS Malaysian Grand Prix in 1999, six drivers have won:

- Eddie Irvine (1999)
- Michael Schumacher (2000, 2001 and 2004)
- Ralf Schumacher (2002)
- Kimi Raikkonen (2003)
- Fernando Alonso (2005 and 2007)
- Giancarlo Fisichella (2006)

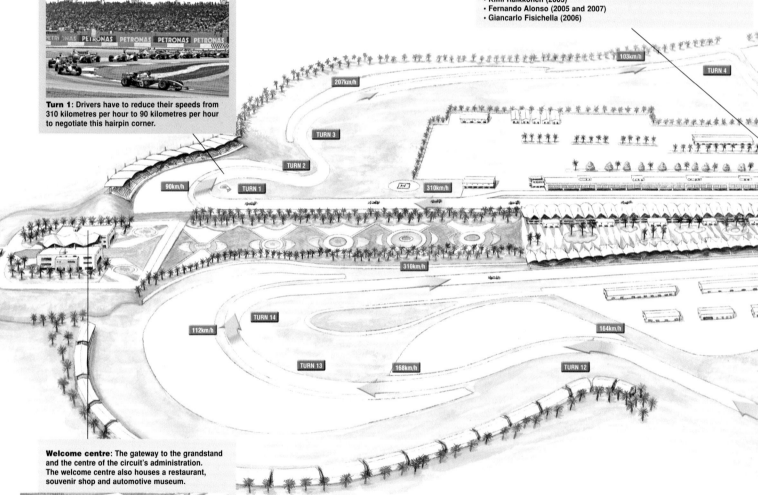

Turn 1: Drivers have to reduce their speeds from 310 kilometres per hour to 90 kilometres per hour to negotiate this hairpin corner.

Welcome centre: The gateway to the grandstand and the centre of the circuit's administration. The welcome centre also houses a restaurant, souvenir shop and automotive museum.

The Sepang International Circuit

The construction of the Sepang International Circuit began in November 1997 and was completed 14 months later. It was officially opened by Prime Minister Dato' Seri Dr Mahathir Mohamad on 9 March 1999. The 5.543-kilometre track features 15 turns and 8 straights, and has a width of 16–22 metres, allowing ample opportunities for overtaking. The circuit, managed by Sepang International Circuit Sdn Bhd, hosted Malaysia's first Formula One race, the PETRONAS Malaysian Grand Prix, on 17 October 1999.

Apart from the F1 Grand Prix, the circuit has also been the venue of the FIM World Motorcycle Grand Prix Championship, Super GT International Series, Merdeka Millennium Endurance Race, Sepang Drag Race, Asian Festival of Speed (comprising the Asian Touring Car Series, Formula V6 Asia, Formula BMW Asia Series and Porsche Carrera Cup Asia Series), A1 Grand Prix, Malaysian Super Series for Cars and Bikes and the SIC-AAM Malaysian Motocross Championship.

The track can accommodate 130,000 spectators, with 32,000 in the main grandstand alone. Of the events hosted by the circuit, the Formula One race receives the most attention—the 2007 grand prix was attended by more than 115,000 motorsports fans.

Pit building: The heart of the circuit, the pit building faces the main grandstand and is where all of the racing facilities are housed. It comprises 33 pits, a race control centre, time-keeping room, paddock clubs and race management offices.

The tower: Located between the front and back straights, spectators at the tower have a view of nearly 80 per cent of the race. One of the most thrilling moments is watching the cars racing up the back straight at speeds of up to 310 kilometres per hour and braking hard into the corner of Turn 15 before zooming away at top speed towards the finish line.

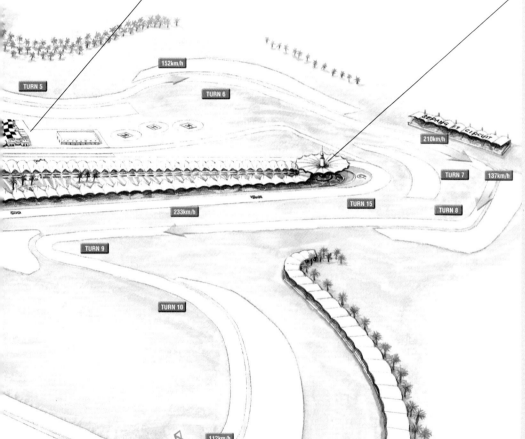

A1 Team Malaysia driver Alex Yoong in action during the Australian leg of the A1 GP 2005–06 season.

The A1 Grand Prix

The A1 GP World Cup of Motorsports (formerly known as the A1 Grand Prix) is contested by national teams instead of competing constructors as is the case in other formula grand prix, including Formula One. All of the teams must use identical cars to maintain a level playing field. The cars are designed to limit performance and reduce cost in order to ensure that no team has an advantage over the others. At the end of the season, the country with the most points is awarded the World Cup of Motorsport trophy.

Twenty-five countries took part in the first season of the A1 GP which ran from September 2005 to April 2006. The Malaysian leg was held in November 2005 at the Sepang International Circuit. A1 Team Malaysia, represented by drivers Alex Yoong and Fairuz Fauzy, finished fifth overall in the first A1 GP season. The second A1 GP season started in October 2006 and ended in April 2007. The Sepang edition was held in November 2006. Team Malaysia finished in sixth place at the conclusion of the season.

A1 Team Malaysia driver Alex Yoong remains the only Malaysian to have driven in Formula One, racing for Team Minardi in 2001 and 2002.

LEFT: Motorcyclist racing in the PETRONAS Sprinta FIM Asian Grand Prix at the Sepang International Circuit, 2007.

ABOVE: Prime Minister Dato' Seri Dr Mahathir Mohamad (centre) sitting in a Red Bull-Sauber PETRONAS Formula One car before the inaugural PETRONAS Malaysian Grand Prix, 1999. On his left are drivers Pedro Diniz and Jean Alesi, and on his right is Youth and Sports Minister Tan Sri Muhyiddin Yassin.

ABOVE: Cars racing in the Super GT International Series at the Sepang International Circuit, 2006.

RIGHT: The official guide to the Sepang F1 Circuit, published in 2007.

Cycling

Cycling competitions have been formally organized in the country since 1938. The Malaysian National Cycling Federation (MNCF) was formed in 1953 and Malaysian cyclists have achieved international success since the 1960s. The annual Tour de Langkawi, inaugurated in 1996, is an important event on the international cycling calendar and draws participants and spectators from Malaysia and beyond.

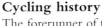

Top: Cyclists making a final sprint for the finish line of stage nine of the 2005 Tour de Langkawi. The fifth stage of the tour from Kota Bharu to Kuala Terengganu attracted an estimated 100,000 spectators along the route.

Above: Cyclists taking part in a race at a velodrome in Kuala Lumpur.

1. Daud Ibrahim was one of the first two local cyclists to win an Asian Games gold medal in 1970.

2. In 1985, Rosman Alwi made history by being the first cyclist to win double gold at the Asian Championships.

3. Josiah Ng in action at the velodrome in Athens during the 2004 Olympic Games.

4. In 2005, Noor Azian Alias became the first Malaysian woman to win the road race at the SEA Games in Manila.

Cycling history

The forerunner of the modern bicycle was invented in France in the late 18th century and cycling was included in the first modern Olympics in 1896. The world's most prestigious annual cycling race, the Tour de France, was first conducted in 1903.

Bicycle racing was introduced to Malaya by the British in the early 20th century. The first organized road races were held in Kuala Lumpur in 1938. The first local cycling association was formed that same year in Selangor by clubs called the Rough Riders and Agas Wheelers. Cycling associations were also set up in Melaka, Perak and Penang.

Track races, the most popular form of bicycle racing at the time, were first held in the 1950s on grass tracks and at the Lucky World Park in Kuala Lumpur, which had a plank track. In 1947, the Kuala Lumpur to Ipoh Race was inaugurated. This was superseded by the longer Kuala Lumpur to Alor Star Race in 1970. The longest-running national race is the annual Tour de Malaysia, which started in 1964.

Asia's most prestigious stage race, the Tour de Langkawi, was first held in 1996. The brainchild of Prime Minister Dato' Seri Dr Mahathir Mohamad, the Tour de Langkawi has evolved into a fixture on the international cycling calendar.

Malaysian National Cycling Federation

The formation of the Malayan Cycling Federation (MCF) in 1953 was initiated by Gurchan Singh, a police officer, and Captain C.O. Jennings, an officer with the New Zealand Regiment. The founding MCF members were the cycling associations of Selangor, Melaka, Perak and Penang. In 1960, the MCF became affiliated to the Union Cycliste Internationale (UCI), the world governing body of the sport. The MCF was renamed the Malaysian National

Cycling Federation (MNCF) in 1963. The Asian Cycling Confederation (ACC) was formed in 1962 with the Philippines, Thailand, Iran, Indonesia, Japan, Hong Kong, Taiwan and Malaya as its founding members and Gurchan Singh as its first president.

Tour de Langkawi

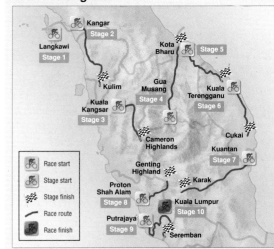

The Tour de Langkawi is a 10-day, 10-stage race covering approximately 1200 kilometres, the highlight being a gruelling climb up Genting Highlands. The 2007 Tour de Langkawi route was similar to those in previous years. Its various stages traversed a large portion of Peninsular Malaysia, starting on Langkawi Island. The 10th and final stage took place in Kuala Lumpur.

Logo of the Malaysian National Cycling Federation.

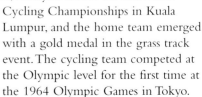
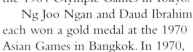
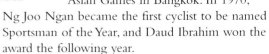

Founding president of the MCF Gurchan Singh.

President of the MNCF as at 2008 Abu Samah Abd. Wahab.

National cycling achievements

Malayan cyclists competed in the inaugural SEAP Games in Bangkok in 1959 and the 1962 Asian Games in Jakarta, winning a bronze medal in the team road race event. In 1963, Malaysia hosted the first Asian Cycling Championships in Kuala Lumpur, and the home team emerged with a gold medal in the grass track event. The cycling team competed at the Olympic level for the first time at the 1964 Olympic Games in Tokyo.

Ng Joo Ngan and Daud Ibrahim each won a gold medal at the 1970 Asian Games in Bangkok. In 1970, Ng Joo Ngan became the first cyclist to be named Sportsman of the Year, and Daud Ibrahim won the award the following year.

Cyclist Rosman Alwi was Sportsman of the Year in 1985 following his double gold medal feat at the Asian Championships of that year. M. Kumaresan and Shahrulneeza Mohd Razali both received the award in 1987 and 1999 respectively.

Josiah Ng competed in the Olympic Games for the first time in 2004. He qualified for the keirin finals, and took fifth place. In 2003 and 2006, Josiah finished as the overall winner in the World Cup keirin event, making him the only cyclist to have ever won the competition twice. At the 2006 Asian Games in Doha, Josiah captured a silver medal in the keirin event.

Malaysia struck gold at the Asian Championships in 2006 with Mohd Rizal Tisin emerging victorious in the keirin event, and again in 2007 with Azizul Hasni Awang capturing the keirin title.

Off-road and rally racing

Off-road racing arrived in Malaysia in the mid-1980s and proved popular among the local community. Taking advantage of Malaysia's diverse terrain, 4x4 clubs organize off-road challenges as well as overland journeys out of the country. Rally racing is equally popular in Malaysia and the nation has produced a world champion in Karamjit Singh.

Driver negotiating a slope during the 2006 Rainforest Challenge in Terengganu.

Extreme off-road racing

In the 1980s and 1990s, 4x4 challenges (also known as 'extreme off-road racing') were popularized in the United States and gained worldwide attention through events such as the Camel Trophy.

In Malaysia, 4x4 challenges were spurred by Yamin Vong, who initiated the formation of the Adventure Club of Kuala Lumpur (ACKL) in 1987. In the same year, the ACKL became the first 4x4 driving club to be registered with the Registrar of Societies, with Taib Khamis as its inaugural president. The president of ACKL as at 2008 is Mohd Isa.

The club launched the Trans Borneo in 1988, which followed a route from Kuching to Kota Kinabalu. The second Trans Borneo was held in 1989. The Trans Peninsula began in 1990 and continued until 1992. The Monsoon Challenge was the last club event to start in 1996. The International Rainforest Challenge (RFC) was created by Luis Wee in 1997. The RFC has grown steadily over the years to become the largest 4x4 event in the world in terms of the number of participating countries.

Rally racing

Rally racing involves modified or specially produced road cars. Races take place on public or private roads, and are not conducted on a formal circuit, but rather in stages from one starting point to another. A rally car contains a driver and navigator, who must communicate and work together to succeed.

Rallying began in Malaysia in the 1960s, when cars raced on informal routes throughout the country. The first Rally of Malaysia, now known as the Malaysian Rally, was organized in 1977, and saw the introduction of the international stage format. The Malaysian Rally Championship (MRC), inaugurated in the late 1960s, attracted both local and foreign drivers. The 2007 MRC is divided into five stages—each in a different month of the year and in a different state in the country.

TOP: Driving across a log bridge during the 2005 Rainforest Challenge in Terengganu.

ABOVE: One of the participants of the 2000 Rainforest Challenge gets a helping hand in Terengganu.

LEFT: Cars starting a stage of the Rainforest Challenge in Terengganu, 2005.

The International Rainforest Challenge (RFC)

Held in a different state in Malaysia every year, usually during November and December, the International Rainforest Challenge (RFC) is usually 800 kilometres long and takes participants through difficult terrain over a period of 10 days. The RFC is also the country's only international class 4x4 challenge trophy and is open to all types of 4x4s.

2007 International Rainforest Challenge course

Opening Ceremony (D-Day)
1 December (Jertih)

Prologue Special Stages
1–2 December (Kampung Bintang)

Predator Zone

Terminator Zone

Beach Finale
30 December
Kuala Terengganu
(Batu Buruk Beach)

Kuala Terengganu

Twilight Zone

The Dark Side Zone

Closing Ceremony
30 December
Kuala Terengganu
(Primula Hotel)

South China Sea

TERENGGANU

TERENGGANU

Strait of Melaka

Peninsular Malaysia

N

0   200 km

RAINFOREST CHALLENGE
RFC logo.

Karamjit Singh (left) and Allen Oh celebrating their win in the Rally of Cyprus in 2002. The duo made history that year by becoming both world and Asia Pacific champions.

World rally champion

Karamjit Singh is the most accomplished rally driver in Malaysia and the Asia Pacific. Singh and his partner Allen Oh were the first Asians to win the Fédération Internationale de l'Automobile (FIA) Production Car World Championship for Drivers, doing so on their first try in 2002. They secured another milestone that year when they became the first drivers to win both the World and Asia Pacific Rally Championship titles in a single year. Oh and Singh were named National Sportsmen of the Year in 2002.

1. Canoeing expedition paddling up the Sarawak River to the Kuching Waterfront, 2006.

2. Powerboats racing in the 2004 Formula One World Championship Grand Prix in Putrajaya.

3. Daniel Bego (in lane 3) competing in the 200-metre butterfly event at the 15th Asian Games in Doha, 2006. In 2007, he qualified for the 2008 Olympics in Beijing in two events.

4. White water rafting in Kedah, 2000. Malaysia's natural terrain offers white water rafting challenges of all degrees of difficulty.

5. Yachts waiting to start at the inaugural Raja Muda Selangor International Regatta off Port Klang, 1990. More than 30 yachts from eight countries, including Malaysia, took part in the seven-day regatta.

6. A scuba diver in the waters off Layang Layang Island, Sabah.

WATER SPORTS

The pristine seas surrounding Malaysia are renowned among divers for their marine life. Divers can see beautiful coral formations, a large variety of fish and even swim with whale sharks. The country has 40 marine parks that may be explored by the intrepid diver. Snorkelling is another leisure activity enjoyed by many.

Angler (left) with his trophy blue marlin caught in the waters off Kennedy Bay in Sabah, 1967.

It is estimated that there are one million recreational anglers in Malaysia. Previously a form of food-gathering, angling has become a favoured activity of leisure and a sport for those seeking a challenge. Again, Malaysia is naturally blessed, with rich sea and river life that attracts anglers from all over the world.

Divers and anglers are not the only ones attracted to Malaysian waters—sailors also find much to challenge them here. The country is host to a number of regattas including the Royal Selangor Yacht Club's Raja Muda Selangor International Regatta, the Royal Langkawi Yacht Club's Royal Langkawi International Regatta, the Borneo International Yachting Challenge and the recently inaugurated Monsoon Cup.

Modern canoeing was introduced before World War II and started to catch on in the 1980s. There are now an increasing number of events organized, including the Putrajaya Canoe Carnival, the National Slalom Championship at Chamang Waterfalls, Bentong, Pahang and the Labuan Round Island Kayak Race. Canoeing events are also held during the annual National Water Festival. Malaysia hosted the 2001 South East Asia Canoeing Championship and the 2005 Asian Canoeing Championship. More recently, the Malaysia International Kayak Endurance competition was held in August 2007 in conjunction with the 50th anniversary of the nation's Independence.

White water rafting is another popular water sport. Malaysia's natural terrain makes this an interesting activity, with rivers ranging from those suitable for a family excursion to raging waters which provide thrills and spills for the hardcore outdoor enthusiast. Excitement can also be found in sports such as powerboat racing and jet skiing.

Organized aquatic sports were introduced to the country in Penang in the early 1900s and have continued to grow in popularity. Initially the focus was on swimming, but water polo was also played. Malaysians have been competing in international aquatics events since the 1950s achieving particular success in regional competitions with the discipline of diving showing considerable progress in recent times. Malaysian aquatics athletes have qualified for the 2008 Beijing Olympics.

Leong Mun Yee (foreground) and Elizabeth Jimie in the synchronized platform diving event at the 15th Asian Games in Doha, 2006.

Aquatics

Aquatic sports in Malaysia include the disciplines of swimming, diving, synchronized swimming, water polo and open water swimming. Introduced to the country in the early 20th century by Europeans, organized aquatics has steadily grown in popularity. Since the 1950s, Malaysians have been participating in international aquatic events, and have achieved significant success in regional competitions.

ABOVE: Logo of the Amateur Swimming Union of Malaysia (ASUM).

ABOVE RIGHT: ASUM president as at 2008 Dato' Seri Shahidan Kassim.

RIGHT: ASUM founding president T.H. Tan.

Early history

Organized swimming in Malaya started in Penang in 1903, when a group of young Europeans on the island decided to form a swimming club. A small clubhouse was erected for this purpose in 1904 at Tanjung Bungah. In 1927, Lee Fong Lim, a member of the Singapore Chinese Swimming Club, came to Penang and taught a small group of swimming enthusiasts the front crawl stroke and the game of water polo. In 1928, these swimmers set up the Penang Chinese Swimming Club. A small residential building situated in Tanjung Bungah bay was rented and became the club's premises.

In 1931, the First Malayan Chinese Olympiad was held in Singapore and swimming and water polo were included in the event. The participants in the meet comprised swimmers from Penang and Singapore. The Third Chinese Olympiad, organized in 1935 in Penang, saw the participation of Selangor and Johor. In the same year, the first contingent of Malayan swimmers left for Shanghai to participate in the Chinese National Olympiad.

In 1936, the formation of the Kinta Swimming Club in Ipoh led to the establishment of the Easter Triangular Swimming Meet with participants from the Singapore, Penang and Kinta clubs.

Prior to the formation of Malaysia, swimming was governed by the Federation of Malaya Amateur Swimming Association. In the early 1960s, the Amateur Swimming Union of Malaysia (ASUM) was formed to regulate the aquatic sports of swimming, diving, synchronized swimming, water polo and open water swimming in the country. The first president of ASUM was T.H. Tan, while its president as at 2008 is Dato' Seri Shahidan Kassim.

The opening of the Kinta Swimming Club in Ipoh in 1936 and the formation of the Easter Triangular Swimming Meet drew swimmers from Perak, Penang and Singapore.

Aquatics success

In 1959, Lim Heng Chek became the nation's first SEAP Games swimming gold medallist when he won the 100-metre backstroke and 100-metre butterfly events.

The 1971 SEAP Games in Kuala Lumpur saw Malaysia winning gold medals

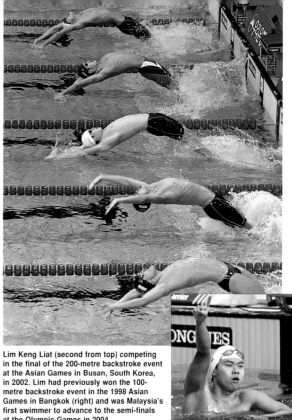

Lim Keng Liat (second from top) competing in the final of the 200-metre backstroke event at the Asian Games in Busan, South Korea, in 2002. Lim had previously won the 100-metre backstroke event in the 1998 Asian Games in Bangkok (right) and was Malaysia's first swimmer to advance to the semi-finals at the Olympic Games in 2004.

through Liew Chun Wai (1500-metre freestyle) and Ong Mei Lin (100-metre backstroke and 200-metre individual medley). Six gold medals were obtained at the 1975 SEA Games in Bangkok.

In the 1980s, swimming in Southeast Asia was dominated by Nurul Huda Abdullah. Her record of 22 SEA Games gold medals remains unparalleled, as is her feat of being named National Sportswoman of the Year for five consecutive years from 1985 to 1989. Other significant swimmers from that period include Helen Chow, May Tan Seok Khoon and Jeffrey Ong Kuan Seng.

Malaysia's first Asian Games gold medal in swimming was clinched by Lim Keng Liat in 1998 in Bangkok, when he won the 100-metre backstroke event. Lim also became the country's

Aquatics medals

1986 Seoul Asian Games
400m freestyle	Nurul Huda Abdullah (silver)
800m freestyle	Nurul Huda Abdullah (silver)
200m freestyle	Nurul Huda Abdullah (bronze)
200m medley	Nurul Huda Abdullah (bronze)

1990 Beijing Asian Games
1500m freestyle	Jeffrey Ong Kuan Seng (silver)

1998 Bangkok Asian Games
100m backstroke	Lim Keng Liat (gold)
200m backstroke	Lim Keng Liat (silver)
100m breaststroke	Elvin Chia (bronze)

2002 Busan Asian Games
100m backstroke	Lim Keng Liat (silver)
3m springboard	Yeoh Ken Nee (bronze)
3m synchronized	Yeoh Ken Nee and Rosharisham Roslan (bronze)
3m synchronized	Leong Mun Yee and Farah Begum Abdullah (bronze)

2002 Manchester Commonwealth Games
50m backstroke	Lim Keng Liat (silver)
100m backstroke	Lim Keng Liat (bronze)

2006 Doha Asian Games
3m springboard	Yeoh Ken Nee and Rosharisham Roslan (silver)
3m synchronized	Leong Mun Yee and Elizabeth Jimie (bronze)
1m springboard	Elizabeth Jimie (bronze)
3m springboard	Leong Mun Yee (bronze)

2006 Melbourne Commonwealth Games
1m springboard	Yeoh Ken Nee (silver)
10m synchronized	Bryan Nickson and James Sandayud (silver)

first swimming medallist in the Commonwealth Games when he brought home a silver in the 50-metre backstroke competition and a bronze in the 100-metre backstroke event in Manchester in 2002.

In 2006, Daniel Bego became the first Malaysian to capture a medal at a world-level swimming competition when he finished second in the 100-metre butterfly event at the World Youth Swimming Championships held in Rio de Janeiro. At the age of 17, he has qualified for the 2000-metre freestyle and 200-metre butterfly events in the 2008 Beijing Olympic Games.

Diving has shown marked progress in recent years, notably during the 2001 SEA Games in Kuala Lumpur when, led by Yeoh Ken Nee and Leong Mun Yee, Malaysian divers swept all the eight gold medals on offer. In fact, the first Malaysian to qualify for the 2008 Beijing Olympic Games was diver Bryan Nickson, who had previously competed in the 2004 Athens Olympics at the age of 14. At the 2007 SEA Games in Thailand, the Malaysian diving team emerged as the overall champion, winning seven gold, two silver and two bronze medals.

ABOVE LEFT: Jeffrey Ong Kuan Seng (left) and Nurul Huda Abdullah after being named 1988 Sportsman and Sportswoman of the Year. From 1985 to 1993, the duo won a total of 30 gold medals for Malaysia in the SEA Games. They were also the country's first swimmers to win medals at the Asian Games.

ABOVE: Daniel Bego in the 100-metre butterfly swimming heats at the 2006 Asian Games in Doha.

LEFT: Bryan Nickson performing a tuck during a dive at the 2007 World Aquatics Championships in Melbourne. His impressive performance helped make him the first Malaysian to qualify for the 2008 Olympics.

Competitive aquatics

Swimming and water polo have been part of the Olympic Games since 1896 and 1900 respectively. Diving became an official event in 1904, synchronized swimming in 1984 and synchronized diving in 2000. In 2008, the Olympic programme will include an open water swim event, a ten-kilometre race, for the first time.

LEFT: Helen Chow successfully competed in freestyle, backstroke and individual medley events in many competitions in the 1980s.

BELOW: Siow Yi Ting swimming in the women's 200-metre individual medley heats at the Olympic Aquatic Centre in Athens, 2004. Her other speciality is breaststroke.

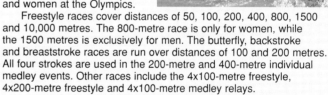

Diving

Leong Mun Yee and Cheong Jun Hoong (foreground) took the gold in the women's 10-metre synchronized platform event during the 2005 SEA Games in Laguna.

Diving competitors are judged on a series of dives and are awarded points based on their elegance and skill. The points are then adjusted according to the degree of difficulty—the number and types of manoeuvres attempted, such as somersaults, pikes (knees straight but a tight bend at the hips), tucks (body folded with hands holding the shins and toes pointed) and twists.

A panel of seven judges scores a dive, looking into elements such as approach, take-off, execution and entry into the water. There are nine judges for synchronized diving—four for execution and the rest for synchronization.

There are four diving events in the Olympic Games: the 10-metre platform, 3-metre springboard, 10-metre platform synchronized and 3-metre springboard synchronized.

Water polo

Water polo combines elements of swimming and handball. Two teams of seven players, including a goalkeeper, strive to score as many goals as possible. Each match is divided into four periods and, at the Olympic Games, each period is seven minutes long. Although water polo first appeared in the 1900 Olympics in Paris, a women's category was only introduced 100 years later at the Sydney games.

Water polo match between Malaysia and Singapore at the 2001 SEA Games in Kuala Lumpur. Players are not allowed to touch the bottom or side of the pool during the game.

Swimming

The four competitive swimming strokes at the Olympic Games are the butterfly, breaststroke, backstroke and freestyle (also known as the front crawl). Presently, there are 16 swimming events for both men and women at the Olympics.

Freestyle races cover distances of 50, 100, 200, 400, 800, 1500 and 10,000 metres. The 800-metre race is only for women, while the 1500 metres is exclusively for men. The butterfly, backstroke and breaststroke races are run over distances of 100 and 200 metres. All four strokes are used in the 200-metre and 400-metre individual medley events. Other races include the 4x100-metre freestyle, 4x200-metre freestyle and 4x100-metre medley relays.

Synchronized swimming

Synchronized swimming has been known, variously, as water ballet, ornamental and figure swimming. A fusion of swimming, gymnastics and dance, synchronized swimming tests the competitors' strength, artistry and breath control. Judging is based on the performers' technical merit and artistry. Only duet and team events (eight swimmers) are contested at the Olympic Games and the sport is only open to women.

Suzanna Ghazali Bujang (left) and Sara Kamil Yusof performing in the 2001 World Aquatics Championships in Japan. The pair won the synchronized swimming duet event at the 2001 SEA Games and Suzanna won the free solo event.

Sailing

Malaysia's harbours are home to splendid watercraft owned and used by those who enjoy the challenges of the sea or by people simply seeking a holiday out on the open water. Although sailing is a recreational pastime for many, regatta competitions organized in Malaysia attract the participation of local and international sailors.

Above left: MYA founding president Tan Sri Vice Admiral (retired) Abdul Wahab Nawi.

Above right: MYA president as at 2008 Tan Sri Dato' Muhammad Ali Hashim.

Sailing through history

Since time immemorial, people have gone to sea in a variety of makeshift watercraft such as boats made from animal skins draped over baskets, tree trunks lashed together to form rafts and hollowed-out logs fashioned into canoes. By the Middle Ages, larger vessels powered by oars and sails were capable of transporting cargo and people over the seas. Modern sailing vessels were developed from early Egyptian trading boats and Phoenician warships, which over time became larger and proved more effective.

The first boats designed solely for pleasure and sport were commissioned by Dutch nobles in the 17th century. The word 'yacht' is of Dutch origin, meaning 'hunting ship'. The English monarch Charles II popularized the sport in England after receiving a yacht as a gift from the Dutch. In 1720, the first formal organization of yacht devotees, the Cork Water Club, now known as the Royal Cork Yacht Club, was founded in Ireland.

Mixed fleet heading downwind during the Royal Langkawi International Regatta in 2005.

The New York Yacht Club, founded in 1844, financed the construction of the 30-metre schooner *America* which won the 100 Guinea Cup, now known as the America's Cup, in England in 1851. The fine lines of *America* changed subsequent yacht designs forever and the America's Cup event has become the premier international sailing event.

The growing number of yacht builders produced a large variety of moderately-priced, power-driven craft, revolutionizing yachting in the late 19th century. Sailing races were first introduced to the Olympic Games in 1900 in Paris and have been part of the Olympic programme ever since.

Organization and facilities

The Malaysian Yachting Association (MYA) was formed in 1968 to promote and develop the sport of sailing in the country. The MYA conducts development programmes to prepare sailors for forthcoming contests. Sailors are sent to compete in Optimist, Laser and 420 dinghy class world titles and other international competitions. In 2005, the MYA training base was constructed at the Regency Tanjung Tuan Beach Resort in Port Dickson. State sailing associations organize annual sail training and racing programmes for beginners and children.

Logo of the Malaysian Yachting Association (MYA).

International achievements

Malaysia has consistently produced world-class sailors in the Optimist Class. In addition, Dr Kevin Lim, who competes in Laser class, is among the top sailors in Southeast Asia. Lim has participated in the Olympic Games three times, and won two silver medals at the 1998 and 2002 Asian Games in Bangkok and Busan respectively.

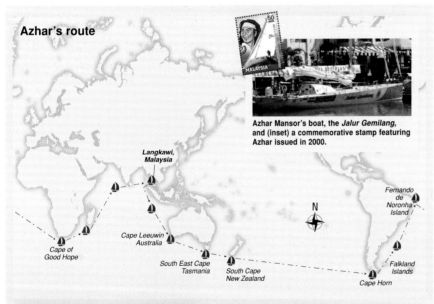

Azhar's route

Langkawi, Malaysia

Cape Leeuwin Australia

Cape of Good Hope

South East Cape Tasmania

South Cape New Zealand

Cape Horn

Falkland Islands

Fernando de Noronha Island

N

Azhar Mansor's boat, the *Jalur Gemilang*, and (inset) a commemorative stamp featuring Azhar issued in 2000.

Azhar Mansor (right) being greeted by Prime Minister Dato' Seri Dr Mahathir Mohamad upon his return in 1999.

Sailing around the world

Forty-one-year-old Azhar Mansor from Perlis successfully sailed solo around the world without engine propulsion on an east-west route. In 190 days, beginning on 2 February 1999, he sailed the RM2-million *Jalur Gemilang* over 21,600 nautical miles. The main mast of *Jalur Gemilang* broke while attempting to go around Cape Horn off the coast of South America, but Azhar managed to reach the Falkland Islands for repairs without further incident. He arrived safely at the Awana Porto Malai Resort in Langkawi on 11 August 1999.

Ryan Tan won a gold medal at the Asian Games of 1994 in Hiroshima. He also clinched two gold medals in the SEA Games, as well as three Asian Optimist championships. Rufina Tan Hong Mui, a 15-year-old, entered the international sailing scene in 2006, winning gold medals in the women's Optimist event at the Asian Games and Asian Championships in Doha.

The best overall performance by a Malaysian sailing team was at the Kuala Lumpur SEA Games in 2001, when the country won five gold, three silver and two bronze medals.

In 1999, Perlis-born mariner Azhar Mansor became the first Malaysian to sail solo around the globe in the *Jalur Gemilang*, and the first person to set a new solo west–east circumnavigation route to and from Langkawi.

LEFT: **Rufina Tan Hong Mui competing in the Doha Asian Games in 2006.**

ABOVE: **Dr Kevin Lim won the gold medal in the Laser event at the 2001 Kuala Lumpur SEA Games.**

Marina building

During the late 1990s, the Malaysian government embarked on a massive marina-building programme linking coastal townships along the Strait of Melaka from Sebana Cove in Johor to Langkawi.

In a significant move to open up the South China Sea to cruising yachts, marinas are being built in Sabah and Sarawak to encourage sailing regattas and chartered yachts to visit these states' magnificent offshore tropical islands.

Yachting regattas and sailing events

Sailing events

1. Royal Langkawi International Regatta (RLIR)
2. International Regatta Access Class Race
3. Raja Muda Selangor International Regatta (RMSIR)
4. The Monsoon Cup
5. Borneo International Yachting Challenge

Initiated by Prime Minister Dato' Seri Abdullah Ahmad Badawi during a fishing trip to Terengganu, the inaugural Monsoon Cup was held at Pulau Duyung in Terengganu in 2005. The competition was included as the 50th official event of the World Match Racing Tour, which comprises a circuit of the premier international regattas. The 2006 Monsoon Cup boasted a prize purse of RM1 million, making it the richest match racing event in the world.

Other major annual events in the country include the Royal Selangor Yacht Club's Raja Muda Selangor International Regatta (RMSIR) and the Royal Langkawi International Regatta (RLIR) hosted by the Royal Langkawi Yacht Club. RMSIR and RLIR competitors have included visiting racing and cruising boats from Hong Kong, Phuket, Singapore and Australia, as well as representatives from the Royal Selangor Yacht Club and the Royal Malaysian Navy.

The RMSIR, established in 1990, is part of of the Perpetual Cup Series that includes the Phuket King's Cup and the Singapore Straits Regatta. The highest-scoring boat in the top racing class of yachts in the three regattas wins the Perpetual Cup. The trophy is kept in Republic of Singapore Yacht Club and is awarded annually at the end of the Singapore Straits Regatta.

The annual Borneo International Yachting Challenge was established in 2003. The event begins in Labuan before making its way to Miri, Sarawak.

The Penang Municipal Council–Penang Swimming Club International Regatta Access Class Race, inaugurated in 2005, is a unique event tailored specially for disabled sailors.

RIGHT: **Prime Minister Dato' Seri Abdullah Ahmad Badawi (right) is assisted by Terengganu Chief Minister Datuk Seri Idris Jusoh in carrying the Monsoon Cup, 2005.**

BELOW: **Racing Class starting the 2006 Raja Muda Selangor International Regatta in Port Klang.**

Yachts sailing in the waters off Pulau Duyung, Kuala Terengganu during the 2007 Monsoon Cup.

Yachts moored at a yacht club in Port Dickson, Negeri Sembilan.

Paddle sports

The most popular paddle sports in Malaysia are canoeing and white water rafting. Canoeing has seen rapid development in the country, especially in the organization of regional and local competitions. White water rafting is a relatively new sport in Malaysia, but many enthusiasts have taken to the country's rivers in search of adventure. Both canoeing and white water rafting offer participants the chance to explore the country's natural environment and locations.

Rowers taking off from a waterfront in Tanjung Bunga at the start of the three-day Penang Round Island Kayak Rally, 1994.

TOP: MASCA logo.

ABOVE LEFT: Shaharuddin Hashim, founding president of MASCA.

ABOVE RIGHT: Tan Sri Vice Admiral (retired) Abdul Wahab Nawi, president of MASCA as at 2008.

Canoeing

Traditional boat and sampan races have been popular events at social gatherings, festivals and royal celebrations on the Malay Peninsula since the 15th century (see 'Traditional water sports').

Modern canoeing was introduced before World War II by British sailors based in Singapore. A formal canoeing programme began with the establishment of the Lumut Outward Bound School in Perak in 1952. The school's training modules included rigorous canoeing expeditions designed to enhance the fitness of its students.

With the launching of the 'Sport for All' programme by the Ministry of Youth and Sports in the 1980s (see 'Sport for all'), canoeing experienced a surge in popularity. Outdoor recreational associations all over the country offered canoeing as one of their main activities. In 1988, Abdul Wahab Ibrahim and Hairuddin Ahmad Jabbar became the first canoeists to make their way around the Malay Peninsula.

The Malaysia Canoe Association

The Malaysia Canoe Association (MASCA) was formed in 1992 with a membership of 14 state canoe associations. MASCA has been an affiliate of the International Canoe Federation since 1995. Canoeing competitions began to be formally

The 1997 Marlboro Rafting Adventure Team plying their way through rough waters in Jeram Besu, Pahang.

organized in 1992 following the establishment of MASCA. The most popular canoe racing event in Malaysia is the annual Putrajaya Canoe Carnival. This carnival, introduced in 2000, attracts more than 600 canoeists from all over the country each year. The carnival involves the four major canoeing events: canoe sprint, canoe slalom, canoe polo and canoe marathon.

The Southeast Asian Canoeing Championships and Asian Canoeing Championships were held in Putrajaya in 2001 and 2005 respectively.

In 2007, MASCA hosted the inaugural Peninsular Challenge, the first-ever international kayak endurance race to be organized in Malaysia. The five-stage competition started in Langkawi and finished at Putrajaya Lake.

MASCA also oversees the regulation and development of white water rafting in the country.

Malaysian canoeing achievements

Abdul Aziz Ahmad won the bronze medal in the 1000-metre TK1 (single-touring kayak) race at the 1990 Asian Canoe Championships held in Japan. Sallehuddin Ayub qualified for the men's K1 slalom (single slalom) event at the Atlanta Olympic Games in 1996. Malaysia won four silver medals at the 1999 Southeast Asian Canoe Championships in Myanmar and its first international canoeing gold medal in

Competitive canoeing and kayaking

Although paddling in a kayak is called 'kayaking', 'canoeing' is sometimes used as an umbrella term to include both sports. There are, however, distinctions between the two sports. A kayak (below right) is a closed-cockpit boat in which the paddler sits with legs straightened. The boat is propelled by a double-blade paddle. The variation of the canoe (below left) that is used in competitions is an open-cockpit boat in which the paddler rests on one knee. The boat is propelled by a single-blade paddle.

The Nenggiri Challenge

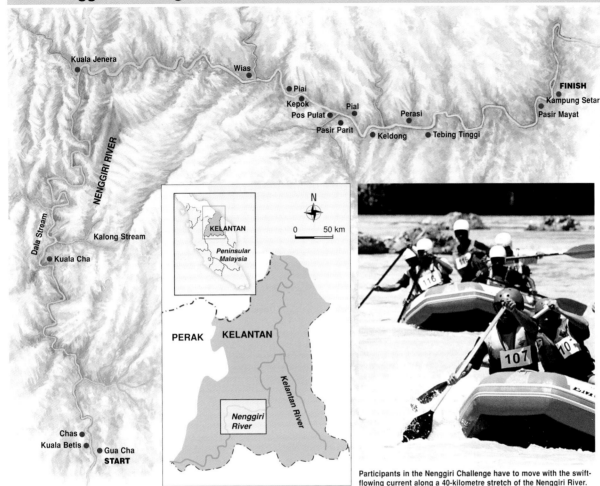

The only white water rafting competition held in Malaysia, the Nenggiri Challenge was inaugurated in 2001. The race, featuring competitors from Malaysia and abroad, comprises two categories: rubber dinghies for teams of five participants and kayaks for individual participants.

The Nenggiri Challenge begins in the upper reaches of the Nenggiri River, which is a tributary of Kelantan River in the district of Gua Musang, Kelantan. The starting point of the race is Gua Cha, a cave well known for the archaeological evidence of prehistoric inhabitation found there. The race route involves an overnight stop at Pos Pulat, an Orang Asli settlement, and ends in the Malay village of Kampung Setar, approximately 40 kilometres downriver.

Participants in the Nenggiri Challenge have to move with the swift-flowing current along a 40-kilometre stretch of the Nenggiri River.

the K4 500-metre (four-person kayaking team) event in the 2001 Asean Junior Championship in Putrajaya with a team comprising Ooi Yee Khun, Fajjan Satta, Mohammad Afri Aziz and Yusri Amad.

White water rafting

Modern rafting started in 1842, when Lieutenant John Fremont of the United States army commenced his explorations of the Platte River. He used a rubber raft, called an air army boat, with varying degrees of success, surviving rapids that would have destroyed wooden rafts, but frequently capsizing nonetheless.

The dry season in Malaysia, from January to May, is a good time for novices to get acquainted with white water rafting because there are slower rapids and the water level is typically low. Suitable rivers for beginners are Sungai Sungkai in Perak, Sungai Sedim in Kedah, or any other river which has a low gradient and thus flows at a slower velocity.

For more experienced rafters, the best season to shoot the rapids is during the rainy season from May until September. Sabah and Sarawak experience the same general weather patterns, but the rapids in these two states are more dangerous than those of the Peninsula and suitable only for more experienced rafters. White water rafting in Sabah is organized as both a recreational activity and a tourist attraction.

FAR LEFT: White water rafting on Sungai Sedim in Kedah.

LEFT: Canoe polo match at the 11th Asian Canoe Championship held in Putrajaya in 2005. Canoe polo pits two teams of five people in kayaks against each other. The objective of the game is to outscore the opposing team using a water polo ball. Players may use their hands to pass the ball or score, and are allowed to hit the ball with their paddles.

Scuba diving

Scuba diving is a popular pastime which enables close-range observation of marine life. In Malaysia, divers encounter a myriad of life forms that exist only in the tropical seas. The Malaysian Sport Diving Association (MSDA) oversees the development and regulation of scuba diving in the country, and various local agencies offer international certification courses.

Scuba divers beholding the abundance of marine life around a coral reef near Layang Layang Island in Sabah.

Miniature sheets issued in 2001 and 2003 showcasing the beauty and diversity of Malaysian islands and marine life.

Diving inventions

In 1535, Guglielmo de Lorena created and used the first modern diving bell. However, the concept of an underwater breathing apparatus was only fully realized in 1943 when renowned diver Jacques Cousteau and engineer Emile Gagnan designed and tested the first 'aqualung'. Scuba (Self Contained Underwater Breathing Apparatus) equipment then became widely used by recreational divers and, by 1949, aqualungs were made available around the world.

First Malaysian scuba divers

One of the first Malaysians to be involved in scuba diving was flying instructor Captain Sim Yong Wah, who joined the Malayan Sub-Aqua Club and trained under foreign divers in 1971 on Pulau Pangkor.

In 1978, Jim Tolar, a National Association of Underwater Instructors (NAUI)-qualified dive instructor, started conducting free courses at the International School of Kuala Lumpur. Sim and Michael Tong were among the first Malaysians to gain NAUI and Professional Association of Diving Instructors (PADI) certification.

MSDA logo.

MSDA founding president and president as at 2008 Datuk Mukhriz Mahathir.

Malaysian Sport Diving Association

In 1996, the Malaysian Sport Diving Association (MSDA) was formed by dive operators to promote the growth and development of scuba diving in the country. The MSDA is also responsible for defining and reviewing the high standards of scuba diving safety, service and training, as well as care for the environment.

Since 1998, MSDA members, under the banner of Tourism Malaysia, have taken part in the annual Asian Dive Expo (ADEX) held in various countries in the region. To further promote the scuba diving industry, the Malaysia International Dive Expo (MIDE) was held in 2006 and 2007.

Other events which have been organized by the MSDA include the Malaysian Heritage Festival, Malaysian Dive Challenge, Pesta Laut, How Safe Is Diving in Malaysia? campaign, Asian Boat Show, Asia Dive Exhibition, Underwater Malaysia National Photo Contest, and the Tag Heuer Under Pressure and Celebrate the Sea underwater imagery exhibitions.

Amazing underwater world

The tropical waters of Malaysia offer some of the world's best scuba diving. Divers can swim with whale sharks, hover around immense coral gardens and walls and dive on hulking World War II shipwrecks. Malaysia is home to 40 marine parks with crystal clear waters teeming with vividly hued coral reefs and a wealth of underwater life.

Among the most popular scuba diving sites in the country are Pulau Sipadan and Pulau Perhentian. Pulau Sipadan, off the coast of Sabah, features caves, walls, canyons, plateaus and overhangs. Sea turtles and one of the largest schools of barracuda in the world inhabit the area. Pulau Perhentian is located off the coast of Terengganu. Divers prize Perhentian's small constellation of rocky islets for their giant soft corals, large schools of pelagic fish and nocturnal sea shells.

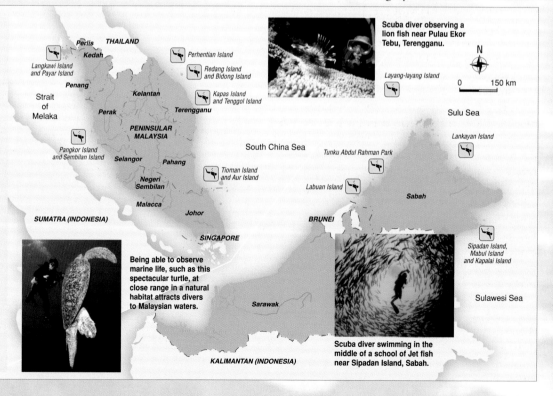

Scuba diver observing a lion fish near Pulau Ekor Tebu, Terengganu.

Being able to observe marine life, such as this spectacular turtle, at close range in a natural habitat attracts divers to Malaysian waters.

Scuba diver swimming in the middle of a school of Jet fish near Sipadan Island, Sabah.

Angling

Initially practised as a means of gathering food, fishing or angling has evolved into a recreational activity and competitive sport. Malaysia's tropical waters are home to about 380 freshwater and 700 saltwater fish species, making them a prime destination for anglers. Locally organized angling competitions draw participants from near and far.

Participants at the 12th Angling Competition organized by the Penang Angling Association near Bayan Lepas Coastal Road, 2007.

Early angling

Fishing with a bamboo rod and line has been practised by the Malays and other indigenous people for many centuries along with other methods such as net casting and fish trapping. Modern angling was introduced to Malaya in the early 1900s by the British, who pioneered the use of cane rods and spinning reels. After World War II, anglers often used 'aerial rods' constructed from the steel aerials of military tanks.

Giant fish caught off the shore of Perak in 1922. The British introduced modern angling to Malaya, resulting in the activity becoming a popular pastime among locals.

Local angling organization and industry

In the 1950s, the Malayan Angling Association was formed by members of the British community with a small group of locals. The post-Independence era, however, saw the demise of this organization as many expatriates left the country.

Angling, as a sport, experienced a revival in 1990 with the formation of the Malaysian Angling Association (Persatuan Memancing Malaysia or PeMM). Established by a group of anglers in the Klang Valley, the PeMM has since become the official representative body for Malaysian anglers. The association regularly holds angling events and seminars and issues publications which communicate rules and codes of ethics in an effort to promote sportsmanship and conservation.

It is estimated that there are more than one million recreational fishermen in the country who generate millions of Ringgit worth of business in the fishing tackle, travel and hospitality industries. Malaysia has also become an increasingly popular destination for 'angling holidays'. Private companies offer tourists the chance to land the catch of a lifetime at various marine and inland destinations. Favoured targets include sailfish, black marlin, amberjack and dogtooth or yellowfin tuna in the seas and the giant snakehead, Malaysian red mahseer and jungle perch in the rivers and lakes.

Many local clubs have been formed to serve the interests of Malaysian anglers. These include the Penang Angling Association and the Kelah Action Group of Malaysia (KAGUM), a voluntary organization focused on conserving Malaysian rivers and their sport fishes.

Angling competitions

Fishing competitions and tournaments are held regularly in Malaysia. Popular among these are beach fishing competitions which offer substantial prize money, such as the 'Ultra-Friendly Series', where freshwater-lure- and fly-fishermen compete on a catch–and–release basis, and the Puspafish Fishing Carnival. Among the offshore competitions, the premier tournament is the annual Labuan Classic, which is on the itinerary of the International Game Fishing Association's Rolex Classic series.

The fishing tackle industry and local fishing magazines also get involved in fishing competitions and seminars. Highlights of the annual angling calendar are the Malaysian Angling and Outdoor Recreation Fair organized by *Rod & Line* magazine and the annual GP Joran and Royal Pahang Billfish tournaments organized by *Joran*, an angling supplement in the *Berita Harian* newspaper.

PeMM logo.

PeMM founding president Dato' Mohamed Darus Haji Mahmud.

PeMM president as at 2008 Major (retired) Ismail Jr Feizol.

Angling records set by Malaysians		
Name	Species and weight	Location and type
Faiz Karim	Striated snakehead (3.5kg)	Selangor Freshwater
Peter Choy Mean Sang	Great snakehead (3.55kg)	Pahang River Freshwater
Teh Ah Teck	Hampala barb or Malaysian jungle perch (6.5kg)	Temengor Lake, Perak Freshwater
Christopher Tan	Giant snakehead (10.0kg)	Dengkil, Selangor Freshwater
Zainuddin Ibrahim	Red mahseer (*kelah*) (12kg)	Jeram Besu, Pahang Freshwater
Vincent Yeo Hock Boon	Humphead Maori wrasse (19.8kg)	Maldives Saltwater
Anthony Webb	Ruby snapper (25.25 kg)	Spratly Islands Saltwater

Teh Ah Teck with his record 6.5-kilogram hampala barb caught in Temengor Lake, Perak.

Anthony Webb with his record breaking 25.25-kilogram ruby snapper, caught off the Spratly Islands.

CONTACT SPORTS

Chinese immigrants brought wushu—the term encompasses martial arts as well as activities such as Lion Dance and *qigong*—to this country where it is still practised as a form of recreation and exercise. Malaysians have also excelled in competitive wushu, with world champions in Ho Ro Bin, Lim Yew Fai, Pui Fook Chien and Chai Fong Ying.

Silambam, the art of stick fighting, is believed to be 5000 years old. Indian immigrants are responsible for introducing it in the country. Another ancient Indian martial art originating from Kerala, kalari payat, is a form of combat primarily directed at self defence. It too has an increasing number of Malaysian practitioners.

In fact a whole host of martial arts have taken hold and are practised here including aikido, ninjutsu, kendo and various forms of kickboxing. Judo was introduced by occupying Japanese forces during World War II and became established in the early 1950s. Its popularity grew to the point where Malaysian judo exponents participated in the 1964 Tokyo Olympics, where the sport was contested for the first time. The Japanese also introduced karate here. Malaysians who studied karate in Japan helped to spread the art when they returned home and set up karate schools. Competitively, Malaysians have achieved international success at the Asian Games and the World Karate Championships. The martial art of taekwondo was introduced to Malaysia in the 1960s by the then Korean Ambassador to Malaysia General Choi Hong Hi. National and inter-club championships are held regularly, while national exponents have succeeded at all levels all over the world.

The country's national fencing body was formed in 1959 and succeeded in sending a fencer to the 1964 Tokyo Olympics. Local fencers have had success at the regional level, particularly from the 1980s. Fencing has been included in Sukan Malaysia since 2002.

Boxing is a riveting spectator sport which tests the skill, speed and mental tenacity of its participants. The most significant boxing event ever held in Malaysia was the heavyweight title fight between Muhammad Ali and Joe Bugner in 1975. Malaysian amateur national boxers have punched their way to glory at the Commonwealth Games.

Chai Fong Ying on her way to winning the gold medal in the women's wushu *taiji quan* event at the 2006 Asian Games in Doha, the first Malaysian woman to win gold in this event at the Games.

The ancient South Indian art of silambam, a form of stick fighting, is described in Tamil mythology. It was introduced to Malaysia in the late 19th century by labourers from Tamil Nadu who came to work in agricultural estates.

1. Malaysia's M. Sri Rajeswari (right) attacking her opponent from Vietnam in the 53-kilogram women's karate-do kumite individual competition at the 2001 SEA Games in Kuala Lumpur. Sri Rajeswari won the gold medal after winning the bout 6–1.

2. Large crowd at the Malawati Stadium in Shah Alam to watch Sapok Biki battle Moses Kinyua of Kenya at the 1998 Commonwealth Games 48-kilogram finals. Biki went on to win Malaysia's first ever Commonwealth boxing gold medal.

3. Aikido master K. Thambirajah demonstrating his martial prowess with the help of his students. Thambirajah was the first Malaysian to be graded the rank of 'Shodan' (first-dan) by the Japanese government in 1957.

4. Malaysia's Lim Teng Piao (right) sparring with an opponent from Singapore on his way to winning the gold medal in the men's individual foil in the 1989 SEA Games in Kuala Lumpur.

5. Taekwondo trainee exhibition in 1967 by army participants. An exponent demonstrates how to break planks with his feet while jumping high into the air.

Fencing

Introduced to Malaya in the late 1950s, the sport of fencing rapidly established itself locally. In 1964, the Malaysian Fencing Federation (MFF) was formed and a Malaysian fencer took part in the Tokyo Olympic Games. Since the 1980s, local duellers have consistently distinguished themselves in competitions at the regional level.

Persekutuan Lawan Pedang Malaysia
Malaysian Fencing Federation

Top: MFF logo.

Above left: MAFA founding president Ronnie Theseira.

Above right: MFF president as at 2008 Ahmad Farik Haji Abdul Hamid.

The fencing tradition

An extension of the traditional use of swords in battle, fencing as a sport was introduced in Europe. It was a popular pastime among members of the nobility. In the late 15th century, Spain pioneered the modern sport of fencing and published the first two fencing manuals. The sport was further refined in Italy with the introduction of fencing positions such as the lunge. In the 16th century, Queen Catherine de Médicis invited many Italian fencing masters to France in order to develop fencing there. This resulted in the formation of the French Fencing Academy in 1567, leading to even more noblemen killed in duels than in war. French and Italian masters proceeded to popularize the sport throughout the world with the introduction of the épée and foil to replace the rapier.

Two participants battling it out during the 2006 Malaysian Open fencing championship at Stadium Putra in Bukit Jalil.

Fencing developments

The Malayan Amateur Fencing Association (MAFA) was formed in Melaka in 1959 with Ronnie Theseira as its first president. In the same year, the first recorded fencing competition in Malaysia took place in Melaka. This foil event was won by Jane Tan Beng Siew, the only woman to compete in the competition.

MAFA subsequently changed its name to the Malaysian Fencing Federation (MFF) in 1964, and became affiliated to the Asian Fencing Confederation (AFC) and the sport's world governing body, Fédération Internationale d'Escrime (FIE). The Malaysian team went on to participate in the 1964 Olympics in Tokyo. As at 2008, the MFF comprises 12 state associations.

In 1988, Malaysia participated in the inaugural Southeast Asian Fencing Federation (SEAFF) Games in Jakarta, and won one gold, one silver and one bronze. In 1998, the Commonwealth Fencing Championships were organized in Shah Alam in conjunction with the Commonwealth Games held in Kuala Lumpur. The first large-scale Malaysian

Fencing techniques and equipment

Equipment and scoring

The Olympic sport of fencing comprises three electrified weapons: the foil, épée and sabre. Fencing bouts are contested by two competitors on a rectangular strip and fenced one touch (valid hit) at a time until one fencer scores enough touches with his weapon to win. Electronic scoring aids are normally used to assist in the detection of touches.

The rules governing these three weapons are determined by the International Fencing Federation (FIE). Fencers wear highly protective special clothing that covers their entire body.

Techniques

Lunge

1. The foil is extended and the point aimed directly at the target until the arm is fully extended.

2. As the front foot steps out across the floor, the body falls forward and down, staying as upright as possible. The left arm is kept erect and behind.

3. After the weapon-arm is extended, the front foot kicks out, heel leaving the floor first, staying as close to the floor as possible. The back foot remains flat on the floor, but can drag a little to extend the reach if necessary.

4. Forward motion is stopped by the landing of the front foot, which will travel forward about three foot-lengths from its original position. The majority of the forward momentum should stem from the energy of the front foot and body pushing forward while the back leg straightens. The front leg should not bend beyond 90 degrees.

Parry

A specific defensive manoeuvre to deflect an opponent's weapon.

Riposte

An offensive action following the successful parry of an attack.

Duelling weapons

90 centimetres

88 centimetres

Foil: A thin weapon with a blunted or 'foiled' tip that is used for thrusting at an opponent.

Épée: Similar to the foil but with a stiffer and heavier triangular shaped blade.

Sabre: A slashing weapon with a curved guard and a triangular shaped blade.

Set-up of a fencing strip or 'piste'

The **spring-loaded spool** shortens or lengthens the cable according to the movement of the fencer and sends signals to the electronic scoring apparatus.

The **retractable cable** connects the metallic jacket to the spring-loaded spool.

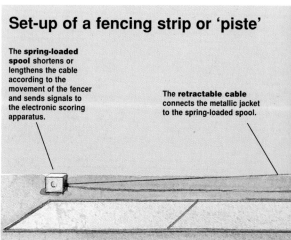

Notable fencers

1. Ronnie Theseira in 1967. He was instrumental in introducing and promoting fencing in Malaysia.

2. Jane Tan Beng Siew (front, centre), champion of the foil event in the first Malaysian fencing competition in 1959, with other local pioneer fencers.

3. Zairul Zaimi Mohd Arsad (right and inset) competing in the men's foil event at the SEA Games in Thailand, 2007. He clinched a bronze medal in the competition.

4. Lim Teng Piao being held aloft after winning a gold medal in the men's individual foil event at the Kuala Lumpur SEA Games in 1989.

5. Malaysian men's épée team (back row, right), winners of a bronze medal at the 2007 SEA Games in Thailand, with the other medal-winning épée teams.

Open was held in 2006 with the participation of fencers from Singapore and Thailand. The same year, the Asian Youth Championship and Asian Fencing Championship (AFC) were both hosted in Malaysia.

Among the national fencing competitions is the National Grand Prix, an annual trio of tournaments initiated in 2005 by the MFF to create a more competitive environment with ranking points awarded to local fencers. After the events, the top 16 fencers with the most accumulated points move on to compete in the National Grand Prix finals. The biennial national games, Sukan Malaysia (SUKMA), has featured fencing as an event since 2002.

The nation's top duellers

Ronnie Theseira represented the country at the 1964 Tokyo Olympics, becoming the only Malaysian fencer thus far to have taken part in the Olympic Games. He also took part in the 1970 Commonwealth Games in Edinburgh and the 1986 World Fencing Championship in Bulgaria.

Kok Sai Hoong won a bronze medal in the epee event at the inaugural Asian Youth Championships held in Kuala Lumpur in 1989 at the age of 16. At the 1989 SEA Games in Kuala Lumpur, Lim Teng Piao captured the gold medal in the men's individual foil event and also won the gold at the second SEAFF meet in Bangkok the following year. At the first SEAFF Games in Jakarta in 1988, the men's team of Mok Chek Wong, Loh Kin Kien, Ong Chuan Hock and Ong Chin Chye clinched the gold in the foil event. Foo May Lan won the silver medal in the individual épée event at the 1989 SEA Games.

At the 2007 SEA Games in Thailand, Zairul Zaimi Mohd Arsad won a bronze medal in the men's foil event and men's team captured a bronze medal in the épée event.

Primary school students practising fencing at Alice Smith School in Kuala Lumpur, 2006.

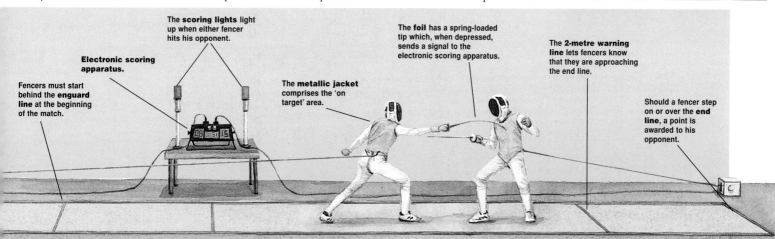

The **scoring lights** light up when either fencer hits his opponent.

Electronic scoring apparatus.

Fencers must start behind the **enguard line** at the beginning of the match.

The **foil** has a spring-loaded tip which, when depressed, sends a signal to the electronic scoring apparatus.

The **metallic jacket** comprises the 'on target' area.

The **2-metre warning line** lets fencers know that they are approaching the end line.

Should a fencer step on or over the **end line**, a point is awarded to his opponent.

Taekwondo

Taekwondo was founded as a martial art in Korea approximately 5000 years ago. The first Malaysian students of the art learned from General Choi Hong Hi, a prominent figure in the global development of taekwondo as an organized sport. Malaysian taekwondo exponents have brought home medals from major international competitions.

Taekwondo exponent jumping over 10 people to break a plank during a demonstration at the 2005 Martial Arts Festival in Kuching, Sarawak.

Logo of the Malaysia Taekwondo Association.

ABOVE LEFT: Logo of the Malaysia Taekwondo Federation.

ABOVE RIGHT: Logo of the Malaysia Taekwondo Clubs Association.

Ancient origins

Taekwondo has a 5000-year old history with its origins tracing back to South Korea. It began as a self-defence martial art called 'subak' or 'taekkyon' as tribal communities fought against each other to gain supremacy. Literally translated, *tae* means to smash with the feet, *kwon* denotes striking with the hands, and *do* means a method or way. The International Taekwondo Federation was founded in 1966, and taekwondo sparring was included as a demonstration sport at the Olympic Games in 1988 and 1992, and as an official event from 2000.

Taekwondo in Malaysia

Taekwondo was brought to Malaysia in 1963 by General Choi Hong Hi, then Ambassador of the Republic of Korea to Malaysia and founder of the International Taekwondo Federation. The Selangor Taekwondo Association was formed in 1963.

The Malaysia Taekwondo Association (MTA) was formally registered in 1974 and became an affiliate of the World Taekwondo Federation (WTF) in 1975. Two other local governing bodies are the Malaysia Taekwondo Clubs Association (MTCA) and the Malaysia Taekwondo Federation (MTF), both of which organize annual events such as the MTF National Taekwondo Championships, the MTCA Inter-club Championships and the Junior Taekwondo Championships.

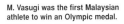
M. Vasugi was the first Malaysian athlete to win an Olympic medal.

Achievements

R. Selvamuthu was the first Malaysian exponent to excel at a major international taekwondo meet when he won a silver medal in the men's flyweight category at the 1986 Asian Games in Seoul. Two years later, M. Vasugi became the first Malaysian athlete, albeit in a demonstration event, to win an Olympic medal when she captured a bronze in the women's flyweight category at the 1988 Olympic Games in Seoul. The following year, Malaysia clinched 10 gold medals in taekwondo events at the SEA Games in Kuala Lumpur.

In 1992, taekwondo was again contested as a demonstration sport at the Olympic Games, and Hii King Hung took the women's bantamweight bronze medal at the competition in Barcelona. The same year, Sarah Chung became the first Malaysian Asian Championships gold medallist when she won the women's heavyweight category in Kuala Lumpur.

Elaine Teo represented Malaysia at the 2004 Olympic Games in Athens in the 49-kilogram women's event. She qualified for the Olympics after winning a silver medal at the Asian Taekwondo Olympic Qualifying Games that year. Also in 2004, Teo won gold medals at the Korean and Austrian International Opens. Following her Olympic Games participation, she was named the 2004 Sportswoman of the Year.

ABOVE LEFT: Joyce Ong (left) sparring with R. Selvamuthu in 1989. Ong won the SEA Games taekwondo welterweight title in 1987 and 1989. Both Ong and Selvamuthu were part of the Malaysian taekwondo team that won ten gold medals in the 1989 SEA Games in Kuala Lumpur.

ABOVE RIGHT: Hii King Hung with the bronze medal she won in the 1992 Olympic Games.

BELOW LEFT: Sarah Chung was Malaysia's first gold medallist in the Asian Taekwondo Championships in 1992.

BELOW RIGHT: Elaine Teo (right) taking on Guatemala's Euda Carias at the 2004 Olympic Games in Athens.

BOTTOM: The Malaysian taekwondo team which won 10 gold medals at the 15th SEA Games in 1989.

Karate

Introduced to Malaysia in the 1960s by Japanese instructors and developed by overseas-trained locals, karate experienced a surge in popularity locally in the 1970s with the formation of numerous clubs and associations. Malaysian karate exponents have been winning medals in international competitions since 1985.

Students sparring at the first Perak Open Koshiki Championship in 2003 at the Sekolah Jenis Kebangsaan Chung Tack in Ipoh.

The early days

Karate's history in Malaysia can be traced back to the early 1960s with the arrival of Japanese instructors including Y. Ishigawa, who brought with him the *Shito-Ryu* karate style. In 1965, a few of his students from Universiti Malaya formed the Universiti Malaya Karate-Do Club. In addition, Malaysians who had learned karate in Japan brought this knowledge back and began teaching others. Most of the karate clubs in Malaysia were formed according to their respective styles such as *Goshin-Ryu*, *Shorin-Ryu*, *Shito-Ryu*, *Kyokushin-Kai* and *Shotokan*.

In 1972, the Malaysian Association of Shito-Ryu Karate and the Universiti Malaya Karate-Do Club spearheaded the formation of the Federation of Malaysia Karate-Do Organizations (FEMKO). Malaysia first participated in the World Karate Federation championships in 1972 in Paris and was represented by Sheikh Naser Anuar and Raymond Tan with Ravee Raghavan as coach. The following year, the national team took part in the first Asia Pacific Union of Karate-Do Organizations (APUKO) Championship in Singapore.

The Malaysian Karate Federation (MAKAF), which succeeded FEMKO, was formed in 1978 with the participation of all of the registered karate clubs in the country from the various styles. The first national senior karate championship was organized by the MAKAF in 1981, while the national junior/cadet championship was inaugurated in 1991.

Karate success

Malaysia's first karate SEA Games gold medals were won in 1987 by P. Arivalagan in the men's *kumite* 60-kilogram event, Chan Foong Ching in the women's *kumite* 60-kilogram event, and Wong Yik Ling in the women's *kumite* over-60-kilogram event. In 1998, C. Muralitharan and R. Muniandy clinched the country's first Asian Games karate gold medals in the men's *kumite* below-55-kilogram and below-75-kilogram competitions respectively.

At the APUKO Championships in 1985, which were held in Kota Kinabalu, the men's team took the *kata* gold, and Ang Lye Hong and Angie Chan won bronze medals in the *kumite* event.

The highest individual achievement by a Malaysian came at the 2002 Karate World Championships in Madrid when S. Premila won a bronze medal in the women's open *kumite* event; the national team returned with two gold and four bronze medals.

S. Premila and R. Puvaneswaran also won gold medals in the women's *kumite* under-63-kilogram and men's *kumite* below-55-kilogram events at the 2002 Asian Games in Busan. Malaysian exponents also captured one silver and two bronze medals. At the 2006 Asian Games in Doha, the national team won four silver and three bronze medals.

At the Asian Senior Karate-Do Championships, Malaysia won three silver and seven bronze medals in 1998 in Singapore; three gold, four silver and six bronze medals in 2001 in Malaysia; and four silver and three bronze medals in 2004 in Macau.

MAKAF founding president Dr Leong Kwok Onn.

MAKAF president as at 2008 Datuk Seri Zulkipli Mat Noor.

Logo of the Malaysian Karate Federation.

Karate events

Kumite: A sparring contest between two competitors.

Kata: A set sequence of movements performed by competitors to demonstrate karate techniques.

1. Ku Jin Keat in his gold medal *kata* performance at the Manila SEA Games in 2005. The Malaysian team won four golds at the 2005 event, and eight golds at the 2007 SEA Games in Thailand.

2. S. Premila celebrates after landing a punch in the women's *kumite* 60-kilogram final during the 2002 Asian Games in Busan. Premila proceeded to win Malaysia's first gold medal in an Asian Games karate event.

3. The women's *kumite* team (from left) comprising Agnes Tan, M. Sri Rajeswari, Ng Chai Lin and S. Premila after their gold-medal-winning performance in Genting Highlands during the 2001 Asian Senior Karate-Do Championship.

4. R. Puvaneswaran overwhelming his opponent during the karate men's 55-kilogram *kumite* semi-final at the 2002 Asian Games in Busan. Puvaneswaran advanced to the final and won the gold medal.

Wushu

Wushu encompasses the many diverse forms of traditional Chinese martial arts. Brought to the country by Chinese immigrants in the 1800s, wushu has become popular as both a recreational and competitive activity in Malaysia. National exponents have reached the pinnacle of the sport, winning five titles at the World Wushu Championships.

Malaysian wushu team showing off the medals that they won at the SEA Games in Manila, 2005.

ABOVE LEFT: WFM founding president Tan Koon Swan.

ABOVE RIGHT: WFM president as at 2008 Dato' Seri Kee Yong Wee.

WFM logo.

The Chin Woo Association set up a branch in Kuala Lumpur in the early 1920s and was one of the first wushu schools in the country. The current Chin Woo Stadium (above) was built in 1962 and is located in Kuala Lumpur.

Chinese martial arts

Wushu, often colloquially referred to as 'kung fu', means martial arts in Chinese. Wushu comprises all forms of Chinese martial arts and martial arts-inspired activities, including the lion dance, dragon dance, *qigong,* acrobatics and *taiji quan* (see 'Traditional Chinese recreation'). However, as a sport, it consists of two disciplines: *taolu* (routines) and *shanshou* (combat). In 1990, the International Wushu Federation (IWUF) was formed in Beijing.

Wushu in Malaysia

Wushu most likely arrived with the wave of Chinese immigration to Malaya in the early 1800s, and was initially practised as a cultural pastime and form of exercise among the Chinese community. In 1973, the Kuala Lumpur Chee Fee Tai Chi Association, along with ten other associations, organized the 3rd Southeast Asia Wushu Championships. The Wushu Federation of Malaysia (WFM) was subsequently established in 1978.

Notable exponents

In 1992, 46-year-old Lim Chew Ah won the gold medal in the women's *taiji* boxing event at the World Grand Wushu Festival in Shanghai. Lim remains one of the leading women's wushu exponents in Malaysia, acting as team manager at the 2003 Asian Junior Championship in Beijing. In 2005, she was awarded the Olympic Council of Malaysia's Women in Sport Award.

Ho Ro Bin won the *nandao* gold at the 1995 World Wushu Championships in Hong Kong. At the 2002 Asian Games in Busan, he took the gold medal in the *nanquan* competition. At the 2004 Asian Championships in Yangon, Ho captured two gold medals and one silver medal.

At the Wushu World Championships held in 2005 in Hanoi, Malaysia won an impressive four world titles—*nandao* (Ho Ro Bin), *nanjian* (Lim Yew Fai), *nangun* (Pui Fook Chien) and *taiji quan* (Chai Fong Ying)—and finished third in the overall medal tally. Chai Fong Ying also brought home a gold medal after emerging victorious in the women's *taiji quan* competition at the 2006 Asian Games in Doha. She repeated the feat in the same event at the 2007 World Wushu Championships in Beijing.

Since being included as a SEA Games event in 1991, Malaysians have consistently won wushu medals. The country's best performance was at the SEA Games in 2001 in Kuala Lumpur, when local exponents picked up six gold, two silver and five bronze medals. Lim Kin, Ho Ro Bin and Oh Poh Soon bagged one, two and three gold medals respectively.

Wushu *taolu* (routines) events

劍 術 jianshu
(sword play)
Pictured: Lim Yew Fai

南拳 nanquan
(southern style boxing)
Pictured: Pui Fook Chien

槍 術 qiangshu
(spear play)
Pictured: Bryan Sonylah

長拳 changquan
(long range boxing)
Pictured: Ang Eng Chong

太極劍 taiji jian
(taiji sword play)
Pictured: Chai Fong Ying

南棍 nangun
(southern cudgel play)
Pictured: Ho Ro Bin

刀 術 daoshu
(broadsword play)
Pictured: Ng Say Yoke

太極拳 taiji quan
(taiji boxing)
Pictured: Lee Yang

南刀 nandao
(southern broadsword play)
Pictured: Diana Bong

棍 術 gunshu
(cudgel play)
Pictured: Chai Fong Wei

Silambam

Silambam, the ancient Indian art of stick fighting, is one of the oldest forms of martial arts, originating approximately 5000 years ago. Brought to the Malay Peninsula in the 15th Century by Indian traders, silambam has remained popular locally. The Malaysian Silambam Association, formed in 1976, has spearheaded the development of the martial art in the country.

Silambam demonstration by two exponents from the Malaysian Silambam Association during the 2007 Ponggal Festival in Melaka.

Competitive silambam

Display at the 8th National Silambam Championship in Penang, 2004.

Weapons

Silambam is the art of fighting using sticks of varying lengths depending on the height of the practitioner. Other weapons are also sometimes utilized including spear-like sticks with blades attached, short sticks used in pairs, swords and clubs.

Competitions

Silambam competitions are contested in a circular area between 6.1 and 7.6 metres in diameter. Individual competitors are categorized according to their gender, age and weight class. There are three rounds in a competition. In the first round, competitors perform a routine for two minutes to demonstrate their skills and knowledge of attack and defence techniques. A total of 20 points are awarded in this round. In the second and third rounds, which each last for one and a half minutes, competitors engage in a stick fight with each other.

Silambam exponent lying on a board covered with nails to demonstrate strength and mental focus at a festival in Kuala Lumpur, 1995.

A point is awarded to the competitor who, holding his stick with two hands, hits his opponent on the leg, chest, abdomen, upper arm, back or buttocks. The competitor with the most points at the end of three minutes is declared the winner.

Competitors must keep moving inside the ring and spinning the stick in a continuous motion until the end of the match. Failure to do so will result in a warning or points deduction. It is an offence to hit an opponent with great force or recklessness or to hit an opponent on the head, from the waist to thigh and from finger to elbow. If a competitor dislodges the stick from the hands of his opponent, he is automatically declared the winner of the match.

Malaysian Silambam Association exponents fighting with knives in Perak, 2006.

Origins of silambam

According to Indian legend, silambam originated in the state of Tamil Nadu approximately 5000 years ago. In this martial art form, a stick, sometimes with a small blade attached, is used to execute many attacking and defensive combat manoeuvres.

Silambam in Malaysia

In the early 15th century, silambam was introduced to Southeast Asia by Indian traders who came to Melaka and other ports throughout the region. In the late 19th century, Tamil labourers were

Master Mahalingam, with his book *Silambattam*, the first comprehensive book on silambam published in Malaysia.

brought to Malaya from India to work in rubber estates, and these immigrants spread silambam throughout the country. By the 1920s, masters of silambam, called 'gurus', could be found in Malaya.

The Malaysian Silambam Association (MSA) was formed in 1976 with Datuk V.L. Kanthan as its founding president. In 1989, the MSA organized the first annual national-level silambam competition at Stadium Negara, attracting nearly 500 members from all over the country. In that same year, the MSA launched an instructional manual on silambam. In 1991, a district- and state-level silambam competition was organized with approximately 2000 participants. Silambam was officially recognized as a sport under the Sports Development Act 1997. The popularity of the martial art in Malaysia has steadily increased over the years, and, as at 2008, there are nearly 300 silambam classes with 7000 students in the country. The MSA currently comprises 12 state associations.

A silambam student needs to learn various strategies and skills to qualify as a silambam exponent. The MSA has taken the initiative to draw up a silambam syllabus. Through this comprehensive system, a student can become a qualified exponent within two years.

The belt and uniform system and the basic guidelines for international tournaments were introduced in Malaysia by the MSA and subsequently adopted by the International Association of Silambam.

MSA logo.

MSA president as at 2008 Dr N.G. Baskaran.

ABOVE: Malaysian Silambam Association exponents performing the Fire Act, one of the techniques in silambam.

BELOW: Silambam practitioners performing a ceremonial snake style routine. According to tradition, silambam has both physical and spiritual aspects.

Judo and other martial arts

Unlike karate and taekwondo, judo does not involve any kicks, aerial movements or punches. A judo exponent tries to subdue his opponent by gripping his uniform and using the forces of balance, power and movement. The first judo school was established in 1882 in Japan, while Malaysia's first training centre was opened in 1951. Malaysia is also home to practitioners of a myriad of other martial arts which include aikido, ninjutsu, kendo, kalari payat and forms of kickboxing.

Malaysian judo exponents battling it out at the 6th Eagle Cup Judo Championship in Kuala Lumpur, 2006.

MJF logo.

MJF president as at 2008 Mohamad Taufik Haji Omar.

Goh Wing Wai receiving a gold medal after winning the judo heavyweight category at the 1977 SEA Games in Kuala Lumpur.

Judo achievements

Since 1964, Malaysian exponents have competed regularly at the SEAP, SEA and Asian Games as well as the World Championships. The highest achievements were by Nordin Hamzah and Goh Wing Wai. Both were double gold-medal winners at the SEAP Games, with Nordin taking a gold in 1971 in the middleweight category and in 1973 in the light heavyweight category, while Goh won at the SEA Games in 1977 in the heavyweight category and in 1979 in the open category. Malaysia's two other SEA Games gold medals in judo came from women exponents—Liew Mei Ling in 1977 in the middleweight category and Peggy Evelyn Nicholas in 1981 in the heavyweight category.

Judo history and local development

Judo was founded in Japan in the late 19th century by Kano Jigoro, a martial arts instructor who devised his own style and system of combat. At its most basic level, judo involves two exponents (*judokas*), who by grabbing the judo uniform (*judogi*), attempt to throw or topple each other to the ground or otherwise apply a manoeuvre to drive the opponent into submission. Translated literally from Japanese, judo means 'the way of gentleness', referring to the art's emphasis on the indirect application of force and use of trickery.

Judo was introduced to Malaya by Japanese occupying forces during World War II. In 1951, the first judo club, the Selangor Judo Club, was founded. The club's first instructors were Khor Ghoon Hoe and Chew Choo Soot. The club hired Hiroshi Ichijima, a seventh-*dan* instructor from Tokyo, as its chief instructor. During his tenure, the Selangor Judo Club trained four first-*dan* practitioners. In 1961, the Selangor Judo Club and the 22nd Commonwealth Brigade Judo Club formed the Malaysia Judo Federation (MJF) with Dr N.S. Chin as its inaugural president.

ABOVE LEFT: Aikido instructor training a student in the art's attack and defence movements.

ABOVE RIGHT: Demonstration of the southern Indian combat and self-defence art of kalari payat.

LEFT: Contestants taking part in a Thai Kickboxing (Muay Thai) match in Kelantan, 2006. Aside from being a serious sport, kickboxing is also popular in Malaysia as a form of exercise.

In 1963, the MJF became affiliated to the Judo Union of Asia and the International Judo Federation. The following year, judo exponents Ang Teck Bee and Moorthy Kanapathy Sathia participated at the Olympic Games in Tokyo. The MJF also sent several athletes to compete in the 1965 and 1971 World Judo Championships in Rio de Janeiro and West Germany respectively.

The national judo championships have been held annually by the MJF since 1963. In 1976, the MJF organized the inaugural Association of Southeast Nations Judo Championships in Penang.

Other martial arts

A diverse range of martial arts have been introduced to Malaysia and are gaining increasing numbers of practitioners. Aside from the physical benefits of participating in these sports, to some their spiritual or cultural aspects are also compelling.

Aikido, of Japanese origin, dates back to the 14th century CE. It involves hand-to-hand and weapon combat. While similar to judo, aikido focuses more on redirection of an attacker's momentum through a series of throw and lock techniques. One translation for aikido is 'the way of harmonious spirit'. It was introduced to Malaya around 1960. The Malaysia Aikido Association was formed in 1994.

The Japanese feudal martial art of ninjutsu dates back to the 6th century CE and has more than 300 practitioners in Malaysia since being introduced in the early 1990s. It developed from special techniques for survival including the art of concealment, disguise, information-gathering, and expertise in all forms of fighting and weapons. Kendo, the Japanese martial art of fencing, places emphasis on mental and physical strength. It also has a local following.

Kalari payat, an ancient art of combat and self-defence originating in Kerala in southern India, is popular in Malaysia. Its thousands of techniques include various types of chops, kicks, punches, locks, throws and tactics targeting pressure and vital points. It also has elements of yoga, gymnastics, acrobatics and wrestling as well as spiritual aspects.

Kickboxing, has many variations, but typically combines the use of kicks, punches and throws.

Boxing

Introduced to the country in 1947, boxing is organized in Malaysia on the amateur level. A number of competitions are conducted locally reflecting the popularity of the sport. Malaysia's amateur boxers are a prominent force in the lighter-weight categories and have achieved international success.

Adnan Jusoh (left) on the attack against his opponent from China during the 2003 Senior World Boxing Championships in Thailand.

Fist fighting
Fist fights were first included as a sport in the ancient 23rd Olympic Games in Greece in the year 688 BCE. In 18th-century England, these fights were given some regulation by Jack Broughton who introduced rules in which a round lasted until a man was knocked down and, if he could not continue after 30 seconds, the fight was over. In 1839, the London Prize ring rules provided that bouts be fought in a 24-square foot ring with ropes surrounding it. In 1867, a Scottish aristocrat, John Sholto Douglas, the eighth Marquis of Queensbury, published the 'Queensbury Rules', which remain the basic framework governing glove boxing. Amateur boxing competitions were included for the first time in the modern Olympic Games in London in 1904 and have been a modern Olympic event ever since.

Early local ringfights
Foo Yeow Teng, a volunteer with the Third Battalion Special Service Volunteer Force in Penang, introduced amateur boxing to the public in 1947 at a fund-raising event. Shaw Brothers Studios, a movie production and distribution company, were the main sponsors for this event. In Kuala Lumpur, the Bukit Bintang Park, equipped with a makeshift ring, was home to professional boxing during this time. Other venues for professional boxing owned by the Shaw Brothers included the Jubilee Amusement Park and the Great World Parks in Alor Setar and Penang, which held fights watched by crowds of families looking for amusement.

Malaysia Amateur Boxing Federation
The Malaysia Amateur Boxing Association (MABA) was formed in 1964 and is affiliated to the Association Internationale de Boxe Amateur (AIBA). In 1992, the MABA was deregistered by the Malaysian Registrar of Companies and, in its place, the Malaysia Amateur Boxing Federation (MABF) was founded.

Boxing events and developments
The main amateur boxing competitions organized annually by the MABF for its affiliates are the Malaysia Cup, the National Cadet Championships and the National Junior Championships. Boxing is also an event in the biennial Sukan Malaysia (SUKMA). Another popular series of events is the NSC–MABA–Milo National age group boxing circuit.

The only international-level professional boxing event that has been organized in Malaysia was on 1 July 1975 when the Joe Bugner and Muhammad Ali world heavyweight title fight was held at Stadium Merdeka.

Amateur women's boxing was introduced in Malaysia in 2006.

MABF logo.

ABOVE LEFT: MABF founding president David Choong.

ABOVE RIGHT: MABF president as at 2008 Tan Sri Mohd Isa Samad.

More than 10,000 boxing fans packed Stadium Merdeka to watch Muhammad Ali (left) successfully defend his heavyweight title against Joe Bugner in 1975. The match was televised live around the world.

Successful Malaysian boxers

The first successful local amateur boxer was Captain Terence Stahlman of the Malaysian Armed Forces, who won gold medals in the welterweight category at the 1965 and 1967 SEAP Games. Stahlman also won a bronze medal in the same category at the 1966 Asian Games. The same event also saw Ahmad Mokhtar win a bronze in the flyweight category.

In 1977, Malaysians made their first breakthrough at the SEA Games held in Kuala Lumpur, when five local boxers made it into the finals of their respective divisions. These boxers were Abe Rahim Salim (light flyweight), Syed Mohd Azam (featherweight), Koo Chan Lee (light welterweight), Ibrahim Mardek (middleweight) and Abdul Kader P.V. (heavyweight). All five won silver medals.

In 1998, Sapok Biki won the light flyweight (48 kilograms and below) gold medal at the 16th Commonwealth Games held in Kuala Lumpur, beating Moses Kinyua of Kenya. Sapok also won a silver medal in the 1999 SEA Games in Brunei. Sapok was inducted into the OCM Hall of Fame in 2004.

Adnan Jusoh, a 60-kilogram lightweight event contender from Kelantan, is another prominent Malaysian boxer. At the 1998 Commonwealth Games in Kuala Lumpur, Adnan clinched a bronze medal in the lightweight category. In 2002, he defeated Thai boxer Somluck Kamsing, an Olympic gold medallist, in the semifinals of the 21st Asian Amateur Boxing Championship held in Seremban before defeating Syria's Hmeili Youssef to win Malaysia's first-ever gold medal in the series. In 2003, he again scored another first after winning the Commonwealth Amateur Boxing Championship at Titiwangsa Stadium in Kuala Lumpur, defeating S. Ramanand of India.

Another successful boxer is Zamzai Azizi Mohamad who won a bronze medal in the 48-kilogram light flyweight category at the 2002 Manchester Commonwealth Games. In 2005, he won a gold medal at the Kyrgyzstan Open and a bronze medal at the Kazakhstan Open.

Sapok Biki raises the Malaysian flag at the 1998 Kuala Lumpur Commonwealth Games after winning the nation's first-ever Commonwealth boxing gold medal

Zamzai Azizi Mohamad (left) in action against Namibia's Joseph Jermia during the 48-kilogram category of the 2002 Commonwealth Games.

1. A freestyle motocross event at the 2006 Asian X Games at Sunway Lagoon.

2. Contestants abseiling down a mountain during the 2000 Eco-Challenge race held in Sabah.

3. Paintball players taking part in the World Cup Asia 2006 in Kuala Lumpur.

4. Competitor about to go airborne on his skateboard with the PETRONAS Twin Towers in the background during the 2002 Asian X Games in Kuala Lumpur. Over 300 athletes from Asia-Pacific region competed in skating, skateboarding, bicycle stunt, sport climbing and wakeboarding events during the seven-day competition.

5. Female competitors off to a blazing start at the beginning of the World Mountain Running Trophy on Mount Kinabalu in Sabah, 1999. The race involved running up and down the mountain, a total distance of 21 kilometres. A total of 367 participants from 33 countries took part.

6. Miniature sheet issued in 2000 as a part of the New Millennium series featuring stamps showing (from left) M. Magendran and N. Mohandas, the first Malaysians to reach the peak of Mount Everest in 1997; Gerald and Justin Read, the first Malaysians to walk the North Pole in 1999; and the Malaysian skydiving expedition which landed on the North Pole with a Proton Wira in 1998.

START / FINISH
World Mountain Running Trophy
SABAH, MALAYSIA

ADVENTURE AND EXTREME SPORTS

The terms 'adventure' and 'extreme' sports are generally used to describe activities that are perceived to have a heightened level of risk and danger. These sports are typically individual rather than team activities, require the use of special equipment, and often involve the individual pitting himself against nature to test the limits of his abilities.

Trekking is one of the most basic forms of adventure sports. It can be a simple one-day affair, with nothing more than a walking stick and bottle of water to help the trekker reach the desired destination. Trekking can also be a multi-day event, with more elaborate equipment and against more challenging terrain and weather. Malaysia offers a wide range of terrain and eco-habitats, ranging from tropical rainforests to limestone caves. Malaysian trekkers have also travelled overseas, venturing, as in the case of Datin Paduka Sharifah Mazlina, all the way to the Antarctic.

Mountaineering shares many similarities with trekking, especially in fulfilling the inherent human need to challenge adverse terrain and weather conditions. Malaysians have sought to conquer the mightiest mountains, not only at home, but also abroad, all the way to the top of the world, Mount Everest.

Skydiving was introduced to Malaysia in the late 1970s and its steady growth is indicative of Malaysians' growing appetite for activities that are high on excitement. Similarly, paragliding and paramotoring, both introduced in the 1990s, have also become increasingly popular. The novelty of these activities as well as the challenge of conquering the air make them attractive to those seeking an adrenaline surge.

Skateboarding is a more down-to-earth activity. Skateboarders thrill in completing stunts that demonstrate both their creativity and courage. Skateboarding has come a long way since the days when skateboards were constructed from roller skate wheels and planks. Improvements have made the skateboard more durable and easier to control, contributing to the sport's burgeoning popularity.

Skydiver BASE jumping from the Kuala Lumpur Tower during the Malaysia International Championship of Extreme Skydive and World BASE Cup in 2004.

First developed in the United States in the 1980s, paintball is a team, rather than an individual, form of recreation. It has caught on quickly since its introduction to Malaysia in 2000, with an annual national tournament first organized in 2005. Paintball is seen by many as a means to foster team spirit as it emphasizes strategy and communication.

Mountaineering

Many of Malaysia's highlands were mapped by British explorers in the 19th century. Malaysians today continue the tradition of discovery and adventure over rough and challenging terrain in the country and beyond. In 1997, the nation reached the pinnacle of mountaineering when two Malaysians reached the peak of Mount Everest.

In 1997, M. Magendran (right) and N. Mohandas became the first two Malaysians to reach Everest's peak.

Participant making his way up Mount Kinabalu during the 2005 International Climbathon.

PERSATUAN KEMBARA NEGARA

ABOVE LEFT: Logo of the National Adventure Association of Malaysia (NAAM).

ABOVE RIGHT: NAAM founding and current president Dato' Khalid Yunus.

Mountaineering

The highest peak in Malaysia, Mount Kinabalu, was only truly conquered after three attempts. British officer Hugh Low tried in 1851 and 1858, the latter expedition with Spenser St John. Believing that they had reached the highest peak, they named it St John's Peak. However, 30 years later, John Whitehead's scientific expedition stumbled upon what was then revealed to be the highest point of the mountain, located at 4095 metres above sea level. In 1997, satellite technology revealed that Mount Kinabalu's summit is actually six metres higher, putting its official height at 4101 metres.

In another early episode of mountaineering, British officer William Cameron was commissioned to map the Malayan highlands in 1882. With the help of locals, Cameron's expedition was a huge success and, within two years, he had mapped out the majority of the Malay Peninsula. He left behind records of the area, which eventually led to the discovery of Cameron Highlands in 1908 by H.C. Robinson and C. Borden Kloss.

Other great peaks were scaled in the early 20th century, including Mount Tahan (the highest point in Peninsular Malaysia at 2187 metres above sea level), and Mount Mulu, Mount Batu Lawi and Mount Murud in Sarawak. Although there is little territory left uncharted in the country's

Conquering Mount Everest

On the team's first attempt on the summit on 9 May 1997, inclement weather forced them to return to their base camp. Four team members were then selected for the final attempt: M. Magendran, N. Mohandas, Mohamad Fauzan Hj. Hassan and Gary Choong Kin Wah. The team left again on 18 May and, after further weather delays, reached Camp Four at 1.30 p.m. on 22 May. At 11.00 p.m. on the same day, they headed for the summit. It was -40°C, according to Magendran's temperature gauge, and the wind blew at 80 kilometres per hour. Mohamad Fauzan and Choong Kin Wah succumbed to altitude sickness and turned back after reaching 8400 metres. Magendran and Mohandas continued their ascent and reached the summit of Mount Everest on 23 May.

highlands, many Malaysians still find great joy in the adventure of mountaineering.

Scaling new heights

Zaini Sharani was the first Malaysian to attempt to climb Mount Everest. He made his attempt in 1978, reaching a height of 7376 metres before having to turn back due to lack of equipment. The first Malaysians to reach the mountain's 8400-metre summit were M. Magendran and N. Mohandas on 23 May 1997. After an ordeal that saw their other eight team members succumb to exhaustion and illness, the duo planted the Malaysian flag atop the highest peak in the world. Other Malaysians have subsequently succeeded in conquering Mount Everest.

Mountaineering programmes

The National Adventure Association of Malaysia (NAAM) was registered in 2005. The primary goal of the association is to identify Malaysian climbers to scale Mount Everest once every four years.

In 2007, Marina Ahmad became the first Malaysian woman to reach the summit.

Marina Ahmad, the first Malaysian woman to conquer Mount Everest.

The Circuit Kembara Negara, or Malaysian Adventure Circuit, was first organized in 2005 to promote mountain running amongst Malaysians. Four mountain runs were conducted at Mount Cenuang in Ulu Langat, Mount Angsi in Negeri Sembilan, Mount Tebu in Terengganu and Mount Jerai in Kedah. Each event attracted more than 250 participants. In 2006, three events, plus an elite final event, were held at the same sites to determine the winner of the title of 'King of the Mountains'.

Mount Kinabalu International Climbathon

Among the annual mountain running events in the country is the Mount Kinabalu International Climbathon, which was initiated in 1987 by former national athlete Balwant Singh Kler, the Sabah Amateur Athletic Association and the Sabah Tourism Board. The 21-kilometre event was accepted in 1995 at the World Mountain Racing Association (WMRA) congress. Since 2002, the Mount Kinabalu International Climbathon has been the final race of the Buff Sky Runner World Series circuit and is one of only two races in the circuit that is held outside Europe. The Buff Sky Runner World Series is regulated and coordinated by the Federation for Sport at Altitude (FSA), an organization which is extremely selective in the choice of the six annual races which comprise the World Series.

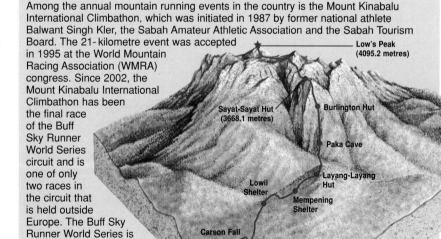

Low's Peak (4095.2 metres)

Sayat-Sayat Hut (3668.1 metres)

Burlington Hut

Paka Cave

Lowii Shelter

Layang-Layang Hut

Mempening Shelter

Carson Fall

Start

Finish

Trekking

Trekking normally refers to a multi-day journey on foot through rugged terrain during which participants must survive in the wild. The objective typically is to visit an interesting location such as a waterfall or mountain, or to view wildlife in its natural environment. The varied forests and warm equatorial climate of Malaysia make trekking a popular form of recreation in the country.

Trekkers crossing Tahan River in Pahang. Precautions must be taken during river crossings as flash floods may occur, with the water level possibly rising by 1.5 metres in minutes.

Trekking through Malaysia

One of the earliest accounts of trekking in Malaysia was recorded by A.R. Wallace in his book entitled *The Malay Archipelago*. He set off from Ayer Panas, Melaka, in 1854 and took two days to reach the top of Mount Ledang by what is now known as the Asahan trail. In the early 1900s, many other trekkers braved the elements to explore the uncharted mountains and hinterlands of the Malay Peninsula.

Certain 'black areas' in the jungles of Malaysia were closed to the public at the onset of the Emergency in 1948. Restrictions on permits to enter the jungle were only lifted following the signing of the peace treaty between the Communist Party of Malaya and the governments of Malaysia and Thailand in 1989.

In the 1980s, Malaysians started taking an interest in 'back to nature' trips, and treks to waterfalls and mountains became popular. Excursions such as the Malaysian Heritage and Scientific Expedition Endau-Rompin, conducted by the Malaysian Nature Society in 1985–86, enabled scientists to carry out research, and members of the public were taken to view the Buaya Sangkut waterfall and the exotic flora on Mount Janing in Johor.

Competitive trekking

Raid Gauloises and Eco-Challenge are events in which teams of four to five members attempt to complete a set route in the fastest time. The courses are both located in some of the most rugged terrain in the world. The first Raid Gauloises was held in New Zealand in 1989. Five years later, Sarawak hosted the event, and a team of Malaysian park rangers took part.

Eco-Challenge, started by Mark Burnett in 1995, is similar to the Raid Gauloises, and has been an even greater success, drawing millions of television viewers globally. In 1998, a Malaysian team comprising Chan Yuen Li, Tang Fook Leong, Gary Leong and Corey Ho took part in the Morocco Eco-Challenge as Team 2020. Since then, a number of adventure races have been held in Malaysia including Eco-Challenge, Sabah (2000), AXN Challenge (2003–05) and Nomad's Eco X-Capade, held annually since 2001.

In 2004, Datin Paduka Sharifah Mazlina became the first Asian woman to trek solo across the South Pole. She covered 1100 kilometres in 22 days with ski sails. In 2007, Mazlina trekked 100 kilometres in 10 days, on skis and on foot, across the North Pole, again becoming the first Asian woman to do so.

Participants crossing Tenom River during the Taman Negara Eco-Challenge in Pahang, 2006.

Datin Paduka Sharifah Mazlina on her way to becoming the first Asian woman to trek solo across the North Pole, 2007.

Popular trekking locations

There are interesting areas to trek in nearly every state in Malaysia including the eight-day trek to the summit of Mount Tahan, the highest point in Peninsular Malaysia; the Mat Kilau trail, named after the Malay warrior who fled to Terengganu after attacking the British forts in Kuala Tembeling in 1894; the spectacular waterfalls of Mount Stong in Kelantan; and Mount Ledang in Johor, home of the famed *Puteri Gunung Ledang* of Malay folklore.

In Sabah, Mount Kinabalu holds the distinction of being the highest point in Southeast Asia, and has always been a popular trekking destination. The Kelabit Highlands in Sarawak offer high-country trekking, while in Mulu National Park there is a trek to view the high limestone pinnacles.

Jungle trekking in the Kelabit Highlands in Sarawak is a major draw for eco-tourists to Malaysia.

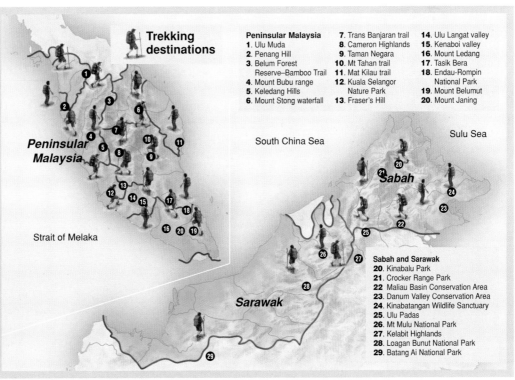

Trekking destinations

Peninsular Malaysia
1. Ulu Muda
2. Penang Hill
3. Belum Forest Reserve–Bamboo Trail
4. Mount Bubu range
5. Keledang Hills
6. Mount Stong waterfall
7. Trans Banjaran trail
8. Cameron Highlands
9. Taman Negara
10. Mt Tahan trail
11. Mat Kilau trail
12. Kuala Selangor Nature Park
13. Fraser's Hill
14. Ulu Langat valley
15. Kenaboi valley
16. Mount Ledang
17. Tasik Bera
18. Endau-Rompin National Park
19. Mount Belumut
20. Mount Janing

Sabah and Sarawak
20. Kinabalu Park
21. Crocker Range Park
22. Maliau Basin Conservation Area
23. Danum Valley Conservation Area
24. Kinabatangan Wildlife Sanctuary
25. Ulu Padas
26. Mt Mulu National Park
27. Kelabit Highlands
28. Loagan Bunut National Park
29. Batang Ai National Park

Peninsular Malaysia

Strait of Melaka

South China Sea

Sulu Sea

Sabah

Sarawak

Paragliding and paramotoring

Paragliding and paramotoring are two adventure sports which have to be undertaken with proper equipment and training. Although still in their infancy in Malaysia, these sports are readily available in the country, and competitions attract participants from all over Malaysia and beyond.

Paragliding through the PETRONAS Twin Towers in Kuala Lumpur.

PTLM logo.

PTLM president as at 2008 Rusnan Saad.

MPA logo.

MPA president as at 2008 Lt Col (retired) Basir Haji Abdul Rahman.

A new way to fly

Recreational paragliding was first developed in France in 1978 and grew rapidly in popularity during the mid-1980s in the French and Swiss Alps. The paramotor was invented in France in the late 1980s as a means of powering a paraglider.

In 1997, Lt Col (retired) Basir Haji Abdul Rahman, a former Royal Malaysian Air Force pilot and skydiver, performed the first paragliding feat in the country when he took off from atop Genting Highlands and landed at the Awana golf course, half way up the hill resort. In 1999, he became the first Malaysian to paraglide down from the summit of Mount Kinabalu in Sabah during the inaugural International Hang Gliding Championships.

Basir spread his knowledge to other Malaysians and foreigners, training more than 500 paramotor pilots over the course of ten years. Learning programmes by Basir and his company are conducted at a training facility in Selangor. Another paragliding centre opened in Seremban in 2007.

In 1998, the Motorized Paragliding Tour Malaysia, covering Kuantan, Kuala Terengganu, Grik and Penang, was organized with the participation of 10 paramotor pilots. Five years later, the tour drew 50 local and foreign pilots who conducted flying demonstrations and coaching sessions at a number of venues around the country. The highlight of the tour was when the participants gracefully guided their machines between the PETRONAS Twin Towers in Kuala Lumpur.

Governing bodies

Formed in 2004, the Malaysia Gliding Association (Persatuan Terbang Layang Malaysia or PTLM) oversees all paragliding activities in the country, while paramotoring is governed by the Malaysian Paramotor Association (MPA), which was founded in 2002. Both are affiliates of the Malaysian Sports Aviation Federation (MSAF), which is recognized by the Fédération Aéronautique Internationale (FAI), the world governing body for all aviation sports.

Competitive events

Although paragliding and paramotoring are still not widely regarded as competitive sports in Malaysia, events such as the Kulim International Paramotor Competition in Kedah in 2005 have raised the profile of the sports locally. A paragliding competition in Selangor began in 2006 with 20 participants. In 2007, it attracted 43 paragliders from 10 countries.

Paragliding and paramotoring

Paragliding and paramotoring

A paraglider is a specially designed wing or parachute enabling a pilot to fly without the need for thrust, which is mandatory for any other type of flying. Basic paragliding equipment consists of the wing, harness, helmet and reserve parachute. A variometer is useful for assisting pilots in finding thermals (rising hot winds which give a paraglider an uplift). A paragliding outfit is made from rip-stop plastic-coated nylon or myla.

Paramotoring, also known as powered paragliding, enables a pilot to fly using a small petrol-driven two-stroke engine for thrust. The motor runs on unleaded petrol mixed with synthetic oil and it can fly for about two hours on average with about eight litres of fuel. Flying at high altitudes requires additional navigational equipment such as a global positioning system, altimeter and variometer.

ABOVE: Two paragliders in the air after jumping off Gunung Ledang (Mount Ophir) during the Ledang Paragliding Challenge in 2005.

RIGHT: The motor used for paramotoring is fixed to the paraglider's back. Here, the paraglider is getting ready for take-off.

RIGHT INSET: Landing during a paramotor event at Pantai Bagan Lalang, Selangor.

Skydiving

Facing great heights and the force of gravity with nothing more than a parachute, skydivers and BASE jumpers must be trained to think and act with measured timing. A world-record breaking BASE jump was performed from the heights of Malaysia's grandest structure, the PETRONAS Twin Towers, as 15 jumpers leapt from one millennium to the next on the eve of the year 2000.

BASE jumper leaping off the Kuala Lumpur Tower during the Malaysia International Championship of Extreme Skydive and World BASE Cup, 2004.

Taking to the skies

The first known jump from an aircraft in flight was in 1797 when Frenchman Andre Jacques Garnerin jumped from a hot air balloon over Paris. Fédération Aéronautique Internationale (FAI), the world's governing body for aeronautical sports was established in 1905.

Skydiving was introduced to Malaysia by Captain (retired) Muid bin Yahya, a qualified skydiving instructor. Upon leaving the Special Forces, Muid formed the Malaysian Sports Parachuting Association (MSPA) in 1979 with his brother Zainal Abidin bin Yahya. In 1982, however, the MSPA had to cease operations due to financial constraints.

One of the most active clubs on the local skydiving scene is the Kuala Lumpur Sports Parachuting Club, better known as Wilayah Skydivers. Since its inception in 1980, the club has trained more than 1000 jumpers, many of whom have represented the country in both national and international competitions. Along with three other clubs—the Pahang Parachute Club, Perak Parachute Club and Selangor Parachute Club—Wilayah Skydivers formed the Malaysian Parachuting Federation (MPF) in 1997. The Malaysian Sports Aviation Federation (MSAF) was formed in 2003 as an umbrella body to regulate all aviation sports in Malaysia.

Events and achievements

Accuracy and Canopy Relative Work (CRW) are the only two skydiving events contested in the country, although Malaysians compete in other events in international meets.

Since 1983, the Malaysian Armed Forces have organized the annual Malaysian Parachuting Championship, welcoming foreign teams primarily from ASEAN countries. The inaugural Melaka Open Skydiving Championship was held in 2006 with around 250 participants from all over the world.

Local skydivers are regularly invited to take part in events such as Merdeka Day and Kuala Lumpur

MPF logo.

MPF founding and current president Datuk Abdul Rahim Dahalan.

City Day celebrations. One memorable event for Malaysian skydivers was during the opening ceremony of the 1998 Commonwealth Games at the National Stadium in Bukit Jalil, when 16 skydivers safely touched down on the field.

On 21 April 1998, a group of 23 Malaysian parachutists successfully landed on the North Pole at 60 metres above sea level. The expedition team brought with them a Malaysian-made car, a Proton Wira, and planted the Malaysian flag at the North Pole.

The youngest Malaysian skydiver on record is Haziq Azlan, who made his first jump in 2002 at the age of 14. He was also the youngest competitor when he represented the country at the 2004 Saudi Arabia Parachuting Championships in Jeddah.

The first recorded BASE jump in Malaysia was by Canadian Martin Dumas in 1999, who jumped from the viewing deck of the Kuala Lumpur Tower. Aziz Ahmad jumped after him, becoming the first Malaysian to BASE jump. Azlan Ismail became the first local BASE jumper to leap from the PETRONAS Twin Towers in 1999 and the Alor Star Communications Tower in 2000.

On new year's eve in 1999, 15 BASE jumpers from the Skyventure Transmillennium team successfully set three world records—the largest number of jumpers to jump off a building simultaneously, leaping off the highest building at that time (the PETRONAS Twin Towers), and 'leaping' from one millennium to the next. Telekom Malaysia has been actively promoting the sport since 2000 by organizing annual four-day BASE jumping events that attract a large number of local and international jumpers. In 2004, the country hosted the Malaysia International Championship of Extreme Skydive and World BASE Cup, which saw 54 participants from all over the world BASE jump from the PETRONAS Twin Towers and Kuala Lumpur Tower.

TOP: Members of the skydiving expedition team that landed on the North Pole, 1998.

ABOVE: Members of Skydive Kuala Lumpur jumping from a helicopter with the city of Kuala Lumpur below. Skydivers can reach speeds of up to 320 kilometres per hour.

Skydiver carrying the Malaysian national flag lands at the National Stadium in Bukit Jalil during the opening ceremony of the Commonwealth Games, 1998.

Skydiving and BASE jumping

Skydiving, or recreational parachuting, involves jumping from an aircraft with a deployable parachute made from thin, lightweight fabric, support tapes and suspension lines. The lines are usually gathered through loops or rings at the ends of several strong straps called risers which are in turn attached to the harness containing the chute load. Skydivers are securely attached to a 'static line', which is designed to automatically open the parachute as they exit the aircraft.

BASE (Building, Antenna, Span and Earth) jumping features spectacular leaps from fixed objects such as buildings, bridges and cliffs. BASE jumping is not formally recognized by local skydiving organizations due to its high risk factor. In BASE jumping, because of the low altitude and the limited time available for chute deployment, jumpers only have the use of the main chute with no reserve chute. It is packed so as to allow rapid deployment.

Paintball

Since its introduction in 2000, paintball has grown to become a popular and established pastime in the country. In addition to an annual national tournament series, the Malaysian Paintball Official Circuit, Malaysia also organizes international events such as the Paintball Asia League Series and the Asia Pacific Paintball Championship (APPC).

Paintballers taking part in the Asia Pacific Paintball Championship at Xtion Paintball Park in Kuala Lumpur, 2005.

ABOVE: Team from Selangor battling during a recreational paintball challenge in Shah Alam, 2006.

BELOW: Members of the Sogo Ball Busters, the first all-female team to enter the final of a local tournament, receiving their prizes after emerging second in the All-Ladies Division of the World Cup Asia 2006.

Early development

The original paintball gun was invented in the United States in 1970 for farmers to mark trees and livestock. In 1981, the first official paintball game was played during which 12 players competed against each other with the objectives of avoiding being hit by paintballs and capturing the opposing team's flag.

Paintball was brought to Malaysia by local conglomerate Berjaya Group Berhad in 2000 with the opening of the Tag Paintball Centre in Pahang. The sport was initially used as a team-building tool, and its arrival did not garner much exposure on the national level. In 2003, with the establishment of Xtion Paintball Park, now located in Bukit Jalil, Kuala Lumpur, the sport received more publicity. In 2004, the first official tournament in

Player competing during the Malaysian Paintball Official Circuit in 2006.

Malaysia, the Nation Cup, was conducted. It attracted participants from eleven countries and was refereed by marshals from the United Kingdom.

Many paintball centres subsequently emerged, leading to the formation of the Malaysian Paintball Operator Circuit in 2005. Individual operators conducted tournaments in order to provide rankings to teams in the country and give a certified structure to the sport. In 2006, the circuit, however, was restructured and renamed the Malaysian Paintball Official Circuit (MPOC). Organized as an annual tournament series by Xtion Paintball Park, the MPOC features international standard-tournament set-ups, qualified marshals and command centres, state-of-the-art equipment and facilities as well as participation from the country's top paintball players.

Playing paintball

The game is played between two teams of equal numbers of players. The objective is to capture the opponent's flag and eliminate opposing players by tagging them with paintballs. The paintballs are propelled from airguns known as 'markers'.

A paintball is a round, thin-skinned gelatine capsule filled with coloured liquid. The paint inside the ball is non-toxic, non-caustic, water-soluble and biodegradable. Paintballs are the ammunition for the markers, which come in

Equipment used to play the sport of paintball. Paintball markers fall under the Malaysian Firearms Act and operators must acquire a licence from the Royal Malaysian Police to purchase them.

different shapes and styles, and are powered by carbon dioxide or compressed air, which allows the paintballs to be propelled at a high velocity.

Tournaments in Malaysia are played in the five-a-side format in accordance with the Paintball-Asia League Series (PALS) rules, which dictate game play guidelines including equipment, duration and safety requirements.

The field of play ranges from 40 to 60 metres in length and 25 to 40 metres in width. Inflated bunkers are placed all over the field as obstacles in the game. These bunkers are manufactured specifically for tournament purposes.

International events

The country's first official tournament, the Nation Cup, evolved into the Asia Pacific Paintball Championship (APPC) in 2005. Recognized by international paintball bodies, the APPC established Malaysia on the international paintball scene.

Promotional posters for the Nation Cup 2004 (below) and World Cup Asia 2006 (above).

The Paintball Asia League Series (PALS) was founded in 2005 to create uniform guidelines for paintball competitions in the region. The 2006 PALS comprised the Taiwan International Paintball Circuit, International Thailand Paintball Circuit and World Cup Asia, which was organized in Malaysia.

Skateboarding

Widely popular as a pastime among Malaysian youth, skateboarding has also taken off as a competitive sport in the country. Malaysia has hosted the Asian X Games on four occasions, and local skateboarders have emerged victorious in numerous international competitions.

Participant taking part in the skateboarding event at the Asian X Games held at Sunway Lagoon, 2006.

Skateboarding history

The skateboard was introduced in the United States in the 1950s as a children's toy. Over the years, the sport of skateboarding has grown into a multi-billion dollar industry worldwide and has given rise to various spin-offs such as snowboarding, wakeboarding and other board-related activities.

Children of expatriates first introduced skateboards to Malaysia in the early 1980s. Local urban youths became fascinated with these new playthings and enthusiastically embraced skateboarding. By the mid-1980s, skateboarding had become popular among local youths.

A local publication entitled *Revolution Skateboarding Magazine* was produced in 1999 and helped spur interest in skateboarding by providing skateboarding-related stories and news from all over the nation.

Organization and events

The Extreme Sports Association of Malaysia (ESAM) was formed in 2002. It is responsible for planning, coordinating and conducting programmes and events for extreme sports such as skateboarding, BMX biking, inline skating and other similar activities in Malaysia. The ESAM's aim is to promote extreme sports and nurture local talent.

Malaysia has played host to a prestigious extreme sports event, the Asian X Games, in 2002 at the Kuala Lumpur City Centre Park, in 2003 and 2004 at Putra Stadium, and in 2006 at Sunway Lagoon.

Skateboarding venues

Skate parks are provided by the government to encourage the development of local skateboarders. Skate parks are specially designed obstacle courses for extreme sports, and often contain everyday street objects such as banks, ledges, rails and stairs. Well-known skateboard parks in Malaysia include Kampung Batu in Kuala Lumpur, Arena MPPJ in Petaling Jaya, KBS Skate Park at Mont Kiara and Batu Buruk Skate Park in Kuala Terengganu.

Skaters practising at the KBS skate park in Kuantan.

Local skateboard champions

Ahmad Fadzil Musa, known by the moniker of 'Pa'din' (left), from Butterworth, Penang, is one of the most accomplished skateboarders in Malaysia. Pa'din has been actively involved in the Malaysian skateboarding scene since 1992. He has travelled throughout Malaysia to participate in local skateboard competitions. Pa'din made history when he became the first Asian skateboarder to win a gold medal in the 2001 Asian X Games in Thailand. He repeated the feat at the Asian X Games in Kuala Lumpur in 2004. Pa'din was invited to participate in the X Games final in Los Angeles that year and managed a respectable top-ten finish.

Eliss Tahir (right) is one of Malaysia's latest crop of skateboard standouts. Eliss was among the first skateboarders to utilize the Arena Skatepark in Petaling Jaya when it opened in 2001. He joined the MBPJ Rakan Muda team and was sent to compete in competitions throughout Malaysia. Eliss was invited to join a reputable skateboard team in Malaysia, Shut Up, and now regularly competes on the Asian skateboarding circuit.

From 1990 to 2000, many Malaysian skating tournaments were won by **Johary Fitry Khairuddin** (above). Known as 'Joe Ipoh', Johary's specialty is on transitions (the curve of a ramp). Joe has won numerous competitions both locally and abroad. Internationally, his best achievement was winning the silver medal in the 2004 Asian X Games in Kuala Lumpur. Now retired, Joe is often invited to judge competitions or give talks to aspiring youth in skateboarding clinics organized by the Ministry of Youth and Sports.

1. Chrystal Lim Wen Chean performing in the individual all around final of the Commonwealth Games in Melbourne, 2006.

2. Matin Guntali showcasing his strength at the Commonwealth Games in Melbourne, 2006.

3. Malaysian dancesport participants took part in the Latin American category at the 2007 Asian Indoor Games in Macau.

4. The Malayan weightlifting team comprising (from left) Tho Fook Hung, Koh Eng Tong, Thong Saw Pak and Tan Kim Bee emerged as the unofficial team champions after winning four medals at the 1950 British Empire Games.

5. Malaysia's premier bodybuilders of the 1960s including (from right) Clancy Ang, Paul Sta Maria, Sunny Phua, Kong Chew, Osman Ali, Pak Wai Phung and Oh Kim Hai.

6. Malaysian ice skaters practising their moves at Sunway Pyramid Ice Rink.

STRENGTH AND MOVEMENT

Several disciplines are best categorized as requiring and enhancing strength and movement. For example, gymnastics demands skill and endurance as well as grace and flexibility. It has its roots in ancient Greek practices and was revived as a competitive sport in the late 19th century. Basic gymnastic activities were first introduced to Malayan schools in the early 20th century, but it was only in the late 1980s, with the support and guidance of the Malaysian Gymnastics Federation (MGF), that Malaysian gymnasts began to make an impact on the international scene.

Men's artistic gymnastic team showing off their gold medals at the 2001 SEA Games in Kuala Lumpur.

Besides extreme strength, weightlifting requires technique, speed and dexterity. Weightlifting was introduced to Malaya in the 1920s, and contributed to national pride with a spectacular outing at the 1950 British Empire Games in which Malayan weightlifters won two gold medals, one silver medal and one bronze medal. The Malayan Amateur Weightlifting and Bodybuilding Federation was formed in 1955, and local lifters have carried on the tradition of success in international events.

At the core of bodybuilding is weight training, along with a caloric diet and rest in order to achieve an aesthetically pleasing physique. Its history in the country goes back to the early 1900s. The sport was initially under the stewardship of the Malayan Amateur Weightlifting and Bodybuilding Federation before its own governing body was formed in 1969. The inaugural Mr Malaya contest was in 1946. Malaysian bodybuilders have shone in international competitions, winning the Mr Asia and Mr Universe titles 15 and five times respectively.

Although dancing has long been a social and recreational activity in Malaysia, dance as a sporting event is a relatively recent development locally. The country's governing body, Malaysian DanceSport Berhad, formed in 1993, has been active, organizing a number of national-level events and preparing Malaysian dancers for international competitions.

Malaysia's tropical climate—and the fact that only one ice rink is operational in the country—has not prevented the growth of ice skating and ice hockey. The 2007 edition of the annual Skate Malaysia, held at Sunway Pyramid Ice Rink, attracted more than 300 ice skaters from six countries. The Sunway rink also manages the Ice Skating Academy, which offers skating classes and prepares participants for competitions both locally and internationally. Ice hockey has also witnessed impressive growth since the rink was opened in 1999. An annual league has been in place since 2000 and the rink has hosted the World Ice Hockey Fives on four occasions.

KL Wildcat forward (right) playing in the World Ice Hockey Fives tournament in Selangor, 2005.

Gymnastics

Introduced to Malaya by the British as a means of promoting physical education among schoolchildren, gymnastics rose to prominence locally through the medal-winning performances of Malaysian gymnasts in the 1990s. The Malaysian Gymnastics Federation (MGF), founded in 1978, has spearheaded the growth and development of the sport in the country. In both artistic and rhythmic gymnastic competitions, Malaysians have distinguished themselves at the international level.

Ng Shu Wai performing on the pommel horse at the 2006 Commonwealth Games in Melbourne.

Ng Shu Wai

Ng Shu Wai finished 35th in the men's artistic all-around finals and 8th in the floor apparatus event at the 2002 World Gymnastics Championships, and became the first Malaysian male gymnast to qualify for and participate in the Olympic Games in 2004. At the 2005 SEA Games in Manila, he won four gold medals (floor exercise, high bar, all-around individual and team). Ng won Malaysia's first-ever Asian Games gymnastics medal in 2006 in Doha, taking the silver medal in the vault event. At the Melbourne Commonwealth Games in the same year, he captured the silver medal in the floor exercise competition.

History of gymnastics

Drawings from ancient Egypt show acrobats forming human pyramids and showcasing balancing skills for an audience over 7000 years ago, while athletes vaulting over a bull were depicted in Greek frescos dating back to 2700 BCE. Ancient Chinese and Persians also practised acrobatic activities.

In ancient Greece, male athletes trained and competed without clothing. Thus, the word 'gymnastics' was derived from the ancient Greek word *gymnos* meaning 'naked art'.

In the 19th century, a German, Johann Friedrich GutsMuths, devised a formalized set of exercises that became popular for the teaching of physical education, emphasizing the development of balance, agility and muscular strength. Later, Friedrich Ludwig Jahn, a teacher, invented the high bar, parallel bars and rings as well as a precursor of the balance beam—a long pine log suspended on supports.

The international governing body, the Fédération Internationale de Gymnastique (FIG), was formed in 1881, and tasked with standardizing the rules of the

Schoolboys performing a balancing exercise during a rally at Stadium Merdeka, 1964.

sport. In 1903, the first annual World Gymnastics Championships were organized.

Gymnastics was included in the first modern Olympic Games in Athens in 1896. The discipline of rhythmic gymnastics, featuring dance movements along with tumbling and juggling, was recognized by the FIG in 1962 and became an Olympic sport in 1984. The International Trampoline Federation merged with the FIG in 1999 and trampolining was included as a part of the gymnastics Olympic programme in 2000.

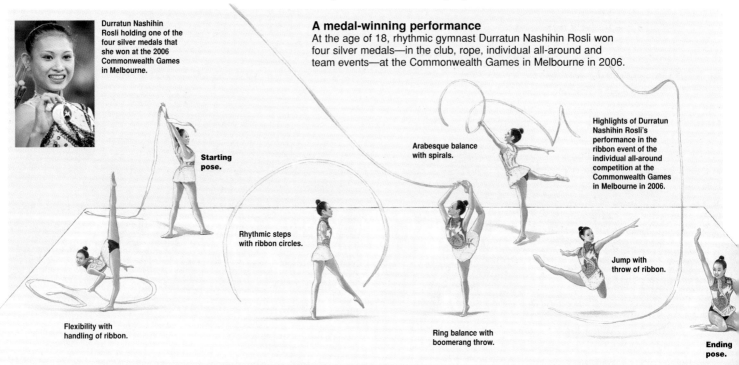

Durratun Nashihin Rosli holding one of the four silver medals that she won at the 2006 Commonwealth Games in Melbourne.

A medal-winning performance

At the age of 18, rhythmic gymnast Durratun Nashihin Rosli won four silver medals—in the club, rope, individual all-around and team events—at the Commonwealth Games in Melbourne in 2006.

Highlights of Durratun Nashihin Rosli's performance in the ribbon event of the individual all-around competition at the Commonwealth Games in Melbourne in 2006.

Starting pose.

Arabesque balance with spirals.

Rhythmic steps with ribbon circles.

Jump with throw of ribbon.

Flexibility with handling of ribbon.

Ring balance with boomerang throw.

Ending pose.

Local development of the sport

Gymnastics was brought to Malaya by the British as a form of physical education for schoolchildren. However, only basic gymnastic activities such as the vaulting horse and parallel bars were introduced in local schools.

The Malaysian Amateur Gymnastics Association (MAGA) was formed in 1969, and the national gymnastics team participated in the SEAP Games in Burma in that same year, bringing home the bronze medal in the vaulting event. But due to internal problems, the MAGA was deregistered in 1971. In 1978, Dr Zakaria Ahmad and others initiated the formation of the Malaysian Gymnastics Federation (MGF). The MGF became a member of the FIG in 1979 and has been a driving force behind the steady growth of the sport in the country.

MGF logo.

Founding and current MGF president Professor Dato' Dr Zakaria Ahmad.

The MGF, comprising 11 state gymnastics associations, conducts programmes in men's and women's artistic gymnastics, rhythmic gymnastics, aerobic gymnastics and gymnastics for all (also known as general gymnastics). The MGF pioneered the formation of the Southeast Asian Gymnastics Confederation (SEAGCON) in 1985, and N. Shanmugarajah from Malaysia was elected as its Honorary Secretary General. In recognition of his efforts in promoting gymnastics in Asia, Dr Zakaria Ahmad was awarded the Order of Merit for Leadership by the International Gymnastics Hall of Fame in 2004.

International achievements

The MGF introduced rhythmic gymnastics to the country and progressively developed it locally. Rhythmic gymnastics was included for the first time in the 1989 SEA Games in Kuala Lumpur, at which Faiznur Miskin captured a total of five gold medals in team and individual events. Although Faiznur retired from competitive gymnastics soon after, her breakthrough performance garnered unprecedented media attention for gymnastics in the country.

In 1990, the MGF shifted its focus to developing artistic gymnastics. This effort paid dividends when Kau Git Kaur won the men's gold medal in the vault at the 1991 SEA Games in Manila and Lim Wai Chi bagged the women's gold medal in the same event at the 1993 SEA Games in Singapore. At the 1998 Commonwealth Games in Kuala Lumpur, Thye Chee Kiat, El Regina Tajuddin, Sarina Sundara Rajah and Carolyn Au Yong collectively won the women's rhythmic gymnastics team gold. After being honoured as the OCM Female Olympian of the year in 1997, Au Li Yen became the first local gymnast to qualify for the Olympic Games, making it to the competition in 2000 in all four artistic events. Malaysia firmly established itself on the international

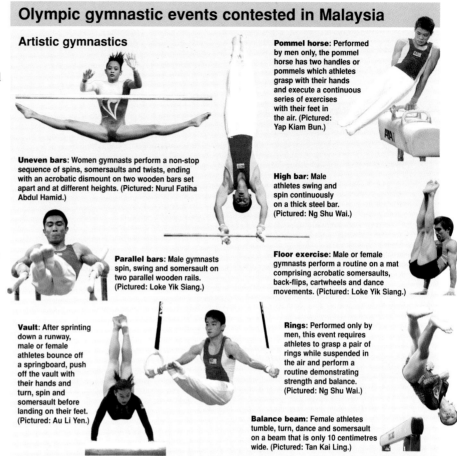

Olympic gymnastic events contested in Malaysia

Artistic gymnastics

Pommel horse: Performed by men only, the pommel horse has two handles or pommels which athletes grasp with their hands and execute a continuous series of exercises with their feet in the air. (Pictured: Yap Kiam Bun.)

Uneven bars: Women gymnasts perform a non-stop sequence of spins, somersaults and twists, ending with an acrobatic dismount on two wooden bars set apart and at different heights. (Pictured: Nurul Fatiha Abdul Hamid.)

High bar: Male athletes swing and spin continuously on a thick steel bar. (Pictured: Ng Shu Wai.)

Parallel bars: Male gymnasts spin, swing and somersault on two parallel wooden rails. (Pictured: Loke Yik Siang.)

Floor exercise: Male or female gymnasts perform a routine on a mat comprising acrobatic somersaults, back-flips, cartwheels and dance movements. (Pictured: Loke Yik Siang.)

Vault: After sprinting down a runway, male or female athletes bounce off a springboard, push off the vault with their hands and turn, spin and somersault before landing on their feet. (Pictured: Au Li Yen.)

Rings: Performed only by men, this event requires athletes to grasp a pair of rings while suspended in the air and perform a routine demonstrating strength and balance. (Pictured: Ng Shu Wai.)

Balance beam: Female athletes tumble, turn, dance and somersault on a beam that is only 10 centimetres wide. (Pictured: Tan Kai Ling.)

Rhythmic gymnastics

Contested only by female athletes, rhythmic gymnastics comprises five separate events—ball, club, hoop, ribbon and rope. Individually and with team-mates, gymnasts perform a routine to music on a 13x13-metre carpeted area. The apparatus are thrown in the air and caught, or manipulated while the athletes perform dance-like moves, some acrobatics and tumbling. (Pictured: Lee Yoke Jeng.)

gymnastics scene when the national gymnastics team won 16 gold, eight silver and three bronze medals to emerge as the overall team champion in the 2001 SEA Games in Kuala Lumpur. Carrying on this winning tradition, local gymnasts brought home nine gold, eight silver and four bronze medals from the 2003 SEA Games in Vietnam, ten gold, seven silver and five bronze medals from the 2005 SEA Games in Manila, and six gold, four silver and nine bronze medals from the 2007 SEA Games in Thailand.

Rhythmic gymnast Durratun Nashihin Rosli won four silver medals at the 2006 Commonwealth Games in Melbourne in the club, rope and individual all-around competitions and in the team event with Foong Seow Ting and Chrystal Lim Wen Chean.

ABOVE: Rhythmic gymnastics team comprising (from left) Sarina Sundara Rajah, Thye Chee Kiat, El Regina Tajuddin and Carolyn Au Yong showing off their gold medals at the Commonwealth Games in Kuala Lumpur, 1998.

LEFT: Faiznur Miskin demonstrating rhythmic gymnastic techniques, 1989.

Bodybuilding

With a history in the country dating back to the early 1900s, the sport of bodybuilding has produced a long line of world-class Malaysian competitors. In 1956, Gan Boon Leong became the first local bodybuilder to win the Mr Asia title and Clancy Ang made history by claiming the Mr Universe title in 1962. Since then, Malaysians have remained at the pinnacle of the sport, capturing 15 Mr Asia and five Mr Universe crowns.

MBBF logo.

ABOVE LEFT: MBBF founding president Dato' Harun Idris.

ABOVE RIGHT: MBBF chairman as at 2008 Datuk Wira Gan Boon Leong.

Bodybuilding history

Emerging out of the innate human desire to improve one's body, competitive bodybuilding was born in Prussia in the late 1800s. The International Federation of Bodybuilders (IFBB) was formed in the United States in 1946.

The earliest-known bodybuilding activity in Malaya was in Penang, when the Penang Happy Health Culturists association was formed in 1912 for the promotion of health and fitness through weight-training. Prior to state-level competitions, there were small-scale contests organized at festivals. A Mr Malaya contest was conducted in 1946, and featured a trophy donated by Malayan Union Governor Sir Edward Gent. The winner was Tan Kheng Chooi from the Penang Happy Health Culturists.

Perak was the first state to organize a bodybuilding contest in 1947, but Selangor became the first state to regularly hold such competitions after the formation of the Selangor Amateur Weight-lifting and Bodybuilding Association (SAWBA) in 1953. The inaugural national championships were held in 1955 in Kuala Lumpur. The first national champion, known as 'Mr Malaya', was 16-year-old Robert Teo from Singapore.

Local bodybuilding was initially governed by the Malayan Amateur Weightlifting and Bodybuilding Federation, formed in 1955. However, at the 1968 Mexico Olympics, the International Weightlifting Federation made a decision to remove bodybuilding from its organization and it was recognized as a distinct sport. In 1968, the Malaysian Body-Building Federation (MBBF), the national governing body, was established.

Malaysia has hosted numerous international events including the World Amateur Championships in 1990 and 2000 in Kuala Lumpur and Melaka respectively as well as the Commonwealth, Asian, and ASEAN championships in Melaka.

1. Gan Boon Leong posing with his trophy after winning the Mr Asia title in 1956.

2. Abdul Malek Noor won the heavyweight Mr Asia title six times between 1985 and 1991.

3. Wong Ngai Hong competing in the 2007 Santa Sussana Pro Grand Prix in Spain.

Super Sazali

Sazali Abdul Samad, an officer with the Royal Malaysian Police, won the bantamweight Mr Asia title in 1996, 1998, 1999, 2000 and 2004. In 2000, he won the bantamweight category at the World Amateur Championship held in Melaka, earning him the IFBB Mr Universe title, the first Malaysian to do so since Clancy Ang in 1962. Sazali further distinguished himself by winning the IFBB Mr Universe title in 2004 and 2006. In 2006, Sazali participated in the newly reinstated bodybuilding event at the Asian Games in Doha, and captured a silver medal. After switching to the below 70-kilogram lightweight category. Sazali won the Mr Universe title for the fourth time at the 2007 World Bodybuilding Championship in South Korea.

Malaysian greats

The inaugural Mr Physique—a contest between Malaya, Singapore and Indonesia (and Burma in 1957)—was won by Malayan Ariffin Hassan in 1955. Gan Boon Leong won the Mr Physique Asia title in 1956. Clancy Ang achieved great distinction for the country when he clinched the Mr Asia contest in 1960 and the 1962 National Amateur Bodybuilders Association (NABBA) Mr Universe (Class III) title in London. Pak Wai Phung won the Mr Asia title in 1961. Sunny Phua took the Mr Asia title and third place at the IFBB Mr Universe (Class III) in 1963.

The most notable Malaysian achiever in the IFBB Asian Championships is Abdul Malek Noor from Johor, who won the heavyweight Mr Asia title from 1985 to 1988, and in 1990 and 1991. Wong Ngai Hong became the next dominant Malaysian champion in the heavyweight category, emerging as Mr Asia in 1999. In 2002, Wong had the distinction of becoming one of the first Asians to earn certification to compete on the IFBB profes-sional bodybuilding circuit.

Five-time Mr Asia and four-time Mr Universe Sazali Abdul Samad is the most accom-plished bodybuilder in the nation's history. Sazali was recognized as the 'Best Bodybuilder of the 20th Century in Asia' by the Asian Bodybuilders Federation in 2000 and won the National Sportsman of the Year award in 2000 and 2006.

Cover of a 1961 issue of *Malayan Sports Illustrated* featuring Clancy Ang, the nation's first Mr Universe.

Weightlifting

Introduced to Malaya in the 1920s, weightlifting's popularity increased after World War II when local exponents brought home four medals from the 1950 British Empire Games. The country's weightlifters have carried on this tradition of success: at the 2006 Commonwealth Games in Melbourne, local lifters captured five medals.

Bantamweight Tho Fook Hung competing in the 1950 British Empire Games in Auckland.

Early development of the sport

Stone lifting was practised by many ancient cultures, but it is widely believed that the sport of weight-lifting originated in either the Middle East or Europe. The first weightlifting association was founded in Germany in 1880, while the International Weightlifting Federation (IWF) was formed in 1920. The Olympic Games in 1896 and 1904 incorporated one-and two-handed lifting events.

During the early 1920s, enthusiastic Malayan practitioners tried to emulate the feats of strength and stunts performed by famous strongmen. The most popular lifting techniques at that time were the one-hand snatch and the one-hand clean and jerk. Weights were not available, so lorry wheels were often used instead.

Victory ceremony at the 1950 British Empire Games where Tho Fook Hung (centre) won the weightlifting bantam class competition.

Weightlifting only took off in Malaya after World War II, when enthusiasts of the sport formulated plans to send local weightlifters abroad to compete for international honours. In 1948, a contingent of weightlifters—Koh Eng Tong, Tho Fook Hung, Loong Ah Ting and Loong Wei Teck from the Federation of Malaya and Ho Lye Ying of Singapore—were sent to compete in the All-China Olympics in Shanghai. Each of these competitors clinched the title in their respective weight classes.

The Malayan team emerged victorious again in 1950 at the British Empire Games held in Auckland. Bantamweight Tho Fook Hung and featherweight Koh Eng Tong won gold medals, lightweight Thong Saw Pak won a silver medal and light heavyweight Tan Kim Bee won a bronze medal. Malaya finished as the unofficial overall team champion. Tho Fook Hung was at his peak in 1952 when he lifted a personal best of 305.33 kilograms but due to organizational reasons, he could not compete in the Helsinki Olympic Games held that same year.

The first weightlifting association in Malaya, the Malayan Amateur Weightlifting and Bodybuilding Federation, was established in 1955 with Lim Jit Hee as its founding president. A team manager and three weightlifters joined the 1956 Malayan contingent to the Melbourne Olympics. Tan Kim Bee, placed sixth in the middleweight division, earned Malaya its only point of the games. Tan won a bronze medal in the middle-heavyweight division at the 1958 Asian Games in Tokyo.

The weightlifting team also represented Malaysia at the 1964 Olympic Games in Tokyo. Chung Kam Weng finished 10th in the featherweight division.

At the 1968 Olympic Games in Mexico City, Malaysia argued for the segregation of the sports of weightlifting and bodybuilding, a concept which was agreed to by the IWF members. The Malaysian Amateur Weightlifting and Bodybuilding Federation was subsequently renamed the Malaysian Weightlifting Federation (MWF).

Recent achievements

In 1994, Matin Guntali won the silver medal in the flyweight category at the Commonwealth Games in Victoria. At the 1998 games in Kuala Lumpur, Matin took three bronze medals in the 56-kilogram competition and Mohd Hidayat Hamidon won a gold and a silver medal in the 69-kilogram category.

Amirul Hamizan Ibrahim was the toast of the 2002 Commonwealth Games in Manchester when he made a clean sweep of three gold medals in the 56-kilogram weight category and broke all three Commonwealth Games records in the process.

At the 2006 Commonwealth Games in Melbourne, Mohd Hidayat Hamidon won the silver medal in the 69-kilogram category, Che Mohd Azrol Che Mat took the bronze medal in the men's 105-kilogram event, Abdul Rashid Roswadi took the bronze medal in the men's 62-kilogram event, and Mohd Faizal Baharom and Matin Guntali took the overall gold and bronze medals respectively in the men's 56-kilogram event.

ABOVE LEFT: MWF logo.

ABOVE RIGHT: Malaysian Weightlifting Federation president as at 2008 Datuk Wira Gan Boon Leong.

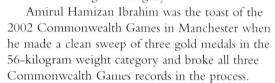

1. Mohd Hidayat Hamidon competing in the 69-kilogram event at the 2006 Commonwealth Games in Melbourne.

2. Amirul Hamizan Ibrahim jumps for joy after setting a new Commonwealth Games record for the clean and jerk event in the 56-kilogram category at the 2002 Commonwealth Games in Manchester.

3. Mohd Faizal Baharom being carried by Matin Guntali after the lifters won the gold and bronze medals respectively in the 56-kilogram event at the 2006 Commonwealth Games in Melbourne.

4. Che Mohd Azrol Che Mat performs a lift in the men's 105-kilogram event at the 2006 Commonwealth Games in Melbourne. He went on to win a bronze.

Dancesport

An extension of the recreational activity of ballroom dancing, dancesport has developed into a competitive event. Dancesport athletes must train rigorously in order to attain the level of skill necessary to compete in formal competitions. Malaysian DanceSport Berhad (MDSB) oversees the growth and development of the sport in the country. Since 1998, Malaysian dancers have taken part in international competitions.

MDSB logo.

ABOVE LEFT: MDSB founding chairperson Chin Chooi Ying.

ABOVE RIGHT: MDSB chairperson as at 2008 Tai Sook Yee.

Tham Cham Soo and Frances Teoh performing a Standard dance routine.

Competitive ballroom dancing

Ballroom dancing has its roots in the 14th-century European folk dances and the 17th- and 18th-century minuets, cotillions and quadrilles of the royal courts and high society in Europe. Changes from the open-couple dance style of the stately dances to the present closed-couple dance style occurred in the 19th century. Evolving out of ballroom dancing, dancesport emerged as a popular form of recreation in the 19th century.

Malaysian grading systems

Dancesport athletes typically begin as social dancers, allowing them to get an all-round initiation into the basics of the dances. Grading is carried out at various dance schools around Malaysia by examiners invited from the Imperial Society of Teachers of Dancing or the National Association of Teachers of Dancing of the United Kingdom.

Competitors are then divided into age groups and a grading system is utilized to decide a dancer's competence level in a specific dance form and the category of competition he or she can participate in. Points are awarded to the finalists of Grade A events in specially-designated competitions. The aggregate number of points accumulated by competitors annually is utilized to rank them on a national basis, and the highest-ranked couples will go on to represent Malaysia in international competitions.

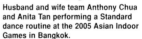

Yong Kwok Leong (right) and Gooi Yee Zhen competing in the Latin American rumba event during the 2007 SEA Games in Thailand. The couple won the bronze medal in the competition.

Dance organizations

In Malaysia, dancesport is governed and regulated by Malaysian DanceSport Berhad (MDSB), which was incorporated in 1993 under its original name, Malaysian Amateur Dance Sport Berhad (MADSB). The MDSB strives to promote competitive dancesport throughout Malaysia and internationally, and to work towards its acceptance as an Olympic sport. An affiliate of the International DanceSport Federation (IDSF) since 1996, the MDSB became an associate member of the OCM in 2001. An application to the Sports Commissioner for registration under the provisions of the Sports Development Act 1997 is still pending as at 2008.

Husband and wife team Anthony Chua and Anita Tan performing a Standard dance routine at the 2005 Asian Indoor Games in Bangkok.

International participation

Beginning with the Asian Sports Festival held in 1998 in China, Malaysia has been participating in a number of international competitions organized by various IDSF members, and some multi-sport events in the Asian region. Other tournaments in which Malaysian national dancers have competed include the 1998 Asian Games in Bangkok, the 2001 World Games in Japan, the 2005 Asian Indoor Games in Bangkok and the 2005 and 2007 SEA Games in the Philippines and Thailand respectively.

Malaysian dancesport standouts

Well into his sixties, Tham Cham Soo and his partner Frances Teoh have the distinction of being admitted into the Guinness Book of World Records in 2002 as the couple who had won the most dancesport competitions in the Southeast Asian and Asia Pacific regions.

At the other end of the spectrum, younger dancers are coming up through the ranks. At 13 years of age, Johnston Lim became the youngest Malaysian male dancesport athlete to win a Malaysia Closed Amateur Standard event when he and his partner, Villy Chai, finished first at the 12th Penang International DanceSport Open Championship in 2005.

At the 2007 SEA Games in Thailand, the pair of Yong Kwok Leong and Gooi Yee Zhen clinched Malaysia's first dancesport medal in a major multi-sport event, winning a bronze in the Latin-American rumba event.

Disciplines

Dancesport can be broadly categorized into social dancing, exhibition-style dancing and competitive dancing and is divided into four different disciplines:

- **Standard**: Five international dances—the waltz, tango, Viennese waltz, slow foxtrot and quickstep.

- **Latin American**: Five Latin American dances—the samba, cha cha cha, rumba, paso doble and jive.

- **10 Dance**: Comprising all of the above 10 dances performed at a one-day event.

- **Formation**: Featuring eight couples dancing in a formation team in either the Standard or Latin American disciplines.

In Malaysia, dancesport competitions are typically held in the Standard and Latin American disciplines.

Benedict Lau (right) and Jovienne Ee competing in the Latin American discipline at the 2005 Asian Indoor Games in Bangkok.

Ice sports

Ice skating and ice hockey are sports that were, until recently, foreign to the Southeast Asian region. Malaysians, however, have embraced both enthusiastically. Malaysian ice skaters have been selected to perform in international stage productions, while a long-running ice hockey league augurs well for the sport's future.

Malaysia's only public ice skating rink, Pyramid Ice at the Sunway Pyramid shopping complex, hosts both ice skating and ice hockey events.

Ice sports origins

Ice skating in its raw form is believed to have originated with the Vikings in Sweden over 1200 years ago. Runners and blades were made of bones that were ground down, and then tied to the feet with thongs.

Figure skating traces its origins back to the United States in 1840, when a skating craze swept the country. The International Skating Union (ISU), founded in 1892, is the world governing body for the sport. Ice skating was first included in the Olympic Games programme in 1908.

Besides being a popular form of winter recreation, ice skating has developed into three sporting formats: speed skating, ice dancing and figure skating. In speed skating, competitors attempt to cover a certain distance over the ice as quickly as possible. Ice dancing involves performing various dance routines on ice. Figure skating is an event in which individuals, mixed couples or groups perform spins, jumps and other moves on the ice, often to the rhythm of music.

Ice hockey originated around 1800 in Canada when students adapted the Irish field game of hurling to ice ponds, thereby creating a new winter game. The rules of modern ice hockey were devised in the 1870s. The International Ice Hockey Federation (IIHF) was founded in 1908, and ice hockey was introduced as an Olympic event in 1920.

Malaysian ice skating

The Ice Skating Association of Malaysia (ISAM), formed in 2000, governs all competitive and recreational aspects of ice-related sports: figure skating, ice hockey, ice theatre as well as speed racing and curling. The ISAM also organizes and sponsors competitions for the purpose of stimulating public interest in the sport.

Although Malaysians have not made any headway on the international competitive ice skating circuit, there have been local skaters who have been hired to perform in international stage productions. Tina Harlina Ramli became the first Malaysian ice

Rachel Ng striking a swan pose in the 2005 Skate Malaysia competition.

skater to participate in an international production, 'Magic On Ice', which was held at the Genting International Showroom in 2001. Phua Hoong Yee followed suit when he was offered a role in the 'Disney on Ice' North American tour in 2004.

Malaysian ice hockey

Kelab Hockey Ice Saga (KHAS) is the only ice hockey club in Malaysia. It was established in 1998 by a group of former ice hockey players to manage and organize league games, training sessions, international tournaments and other group events. There are five ice hockey teams under KHAS—the KL Wildcats, Inferno Ice, KL Slayers (women's team) as well as the KL Tigers and KL Thunders (junior teams).

Since 2000, KHAS has been organizing an annual ice hockey league for its Division One (locals and expatriates) and Division Two (juniors and beginners) teams. Starting out in 2000 with only three teams and 40 players, the 2006 league saw the participation of 200 players from 18 teams. Malaysia hosted the World Ice Hockey Fives, the largest five-a-side ice hockey tournament in Asia for amateur players, in 2001, 2002, 2005 and 2006 at the Sunway Pyramid Ice Rink. The country was represented by the national team as well as by the KL Wildcats, Inferno Ice and KL Slayers.

In 2002, the KL Wildcats emerged as champions at the World Ice Hockey Fives tournament in the Asian Division B, beating the Hong Kong All Stars in the final. The team repeated the same feat in 2006 after defeating Macau.

A representative team was sent by KHAS to play at the 2007 Asian Winter Games in China. They defeated Hong Kong 7–3 in their first match, but lost to South Korea, North Korea and Kuwait in their ensuing contests.

ISAM logo.

ABOVE LEFT: ISAM founding president Datuk Razman Hashim.

ABOVE RIGHT: ISAM president as at 2008 Datin Laila Abdullah.

ABOVE: Action in front of the goal during a KHAS league match between the KL Wildcats (in white) and the Cobras.

LEFT: The KL Wildcats celebrating after defeating Macau to win the World Ice Hockey Fives tournament, 2006.

PARALYMPIC SPORTS

When disability sports in Malaysia started in the 1970s, the early sports were basketball, table tennis, badminton, darts and carrom. The Malaysian Paralympic Council (MPC), established in 1989, is the umbrella body for disability sports in the country. A unit under the Ministry of Youth and Sports oversees the development of these sports.

Miniature sheet issued in 2006 during the 9th FESPIC Games held in Kuala Lumpur.

Athletics and swimming were the first two disability sports to be introduced competitively in the country. Malaysians with a disability now compete in more than 20 sports. Rowing and wheelchair rugby are the only official Paralympic sports that are not played locally.

In addition to introducing new sports, the MPC also trains coaches, classifiers and technical officials. Malaysia has internationally accredited classifiers in wheelchair basketball, badminton, tenpin bowling and powerlifting as well as accredited technical officials for athletics, table tennis, wheelchair basketball and goalball.

Malaysia has been taking part in international disability sports competitions since the 1970s, including multi-sports and multi-disability competitions, single-disability competitions as well as single-sport competitions. The nation's world-class athletes with a disability include Wong Chee Kin, three-time Paralympic Games swimming finalist; Mohd Khassery Othman, Paralympic Games bronze medallist for high jump in 1992; and powerlifters P. Mariappan, two-time Paralympic Games bronze medallist, Siow Lee Chan, two-time gold medallist in the ASEAN Para Games and Cheok Kon Fatt, ASEAN Para Games gold medallist.

Malaysia has hosted various international events including the first ASEAN Para Games in 2001 and the ninth FESPIC (Far East and South Pacific Games for the Disabled) Games in 2006, where the country finished fourth with 44 gold, 60 silver and 71 bronze medals, the best ever outing for Malaysia at a FESPIC Games.

Malaysia participated in the formation of the ASEAN Para Sports Federation (APSF) in 2000 and the Asian Paralympic Council in 2002. The secretariats for both organizations are based in Kuala Lumpur.

Malaysian athletes Jap Soon Hung (front) and Mat Sani Kasbun training for the 9th FESPIC Games held in Kuala Lumpur in 2006.

1. The 50-metre freestyle swimming event at the 2004 Malaysian Paralympiad. The biennial Malaysian Paralympiad was originally known as the National Sport for the Disabled and was first held in 1982.

2. Dato' Napsiah Omar (left), Minister of National Unity and Social Development, handing over the Malaysian flag to Zainal Abu Zarin, chef-de-mission of the 1992 Paralympics contingent. The Malaysian paralympians returned from Barcelona with one silver and two bronze medals.

3. Wheelchair fencing competition organized during a sports carnival in Shah Alam in 2000.

4. Powerlifter P. Mariappan with the bronze medal he won at the 1988 Paralympics held in South Korea. He repeated the feat at the 1992 Barcelona Paralympics. A multiple international gold medal winner, Mariappan is one of Malaysia's most successful Paralympians.

5. The oath-taking ceremony of the 2006 Kuala Lumpur FESPIC (Far East and South Pacific Games for the Disabled) Games at the Cheras Football Stadium.

Paralympic organizations and national competitions

Malaysia has been active in the international development of disability sports. The nation played a leading role in the formation of the ASEAN Para Sports Federation and the Asian Paralympic Council, while the Malaysian Paralympic Council organized the 2006 FESPIC Games, the largest disability sports event ever held in the Asia-Pacific region. Local disability sports competitions have been conducted since 1982.

Malaysian athlete rebounding the ball in a game against China during the first Asia Paralympic Wheelchair Basketball Cup held in Malaysia, 2005.

The 100-metre wheelchair race at the Handicapped Athletics Championships in Kuala Lumpur, 1986.

MALAYSIAN PARALYMPIC COUNCIL

Top: Logo of the Malaysia Paralympic Council (MPC).

Above: Dato' Zainal Abu Zarin, founding and current MPC president.

International and regional organization

The International Paralympic Committee (IPC) is the world governing body of the Paralympic Movement and organizes the Paralympic Games. It was founded in 1989 as a non-profit organization with its headquarters in Germany.

The Paralympic Games, the largest multi-disability and multi-sport competition for athletes with disabilities, are held every four years following the cycle of the Olympic Games. In 1960, the inaugural Paralympic Games were held in Rome. Since 1988, the Paralympic Games have been held in the same city that hosts the Olympic Games, approximately three weeks after the closing ceremony of the Olympics.

Athletes who take part in the Paralympic Games are classified into six disability categories: amputee, cerebral palsy, visually impaired, wheelchair, intellectually disabled and *les autres* (which comprises athletes who do not fit into the other categories).

Disability sports in the Asian region started with the formation of the Far East and South Pacific Games for the Disabled (FESPIC) Federation in 1974. The quadrennial FESPIC Games, the largest competition for athletes with a disability in Asia and Oceania and the second largest in the world after the Paralympic Games, are held in the same year as the Asian and Commonwealth Games. Malaysia hosted the 2006 games in Kuala Lumpur (see 'International paralympic events and achievements').

In 2002, the Asian Paralympic Council was established in Busan with Dato' Zainal Abu Zarin, president of the Malaysian Paralympic Council (MPC), as the founding president of the new organization. In 2006, the Asian Paralympic Council merged with the FESPIC Federation to form the Asian Paralympic Committee. Dato' Zainal was again elected president of this new body. This merger resulted in the creation of the Asian Para Games which will, beginning in 2010, replace the FESPIC Games. The biennial ASEAN Para Games are held just after the SEA Games in the same host city.

Local organization

The Malaysian Sports Council for the Disabled, a non-profit organization, was established in 1989. It was renamed the Malaysian Paralympic Council (MPC) in 1996.

The MPC has seven affiliates, comprising disability organizations as well as disability sports organizations, which represent six disability categories: the visually impaired, intellectually disabled, physically disabled, hearing impaired, dwarfs and cerebral palsy.

Three sports associations for paralympians have been established in Malaysia for wheelchair tennis, lawn bowls and wheelchair basketball.

National competitions

A national multi-sport and multi-disability sports competition has been organized biennially in Malaysia since 1982. Originally called the National Sport for the Disabled, the name of the competition was changed to the Malaysian Paralympiad in 1998. From 1982 to 1996, only athletics and swimming competitions were held. The number of sports which are contested has subsequently increased; in 2006, 20 sports—judo, athletics, swimming, sitting volleyball, archery, wheelchair tennis, wheelchair basketball, lawn bowls, badminton, powerlifting, table tennis, goalball, fencing, boccia, cycling, football, shooting, tenpin bowling, sailing and chess—were included in the Malaysian Paralympiad programme. From 550 participants at the first games in 1982, the number of athletes increased to 1207 in 2006. In 1990, ASEAN countries participated in the national games and, in 2002, participation grew to include countries from the wider Asian region.

The national games have been held in various states in Malaysia. Since 1992, the event has been organized with support from the respective state governments, the Ministry of National Unity and Social Development, the Ministry of Youth and Sports and the state Athletics Amateur Associations. Since 2000, the Malaysian Paralympiad has been held in Kuala Lumpur. An important objective of the Malaysian Paralympiad is also to identify talent and increase the number of local coaches, technical officials and classifiers.

Paralympic events

The Paralympic Games programme comprises 27 events. While Paralympic athletes can be generally classified into six categories of disability—amputee, cerebral palsy, visually impaired, wheelchair, intellectually disabled and *les autres*—they are also grouped into classes based on their different levels of impairment for competitive purposes, ensuring a level playing field for all athletes taking part in a given event.

There are guidelines for athlete classification that differ from sport to sport and sometimes include physical and technical assessments of the athletes. Certified individuals, known as classifiers, are responsible for placing athletes into appropriate classes. Classification, however, is not absolute and an athlete's class is reviewed throughout his or her sporting career and changed if necessary.

Volleyball
Although there are two volleyball events for athletes with a disability—standing and sitting—only sitting volleyball is contested in the Paralympic Games. In sitting volleyball, athletes are not classified into groups; instead, they must meet minimal disability requirements. The game is played on a smaller court and, at all times, the athletes' pelvises must be touching the ground.

Shooting
The classification system in shooting allows athletes from different disability classes, but with the same abilities, to compete together. There are three classifications in shooting: SH1, SH2 and SH3. SH1 athletes do not require a shooting stand, while SH2 athletes do. Athletes classified as SH3 are visually impaired.

Football
Two versions of disability football are played. Five-a-side football is open to visually impaired athletes. Players other than the goalkeeper are blindfolded and are guided by bells in the ball. Seven-a-side football is open to athletes with cerebral palsy.

Wheelchair tennis
Open to athletes with substantial or total loss of function in one or both legs. There is also a quad division open to athletes with disability in three or four limbs. Normal tennis rules apply although wheelchair tennis players are allowed two bounces of the ball before having to return it.

Cycling
Athletes are classified into four groups of disability—visually impaired, locomotor disabilities, cerebral palsy and handcycling athletes—as well as functional categories. Visually-impaired cyclists compete on tandem bicycles with a sighted pilot.

Goalball
Created for visually impaired athletes, goalball participants wear eye patches and shades to ensure they participate on equal terms. Bells in the ball help players track its direction.

Swimming
Athletes are classified according to disability and degree of disability, for example, the degree of vision loss. Not all events are open to all classes.

Powerlifting
Open to athletes with a physical disability who are divided into weight categories. Participants, however, must be declared physically fit by a physician before competing.

Athletics
Events are open to all disability categories. Athletes are classfied according to the level of their disabilities. During competitions, the visually impaired are permitted accompanying guides, who are attached to runners with either an elbow lead or a tether.

International paralympic events and achievements

Malaysian athletes have participated in international paralympic sports events since the 1972 Stoke Mandeville Games, the precursor to today's Paralympic Games. In recent times, Malaysian athletes with a disability have given medal-winning performances around the world. At the 2006 FESPIC Games held in Kuala Lumpur, Malaysian athletes won 44 gold medals.

Deputy Prime Minister Dato' Sri Najib Tun Razak (second from right) receiving a souvenir from national powerlifter Cheok Kon Fatt after launching the 2006 FESPIC Games.

Hosting international events

Malaysia has hosted two major multi-sport and multi-disability competitions: the first ASEAN Para Games in 2001 and the ninth FESPIC (Far East and South Pacific Games for the Disabled) Games in 2006.

The ASEAN Para Games were organized in Kuala Lumpur from 25 to 30 October 2001. Athletics competitions were conducted at the National Stadium in Bukit Jalil, while swimming competitions were held at the National Aquatic Centre. A total of 548 athletes from the ASEAN countries—Brunei, Cambodia, Indonesia, Laos, Malaysia, Myanmar, the Philippines, Singapore, Thailand and Vietnam—participated in the competition. Malaysian competitors succeeded in setting 11 new regional records in athletics.

Flag-bearers entering the Kuala Lumpur Football Stadium in Cheras at the opening ceremony of the 2006 FESPIC Games.

Malaysia hosted the FESPIC Games from 25 November to 1 December 2006. Nearly 2300 athletes from 46 Asian and Oceanic countries took part in the competition. It was also the first time that countries from West Asia participated in the FESPIC Games. Athletes from the four major disability categories—the visually impaired, wheelchair and amputees, cerebral palsy and the intellectually disabled—competed in 19 events held

National Paralympians of the Year

In 2005, the National Sports Council (NSC) began recognizing the nation's top male and female athletes with a disability with a yearly award equivalent to the National Sportsman and Sportswoman of the Year awards.

In 2006, Faridul Masri was named Male Paralympian of the Year by the NSC after capturing three gold medals in the javelin, discus and shot put events at the 9th FESPIC Games in Kuala Lumpur.

In 2005, Mohd Salam Sidik was named Male Paralympian of the Year by the NSC after winning three gold medals in the World Wheelchair Archery Championship held in Rio de Janeiro. Mohd Salam won the 50-, 70- and 90-metre events.

Powerlifter Siow Lee Chan, who created a new record at the Manila ASEAN Paragames in 2005 when she won the 92.5-kilogram category, was named 2005 Female Paralympian of the Year by the NSC. Siow also won a silver medal in the 75-kilogram category at the inaugural 2005 Asian Powerlifting Championship held in Kuala Lumpur.

The 2006 Female Paralympian of the Year was Zainab Mohamad Ashari who won gold medals in the 100-, 4x100- and 4x400-metre events, two silvers in the 200-metre and long jump competitions and one bronze in the 400-metre race at the 2006 FESPIC Games.

at venues in and around Kuala Lumpur. During the competition, 27 International Paralympic Committee (IPC) world records were broken, while more than 60 new FESPIC Games records were set.

Malaysia has also played host to international Paralympic single sport competitions including the 2002 IPC World Powerlifting Championship, 2004 Asia and South Pacific Archery Championship, 2004 IPC World Bowls Championship, 2004 Asian Paralympic Badminton Cup, and the Asia and South Pacific Table Tennis Championship and Asia Tenpin Bowling Championship in 2005.

A tradition of success

Malaysia first took part in the third FESPIC Games in Hong Kong in 1982. Malaysian athletes in three disability categories—physical disability, visually impaired and cerebral palsy—participated in the event. Since then, Malaysia has taken part in all the subsequent FESPIC Games, which are held every four years. Malaysia has won medals in all the FESPIC Games in which it has participated. However, the best performance was at the 2006 FESPIC Games in Kuala Lumpur when Malaysia won 44 gold, 60 silver and 71 bronze medals.

Malaysia has been taking part in the Paralympic Games since 1988. The Malaysian contingent participated in athletics, swimming and powerlifting at the 1988 Paralympics in Seoul, and P. Mariappan won the country's first Paralympic medal, a bronze, for powerlifting. Malaysia also brought home medals—one silver and one bronze in powerlifting and one bronze in athletics—from the Barcelona Paralympic Games in 1992. These games marked the first time that medal-winning Malaysian athletes with a disability received cash incentives from the government.

Since 2002, the Commonwealth Games has integrated events for elite athletes with a disability (EAD). Malaysia sent EAD participants to both the 2002 Manchester and 2006 Melbourne editions of the Commonwealth Games. In 2002, Malaysia won one silver medal in athletics, two bronze medals in lawn bowls and one bronze medal in powerlifting.

Visually impaired athlete Mohd Hisham Khaironi (in yellow) running in the 100-metre race at the 2006 Commonwealth Games in Melbourne. Four years earlier in Manchester, Mohd Hisham won a silver medal in the same event.

Other disability sports events

The Special Olympics is a separate programme from the Paralympics. Whereas the latter has, since its 2000 edition in Sydney, been open only to athletes with a physical disability, the Special Olympics caters to athletes with intellectual disabilities. The Special Olympics World Games, like the Paralympic Games, take place once every four years. Malaysia participated in its first Special Olympics World Games in Ireland in 2003.

The first Special Olympics state body in Malaysia was established in Sabah in 1986, and, as of 2006, Sarawak, Penang, Selangor and Perak also have their own governing bodies. Special Olympics Malaysia is awaiting registration under the Sports Development Act 1997 to be recognized as the national governing body of the Special Olympic programme. The first Special Olympics event in Malaysia, held in Kuala Lumpur in 1992, offered track and field events. The inaugural National Games for the Special Olympics were held in Sabah in 2006.

The hearing impaired do not take part in the Paralympic Games, but in the Deaflympics, which is a single-disability competition. Hearing-impaired athletes play the full spectrum of sports which the able-bodied play. In Malaysia, hearing-impaired sports are governed by the Malaysia Sports Federation of the Deaf.

The Malaysian contingent at the opening ceremony of the 2007 Special Olympics World Summer Games in Shanghai. The 20 athletes returned home with a medal haul of four gold, eight silver and seven bronze medals from the athletics, bocce and bowling events.

1. Visually impaired Lee Sheng Chow led the oath recitation at the opening ceremony of the 1998 FESPIC Games. He finished the competition with two gold medals in javelin, shot put and a silver medal in the discus.

2. Wong Chee Kin, a gold medallist at the 2006 FESPIC Games in Kuala Lumpur, bagged five medals—a gold, three silver and a bronze—at the 2001 CP World Games in Nottingham.

3. Azmi Lamin was a member of the trio that won a lawn bowls bronze medal in the men's triples physically disabled event at the 2002 Commonwealth Games in Manchester.

4. A two-gold medal winner at the 2006 FESPIC Games, Nursyafawati Arshukri had previously won gold medals in the 100-metre and long jump events at the ASEAN Para Games in Manila in 2005.

5. Mat Sani Kasbun (left) edging Mohd Sani Harun in the 200-metre wheelchair race at the Malaysia Paralympics Athletics Open, 2005.

6. Malaysian powerlifters (from left) P. Mariappan, Benson Patta and Cheok Kon Fatt returning home after winning seven gold and two silver medals at the 1993 World Wheelchair Games in England.

1. Schoolchildren form the logo for the 16th Commonwealth Games during the 40th National Day celebrations at Dataran Merdeka in Kuala Lumpur, 31 August 1997.

2. Commemorative miniature sheet issued during the 1998 Commonwealth Games in Kuala Lumpur, the largest multi-sport event held in Malaysia to date.

3. The golf course at Berjaya Tioman Resort, Pulau Tioman. The country's 207 golf courses are a major attraction for sports tourists to Malaysia.

4. Tun Abdul Razak (third from left) addressing members of the organizing committee of the 1965 SEAP Games, including (from left) Lum Mun Chak, Lim Kee Siong, Thong Poh Nyen and A.T. Rajah.

5. Prime Minister Tunku Abdul Rahman, who was also the nation's first Minister of Youth and Sports, addressing sports associations at the Dewan Tuanku Abdul Rahman in 1964.

6. Qabil Ambak (second from left) celebrates being named the Best Sportsman of the 2001 SEA Games in Kuala Lumpur. With him are (from left) president of the Olympic Council of Malaysia Tunku Tan Sri Imran Tuanku Ja'afar, then Prime Minister Dato' Seri Dr Mahathir Mohamad, and then Minister of Youth and Sports Dato' Seri Hishammuddin Tun Hussein.

7. Universiti Utara Malaysia athlete Rozi Zakaria leading the oath taking at the opening of the 1997 Intervarsity Games.

8. Opening ceremony of Stadium Merdeka, 30 August 1957.

THE ORGANIZATION AND GOVERNANCE OF SPORTS

The National Sports Policy of the country seeks to develop an active, healthy and fit society through sports and physical recreational activities as an effort towards nation building. It postulates that sports are as important as other social areas of development, such as education, transport, housing and health. The government has promoted the development of sports through means such as hiring foreign coaches for national teams, allowances to athletes during training, the building of sports schools and state-of-the-art facilities for sports, and the hosting of international sporting events.

A systematic structure exists with both governmental and non-governmental organizations working together at various levels for the development of sports in the country. This structure is headed by the Ministry of Youth and Sports, with the National Sports Council (NSC) as the promoting body, and is supported by the Ministry of Education, the Malaysian Government Services Welfare and Recreation Council and the Olympic Council of Malaysia (OCM). The NSC, the Malaysian Schools' Sports Council, the OCM and the national sports associations work towards promoting high performance sports. State and district sports councils have been set up throughout the country to carry out NSC programmes. The umbrella body for all national sports associations, the OCM, works closely with the Ministry of Youth and Sports in the selection and training of athletes for the Southeast Asian (SEA) Games, the Commonwealth Games, the Asian Games and the Olympic Games.

The Ministry of Education allocates time for physical education classes for all students and develops and coordinates sports activities in schools. The Sports Division of the Ministry of Education also plays a part in promoting mass sports in schools by implementing sports activities for all students. The Malaysian Government Services Welfare and Recreation Council's role is to encourage sports activities in the public service. It provides sports facilities, grants unrecorded paid leave and gives financial subsidies to deserving staff. The Ministry of Youth and Sports encourages a healthy lifestyle among the general population by promoting its 'Sport for All' and Malaysia Cergas (Fitness Malaysia) programmes.

The National Sports Council Act of 1971 and the Sports Development Act of 1997 have facilitated the development and administration of sports in the country by establishing the NSC as the overall coordinating body for all sports bodies and requiring sports associations to register with the Office of the Commissioner of Sports.

Menara KBS in Putrajaya, office of the Ministry of Youth and Sports.

Sports institutions

In Malaysia, sport is an important aspect of national development. The government, through the Ministry of Youth and Sports, promotes competitive sports and sports for the masses. National sports associations oversee the development of sports on an individual basis while other sports bodies have a larger, multi-sport perspective.

Ministers in charge of sports

1. Tunku Abdul Rahman Putra (1964–66)
2. Senu Abdul Rahman (Tan Sri) (1966–68)
3. Hamzah Abu Samah (Tan Sri) (1969–73)
4. Ali Haji Ahmad (Dato') (1973–78)
5. Samad Idris (Tan Sri) (1978–80)
6. Mokhtar Hashim (Dato') (1980–83)
7. Anwar Ibrahim (Dato' Seri) (1983–84)
8. Dr Sulaiman Haji Daud (Tan Sri) (1984–86)
9. Najib Tun Razak (Dato' Sri) (1986–90)
10. Annuar Musa (Dato' Seri Panglima) (1990–93)
11. Abdul Ghani Othman (Dato') (1993–95)
12. Muhyiddin Haji Yassin (Tan Sri) (1995–99)
13. Hishammuddin Tun Hussein (Dato' Seri) (1999–2004)
14. Azalina Othman Said (Dato' Sri) (2004–08)
15. Ismail Sabri Yaakob (Datuk) (2008–present)

Ministry of Youth and Sports

The Ministry of Youth and Sports was officially established in 1964. Its origins, however, date back to 1953 with the establishment of a Cultural Division responsible for youth-related affairs in the Social Welfare Department. The division was transferred to the Ministry of Information in 1964. At the same time, the increasing number of youth activities required the setting up of a separate Youth Division to direct these activities in the country. A division for sports was also formed in the Ministry of Information at the time.

Both the Youth and Sports Divisions were formally established as a ministry on 15 May 1964. In 1972, a Cultural Division was incorporated into the ministry, which changed its name to the Ministry of Culture, Youth and Sports. In 1987, the Cultural Division was transferred to what became the Ministry of Arts, Culture and Tourism.

The Ministry of Youth and Sports' primary objective for sports is to develop an active, healthy and sports-oriented society towards the goals of achieving national unity and progress. Additionally, the ministry also seeks to nurture high-calibre athletes capable of competing at the international level.

Cabinet Committee on Sports Development

In 2004, the government appointed a Cabinet Committee on Sports Development, under the chairmanship of Deputy Prime Minister Dato' Sri Najib Tun Razak, with broad powers to revamp the Malaysian sports scene. The committee recommended wide-ranging changes to enable talented Malaysian sports performers to receive

Deputy Prime Minister Dato' Sri Najib Tun Razak (right) chairing a meeting of the Cabinet Committee on Sports Development in Putrajaya, 2005.

NSC Directors-General

1. Wilfred Vias (1976–81)
2. Noh Abdullah (Dato') (1982–88)
3. Kamalul Ariffin Abd Rahim (Dato') (1988–92)
4. Mazlan Ahmad (Dato' Wira) (1992–2005)
5. Dr Ramlan Abd Aziz (Dato') (2005–07)
6. Zolkeples Embong (Dato') (2007–present)

Minister of Youth and Sports Dato' Sri Azalina Othman Said (foreground, left) chairing a meeting with national sports associations in 2004.

material rewards and government incentives should they excel for the country in the international arena over a sustained period of time.

The changes bode well for high achieving exponents of any one of eight selected core sports—football, badminton, hockey, tenpin bowling, squash, track and field, swimming and gymnastics. The cabinet committee also announced a pension scheme for athletes who win medals at the Olympic Games and a sport scholarship programme to encourage athletes to excel in both the academic and sports arenas.

National Sports Council (NSC)

Parliament passed the National Sports Council Act in 1971 and the NSC was launched in February 1972. The NSC is chaired by the Minister of Youth and Sports, while day-to-day administration is handled by a director-general. An executive board, also chaired by the Minister of Youth and Sports, is responsible for the management of the NSC.

The National Sports Council Act also provided for the establishment of a National Sports Fund to finance the activities of the NSC. In 1982, for example, Malaysian athletes began receiving allowances as an incentive to intensify their training and increase their competitiveness. The NSC also introduced an Incentive Scheme, through which cash rewards are given to medal-winning athletes in the SEA Games, Commonwealth Games, Asian Games, Olympic Games and Asian, Commonwealth and world championships sanctioned by an international sports governing body.

The National Sports Institute (NSI) was set up as a part of the NSC to promote sporting excellence by providing sports science services, research and education and the systematic preparation of athletes using scientific principles. The NSI became an independent body in 2007.

Commissioner of Sports

The Sports Development Act 1997 was created to promote and facilitate the development and administration of sports in Malaysia. The Act also provided for the appointment, by the Minister of Youth and Sports, of a Sports Commissioner who has the authority to register any association, club, society or company as a sports body. The Sports Commissioner can also impose conditions deemed necessary for the registration of a sports body as well as revoke or suspend its registration.

Commissioner of Sports from 1997 to 2005 Mahamad Zabri Min (Datuk) (top) and Commissioner of Sports from 2005 to present Elyas Omar (Tan Sri) (above).

Olympic Council of Malaysia (OCM)

The oldest of the three bodies that steer Malaysian sport is the OCM. It was formed in 1953 as the Federation of Malaya Olympic Council (FMOC) through an initiative taken by the already existent Federation of Malaya Amateur Athletic Union and the Federation of Malaya Hockey Union. The impetus to create the FMOC arose out of the stirrings of national consciousness among the racially diverse peoples of Malaya who were at that time under British colonial rule. The revival of the quadrennial Olympic Games, staged in London in 1948 and Helsinki in 1952, helped give shape to the desire for national identity and representation.

OCM affiliates: the National Sports Associations

Sport	Association	Sport	Association
Aikido	Malaysia Aikido Association	Netball	Malaysian Netball Association
Aquatics	Amateur Swimming Union of Malaysia	Pétanque	Pétanque Federation of Malaysia
Archery	National Archery Association of Malaysia	Polo	Royal Malaysian Polo Association
		Rowing	Malaysian Rowing Association
Athletics	Malaysia Amateur Athletics Union	Rugby	Malaysian Rugby Union
Badminton	Badminton Association of Malaysia	Sailing	Malaysian Yachting Association
Baseball	Baseball Federation of Malaysia	Sepak takraw	Sepak Takraw Federation of Malaysia
Basketball	Malaysian Amateur Basketball Association	Shooting	National Shooting Association of Malaysia
Bodybuilding	Malaysian Bodybuilding Federation		
Boxing	Malaysia Amateur Boxing Federation	Silambam	Malaysian Silambam Association
Canoeing	Malaysia Canoe Association	Silat	National Silat Federation of Malaysia
Chess	Malaysian Chess Federaton		
Cricket	Malaysian Cricket Association	Snooker	Malaysian Snooker and Billiards Federation
Cycling	Malaysian National Cycling Federation	Softball	Softball Association of Malaysia
Dancesport	Malaysia Amateur Dance Sport Bhd	Squash	Squash Racquets Association of Malaysia
Equestrianism	Equestrian Association of Malaysia		
Fencing	Malaysian Fencing Federation	Table Tennis	Table Tennis Association of Malaysia
Football	Football Association of Malaysia		
Golf	Malaysian Golf Association	Taekwondo	Malaysia Taekwondo Association
Golf (Women)	Malaysian Ladies Golf Association	Tennis	Lawn Tennis Association of Malaysia
Gymnastics	Malaysian Gymnastics Federation		
Handball	Malaysian Handball Federation	Tenpin Bowling	Malaysian Tenpin Bowling Congress
Hockey	Malaysian Hockey Confederation	Triathlon	Triathlon Malaysia
Judo	Malaysia Judo Federation	Volleyball	Malaysia Volleyball Association
Kabaddi	Malaysian Kabaddi Association	Water Skiing	Malaysian Water Skiing Association
Karate	Malaysia Karate Federation	Weightlifting	Malaysia Weightlifting Federation
Lawn Bowls	Malaysia Lawn Bowls Federation	Wushu	Wushu Federation of Malaysia
Mountaineering	Mountaineering Association of Malaysia	X Sports	Extreme Sports Association of Malaysia

Within weeks of its formation, the FMOC, which was recognized by the International Olympic Committee (IOC), began to focus on what has since been its central role: the selection and deployment of a national contingent, in this instance, for the Asian Games in Manila in 1954 and the Melbourne Olympics in 1956. The FMOC became the focal point for the support of national performers by the Malayan public. In 1963, the FMOC was renamed the Olympic Council of Malaysia (OCM).

The OCM is the only sports organization in Malaysia with the right to send athletes to participate in the SEA Games, Asian Games, Commonwealth Games and the Olympics. It also acts as the coordinating body for all sporting organizations in Malaysia and seeks to promote the development of high-performance sport and sport for all through collaboration with national sports associations, government agencies and the IOC for the development and training of athletes, coaches, technical officials and sports administrators.

Officially opened in 1991, Wisma OCM houses the council's offices, the Indoor Sports Centre and Hall of Fame. It is also home to many of the national sports associations affiliated to the OCM.

OCM Presidents

1. E.M. MacDonald (1953–57)
2. H.S. Lee (Tun) (1957–59)
3. Abdul Razak (Tun) (1959–76)
4. Hamzah Abu Samah (Tan Sri) (1975–98)
5. Tunku Imran Tuanku Ja'afar (Tan Sri) (1998–present)

Members of the Federation of Malaya Olympic Council, 1958. Then president Tun H.S. Lee (front row, centre) and immediate past president E.M. MacDonald (front row, third from left) were inducted into the OCM Hall of Fame for their contributions to Malaysian sports. K. Aryaduray (front row, fourth from right), Koh Eng Tong (second row, extreme left), Sum Kwok Seng (second row, fourth from left) and Thong Poh Nyen (back row, third from left) were also inducted into the Hall of Fame (see 'Leaders and Administrators').

Leaders and administrators

Sporting glory belongs as much to the leaders and administrators of sports organizations as it does to athletes. Included in this group are senior politicians, civil servants, corporate figures, members of royal families and former sportsmen, whose influence, background and passion for their respective sports has helped to develop the sports sector.

Prime Minister Dato' Seri Abdullah Ahmad Badawi launching the Olympic Council of Malaysia's Sports Centre and Hall of Fame in 2004.

MAAU President Tun Mohd Ghazali Shafie (left) presenting the women's 400-metre gold medal to Law Kiu Ee at the SEA Games in Kuala Lumpur in 1977.

Hall of Fame

It is fitting that the nation's first two Prime Ministers were among the first six inductees into the Olympic Council of Malaysia (OCM) Hall of Fame. Tunku Abdul Rahman Putra—famous for his interest in golf, football, tennis and racing—was president of the national football association from 1951 to 1974, while Tun Abdul Razak—a sportsman in his youth and a stellar hockey and cricket player—was president of the OCM from 1959 to 1976.

Tan Sri Hamzah Abu Samah, a sportsman and politician, is another inductee into the OCM Hall of Fame. Hamzah served as Minister of Culture, Youth and Sports from 1971 to 1973, during which time he helped establish the National Sports Council (NSC). He was also president of the OCM, the Football Association of Malaysia (FAM), Asian Football Confederation (AFC) and Malaysia Taekwondo Association.

Tun Mohd Ghazali Shafie, another sports leader inducted into the OCM Hall of Fame, was a Cabinet Minister and president of the Malaysian Amateur Athletics Union (MAAU) from 1963 to 1988. Under his stewardship, the MAAU witnessed the success of athletes such as Ishtiaq Mobarak, M. Jegathesan, M. Rajamani, Nashatar Singh, Nur Herman Majid, Saik Oik Cum and Rabuan Pit.

Others who have been inducted into the OCM Hall of Fame for their sports leadership contributions were athletes themselves. Sidique Ali Merican, the first Malayan to break the 10-second barrier in the 100-yard race in 1949 (during his maiden appearance outside Kelantan and his first race wearing a pair of spikes), became director of sports in the Youth and Sports Ministry and was an assistant secretary of the OCM. Datuk Peter

Prime Minister Tunku Abdul Rahman Putra tossing the ball into the air at the opening match of the 1965 Asian Basketball Championships between Malaysia and the Philippines at Stadium Negara.

Velappan, a football player, coach and administrator, served as AFC general secretary from 1978 to 2006.

Other inductees into the OCM Hall of Fame include former champion quarter-miler N.M. Vasagam, the first secretary of the Federation of Malayan Olympic Council (FMOC); K. Aryaduray, the first secretary of the Malaysian Hockey Federation (MHF); Thong Poh Nyen, who served as secretary of the OCM for 31 years before retiring in 1992; journalist and sport official Datuk G.S. Kler, a founder of the Sportswriters Association of Malaysia; and Datuk G. Vijayanathan, MHF secretary for 25 years and an internationally recognized umpire.

Sports Leadership Award

The National Sports Council (NSC) Sports Leadership Award recognizes individuals and organizations that have made outstanding contributions to sports.

The first recipient of the Award in 1987 was Tan Sri Mohd Khir Johari, who assisted in the development of the OCM and the sports of badminton and sepak takraw. A former Cabinet Minister, he was president of the Badminton

ABOVE: Prime Minister and OCM President Tun Abdul Razak (left) presenting Punch Gunalan with the Sportsman of the Year Award, 1975.

LEFT: The 1963 Federation of Malaya Olympic Council members with president Tun Abdul Razak in the centre of the front row.

Association of Malaysia (BAM), Sepak Takraw Federation of Malaysia and Malaysian Bodybuilding Federation. One of Khir's outstanding achievements was leading the national badminton squad to victory in the 1967 Thomas Cup in Jakarta.

Tan Sri Elyas Omar, who received the Sports Leadership Award in 1989, presided over the BAM, the Malaysian National Cycling Federation and the Kuala Lumpur Football Association during the 1980s. He was one of the architects of Malaysia's 1992 Thomas Cup victory.

In 2006, Tunku Imran Tuanku Ja'afar, an influential figure in squash and cricket, became the first Malaysian after Tan Sri Hamzah Abu Samah to be elected as a member of the International Olympic Committee (IOC). Tunku Imran also

Noh Abdullah (second from right), chef-de-mission to the 1985 SEA Games, receiving the Malaysian flag from Culture, Youth and Sports Minister Datuk Dr Sulaiman Daud (left). The handing over was witnessed by OCM deputy president Mohd Khir Johari (second from left) and OCM secretary Thong Poh Nyen (right).

succeeded Hamzah as the OCM president in 1998, a position he still holds. Winner of the Sports Leadership Award in 1990, Tunku Imran is a former Malaysian squash champion who helmed the World Squash Federation from 1989 to 1996.

In 2004, the NSC gave the Leadership Award to journalist Rosmanizam Abdullah, secretary of the Malaysian Malays Cricket Association (MMCA). The MMCA, which fosters the development of young cricketers in the country, was voted by the International Cricket Council as having the best overall development programme in 2003 from among 17 associate and affiliated members in the Asian region.

Dato' Dr P. S Nathan.

Although Dato' Dr P.S. Nathan came late to tenpin bowling—he only picked up the sport in his mid-30s—he achieved many firsts both as a player and an administrator. He was founder of the Malaysian Tenpin Bowling Congress and the first Asian to serve as the president of the World Tenpin Bowling Association, a position which he held from 1987 to 2003. He received the Sports Leadership Award for 2005.

Tan Sri Dato' Seri Ahmad Sarji Abdul Hamid helped turn lawn bowls into a major medal-winner for the country and the Malaysia Lawn Bowls Federation into a respected association. Under his leadership, Malaysia has collected gold medals at

Datuk Hamzah Abu Samah (fifth from right), Minister of Culture, Youth and Sports, chairing the inaugural meeting of the International Games Preparatory Committee of the National Sports Council, 1973.

world championships as well as the Commonwealth, Asian and SEA Games. Four of the world's top 20 lawn bowlers are Malaysians, including Safuan Said (number one in the men's rankings) and Siti Zalina Ahmad, (number three in the women's rankings).

Ahmad Sarji is the founding president of the Asian Lawn Bowls Federation. He is also the deputy president of the Malaysian Malays Cricket Association. He received the NSC Sports Leadership Award for 2006.

Since its inception in 1987, the Sports Leadership Award has also honoured the efforts and achievements of organizations including the Sarawak State Government, the Combined Old Boys' Rugby Association (COBRA) and the Rompin District Sports Council.

BAM President Tan Sri Elyas Omar (second from left) celebrating with players after Malaysia's victory in the 1992 Thomas Cup competition in Stadium Negara.

Other leaders

Datuk Punch Gunalan was an internationally successful badminton player whose exploits on the court led to his induction into the OCM Hall of Fame as a player. He continued to contribute to badminton after his retirement as a player in 1969. He is currently deputy president of the Badminton World Federation (BWF) after having served the BAM in various capacities.

Sultan Azlan Shah, who received the NSC Sports Personality Award for 2006, was president of the MHF from 1981 to 2004. One of the leading hockey tournaments in the world, the Sultan Azlan Shah Cup, is named after him.

Tun Ghafar Baba was president of the Lawn Tennis Association of Malaysia from 1984 to 1999 and served as president of the Asian Tennis Circuit Council and the Malaysian Professional Golfers Association. Ghafar, the founder of the Ghafar Cup Tennis Championship Tournament, was the NSC's Sports Personality for 2005.

Tan Sri Dato' Seri Ahmad Sarji Abdul Hamid, president of the Malaysia Lawn Bowls Federation, holding the World Bowls Challenge Trophy when Malaysia emerged as the overall champion at the 1999 SEA Games in Brunei Darussalam.

MHF Secretary Datuk G. Vijayanathan (left) and MHF President Sultan Azlan Shah at a MHF annual general meeting in Kuala Lumpur, 1984.

Sports leadership awards

Athletes are widely celebrated for their achievements, but the contributions of sports leaders often go unnoticed. The major sports institutions of Malaysia, however, have established awards and accolades to honour the accomplishments of the nation's sports leaders. The Olympic Council of Malaysia Hall of Fame pays homage to administrators' lifetime achievements, while the National Sports Council awards recognize sports leadership excellence in a given year.

Prime Ministers involved in sports

Tunku Abdul Rahman Putra   Tun Abdul Razak   Tun Hussein Onn   Tun Dr Mahathir Mohamad

Four prime ministers have been recognized for their contributions as sports leaders. In 1993, Tunku Abdul Rahman Putra, Tun Abdul Razak and Tun Hussein Onn were inducted into the OCM Hall of Fame. Tun Abdul Razak and Tun Dr Mahathir Mohamad were given the NSC Sports Personality Award in 1988 and 2003 respectively.

Olympic Council of Malaysia (OCM) Hall of Fame

Administrators

1993
- Tunku Abdul Rahman Putra
- Tun Abdul Razak
- Tun Hussein Onn
- Tun Sir Henry H.S. Lee
- Tan Sri Khaw Kai Boh
- N.M. Vasagam

1994
- Thong Poh Nyen
- Koh Eng Tong

2000
- Tan Sri Alexander Lee Yu Lung
- Tan Sri Hamzah Abu Samah

Inductees into the OCM Hall of Fame (from left) Sum Kwok Seng, K. Aryaduray and Sidique Ali Merican, 2002.

2002
- K. Aryaduray
- Sum Kwok Seng
- Sidique Ali Merican
- Tan Sri Mohd Khir Johari
- Lum Mun Chak

2004
- Tun Abdul Ghafar Baba
- E.M. MacDonald
- Tan Sri Abdul Jamil Rais
- Tan Sri Mohd Ghazali Shafie (now Tun)
- Datuk G.S. Kler
- Yap Yong Yih
- Datuk G. Vijayanathan
- Toh Puan Zainon Datuk Hussein

Toh Puan Zainon Datuk Hussein (centre) at the OCM Hall of Fame induction ceremony in 2004.

2006
- Dato' Peter Vellapan
- Norminshah Sabirin

Deputy Minister of Youth and Sports Datuk Liow Tiong Lai presenting an award to Dato' Peter Vellapan (right), 2006.

National Sports Council (NSC) Awards

Sports Leadership Award

1987 Tan Sri Mohd Khir Johari

1988 Thong Poh Nyen

1989 Tan Sri Dato' Elyas Omar

1990 Tunku Tan Sri Imran Tuanku Ja'afar

1991 Tan Sri Dato' Murad Ahmad

1992 Sarawak State Government

1993 Tan Sri Abu Zarim Omar

1994 Padang Midin Secondary School, Kuala Terengganu, for hockey

1995 Rompin District Sports Council

1996 The Combined Old Boys' Rugby Association (COBRA)

1997 Universiti Sains Malaysia Hockey Festival Organising Committee

1999 Datuk Mohamad Taha Ariffin and Dato' Noh Abdullah

2000 Tan Sri Darshan Singh Gill and Datuk Wira Gan Boon Leong

2001 Dr Leonard de Vries and Mary Ong Kwee Kee

2002 Ramlan Dato' Harun

2003 Dato' Peter Vellapan

2004 Rosmanizam Abdullah

Minister of Youth and Sports Dato' Sri Azalina Othman Said (right) presenting Rosmanizam Abdullah with the Sports Leadership Award for 2004.

Tan Sri Dato' Seri Ahmad Sarji Abdul Hamid (right) receiving the 2006 Sports Leadership Award certificate.

2005 Dato' Dr P.S. Nathan

2006 Tan Sri Dato' Seri Ahmad Sarji Abdul Hamid and Dato' Thomas Lee

Sports Personality Award

1988 Tun Abdul Razak

1995 Toh Puan Hajjah Saadiah Sardon

1997 Tan Sri Mohd Khir Johari

1998 Tan Sri Hamzah Abu Samah

1999 Tan Sri Alexander Lee Yu Lung

2002 Tan Sri Mohd Ghazali Shafie (now Tun)

2003 Tun Dr Mahathir Mohamad

2005 Tun Abdul Ghafar Baba

2006 Sultan Azlan Shah

Yang di-Pertuan Agong Sultan Mizan Zainal Abidin (second from left) presenting Sultan Azlan Shah with the 2006 Sports Personality Award.

Special Award

1986 Sidek Abdullah Kamar

1988 1949, 1952, 1955 Thomas Cup teams

1990 Thomas Cup team

1992 Cheok Kon Fatt

1993 Rabia Abdul Salam

1995 Vincent Fernandez S. Vegiyathunmam

1996 Mohd Fathil Dato' Mahmood and Datuk A. Vaithilingam

Mohd Fathil Dato' Mahmood (left) receiving the Special Award for 1996.

1997 S.Kathiravale, Tham Siew Kai, Sharon Low Su Lin and Daniel Lim Tow Chuang

1998 Dr Harjit Singh

1999 Tong Veng Kit, Yap Yong Yih and Ong Hoon Chin

2000 Dato' Kamaruddin Abdul Ghani, Karamjit Singh and Mobarak Ahmad Sher Mohamed

2001 H.R.M. Storey

2002 Malik Jeremiah and A. Perumal Allagappa

2003 Durbara Singh, Loh Beng Hooi and Abdul Majid Muda

2004 S. Satgunam and Chin Mee Keong

2005 Azmi Shaari, M.K. Nathan and Zainal Abu Zarin

2006 Krishnan Thambusamy, Yeoh Cheang Swi and Balwant Singh Kler

Abdul Majid Muda (left) receiving his award from then Minister of Youth and Sports Dato' Seri Hishammuddin Tun Hussein.

Individual recipients of OCM and NSC sports leadership awards*

 Tan Sri Abdul Jamil Rais

 Tan Sri Abu Zarim Omar

 Azmi Shaari

 Balwant Singh Kler

 Cheok Kon Fatt

 Chin Mee Keong

 Tan Sri Darshan Singh Gill

 Dr Leonard de Vries

 Tan Sri Dato' Elyas Omar

 Datuk Wira Gan Boon Leong

 Tun Abdul Ghafar Baba

 Tan Sri Hamzah Abu Samah

 Dr Harjit Singh

 Tunku Tan Sri Imran Tuanku Ja'afar

 Dato' Kamaruddin Abdul Ghani

 Karamjit Singh

 S. Kathiravale

 Tan Sri Khaw Kai Boh

 Datuk G.S. Kler

 Krishnan Thambusamy

 Tan Sri Alexander Lee Yu Lung

 Tun Sir Henry H.S. Lee

 Dato' Thomas Lee

 Daniel Lim Tow Chuang

 Loh Beng Hooi

 Sharon Low Su Lin

 Lum Mun Chak

 E.M. MacDonald

 Malik Jeremiah

 Mobarak Ahmad Sher Mohamed

 Datuk Mohamad Taha Ariffin

 Tan Sri Mohd Ghazali Shafie (now Tun)

 Tan Sri Mohd Khir Johari

 Tan Sri Dato' Murad Ahmad

 M.K. Nathan

 Dato' Dr P.S. Nathan

 Dato' Noh Abdullah

 Hajah Norminshah Sabirin

 Ong Hoon Chin

 Mary Ong Kwee Kee

 Rabia Abdul Salam

 Ramlan Dato' Harun

 Toh Puan Hajjah Saadiah Sardon

 S. Satgunam

 Sidek Abdullah Kamar

 H.R.M. Storey

 Tham Siew Kai

 Thong Poh Nyen

 Tong Veng Kit

 Datuk A. Vaithilingam

 N.M. Vasagam

 Datuk G. Vijayanathan

 Vincent Fernandez S. Vegiyathunmam

 Yap Yong Yih

 Yeoh Cheang Swi

 Zainal Abu Zarin

NSC OCM NSC and OCM

*Some recipients are shown on the facing page. A. Perumal Allagappa and Durbara Singh are not pictured.

Sports and education

The government views sports as a means of promoting a healthy lifestyle, character building and teamwork among Malaysians. The International Charter of Physical Education and Sport states that physical education and sports are essential for overall education. The Malaysian National Sports Policy highlights the roles and responsibilities of various government agencies in promoting sports in schools, polytechnic institutes, colleges and universities.

SMK Sungai Tapang school athletes training in their school compound in Sarawak, 2000.

Players from the Bukit Jalil Sports School (in white) and the Anderson Secondary School competing during a Liga Hoki Remaja tournament at Sultan Azlan Shah Stadium in Ipoh, 2005.

Sports at school level

Schools are an important venue for discovering and nurturing athletic talent at the grassroots level. In addition, school sports provide the starting point for adult participation in sports.

Physical Education is a compulsory subject in Malaysian primary and secondary schools. Its goal is to develop the knowledge, skills, and confidence of young individuals so that they are able to enjoy a lifetime of healthy physical activity. The minimum weekly allocation is 90 minutes for Years 1–3 and 60 minutes for Years 4–6 in primary schools. The minimum weekly allocation for Forms 1–5 is 80 minutes. The Physical Education syllabus is divided into three content areas: fitness, skills and education in sports safety, management, ethics and other issues.

Sports Science is a new subject in the national Sijil Pelajaran Malaysia (SPM) examination. It was first introduced as a subject in the sports schools in 1998. Later, other secondary schools began offering the subject to their Form 4 students. By 2003, 129 schools in 14 states were conducting Sports Science classes. Schools also provide a range of co-curriculum sports activities. Students are encouraged to participate in at least one game or sport as a co-curriculum activity. In 1997, mini-sports for primary schools were launched to develop the physical and psychomotor abilities of children between 8–10 years old. The sports involved are athletics, gymnastics, basketball, netball, touch rugby, cricket, volleyball, football, tennis and sepak takraw.

The Malaysian Schools Sports Council (Majlis Sukan Sekolah Malaysia, MSSM) is in charge of school sports competitions. Formed in 1958, the

Student team that broke the boys' under-15 4x400-metre record to win gold for Johor at the 2005 Malaysian Schools' Sports Council Championships held in Penang.

M. Jegathesan (right) in a 100-yard race at Batu Road School in Kuala Lumpur, 1954. A prominent Malaysian athlete in the 1960s, Jegathesan's success began at the school level.

MSSM finances and prepares students for competitions at home and abroad. The council organizes annual competitions at the national level and supervises competitions by district and state sports councils. Contests are held for three major age groups—under-12, under-15 and under-18—starting among schools at the district level. Athletes who perform well are chosen to represent the district at state-level competitions where athletes qualify to participate at the national competition. Students also take part in international competitions such as the ASEAN School Sports Championship, the Asian School Sports Championship and other international invitational meets.

In addition to organizing competitions, the MSSM also conducts coaching and officiating courses for teachers, carries out centralized training for national school athletes and oversees the standardization of sports rules and regulations at various levels.

The MSSM collaborates with the private sector to provide various sports awards for outstanding students and teachers. Partnerships have also been formed between the MSSM and sports associations, the Ministry of Youth and Sports, the Olympic Council of Malaysia (OCM) and the private sector to identify potential athletes and provide training.

The MSSM also promotes sports in schools through collaborative efforts with organizations such as the Malay Cricket Association of Malaysia and the Malaysia Lawn Bowls Federation.

Sports in universities

Physical Education is not compulsory for pre-university and university students. However, universities conduct various sports and recreational activities for students throughout the year.

Activities are also organized among public and private institutions of higher learning. All 20 public universities are members of the Malaysian Universities Sports Council (Majlis Sukan Universiti Malaysia, MASUM), which encourages sports activities in public institutions of higher education. The council organizes mass programmes such as sports carnivals, walks and cycling events, as well as annual competitions among public institutions of higher education.

MASUM is affiliated to the International University Sports Federation, the Asian Universities Sports Federation and the ASEAN Universities Sports Council. This allows students to participate in international competitions such as the World University Games, the Asian University Games and the ASEAN University Games.

Sports events are also organized among private colleges and universities. They are held by the Sports Committee of the Malaysian Association of Private Colleges and Universities (MAPCU), which also conducts the annual MAPCU Games.

The biennial Malaysian Educational Institutions Games (SIPMA) was first held in 2005. Teams participating in the event come from all levels of educational institutions, and compete for medals in hockey, badminton, football, aquatics, athletics, bowling and squash.

Various public universities offer undergraduate degrees in Physical Education and Sports Science. In 1978, Universiti Putra Malaysia became the first local university to offer a degree in Physical Education, while in 1995, Universiti Malaya became the first local university to offer a degree in Sports Science. Some universities also offer post-graduate degrees in Physical Education and Sports Science up to the doctorate level.

Universiti Putra Malaysia set up a Sports Academy on its campus in 2004 to enhance sports performance through scientific methods. Its goal is to be a one-stop centre for high-performance sports.

Universities also receive technical assistance from national sports organizations such as the Malay

Cricket Association of Malaysia and the Malaysian Lawn Bowls Federation which collaborate with Universiti Kebangsaan Malaysia and Universiti Putra Malaysia respectively.

Promoting sports and education

In 2005, the government allocated RM10 million for sports development programmes in schools. The money was used to develop infrastructure and improve resources for trainers, Physical Education teachers and trainees. The Ministry of Education's Sports Scholarship Scheme enables secondary school athletes who excel in sports and academic work to receive cash awards and training.

The Sports Advisory Panel was established at the Ministry of Education in 2005. The panel consists of members from the private sector and sports associations. This panel acts as a think-tank to plan and implement sports development programmes for mass participation and high-performance sports.

Under the Ninth Malaysia Plan 2006–10, the Ministry of Education aims to seriously develop sports in schools. More Physical Education teachers will be deployed to primary schools and schools will be encouraged to organize after-school sports activities. The plan also includes proposals to hire full-time coaches in schools and set up 15 state sports centres for the eight core sports. Two new sports schools are slated to be built. Additionally, public institutions of higher education will be encouraged to offer more places for sports science degrees as well as programmes to train coaches.

TOP: Over 65 students of higher learning participated in the Universiti Sains Malaysia (USM) Aquathon Challenge in 2005 by performing 50 hours of non-stop swimming at the USM swimming complex, earning themselves an entry in the Malaysian Book of Records.

ABOVE: Students of Universiti Teknologi Malaysia celebrating after winning top placing at the Universiti Tenaga National Rowing Invitational 2005 at Lake Putrajaya Club.

Public universities offering undergraduate degrees in sports

Institution	Degree
Universiti Kebangsaan Malaysia	Sports and Recreation
Universiti Malaya	Sports Science
Universiti Malaysia Sabah	Sports Science
Universiti Pendidikan Sultan Idris	Sports Science and Coaching Science
Universiti Putra Malaysia	Physical Education
Universiti Sains Malaysia	Exercise and Sports Science
Universiti Teknologi Malaysia	Sports Science
Universiti Teknologi Mara	Sports Management and Sports Science

Football match between Universiti Malaya and Indonesia (dark shirts) during the 1979 Intervarsity Games.

Sports schools

Sports schools were established to locate and nurture young, talented athletes. There are currently two sports schools in Malaysia: the Bukit Jalil Sports School, set up in 1996, and the Bandar Penawar Sports School in Johor, established in 1998.

Students are identified through various competitions and talent identification programmes, talent scouting and recommendations by national coaches or sports associations. In addition to athletic prowess, academic performance is also utilized as a selection criterion.

Students in sports schools follow the National School Curriculum and sit for public academic examinations.

Sports school students have represented the country in the SEA, Commonwealth, Asian and Olympic Games and have contributed to the medal tally in all these events.

After leaving the sports schools, students are given the opportunity to pursue sports-related studies in institutions of higher learning or become coaches.

Collaboration between the Ministry of Education and the National Sports Council provides students with the opportunity to pursue their education in selected local universities, allowing them to continue with careers in sport and physical education.

Students at the Bukit Jalil Sports School preparing for classes, 2005. Since it was set up in 1996, the school has nurtured a number of talented young athletes including Olympic diver Bryan Nickson, world wushu champion Chai Fong Ying and Olympic swimmer Daniel Bego.

Sports schools have programmes to develop the following sports:

- aquatics
- archery
- artistic gymnastics
- badminton
- basketball
- cricket
- equestrian
- fencing
- football
- golf
- hockey
- lawn bowls
- netball
- rhythmic gymnastics
- rugby
- sepak takraw
- shooting
- squash
- table tennis
- taekwondo
- tennis
- track and field
- volleyball
- wrestling
- wushu

Sport for All

The National Fitness Council (NFC) was specially set up in 2004 by the Ministry of Youth and Sports to promote a healthier lifestyle among Malaysians. The NFC plays an integral role in providing opportunities for the public to participate in exercise and sports. The two activities that the NFC has chosen to emphasize to promote healthier living to the Malaysian public are gymnasium workouts and aerobics exercises.

Prime Minister Dato' Seri Dr Mahathir Mohamad keeping pace during a 'Senamrobik' exercise at Dataran Merdeka, 2002. As it is easy to conduct for large groups of people, aerobics is suited to the government's initiative of promoting exercise among the Malaysian public.

The 2006 Ultimate Warrior tournament was organized by the NFC to promote all manner of martial arts, and drew large crowds of spectators to its staging in Dataran Merdeka.

Promoting public fitness

Under the National Sports Policy adopted in 1988, a Sport for All programme was initiated to encourage Malaysians to embrace a healthy and active way of life. In 2004, under the auspices of the Ministry of Youth and Sports, the National Fitness Council (NFC) was established as part of the Malaysia Cergas (Fitness Malaysia) campaign. The main objective of the NFC is to raise the standard of physical fitness among Malaysians.

While the National Sports Council (NSC) focuses on promoting and raising the standards of high performance sports in the country, the NFC attempts to bring sports and fitness across all strata of Malaysian society by directing their programmes at educating the public at the grassroots level.

The NFC actively promotes two forms of exercises: gymnasium workouts and aerobics. Via these two general and easy-to-learn exercise forms, the NFC is able to target wider participation from the public. The NFC conducts courses on both gymnasium workouts and aerobics for the general public at government-provided facilities, such as those held in the many Gim Rakyat outlets throughout Malaysia, in order to offer knowledge of these exercises to the public.

The NFC also encourages public participation in its mission, offering certification to volunteer instructors, some of whom may be professionally attached to private organizations and are willing to undergo special training and subsequently offer their services to the NFC. From 17 to 23 July 2006, four trainers from the National Exercise and Sports Trainers Association of the United States were invited by the NFC to train 59 of Malaysia's private gym and aerobics instructors at the Kompleks Rakan Muda in Puchong. After undergoing this training, the instructors received certification from the United States body which enables them to teach anywhere in the world. Private companies may also apply to be endorsed by the NFC for certain sports events that they are organizing.

Although the NFC focuses primarily on sports for the masses, it also works hand-in-hand with other Ministry of Youth and Sports departments, such as in helping to identify new sports talents for the NSC. The NFC is involved in the 'Cari Champions' initiative launched in August 2005, which is a collaborative talent identification programme with the NSC and the Ministry of Education.

The NFC also organizes large-scale events such as the annual Larian Merdeka NFC, a long-distance race around the city of Kuala Lumpur usually held in conjunction with Independence Day.

Larian Merdeka NFC 2006

Above: Deputy Minister of Youth and Sports Dato' Liow Tiong Lai (right) signalling the start of the 2006 Larian Merdeka NFC. A 4.5-kilometre race starting from Dataran Merdeka, the Larian Merdeka NFC was held on 27 August 2006, four days before the actual Independence Day celebrations.

Right: Other sports activities such as basketball were also held in conjunction with the 2006 Larian Merdeka NFC.

Logo of the National Fitness Council (NFC).

The NFC contributed to the Ministry of Youth and Sports anti-drug campaign by actively promoting the *Belia Benci Dadah* (youths hate drugs) slogan at all its sporting activities.

Women's Sports and Fitness Foundation Malaysia

The Women's Sports and Fitness Foundation Malaysia (WSFFM) was established in 1995 to increase the awareness of fitness and sports among Malaysian women as well as promote women in sports and fitness.

Among the activities the WSFFM has organized are the Annual Aerobics Convention and the National Aerofit Challenge. The WSFFM also works together with the National Fitness Council to achieve its objectives.

In 2002, the Miss Fitness pageant was introduced. The contestants were judged not only on their physical looks, but also on how they achieved and maintained their appearance. Participants had to show a commitment to maintaining a healthy lifestyle through correct eating habits. Nutritionists and fitness trainers were enlisted to supervise the contestants on gruelling schedules and daunting physical challenges. Meei Liew, Miss Malaysia Fitness 2004, ranked among the top eight in the Fitness Woman World Championship 2005, which was the first such championship to be held in Malaysia.

The WSFFM successfully organized the first National Women's Games in 2005. Nine events were held at the Games—aquatics, athletics, badminton, bowling, football, gymnastics, hockey, squash and netball—which saw the participation of 3000 athletes and officials. The second National Women's Games were held in 2007 and attracted nearly 3400 athletes and officials.

Minister of Youth and Sports Dato' Sri Azalina Othman Said (right) officiating the closing ceremony of the 2007 National Women's Games at Stadium Juara in Bukit Kiara, Kuala Lumpur.

Aerobics

By definition, aerobics is any activity that can be sustained continuously for at least 25 minutes at a heart rate of between 55 to 85 per cent of the individual's maximum rate per minute. It can also be defined as the ability of the body to take in, transport and utilize oxygen, involving the capacity of the heart and lungs to exchange and deliver oxygen to working muscles during the activity. Thus, aerobics is a cardiovascular workout and a form of cardiorespiratory exercise.

In Malaysia, as in the rest of the world, aerobics has come to be synonymous with a dance fitness or exercise routine that is usually, but not always, executed to the beat of music.

In the early 1980s, jazz dance classes held at various ballet studios mainly located in urban locations, such as Annabelle Ballet School on Jalan Bukit Bintang in Kuala Lumpur, specially catered to women who were looking for some form of physical exercise. This was a forerunner of aerobic dance when it arrived in Malaysia. There was no standard to govern instructors' accreditations at the time. As a result, aerobics spread exponentially beyond the ballet studio to gyms, office conference rooms, city halls, school halls, parks and generally anywhere a group could gather and hold a class.

By the 1990s, classes were better organized and even though instructors were not accredited, aerobic programmes like Jazzercise, a franchised dance fitness programme, were establishing themselves in Kuala Lumpur. Sporting goods giants including Nike and, later, Reebok held workshops for local aerobics enthusiasts to improve their technical knowledge and update themselves on new aerobic innovations like the 'step'.

By the late 1990s, health clubs and fitness centres like Fitness First, California Fitness, Celebrity Fitness and True Fitness began sprouting up throughout the country, offering aerobics classes as part of their exercise programmes.

Malaysian instructors are equipping themselves by attending courses and receiving qualifications and certifications from institutions such as the International Dance Exercise Association (IDEA) and the Aerobics and Fitness Association of America (AFAA).

Jazzercise, like other aerobics dance routines, promotes exercise through a fun group activity.

Aerobics instructors demonstrating a dance routine at the 1999 National Aerobics Championship.

Gym culture

In 1997, gyms and fitness clubs began to be established in all the country's major cities. Gyms and fitness centres located in the heart of business districts in urban and suburban areas became ideal workout places.

The four major gym chains in Malaysia—Fitness First, Clark Hatch International, Sweat Club and Philip Wain Fitness and Beauty—have a total of 19 outlets in the metropolitan Kuala Lumpur area, and three others in major Malaysian cities. There are also many private-member gyms in Malaysia that are sole-proprietorships.

The government has also built public gyms throughout the country known as Gim Rakyat. These facilities are used to promote a healthy lifestyle under the government's social health initiatives.

1. Minister of Youth and Sports Dato' Sri Azalina Othman Said trading friendly punches with Hong Kong movie star Jackie Chan during the launching of the California Fitness gym franchise in Malaysia, 2005.

2. The 2006 Mr Gim Rakyat NFC competition, an annual bodybuilding contest.

3. The gym room at a Fitness First branch in Malaysia outfitted with international standard gym equipment which is open to the paying public.

Major multi-sport events

Malaysia has hosted a number of international single-sport events over the years including the Thomas Cup, World Cup of Golf and Hockey World Cup. The country has also been the venue for international multi-sport events—the SEAP/SEA Games and the Commonwealth Games—as well as numerous national multi-sport events. The benefits of hosting major sporting events include the enhancement of national pride among athletes as well as Malaysians in general, and the spurring of investment in local sports facilities and development.

Rahim Ahmad, a Malaysian track star, bearing the flame during the opening ceremony of the 1965 SEAP Games in Kuala Lumpur.

National games

Sukan Malaysia (SUKMA or Malaysian Games) is a biennial multi-sport event contested by contingents from the various states and federal territories, the Royal Malaysian Police Sports Council, Armed Forces, Malaysian Schools Sports Council and Malaysian Universities' Sports Council (MASUM) as well as Brunei. Initiated by the National Sports Council, the first SUKMA was held in Kuala Lumpur in 1986 and saw the participation of nearly 5000 athletes and officials in 21 events. The 2006 SUKMA was held in Kedah, and the 2008 games will be held in Terengganu. The underlying objective of SUKMA is to scout and identify talented athletes from all over the country who could possibly represent Malaysia at the international level.

The inaugural Borneo Games—featuring teams from the British territories of North Borneo, Sarawak and Brunei—were organized in 1950 in Brunei. Datuk G.S. Kler was a driving force behind the initial staging of the compe-

Opening ceremony of the 11th SUKMA in Kedah, 2006.

tition. A biennial multi-sport event, the Borneo Games ceased to be held regularly after 1967 and stopped altogether after the 1984 event. After more than 20 years, the Borneo Games were revived in 2005 in Sabah. The 2007 games in Sarawak saw the participation of teams from Sarawak, Sabah, Labuan, Terengganu, Kalimantan and Brunei.

Other national multi-sport events include the Malaysian Educational Institution Sports Tournament (Kejohanan Sukan Institusi Pendidikan Malaysia or SIPMA), inaugurated in 2005, and the Federal Territory Games (Sukan Wilayah Persekutuan or SWIP)—contested by contingents from Kuala Lumpur, Labuan and Putrajaya—inaugurated in 2007 (see 'Sports and education').

Regional games

National shooter Chan Kooi Chye running through the streets of Kuala Lumpur with the SEAP Games torch, 1965.

Southeast Asian Peninsular (SEAP) Games

The Southeast Asian Peninsular (SEAP) Games Federation was formed in June 1959, with Burma, Cambodia, Laos, Malaya, Thailand and Vietnam as its founding members. The first SEAP Games were held in Bangkok from 12 to 17 December 1959 with participation by Singapore and all the founding members except Cambodia. Only during the second SEAP Games, held in Rangoon, Burma from 11 to 16 December 1961, did all the founding members compete for the first time.

The next SEAP Games, scheduled for 1963, were cancelled after the designated host Cambodia was unable to organize the event. The same fate seemed about to befall the 1965 event after Laos withdrew, until Malaysia stepped in and decided to host the 3rd SEAP Games, the nation's first ever international multi-sport event. The games took place from 14 to 21 December 1965 in what were at that time the country's two major stadiums, Stadium Merdeka and Stadium Negara, with the former as the main venue. The Specialist Teachers Training Institute and Sultan Alam Shah School in Cheras became the Games Village and housed visiting athletes and officials. Six countries took part in the event—Burma,

Laos, Malaysia, Singapore, South Vietnam and Thailand. To ensure that there were enough participants, each country was allowed to enrol three athletes per sports event, an increase from the usual two. A total of 14 sports were featured in the games. Malaysia, fielding 212 athletes, won 33 gold, 36 silver and 29 bronze medals, finishing second overall.

The 6th SEAP Games were held in Malaysia from 6 to 13 December 1971. The event featured 15 sports and all seven members of the SEAP Federation—Burma, Cambodia, Laos, Malaysia, Singapore, South Vietnam and Thailand. Malaysia, represented by a contingent of 282 athletes, finished second again after winning 41 gold, 43 silver and 55 bronze medals.

Southeast Asian (SEA) Games

The admission of Brunei, Indonesia and the Philippines into the SEAP Federation made up for the non-participation of Cambodia, Vietnam and Laos in the renamed Southeast Asian (SEA) Games in 1977. The 9th edition of the regional games was hosted by Malaysia from 19 to 26 December 1977. The seven nations competed in 18 sports. Malaysia finished fourth when the nation's 381 athletes won 25 gold, 42 silver and 44 bronze medals.

Nine countries—Brunei, Burma, Indonesia, Laos, Malaysia, the Philippines, Singapore, Vietnam and Thailand—took part in the 15th SEA Games, held in Kuala Lumpur from 20 to 31 August 1989. The event featured 24 sports, which were held in various venues including Stadium Merdeka, Stadium Negara, Cheras Aquatic Centre, Cheras Velodrome, Subang Shooting Range and Kent Bowl in Petaling Jaya. Over 3000 athletes and officials participated. Malaysia, represented by 483 athletes, finished second after winning 67 gold, 57 silver and 78 bronze medals.

The success of the 1998 Commonwealth Games in Kuala Lumpur extended to the 21st SEA Games hosted by Malaysia from 8 to 17 September 2001. Eleven countries participated in the games, including, for the first time, Timor-Leste. The events were held in the National Sports Complex in Bukit Jalil as well as other venues in Penang, Johor Bahru, Seremban and Shah Alam. Malaysia fielded 568 athletes in the 32 sports events and, for the first time, finished first in the standings after winning 111 gold, 75 silver and 85 bronze medals, its best-ever performance in the SEA Games.

(From left) May Tan, Magdaline Goh, Jeffrey Ong, Nurul Huda Abdullah and Jong Su Ting were members of the 1989 SEA Games swimming team that won 11 gold medals.

Opening ceremony of the 15th SEA Games.

Bukit Jalil National Sports Complex

Construction of the National Sports Complex (Kompleks Sukan Negara) situated at Bukit Jalil commenced in 1992 and was completed in 1998 when it was utilized for the Kuala Lumpur Commonwealth Games hosted by Malaysia.

The sports complex is the largest in the country and comprises the National Stadium, Putra Stadium, the National Hockey Stadium, the National Aquatic Centre and the National Squash Centre. The headquarters of the National Sports Council and the Bukit Jalil Sports School (see 'Sports and education') are also located nearby.

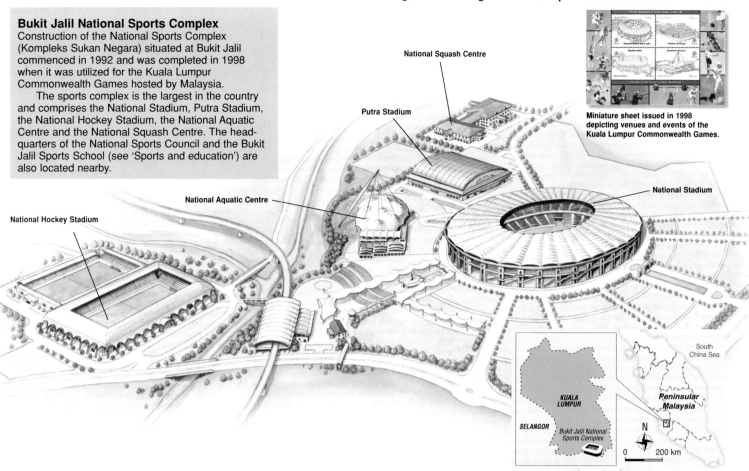

National Squash Centre

Putra Stadium

National Stadium

National Aquatic Centre

National Hockey Stadium

Miniature sheet issued in 1998 depicting venues and events of the Kuala Lumpur Commonwealth Games.

South China Sea

SELANGOR

KUALA LUMPUR

Bukit Jalil National Sports Complex

Peninsular Malaysia

N

0   200 km

Commonwealth Games

On 21 July 1992, Kuala Lumpur won the bid in Barcelona to host the 1998 Commonwealth Games. The official Commonwealth Games contract was signed in Kuala Lumpur on 19 January 1993, confirming the city's hosting of the event and, in the process, the country became the first Asian host in Commonwealth Games history.

Sukom Ninety Eight Berhad was specially set up to handle all organizational aspects of the event. It was chaired by Tan Sri Hamzah Abu Samah, president of the Olympic Council of Malaysia, who appointed General (retired) Tan Sri Hashim Mohamad Ali as chief executive officer. Several high-cost projects were initiated in preparation for the Commonwealth Games, the largest of which were the building of the Bukit Jalil National Sports Complex, comprising the National Stadium, Putra Stadium, the National Aquatics Centre, National Hockey Stadium and National Squash Centre, and the Bukit Kiara Lawn Bowls Complex. The task force for the event involved 5000 people, while 17,000 volunteers participated in the opening and closing ceremonies. Wira, an orangutan, was chosen as the mascot for the games.

The games were held over 11 days from 11 to 21 September 1998. The opening ceremony featured, among other presentations, the cultural diversity of Malaysia, with traditionally inspired dances and costumes. Malaysia's aim for the Commonwealth Games to be the largest in their history was successful. A total of 5000 competitors and officials from a record 70 countries participated in the 1998 Commonwealth Games, which was a large increase from the 3300 participants who had participated in the 1994 edition in Victoria, Canada. The number of sporting events also increased to a record 15, with the addition of hockey, cricket, netball and rugby to the programme.

Ticket sales proved to be high, as an estimated 60,000 spectators flocked to the stadium for the opening ceremony, while the closing ceremony, attended by Queen Elizabeth II (Head of the Commonwealth and Patron of the Commonwealth Games Federation) and the Yang di-Pertuan Agong Tuanku Ja'afar, sold approximately 80,000 seats. Sukom Ninety Eight Berhad reported a sum of RM25 million in ticket sales. Malaysia finished fourth overall after collecting 10 gold, 14 silver and 12 bronze medals, its best-ever performance at the Commonwealth Games (see 'Chronology' and 'Awards and achievements').

ABOVE: (from left) Sarina Sundara Rajah, Thye Chee Kiat, Carolyn Au Yong and El Regina Tajuddin receiving their Commonwealth Games gold medals from Prime Minister Dato' Seri Dr Mahathir Mohamad after winning the women's rhythmic gymnastics team event.

BELOW: 'Wira', the mascot for the Kuala Lumpur Commonwealth Games, in front of the National Sports Complex.

ABOVE: The Yang di-Pertuan Agong Tuanku Ja'afar (second from left) and Queen Elizabeth II inspecting the guard of honour at the closing ceremony of the 16th Commonwealth Games in Kuala Lumpur, 21 September 1998.

LEFT: Inside the National Stadium during the opening ceremony of the Kuala Lumpur Commonwealth Games.

Sports tourism

Sports tourism in Malaysia has become a high-value industry which provides many opportunities for enhancement of local economic activity. A multi-billion Ringgit business for the country, sports tourism is one of the fastest growing areas in the global travel and tourism industry.

Growth of sports tourism

In 2006, just over 17.5 million tourists visited Malaysia. Of this figure, 1.3 per cent were visiting for the purpose of sport-related activities, an increase of 18.2 per cent from 2005. Recognizing its potential, the Malaysian government has made an effort to promote sports tourism. Among the factors encouraging sports tourism in the country are the construction of new resort complexes with sports facilities, the constant availability of water activities and scheduled sports tours. The growth potential of sports tourism in Malaysia is high and the industry is estimated to be capable of contributing up to one-third of the country's tourism receipts by 2015.

A high value industry

National and international sporting events and activities collect tourist revenue at various stages which extend far beyond ticket sales. Officials, participants and spectators utilize hotels, transportation and local entertainment during their visit, and tourist shopping contributes to the economy by injecting money into the commercial sector.

Top: Sutera Harbour Golf Course in Kota Kinabalu, Sabah, is one of many premier golfing locations for tourists visiting Malaysia's Borneo States.

Above: Sipadan Island, one of the best snorkelling and diving locations in Southeast Asia, achieved international fame after being featured in the 1989 documentary *Ghost of the Sea Turtle* by famed diver Jacques Cousteau.

Prime Minister Dato' Seri Abdullah Ahmad Badawi (right) with other dignitaries and officials at the launch of 'Visit Malaysia Year 2007' at Taman Tasik Titiwangsa. Tourist arrivals to Malaysia in 2007 reached 20.97 million, an increase of 19.5 per cent from the previous year.

The sports sector is versatile in that it allows a broad range of participation. Realizing the importance of the link between sports and tourism, the government provides support to event managers, organizers and non-governmental organizations to host selected sports events, especially those which attract fans and spectators in large numbers. The buoyancy of the sports tourism industry encourages the development of market strategies in the promotion of sports events and is supported by professional event managers keen to capitalize on the growing industry. Commercial operators have commenced development of water, land and air-based sports and recreational facilities.

In order to attract sports tourists, most hotels offer activity-based packages, which include sport segments such as golf, sailing and tennis. Tourism has also boosted the growth of sports through the development of better sporting facilities, particularly in coastal and rural areas. In some cases, hotel-owned sports facilities are made available to the paying public through membership schemes.

Well-planned sports activities also help to generate tourism in less visited areas of the country and during off-season periods. The annual Monsoon Cup, a sailing tournament in the state of Terengganu, is a good example of an international event which

Sports event attractions

buoys the tourism economy despite the periodically low tourist traffic of the monsoon season. Shopping outlets, hotels, travel agents as well as the wider public all benefit from this initiative.

Sports tourism initiatives

In the early 1960s, major sports events such as the Merdeka Cup attracted the participation of national football teams from Asian countries. The two-week tournament brought football fans from the neighbouring countries of Thailand and Singapore to witness the matches. Together with local football fans, they packed Stadium Merdeka, the only football stadium in Kuala Lumpur at that time.

Stamps issued in conjunction with 'Visit Malaysia Year 2007' showcasing some of the natural wonders that trekkers and divers can encounter in the country.

Malaysia has hosted other large events in recent years such as the F1 PETRONAS Malaysian Grand Prix at the Sepang International Circuit (since 1999), which has provided the country with an enormous amount of beneficial media attention. The country also plays host to the biggest cycling event in Asia, Tour de Langkawi (since 1996), and the FIFA World Youth Championship was held here in 1997.

Malaysia's rich natural resources are ideal for outdoor sporting pursuits. Over 20 coastal islands and 30 nature parks and marinas (including Langkawi Island, Port Dickson, Penang and Port Klang) provide sporting attractions. Golf is particularly popular—there are 207 golf courses available in the country as at 2008. Scheduled events like bird watching at Fraser's Hill in Pahang and Tanjung Tuan in Negeri Sembilan also attract tourists.

1. International sailors are drawn to Terengganu every year to participate in the Monsoon Cup, one of the region's premier sailing tournaments.

2. Fans cheering on Ferrari race driver Michael Schumacher at the F1 PETRONAS Malaysian Grand Prix at Sepang, a major international sporting event that draws large tourist crowds every year and exposes Malaysia to potential visitors via international media coverage.

3. The Tour de Langkawi, a prestigious international cycling event, receives wide media coverage, showcasing many of the country's sights to viewers across the globe as the peloton tours Malaysia. In 2007, it also served as the curtain-raising sports event for 'Visit Malaysia Year 2007'. The cyclists are seen here passing the Bangunan Sultan Abdul Samad in Kuala Lumpur during the 2006 Tour.

A recent phenomenon is the building of sports facilities next to hotels, for example, the woodball course at the Lanjut Golf and Beach Resort in Pahang, a bowling centre and ice-skating rink at Sunway Resort and Spa in Selangor, and golf courses such as those at the Saujana Golf and Country Club in Selangor, Tanjung Puteri Golf Resort in Johor, Nexus Resort Karambunai in Sabah and the Hornbill Golf and Jungle Club in Sarawak. Silver-haired tourists from Europe may enjoy a game of lawn bowls at the Bayuemas Indoor Bowls Stadium in Klang and at the Bukit Kiara National Lawn Bowls Complex in Kuala Lumpur.

Not surprisingly, the number of sports tourists to Malaysia increases during holiday seasons. These periods provide an effective induction period into sports via the offering of 'sport-tryout' events and promotional schemes which include complimentary 'beginner-training' courses and equipment. The promotion of sports during peak tourist seasons helps to widen participation in sports as well as sustain them.

In 1994, sports tourism was given due recognition by the Ministry of Youth and Sports and the Ministry of Tourism (then Culture, Arts and Tourism), with the creation of the Malaysian Sports Tourism Council. This council advises the founding ministries on matters related to sports tourism. Accordingly, the primary emphasis of sports tourism in Malaysia is to complement and highlight the National Tourism Policy.

The government promoted 1998 as the Year of Sports and Recreation in order to diversify tourism products into sports and recreation events. A sound management structure of sport associations, combined with a supportive public, produced more than 240 sport and recreational events that year. Among the events initiated by the government were an open-fishing competition, extreme sports, international jet skiing, the Super Bikers Tour and a variety of traditional games. A total of 56 international sports events were organized in Malaysia in 2005.

Sports tourism in Malaysia is a high-value, dynamic industry, which energizes the economy. It is has many positive outcomes: the increase of cash capital, the creation of opportunities for new jobs and the improvement of cultural perceptions. Its immediate benefit to the tourism sector is not only measured in cash, but also in the long-term promotion of recurring visits by tourists.

Other sport-related activities

1. A young tourist hangs from pulleys on the 'Bungy Bounce', one of Club Med's many organized outdoor activities. Located at Cherating Beach, the resort is a haven for holiday-goers in search of recreation.

2. A cultural boat race taking place in Kota Bharu, Kelantan. The northern state is a treasure-trove of traditional sports, with public activities held regularly.

3. Parasailing on a beach at Pangkor Island, Perak. Most tourist beaches in Malaysia have private operators who offer various recreational activities.

4. BASE jumpers in freefall from Kuala Lumpur Communications Tower. Kuala Lumpur is one of the few cities in the world that offers legalized BASE jumping activities.

Glossary

Over 1000 participants from all over the Southeast Asian region took part in the Putrajaya bird-singing competition, 2002.

A

All England Open Badminton Championships: One of the oldest and most prestigious badminton tournaments in the world. First held in 1899, they functioned as the unofficial world badminton championships until the 1977 World Badminton Championships.

Asian Games: A multi-sport event held every four years among Asian athletes and regulated by the Olympic Council of Asia (OCA). The inaugural Games were held in New Delhi in 1951.

B

Borneo Games: A biennial multi-sport event initially organized in 1950 in Brunei, the 2007 Borneo Games featured teams from Sarawak, Sabah, Labuan, Brunei, Terengganu and Kalimantan.

British Empire Games: The predecessor of the Commonwealth Games, they were first held in Ontario in 1930. The name was changed to the British Empire and Commonwealth Games in 1954, the British Commonwealth Games in 1970, and the Commonwealth Games in 1974.

C

Cabinet Committee on Sports Development: Formed in 2004 with Deputy Prime Minister Dato' Sri Najib Tun Razak as chairman. Its mission is to revitalize the Malaysian sports scene by planning and implementing various sports programmes and policies.

Cockfighting: A blood sport in which two specially trained cockerels are set in a ring to fight in front of spectators who often place bets on the outcome of the duel. It is outlawed under the Prevention of Cruelty to Animals Ordinance 1962, but government-licensed cockfights continue to be held at certain indigenous festivals.

Commissioner of Sports: A position created by the Sports Development Act 1997. The Commissioner has the authority to register associations, clubs, societies as sports bodies.

Commonwealth Games: A quadrennial multi-sport event involving athletes from the 53 member countries of the Commonwealth organized by the Commonwealth Games Federation (CGF). The 1998 Commonwealth Games were held in Kuala Lumpur.

F

Formula One (F1): The highest class of auto race as designated by the Fédération Internationale de l'Automobile, the world governing body of motor sports. First held in 1950, the F1 World Championship season comprises a series of races, called Grand Prix. The F1 PETRONAS Malaysian Grand Prix was first staged in 1999 at the Sepang International Circuit.

G

Gasing: Malay word meaning 'top'. Top spinning (*main gasing*) is a popular pastime throughout Malaysia, particularly in the Malay communities on the east coast of the Peninsula.

H

H.M.S. Malaya Cup: Two trophies donated in 1921 by the officers and crew of the battleship H.M.S. *Malaya* to inaugurate football and rugby competitions. In 1967, the Malaysia Cup superseded the H.M.S. Malaya Cup as the nation's premier football tournament. The final H.M.S. Malaya Cup rugby competition was held in 1982.

I

International Olympic Committee (IOC): Based in Lausanne, Switzerland, the IOC was founded in 1894. It organizes the summer and winter Olympic Games. IOC membership comprises 205 national Olympic committees from around the world.

International Paralympic Committee (IPC): Founded in 1989 and based in Bonn, Germany, the IPC is the global governing body of the Paralympic Movement and organizer of the summer and winter Paralympic Games. The IPC's membership in 2007 comprised representatives from 162 national paralympic committees, four international organizations of sport for the disabled, five regional organizations and six international sports federations.

M

Malaysian Schools Sports Council (Majlis Sukan Sekolah Malaysia or MSSM): Formed in 1958, the MSSM organizes annual national-level school sports competitions and supervises district and state-level competitions.

Malaysian Universities' Sports Council (Majlis Sukan Universiti Malaysia or MASUM): Founded in 1981 to encourage sports activities in public universities, MASUM trains and sends athletes to regional and international varsity games.

Merbok: Zebra dove or *Geopelia striata*. Also known as *ketitir*. Prized in Southeast Asia for their natural vocal abilities,

Malaysian contingent to the 2007 Blind Sport Association Championship in Brazil.

merbok are bred and trained to sing in competitions.

Ministry of Youth and Sports Malaysia (Kementerian Belia dan Sukan or KBS): Responsible for all youth and sports related affairs in the country, the Ministry of Youth and Sports promotes both recreational and competitive sports and develops local athletes to compete at the international level.

N

National Fitness Council (NFC): Launched in 2004, the NFC seeks to raise the standard of fitness of all Malaysians. It promotes exercises such as gym workouts and aerobics as well as large-scale activities such as the annual Larian Merdeka.

National Sports Council (NSC or Majlis Sukan Negara (MSN): Established by the National Sports Council Act in 1971, the NSC promotes excellence in competitive sports. Apart from training athletes and coaches, the NSC gives annual National Sports Awards to recognize the achievements of outstanding Malaysian athletes and sports leaders.

National Sports Institute (NSI): Set up under the National Sports Council to promote the use of sports science, the NSI became an independent body in 2007.

National Women's Games: First held in 2005, this biennial multi-sport event is organized by the Women's Sports and Fitness Foundation of Malaysia.

O

Olympians of the Year: Awards given by the Olympic Council of Malaysia (OCM) to the most outstanding male and female athletes of Malaysian contingents to multi-sports events under the jurisdiction of the OCM.

Olympic Council of Asia (OCA): One of the five continental sports associations recognized by the International Olympic Committee. Formed in 1982, the OCA is headquartered in Kuwait and has a membership of 45 national Olympic committees from all over Asia.

Olympic Council of Malaysia (OCM): The coordinating body for all sporting organizations in Malaysia. It seeks to promote sports in Malaysia as well as select and enter athletes for multi-sport events such as the Olympic, Asian, SEA and Commonwealth Games. The OCM has 50 affiliate national sports associations as members.

Olympic Council of Malaysia (OCM) Hall of Fame: First proposed in 1974 by then Minister of Culture, Youth and Sports Tan Sri Hamzah Abu Samah, it highlights the progress of sports in Malaysia and honours outstanding athletes and sports officials. Induction ceremonies took place in 1993, 1994, 1995, 2000, 2002, 2004 and 2006.

Olympic Council of Malaysia (OCM) Sports Museum: Opened in 2005, the museum seeks to preserve and display memorabilia related to the nation's outstanding athletes and sporting achievements.

Olympic Games: Quadrennial, multi-sport event organized by the International Olympic Committee (IOC). The inaugural summer Olympics were held in Greece in 1896, the first winter Olympics in France in 1924.

Orang Asli: The indigenous minority peoples of Peninsular Malaysia, comprising 18 ethnic subgroups.

P

Padang: Malay term for 'field'.

Paralympic Games: Multi-sport event for athletes with disabilities organized by the International Paralympic Committee (IPC) every four years. The inaugural summer Games were held in Rome in 1960 and the first winter Games in Sweden in 1976. Since 1988 (summer Games) and 1992 (winter Games), the Paralympics have been held at the same venues as the Olympics.

Perbadanan Stadium Merdeka: A federal statutory body responsible for the management of Stadium Merdeka, the Bukit Jalil National Sports Complex and the Bukit Kiara Sports Complex.

S

Silat: Traditional Malay art of self-defence, comprising numerous different styles and forms.

Southeast Asian Peninsular (SEAP) Games and Southeast Asian (SEA) Games: Biennial multi-sport event organized by, initially, the Southeast Asian Peninsula (SEAP) Games Federation and, after 1977, by the Southeast Asian (SEA) Games Federation. The first SEAP Games were held in Bangkok in 1959, the first SEA Games in Kuala Lumpur in 1977. The SEA Games Federation comprises 11 member countries—Brunei Darussalam, Cambodia, Laos, Indonesia, Malaysia, Myanmar, the Philippines, Singapore, Thailand, Timor-Leste and Vietnam. Malaysia hosted the SEAP Games in 1965 and 1971, and the SEA Games in 1977, 1989 and 2001.

Sports schools: Set up to nurture talented young athletes, there are two sports schools in Malaysia—Bukit Jalil Sports School (opened in 1996) and Bandar Penawar Sports School (opened in 1998).

Sukan Malaysia (SUKMA or Malaysian Games): Biennial multi-sport youth event contested by contingents from the various states and federal territories, the Police, Armed Forces, Malaysian Schools Sports Council and Malaysian Universities' Sports Council as well as Brunei. The first SUKMA was held in Kuala Lumpur in 1986.

T

Thomas Cup: Also known as the World Team Championships. An international badminton competition contested by men's national teams of the member countries of the Badminton World Federation (BWF). Only three countries—Malaysia, Indonesia and China—have won the tournament since its inception in 1948.

W

Wau: Malay word for 'kite'. Initially used for traditional kites of Kelantan and Terengganu, *wau* is now a general term for kites. The term *laying-layang* is also used, particularly in Johor, Negeri Sembilan and Penang to refer to kites.

Women's Sports and Fitness Foundation of Malaysia (WSFFM): Established in 1995 to increase awareness of fitness and sports among Malaysian women. The WSFFM organizes a number of sports-related activities including the Annual Aerobics Convention, National Aerofit Challenge and the National Women's Games.

Wushu: Commonly referred to as 'kung fu', wushu is an umbrella term used to refer to the many different forms of Chinese martial arts.

Selangor celebrating after defeating Singapore 4–2 to win the Malaysia Cup, 1978.

Bibliography

Abdul Aziz Abdan (1991), 'The Role of Sports in Nation Building and Provision of Facilities in Kuala Lumpur', paper presented at the 12th Pacific-Asian Congress of Municipalities, Kuala Lumpur.

Abdul Rahim Ahmad (1976), 'Role of the Ministry of Culture, Youth and Sports in the Development of Football', paper presented at the Seminar Jawatankuasa Teknik dan Kemajuan Persatuan Bolasepak Malaysia, Kuala Lumpur.

Abdul Talib Mohd Zin (1993), 'Pembangunan Sukan di Sekolah-Sekolah', paper presented at the National Seminar on Planning for Sports and Recreation Facilities in the Urbanization Process, Kuala Lumpur.

Ahmad Mustafa (2002), 'International Event Hosting: Motor Sports Venue: the Prospects for Malaysia', paper presented at the National Conference on Sports Tourism, Petaling Jaya.

Ahmad Sarji Abdul Hamid (2005), *Lawn Bowls in Malaysia: The President's Memoir*, Kuala Lumpur: Pelanduk Publications.

Arkib Negara Malaysia (1998), *Sukan Komanwel: Dari Hamilton ke Kuala Lumpur (1930–1998)*, Kuala Lumpur.

Aziz Deraman and Wan Ramli Wan Mohamad (1994), *Permainan Tradisi Orang Melayu*, Kuala Lumpur: Fajar Bakti.

British Malaya, various issues.

Dawson, T. (ed.) (1975), *Who's Who in Sports in Malaysia and Singapore*, Kuala Lumpur: Who's Who in Sports.

Delilkan, Alex (1970), *Cricket: A Malaysian Experience*, Kuala Lumpur: Malaysian Cricket Association.

Gapor Ahmad (2007), *Kejurulatihan dan Sains Sukan*, Kuala Lumpur: Utusan.

Ho Koh Chye (1977), 'Hockey Development Plan', paper presented at the Southeast Asian Games Seminar on Physical Education of Youth and National Development, Kuala Lumpur.

Imran Tuanku Ja'afar, Tunku (1986), 'How Malaysian Sports Ambassadors Can Assist in Promoting Malaysian Tourism', paper presented at the National Tourism Conference, Kuala Lumpur: National Tourism Council Malaysia.

Khairuddin Ayip (1988), *Raja Pecut*, Shah Alam: Marwilis Publisher.

Khoo Kay Kim and Khoo, Selina (2007), *50 Outstanding Malaysian Sportspersons*, Kuala Lumpur: The Writers' Publishing House.

Khoo, Selina (2005), *Sport for All in Malaysia: Policy and Practice*, Kuala Lumpur: Universiti Malaya Press.

Kum Boo (1977), 'Status of Physical Education and Sports in Malaysia', paper presented at the Southeast Asian Games Seminar on Physical Education of Youth and National Development, Kuala Lumpur.

Laila Kadir (ed.) (2001), *Kompleks Sukan Negara Bukit Jalil*, Kuala Lumpur: Jabatan Penerangan Malaysia.

Liponski, W. (2003), *World Sports Encyclopedia*, St. Paul: MBI Publishing Company.

Mathews, Philip (ed.) (2007), *Chronicle of Malaysia: Fifty Years of Headline News*, Kuala Lumpur: Editions Didier Millet.

Megat Ahmad Kamaluddin Megat Daud (2001), 'The Sports Industry in Malaysia', in Mohd Sofian Omar Fauzee (ed.), *Proceedings from Congress on Information Technology towards a Better Asia*, Ampang: Penerbitan Salafi.

Ministry of Culture, Youth and Sports Malaysia (1987), *Know the Game of Sepak Takraw*, Kuala Lumpur: Sports Division, Ministry of Youth and Sports.

Mohd Fadzil, Khoo Kay Kim and Sidique Ali Merican (eds.) (1979), *The Ninth SEA Games Kuala Lumpur '77 Official Report*, Kuala Lumpur: Ninth Sea Games Organizing Council.

Mohd Khir Johari (1980), 'Eighties: A New Challenging Era for Sports Organizations', paper presented at the Seminar on Malaysian Sports in the Eighties, Kuala Lumpur.

Mohd Maidon (1980), 'Private Sector Participation in Promoting Sports Activities', paper presented at the Seminar on Malaysian Sports in the Eighties, Kuala Lumpur.

Mohd Nor Che Nor (1977), 'Concept of Physical Education for Southeast Asia', paper presented at the Southeast Asian Games Seminar on Physical Education of Youth and National Development, Kuala Lumpur.

Mohd Salleh Aman (2004), *Sukan dalam Masyarakat Malaysia*, Kuala Lumpur: Universiti Malaya Press.

—— (ed.) (2006), *Pengurusan Sukan: Aplikasinya di Malaysia*, Kuala Lumpur: Universiti Malaya Press.

Nadhratul Wardah Salman (2001), 'Women and Sport in Malaysia: Opportunities and Barriers', in Mohd Sofian Omar Fauzee (ed.), *Proceedings from Congress on Information Technology towards a Better Asia*, Ampang: Penerbitan Salafi.

National Sports Council (1984), *Sports Science and General Research*, Kuala Lumpur.

National Sports Council, *Annual Report* (various years), Kuala Lumpur.

Nekvapil, Matthew Thomas (2002), 'International Branding for Malaysia: A Sports Tourism Perspective', paper presented at the National Conference on Sports Tourism, Petaling Jaya.

Ng Peng Kong (2003), *Rugby: A Malaysian Chapter*, Kuala Lumpur: Swan Printing.

Noh Abdullah (1982), 'National Sports Council of Malaysia: Aspiration for Nation Building', paper presented at International Seminar on Physical Education and Sports in Nation Building, Kuala Lumpur.

Olympic Council of Malaysia, *Annual Report* (various years), Kuala Lumpur.

Persatuan Penulis Sukan Sarawak (1993), *Sarawak: The Sports Powerhouse*, Kuching: Majlis Sukan Negri Kuching.

Razali Kidam, Amidah Hamim and Abd. Rashid Ahmad (eds.) (2002), *Menjulang Kegemilangan Sukan SEA XXI*, Kuala Lumpur: Jabatan Penerangan.

Sarawak Museum (1983), *Sepak Raga*, Kuching.

Seneviratne, Percy (1993), *Golden Moments of the SEA Games 1959–1991*, Singapore: Dominie Press.

Sheppard, Mubin (1972), *Taman Indera: Malay Decorative Arts and Pastimes*, Kuala Lumpur: Oxford University Press.

Soon Siew Fuang (1990), *Koleksi Permainan Tradisi Kanak-Kanak Malaysia*, Kuala Lumpur: Kementerian Kebudayaan, Kesenian dan Pelancongan Malaysia.

SUKOM Ninety-Eight Berhad (1998), *XVI Commonwealth Games: The Road to Kuala Lumpur*, Kuala Lumpur: Archipelago Press.

Ten Hong Beng, Helen (1992), *Pengelolaan dan Pengurusan Pertandingan Sukan*, Kuala Lumpur: Fajar Bakti.

Wallace, Alfred Russel (1869), *The Malay Archipelago: The Land of the Orang-Utan, and the Bird of Paradise*, London: Macmillan.

Index

Malayan team preparing to sail home from England after winning the inaugural Thomas Cup competition in 1949.

Sazali Samad (centre) celebrating after winning the Mr Universe title in the bantamweight category at the World Amateur Bodybuilding Championships in Melaka, 2000.

Malaysian players celebrating after scoring a goal during the 1975 Hockey World Cup in Kuala Lumpur.

Picture Credits

A. Kasim Abas, p. 16, *gasing piring*. Abdul Rahman Hussin, p. 21, bird cage, raising the cages. Agence France-Presse, p. 14, Nicol David; p. 49, Malaysian team; p. 56, 2006 Asian Games, Gold Cup; p. 68, Nicol David; p. 71, Lee Chong Wei; p. 72, Roslin Hashim, Chin and Wong, Tan and Koo; p. 75, Ong and Azlan, Nicol kissing trophy, Nicol reaching for ball; p. 76, Yao and Liu; p. 78, Siti Zalina Ahmad, archers; p. 83, Iain Steel, Airil Rizman, Lim Siew Ai; p. 87, Ooi Chin Kay, Sam Chong; p. 88, Esther Cheah; p. 90, Mon Redee; p. 91, Irina Maharani, Abdul Mutalib; p. 94, Watson Nyambek, Wong Zee, Nur Herman Majid, Roslinda Samsu; p. 97, steeplechase; p. 99, Zaki Sadri, Ngew Sin Mei, G. Shanti; p. 101, Kimbeley Yap swimming; p. 107, Mahathir on horse, Syed Omar; p. 110, Tour de Langkawi; p. 112, Start/finish line; p. 113, Alex Yoong; p. 114, Josiah Ng, Noor Azian; p. 119, Daniel Bego, synchronized swimmers; p. 131, S. Premila, R. Puvaneswaran; p. 135, Adnan Jusoh; p. 141, Commonwealth Games; p. 146, Ng Shu Wai, Durratun Rosli; p. 147, pommel horse, rings, rhythmic gymnast, parallel bars; p. 149, Amirul Hamizan Ibrahim, Che Mohd Azrol; p. 155, swimming; p. 157, Special Olympics; p. 158, Merdeka Square; p. 171, opening ceremony, Wira. Ahmad Sarji, p. 5, Wong Peng Soon; p. 50, North vs. South, souvenir programme; p. 51, Dollah Don; p. 53, Abdul Ghani Minhat; p. 54, Selangor vs. Perak; p. 55, FMS team, Perak team, Negeri Sembilan vs. Melaka; p. 70, Ismail Marjan; p. 80, Tunku in action, Malaya Golf Society, Challenge Bowl, Ariff Tuah; p. 81, New Club clubhouse, New Club course, Petaling Hill, C.W.H. Cochrane, Thomas Lee, Royal Selangor Golf Club; p. 82, Putra Cup, Amateur trophy, Eisenhower trophy team, ex-Malaya champions; p. 83, World Cup trophy, Nazamuddin Yusoff, R. Nachimuthu, Jalal Deran, Bobby Lim, V. Nellan; p. 84, Nor Hashimah Ismail, esplanade, Nor Iryani Azmi, bowls, national complex, book launch, Siti Zalina Ahmad; p. 85, Siti Zalina Ahmad, Nur Fidrah Noh, Ahmad Sarji, Bayuemas stadium, Saiedah Abdul Rahim, Malaysian team; p. 96, E.M. MacDonald; p. 147, Tho Fook Hung, medal ceremony; p. 163, WBB Challenge Trophy; p. 165, E.M. MacDonald. Alt. TYPE/REUTERS, p. 6, gymnast; p. 30, pole climbing; p. 32, pillow fighting; p. 43, World Cyber Games; p. 47, sepak takraw; p. 49, leaping, passing, holding the ball; p. 56, 2002 Asian Games; p. 62, Ooi Ban Sin; p. 68, All England Championships; p. 72, Hafiz Hashim; p. 76, Ng Sock Khim; p. 97, G. Saravanan; p. 98, Nazmizan Muhamad; p. 99, Lee Kum Zee, Narinder Singh; p. 101, Kimbeley Yap cycling; p. 107, Qabil Ambak; p. 110, F1 Grand Prix; p. 113, Mahathir in car; p. 119, women divers; Bryan Nickson;

p. 126, karate; p. 127, Chai Fong Ying; p. 137, base jumping; p. 144, Chrystal Lim; p. 145, men's team; p. 147, uneven bars, high bar, floor exercise, vault; p. 148, Sazali Samad. Angkatan Koperasi Kebangsaaan Malaysia Berhad, p. 92, 2008 PFM president, launch of pétanque, measuring the distance, jack and *boules*. Arkib Negara, p. 48, Mohd Khir Johari; p. 50, football match, Malaya Cup teams; p. 51, Malaya vs. Burma, Tunku at the Merdeka Tournament; p. 52, 1958 Merdeka team, E.C. Dutton; p. 54, Perak players, Tun Abdul Razak; p. 58, cricket teams; p. 59, Gurucharan Singh; p. 62, Quek Kai Dong; p. 68, national squash trophy; p. 77, Malay Tournament, S.A. Azman; p. 91, Warren Shield, Tan Siew Sin; p. 96, M. Jegathesan with medal; long jump; p. 104, army team; p. 106, jumping competition; p. 109, Sultan Iskandar, Sultan Ahmad Shah; p. 118, founding ASUM president; p. 125, giant fish; p. 126, taekwondo exhibition; p. 134, Goh Wing Wai; p. 135, Muhammad Ali; p. 162, Tunku Abdul Rahman, Ghazali Shafie, Punch Gunalan. AsianYachting.Com, p. 120, Royal Langkawi Regatta; p. 121, Raja Muda Selangor Regatta. Asiapromote Ventures Sdn Bhd, p. 106, FEI World Cup. Associated Press, p. 63, Rashid Sidek. Aznir Malek, p. 125, Anthony Webb, Teh Ah Teck. Badminton World Federation, p. 8, Thomas Cup. Baharuddin Jamil, p. 90, 1978 tournament. Basir Abdul Rahman, p. 140, MPA 2008 president, paragliding through the twin towers, paramotoring. Bernama, p. 7, badminton stadium; p. 13, lawn bowls medals; p. 17, tops on the ground; p. 19, Kelantan festival; p. 23, *junus tunggal*; p. 26, buffalo race; p. 42, SEA Games match; p. 48, Ahmad Ismail; p. 72, Wong Choong Han; p. 77, Si Yew Ming; p. 87, Suhana Dewi; p. 98, Moh Siew Wei; p. 113, pit building; p. 114, Tour de Langkawi; p. 123, Nenggiri Challenge; p. 152, Napsiah Omar, P. Mariappan; p. 153, track athletes; p. 154, MPC president; p. 155, football, volleyball, tennis, athletics, cycling, powerlifting; p. 156, opening ceremony, 2005 and 2006 Paralympians; p. 157, lawn bowls, javelin, long jump; p. 163, Noh Abdullah; p. 165, Zainal Abu Zarim, p. 166, MSSC championships, hockey match; p. 167, Aquathon, rowing invitational; p. 169, National Women's Games, Azalina and Jackie Chan; p. 173, Tour de Langkawi. Bowden, David, p. 140, landing. C.K. Low, p. 139, crossing a river. Chai Kah Yune, p. 17, physics of spinning; p. 31. dragon boat; p. 39, *congkak* game play; p. 49, the service; p. 58, cricket pitch; p. 63, netball court; p. 64, handball court; p. 65, volleyball shots; p. 66, baseball game play; p. 67, softball game play; p. 76, paddle grips; p. 93, Lanjut course; p. 123, Nenggiri course; p. 128, fencing equipment and techniques, fencing strip; p. 138, Mount Kinabalu; p. 171, Bukit

Jalil complex. Chee Yih Yang, p. 45, playing cards. Cobra, p. 61, International Tens. EDM archives, p. 147, 2008 MGF president. Elyas Omar, p. 161, present commissioner. Falconer, John, p. 28, cockfighting. Fam, John, p. 144, dancesport; p. 148, 2007 SEA Games, Latin American routine. Federal Information Department, p.5, sepak takraw; p. 8, top spinning; p. 12, Thomas Cup; p. 14, top spinning; lake gardens festival; p. 28, Iban wrestling; p. 48, *sepak raga jaring*; p. 62, SEAP Games, Asian Basketball Championship; p. 68, table tennis, 1967 Thomas Cup team, S.A. Azman; p. 72, Thomas Cup parade; p. 76, Asian championships; p. 77, Davis Cup; p. 160, Tunku Abdul Rahman, Senu Abdul Rahman, Annuar Musa, Hishamuddin Hussein; p. 164, Tunku Abdul Rahman, Abdul Razak, Hussein Onn, Mahathir Mohamad. Fong Min Yuan, p. 45, Comics Corner. George Gill, p. 109, BRDB team, Tengku Abdullah. Getty Images, p. 83, M. Ramayah. Hasbro Toy (M) Sdn Bhd, p. 40, Monopoly championship. Hash Heritage Foundation, p. 102, foundation building. HBL Network Photo Agency, p.4, drums; p. 5, car; p.7, National Sports Complex; p. 109, polo match; p. 113, motorcyclist; p. 116, powerboats; p. 136, skateboarder; p. 141, base jumper; p. 171, gymnastics team, Agong with Queen Elizabeth. Ice Skating Association of Malaysia, p. 151, ISAM founding president, ISAM 2008 president. Impian Golf and Country Club, p. 83, Rashid Ismail. International Rainforest Challenge, p. 115, a helping hand. Karamjit Singh, p. 110, rally racing, p. 115, Rally of Cyprus. Kelab Hockey Ice Saga, p. 145, KL Wildcats; p. 151, World Fives. Selina Khoo, p, 153, oath taking. King Edward VII School, p. 60, catching a throw-in. Kuala Lumpur Golf and Country Club, p. 81, golf course. Kuala Lumpur Skydiving Association, p. 141, jumping off a helicopter, expedition. Lat, p. 102, Hashing cartoon. Lawn Tennis Association of Malaysia, p. 77, 2008 LTAM president. Lim Joo, p. 17, throwing a top; p. 29, *tibau*; p. 34, *kuri paichal*, p. 36, *batu seremban*, *sepak bulu ayam*; p. 37, *kunda kundi*, p. 38, *jala itik*, *injit-injit semut*, kampung scene; p. 55, hockey field; p. 84, end of pairs; p. 146, a medal-winning performance. Loh Beng Hooi, p. 165, Loh Beng Hooi. M. Magendran, p. 138, conquering Mount Everest. M. Mahadevan, p. 109, centenary celebration. Malay College Kuala Kangsar, The, p. 74, fives, Tuanku Ja'afar. Malaysia Amateur Boxing Association, p. 135, MABF 2008 president. Malaysia Canoe Association, p. 120, Abdul Wahab Nawi; p. 122, Abdul Wahab Nawi, canoeing; p. 123, canoe polo. Malaysia Gliding Association, p. 140, PTLM 2008 president. Malaysia

Weiqi Association, p. 33, weiqi championships. Malaysia Woodball Association, p. 93, founding president, 2008 president, equipment. Malaysian Angling Association, p. 125, founding PeMM president, 2008 PeMM president. Malaysian Amateur Basketball Association, p. 62, MABA president. Malaysian Amateur Volleyball Association, p. 65, founding MAVA president, 2008 MAVA president. Malaysian Body-Building Federation, p. 144, premier bodybuilders; p. 148, Gan Boon Leong. Malaysian Chess Federation, p. 42, junior tournament, Malaysian Chess Festival, international masters, Jimmy Liew. Malaysian Dance Sport Berhad, p. 150, MSDB founding and 2008 chairpersons, Frances and Tham, Anthony and Anita. Malaysian Fencing Federation, p. 128, MFF 2008 president, Malaysian Open; p. 129, 1959 team, Zairul Zaimi, épée team. Malaysian Golf Association, p. 81, 2008 MGA president, p. 82, Seagram Cup. Malaysian Handball Federation, p. 64, 2008 MAHF president. Malaysian Hockey Federation, p. 54, 2008 MHF president. Malaysian Ladies Golf Association, p. 81, 2008 MALGA president. Malaysian Netball Association, p. 63, founding MNA president, 2008 MNA president. Malaysian Rugby Union, p. 60, 2008 MRU president; p. 61, diving for a try, Malaysian team. Malaysian Tenpin Bowling Congress, p. 88, 2008 MTBC president; p. 89, Ben Heng, 2003 champions, 2007 champions, Shalin with trophy, p. 163, P.S. Nathan. Malaysian Silambam Association, p. 133, 2008 MSA president. Ministry of Youth and Sports, p. 159, Menara KBS. Mohd Adam Ismail, p. 143, KBS park, Eliss Tahir. Muzium Negara Malaysia, p. 39, *congkak* board. Natasha Mustapha, p. 104, Mohamed Moiz, Syed Omar; p. 107, Quzandria Nur, Quzier Ambak; p. 109, Shariman Sharir. National Adventure Association of Malaysia, p. 138, NAAM founding president. National Fitness Council, p. 168, Larian Merdeka, basketball; p. 169, Gim Rakyat, jazzercise, Fitness First. National Shooting Association of Malaysia, p. 91, 2008 NSAM president. National Sports Council, p. 63, players celebrating; p. 68, 1992 Thomas Cup; p. 107, Kamaruddin Abdul Ghani; p. 119, water polo; p. 160, Noh Abdullah, Kamalul Ariffin, Mazlan Ahmad, Ramlan Abd Aziz, Zolkeples Embong; p. 164, Ahmad Sarji, Sultan Azlan Shah, Mohd Fathil, Abdul Majid Muda; p. 165, Azmi Shaari, Chin Mee Keong, Vincent Fernandez, Kamaruddin Abdul Ghani, S. Kathiravale, Thomas Lee, Sharon Low Su Lin, M.K. Nathan, Ong Hoon Chin, Mary Ong Kwee Kee, Rabia Abdul Salam, Hajjah Saadiah Sardon, H.R.M. Storey, Mohd Taha Ariffin, Tham Siew Kai, Daniel